D1525591

Praise for *Poor Technology*

Levi Checketts's unique and poignant view of technology—AI in particular—and the poor is fascinating. Checketts uses the experience of poverty to question the narratives of technology and to create a hermeneutic of poverty to pursue the ethical problems specific to AI. In the era of AI, orchestrated by tech capitalism, the concern for the poor is the moral apparatus of twenty-first-century global ethics, and this book will be one of the must-reads.

—Sophia Park, professor emerita of religious studies and philosophy, Holy Names University

Checketts offers a searing critique of both AI enthusiasts and doomsayers, arguing that their utopian and dystopian futures leave the poor and marginalized of the world invisible and voiceless. He argues that AI optimizes capitalist, first-world, patriarchal, and instrumental values, to which he contrasts an alternative technology framed from the worldview and lifeworld of the poor and oppressed—a "poor AI" that enhances rather than transcends our common humanity. It is a fascinating and informative read, especially relevant in light of the recent controversies around the need to regulate generative AI such as ChatGPT, as well as a timely critique of the millennial mirage of "effective altruism."

—Timothy Clancy, SJ, associate professor of philosophy, Gonzaga University

Poor Technology is a unique and important contribution to the landscape of technology studies for several reasons, but two are crucial: First, its analysis of artificial intelligence focuses on the experiences of poor people, which often go unnoticed in other studies of that technology. Second, it offers a nuanced Christian perspective on artificial intelligence, work, and our conceptions of the less privileged. We are so lucky to have Checketts's voice today.

—Lee Vinsel, associate professor of science, technology, and society, Virginia Tech, and coauthor of *The Innovation Delusion: How Our Obsession with the New Has Disrupted the Work That Matters Most*

Poor Technology is a forceful provocation to contemporary AI narratives, whether utopian or dystopian. In clear and illuminating prose, Checketts exposes our reluctance to confront the uncomfortable relationship between our visions of the machine "other" and those of us who have always and everywhere been other: the poor.

—Shannon Vallor, Baillie Gifford Professor in the Ethics of Data and Artificial Intelligence, University of Edinburgh, and author of *Technology and the Virtues: A Philosophical Guide to a Future Worth Wanting*

POOR TECHNOLOGY

POOR TECHNOLOGY

Artificial Intelligence and the Experience of Poverty

LEVI CHECKETTS

FORTRESS PRESS
Minneapolis

POOR TECHNOLOGY
Artificial Intelligence and the Experience of Poverty

Library of Congress Control Number: 2023940018 (print)

Cover image: Antique illustration of mechanical man – stock illustration by ilbusca/ Getty Images, colored by Kristin Miller
Cover design: Kristin Miller

Print ISBN: 978-1-5064-8231-6
eBook ISBN: 978-1-5064-8232-3

To Jiyoung, whose ability to understand me better than myself made this book possible.

CONTENTS

ACKNOWLEDGMENTS

I owe a great many people for this work, for better or worse. In the first place, I owe a great thanks to Eric Schnurer, director of the Greater Good Gathering. His invitation to speak at a conference at Union Theological Seminary was the most direct trigger for leading me to think about this issue. In turn, I owe the people at Union who hosted us, and especially those attending the conference whose remarks after my talk encouraged me to continue in this line of thinking.

I owe a great deal more to many people involved in theology and science who saw potential in me and fostered it. Ted Peters, one of my mentors at the Graduate Theological Union, has been tremendously genial, making recommendations and introductions and opening opportunities for a young scholar like me. Noreen Herzfeld has been a tremendous benefactor to me as well, encouraging my scholarship and inviting me into larger conversations with theologians and thinkers, such as the Dicastery for Culture and Education's Ethical and Social AI Concerns Committee. I am also grateful to Brian Green, Robert Russell, and Braden Molhoek, who have sustained my work and offered me opportunities to present and publish with them as well.

I owe my parents as well. We were poor when I was a child, the experience of which underwrites this book, but my parents were dedicated to ensuring their children were healthy, educated, and happy. While we lacked many things, we did not lack the most important things. Even if I can now recognize how much of our cuisine was "poor food," they ensured we had a balanced diet (even if we did not want to eat our vegetables), and though there were many hand-me-downs and secondhand clothes (and the occasional shoe held together with duct tape), they made sure we had clean clothes to wear. I do not think I would have been able to attend world-class colleges without the care they provided or the support they gave. Indeed, I owe it to their dedicated parenthood that I did not fully understand how poor we were until I attended college. While we experienced scarcity and depravation, they ensured we did not experience insecurity as profoundly as many others in our neighborhood.

My PhD advisor, Lisa Fullam, deserves my thanks as well. The history of ethics as a whole and Catholic ethics in particular is filled with people who "look" like me—cisgender white men. When I entered my PhD program, I lacked any clear idea what I had to contribute, but Lisa was able to see potential in me and took me under her wing. Her openness, good humor, and critical insight have given me hope and inspiration, and I value both her mentorship and her friendship. She opened many opportunities for me to teach at Bay Area institutions and to develop my CV as her research assistant, all critical for developing the sort of cultural capital necessary to succeed in academia.

I also wish to sincerely thank my editor, Carey Newman. Somehow, a paper I delivered online during the COVID-19 pandemic at the Society for Christian Ethics, based off the initial presentation I gave in New York, caught his eye. He saw in my work a potential that I myself didn't see. The practice of talking with him has helped me to think through my ideas in ways that I couldn't do alone, and the practices he has had me work through have helped my thinking overcome obstacles. To the degree that this book contains anything resembling a coherent thesis, he is responsible. If this book reaches anybody at all, it is also due to his own keen understanding of its importance in this current cultural moment.

Many other people, far too many to count, deserve my thanks. I wish to thank many other mentors in my life—Ed Vacek, who gave me the encouragement and hope I needed to stay in Christian ethics; Carl Mitcham, who fostered my work as a young ethicist of technology; Rodolfo John Alaniz, who pushed me to carefully and rigorously tie STS to Catholic ethics; and many others. I wish to thank the faculty of HKBU's Religion and Philosophy Department, who have offered insights into several key portions of the book. I am grateful to Caroline Burns, who offered me opportunities to teach business ethics and further my own scholarship on economic questions. I am grateful to Jordan Wales and Cory Andrew Labrecque, who offered critical feedback for me to develop my work; and Matt Gaudet and Elias Kruger, who both offered opportunities for me to publish early versions of my ideas.

Finally, two important persons deserve my special thanks. The first is my wife, Jiyoung Ko, to whom this book is dedicated. She stuck with me through several years of near-poverty as we studied and struggled as PhD students in Berkeley. She has been a critical voice for reflection, an important conversation partner, and has offered me new insights into problems that I didn't have before. With no exaggeration, she has been the best writing and thinking partner I could have asked for. Second, I am grateful to my dear friend Sophia Park. She pushed me to write from my own experience, to articulate who I really am instead of a generic version of Catholic thought. Like Lisa Fullam, she saw in me what I could not see, and she has opened many doors for me as well, both in employment at Holy Names University and in studying the work of Jacques Lacan. Jiyoung and Sophia together pushed me to recognize how my own interest and scholarship are underwritten by my experience as a child and to use that to articulate my own experience.

PREFACE

The Importance of Stories

I never fully understood what it meant to be poor until I began my undergraduate studies. While I was not the first in my family to go to college, I was the first among my siblings, and only two of us six have gone. After stumbling my way successfully through the application process, I traveled halfway across the US to attend a top-tier private college. When I finished schlepping all of my belongings from the bookstore parking lot, where the airport bus dropped me off, to the far end of the oversized campus, I began to realize my college experience would not be the same as that of my peers. My secondhand clothes and cheap suitcases punctuated my poverty as much as my lack of collegiate swag and dorm room basics. I was perpetually conscious of this difference, and empirical data from the university reinforced my discomfort: more students from the economic top 1 percent attended the school than from the bottom 50 percent. My family had always been in the bottom 15 percent.

The ease at which most of my peers used money was a stark difference from the anxiety I always felt. Football games, cover charges for parties, money for beer runs, off-campus dining, and so forth were very common expenses I either could never afford or could only do so with great pain. The most poignant moment I can recall was when, as a freshman, some upperclassmen were excitedly discussing an upcoming event on campus. I expressed some regret that I didn't think I could afford it. "It's only five dollars," one of them scoffed. But it was true; my wallet was empty, and my bank account did not have enough to withdraw. I can still feel the embarrassment this offhand comment caused me.

Two classes in particular at Notre Dame helped me see the problem clearly. In my first-year composition class (a course required for me because I had not tested out through AP English as most of my peers had), we studied "the American Dream." I was shocked to see myself reflected in the case studies in our readings of the "American poor." What stood out even more, though, was the reality these readings showed: while many poor Americans believe in the logic of capitalism, very few of them actually achieve "the American Dream."[1] The second class was a theology course my senior year on "Radical Catholicism." In reading the work and activity of Dorothy Day and other Catholic Workers, I came to realize the ideas they embraced would have empowered my family tremendously. And yet the ideas of solidarity, of organizing, of pacifist activism conflicted with my family's neoconservative ideology. My decision to study ethics in grad school was entirely motivated by trying to understand how and why my father and older brothers persisted in rejecting politics and strategies that would benefit them as workers.

But then, over the course of the process of undergraduate, master's, and doctoral studies, my thinking, writing, and even speaking changed. While I still had a great deal of anxiety about spending money, my writing was in many ways indistinguishable from that of any other white, male, bourgeois theologian. I could not see this myself, of course—this is the way pedagogy works. When one has been conformed to the dominant scheme of speech or thought, they are unable to retrieve the way they had previously encountered the world. Educators tend to think this is *good*, but it means the educator is unable to understand the perspectives of those still in a poor frame of mind.

The only way I began to be aware of this was due to the gracious assistance of my friend Sophia Park and my wife, Jiyoung Ko. After concluding my doctoral studies, I spent four years applying for full-time academic jobs. One opened in Berkeley that would allow my family to remain in the community we had grown to love, and I threw myself into crafting the best application I could to secure the position. But when Jiyoung and Sophia read my cover letter, they were disappointed. "This isn't you," Sophia told me, frankly. The letter addressed everything online guides say a cover letter should—my teaching experience, my research focus, my contribution to the school. But I had abstracted my work from my experience. This was not how I taught my Oakland students at Holy Names University, and it was not what motivated my research. I spent hours reflecting and crafting and re-crafting the letter to capture the way my experience of poverty shaped my pedagogy, my research, and my approach to education in general. In the end, it was one of the best statements I could have made of myself. Nonetheless, I didn't get the job.

The process of drafting this letter forced me to do something I had avoided explicitly doing for too long: connect my interest in the ethics of technology with my interest in economic issues. I had written a short paper on the topic of work and automation,[2] and I had taught business ethics in one form or another for about seven years, but I had yet to articulate a clear connection between the ways that new technologies have a dangerous bearing on economically vulnerable populations. An invitation to a conference in New York provided a critical opportunity I needed for just that.

Just before COVID-19 was declared a global pandemic, Union Theological Seminary and the Greater Good Initiative hosted a conference entitled "Artificial Intelligence: Implications for Ethics and Religion." I was invited to prepare some remarks for a panel on ethico-religious responses to AI. As I thought about the other invitees, the focus of their research, and the trends in which conversations around AI ethics had been moving, I realized this would be a much-wanted opportunity to bring together my work on technology ethics and my own unique voice. While there had been and are many important views addressing AI's shortcomings from the perspectives of women, people of color, and other marginalized groups (see chapter 2), very little had been written about AI's inevitable impact on the poor, and still less from the perspective of poverty.

My talk at Union was a very truncated version of this book. I considered AI from the perspective of the two Great Commandments—love God and love your neighbor. As some AI evangelists (even the name is telling) predict AI will become God, we have to recognize the absolute weakness of such a vision of God. A god that can be killed by a clumsy technician tripping over a wire, or a god bounded by silicon chips, or a god confined to algorithmic processes is not the ineffable God the Abrahamic faiths have stood before in fearful wonder. But the adverse side of this proposition is that if AI is our image of God, it is also our image of ourselves. The reduction of humanity to rote mathematical processes reinforces an anthropology that equates humanity with normative rationality. Persons with cognitive deviations, mental illness, or simply less education are less "persons" in this model than high-end computers. This is especially troubling given the very real history of eugenics intelligence standards (see conclusion).

I was surprised by the reception of my talk at the conference. Not many of my copresenters had much to say, but many in the audience, which included Union and Jewish Theological Seminary of America students, as well as Riverside Church congregants, told me that my talk resonated with them. In a city like New York, homelessness, mental illness, and poverty stand in stark contrast to the financial hub of Manhattan. In speaking of AI, it is tempting to anthropomorphize the shiny silicon components while ignoring the human-all-too-human poor shivering in the cold.

But I don't believe this oversight is intentional. Indeed, this is the truly damning part; AI is done from *good* intentions. Certainly, there is a fair amount of greed and avarice at play, but few (if any) of the major players in AI research want to inflict harm. However, the "good intentions" of the well-off are responsible for so much of the inequality, injustice, and disaster of the world. Few people really believe themselves to be bad actors. Most are indoctrinated through the process of education, propaganda, primary socialization, religious instruction, deliberate countercultural antithetical identification, and so on. This is the problem of the AI community; it's also the problem of most communities in general. The great liberation theologian Marcella Althaus-Reid notes that, when her parish was discussing ways they could help the poor in their community, they were entirely oblivious to the fact that there were already poor of the community in their midst.[3] Power blinds its wielder to the realities of other persons;

they become convinced that their view is the right view and that it is an omniscient view. The inability of people in power to recognize their own privileged position (myself included) is what makes discussions about whether or not a pile of circuitry should have rights seem legitimate in San Jose while forty miles north, the Port of Oakland is one of the largest sites for human trafficking in the US.[4] It is why Ben Goertzel's robot Sophia was granted citizenship by Saudi Arabia, while human women could not drive in the same country. It is why Francesca Ferrando's philosophy of posthumanism can claim to go beyond anthropocentrism while still granting privilege to the codified human biases of AI.

In other words, AI fascination is theologically telling—mostly it tells us about the reality of human fallenness and our inability to be whole.

I begin this book with my own story because, as Hannah Arendt notes, "*who* somebody is" can only be understood through the "web of relations" they are a part of and the "story" of their life.[5] Our thinking is inherently narratological; not only do we understand the world through narrative shortcuts (as in referring to someone as a "Good Samaritan" or a "Scrooge") and tell stories (no matter how mundane) as part of our bonding and communication but we also understand ourselves and those around us through stories. My late grandfather told stories about his time in the army stationed in Okinawa, Japan, and his occasional visits to Gimpo Airport in Seoul after he met my wife; nobody else in the family had heard these stories before, and they recontextualized the meaning of his life in his sunset years.

Artificial intelligence fits into our stories; it has animated our interest in the form of science fiction since the early 1900s (see introduction) and animates our interest today in stories about new accomplishments in machine learning, new applications to various industries, and new expansions into broader parts of the economy. Throughout this book, I contextualize each chapter with two vignettes meant to set the stage for the chapter. These stories include very recent tales of AI in the public sphere and older tales of the intersection of social change with industrial technologies. Much of the AI narrative itself is reminiscent of what has gone before. But even what is novel in AI shows itself to be less mysterious once contextualized against the broader narrative of socioeconomic and political interests.

The poor are certainly characterized by their stories. Whether theirs is a life of trauma, a history of abuse, a spate of bad luck, a descent into worsening conditions, or a roller coaster of good and ill, their experiences and perspectives of the world are conditioned and contextualized by the stories of their lives. Indeed, this is perhaps the greatest way to humanize those Others we may often wish to keep at bay—to recognize that their lives, too, are tangled within webs of relations, some of which inevitably intersect our own. A series of telling and retelling their own stories makes us recognize that, though the gap between myself and the Other is insurmountable, the Other though ultimately barred from me, has a shared humanity. That humanity is what we must strive to preserve, to fight for, to protect, to empower, to fully humanize (and not romanticize or abstract). The Tennessee Williams line "nothing human disgusts me" can only be true for those who recognize the real humanity in the poor, and this humanity requires that we understand that there are stories behind every dirty face; behind alcoholics' bloodshot eyes; behind flea-infested, ratted beards; behind methamphetamine-rotted smiles; behind greasy double chins; behind child prostitutes' vacant stares.

For Christians, the significance of stories cannot be overstated. Catholics laud the lives of saints, and Protestant sermons rely on the power of myth to convey deeper truths. As I write these words in Advent season, I cannot help but think John's words "The Word became flesh and dwelt among us" (John 1:14 ESV) prefigure his own account of the story of Jesus, a story of how God lived among a particular people in a particular time and suffered a particular death that Christians believe, in its particularity, has universal ramifications.

But AI, at least in its idealized form, is meant to be story-free. There is no life behind the screen. While the most advanced language models can now replicate human writing on a level comparable to college students, the machine itself does not contextualize this information within a broader understanding of itself in the universe. It merely replicates what it has been trained to replicate. Machines do not have understanding because they do not have stories, and they do not have stories because they do not have understanding. And yet, science fiction is replete with examples of AI pleading for its humanity, whether that be *Bladerunner*'s Roy Batty (technically a "replicant") waxing philosophical about the inevitability of death, or *Star Trek*'s Data seeking to grow more human, or even *Portal*'s murderous GLADOS, who is retconned to be a more sympathetic uploaded consciousness in the game's sequel. We humanize these inhuman machines by giving them stories; we tell stories about the inhuman having stories because telling stories is what it is to be human. And yet, AI as such does not have stories; it is rote processing, not narratological thinking. And so, we create stories about the AI; we give it names and history. We anthropomorphize because that is also what humans do.

This work is intended to be read as a story, one with agonists who appear new but are perhaps typified most clearly by personae active in British public consciousness in the 1810s: Dr. Victor Frankenstein and General Ned Ludd. *Frankenstein*, a story of hubris and the mismatch of human ingenuity to human wisdom, is often invoked in the story of AI. But whatever morals Mary Shelley tried to convey in her novel tend to be perverted in the AI project—the appeal of mad Dr. Frankenstein screaming "It's alive!" compels the AI evangelist, despite the protagonist spending the majority of the novel trying to escape his monstrosity. Ned Ludd, on the other hand, is the apocryphal Robin Hood–esque leader of the Luddites, textile manufacturers who sabotaged industrial machinery that was displacing them. While the Luddites themselves were a formidable threat in their time, the techno-optimism inherent in Anglo-culture has reframed these popular heroes as regressive holdouts. Both stories demonstrate the conflict between conceptions of humanity—the unscrupulous self-aggrandizing of Dr. Frankenstein in deciding he has power over life and death, and the effacement of those fighting (and sometimes dying) for the right to not be replaced by machines. The struggles for meaning and human dignity that characterized the early years of the Industrial

Revolution thus frame current discussions, and the reconfiguration of the meanings of these stories should be considered as a cautionary tale.

Let me conclude with a final story. In between my presentation in New York and the present, I moved across the world to Hong Kong, perhaps the most stereotypically bourgeois white move I could make. In my new setting, the cultural referents of western Christianity are not as present as Chinese culture is. The more time I spend here, the more I see the important richness of the stories that frame what Hong Kong is. Let me, then, draw from one Chinese story. In the *Zhuangzi*, Zi-gong encounters a farmer laboriously trying to water his crops. Zi-gong tells the man there is a nifty device that will improve irrigation and save labor. In this section, we read the problem of "scheming heart/mind" (機心, *jixin*, meaning literally "machine mind"). The farmer replies to Zi-gong, "I have heard from my teacher that, where there are ingenious contrivances, there are sure to be subtle doings; and that, where there are subtle doings, there is sure to be a [machine] mind. But, when there is a [machine] mind in the breast, its pure simplicity is impaired. When this pure simplicity is impaired, the spirit becomes unsettled, and the unsettled spirit is not the proper residence of the Dao. It is not that I do not know the contrivance which you mention, but I should be ashamed to use it."

INTRODUCTION

Better Living through Smarter Technology

On June 6, 2022, Blake Lemoine, an engineer at Google, stated he believed their language modeling AI LaMDA was sentient.[1] Modern language modeling programs are impressive in their ability to generate "realistic" speech with just a few prompts. The most recent models, like GPT-4, can even "dialogue" with a person as a highly sophisticated chatbot. Lemoine claimed that the program demonstrated sentience due to what he perceives as self-reflective responses in chat interactions with the program.[2] Lemoine's "interview" with the program does demonstrate that the program provided outputs to his inputs similar to the way a conscious human being might. It would seem that, for Lemoine, this is sufficient to pass the so-called "Turing test," a threshold for machine intelligence initially proposed by AI pioneer Alan Turing whereby a machine successfully convinces a human judge that it is human.[3]

Lemoine was placed on administrative leave and expressed fear that, in revealing the nature of LaMDA, he might be fired the way AI ethics lead Margaret Mitchell was.[4] Mitchell had been fired shortly after her ethics colead Timnit Gebru had been fired over a paper critiquing the same program.[5] Gebru and Mitchell's critique, however, was not that language programs were becoming sentient but, among other things, that they were reinforcing biases (including racism and sexism) common across their sets of training data.[6] In other words, Lemoine's conclusion that AI is sentient reinforces the dangers Gebru and Mitchell highlight, namely, that a sophisticated language program might be taken as conscious when in fact it merely parrots back the biases of its training.

When Google Deepmind's program "AlphaGo" beat world Go champion Sedol Lee in 2016, many believed they were witnessing the birth of true artificial superintelligence. IBM's computer "Deep Blue" had bested world chess champion Garry Kasparov in 1997, but skeptics noted that chess, though a complex game, was one with a necessarily limited number of moves. It was well within the realm of possibilities, though perhaps a bit complicated, to program a computer with every single possible move on a chessboard of thirty-two pieces on sixty-four tiles. Go, on the other hand, involves an ever-changing 361-square board where decision-making has typically been seen as much of an art as it is strategy. It was previously estimated that no computer program was anywhere near complex enough to be successful at Go and wouldn't be until 2024.[7] The fact that computers beat a world-champion Go player eight years before expectations was sensational, to say the least. *Wired* magazine described the event with awe, attributing agency to the machine, suggesting it reckoned the Korean world-champion's strategy and, perhaps inappropriately, articulating the machine's performance as "beautiful."[8]

Lee's loss was felt particularly sharply by his compatriots. While Korea's tech scene includes major consumer electronics corporations like Samsung and LG, the country has lagged behind its neighbor Japan in pursuing AI. Lee's loss then came as a threefold shock: a shock to South Korea's tech strategy, a shock to the Go community, and a shock to Lee himself. Lee retired from Go in 2019, conceding that there was no point to continue when no human can beat AlphaGo. After Lee's defeat, AlphaGo bested every other human it challenged, despite having lost one game to Lee, making AI the undisputed perennial champion of Go. If that were not enough, DeepMind researchers adapted AlphaGo's programming to create "AlphaZero," a program that has itself surpassed AlphaGo, widening the gap between human and machine capabilities far beyond any reconcilable distance.[9] After witnessing the impressive capabilities of AlphaGo, the South Korean government decided to invest one trillion won (about 863 million USD) into AI research.[10]

But Lee's loss sent ripples across the region that are shaping global policy and power dynamics. South Korea's decision to increase AI research was reiterated by their neighbor to the west. In the nineteenth Party Congress in October of 2017, President Xi Jinping declared that AI would be one of China's "strategic industries," the next frontier for economic growth as the increase of manufacturing in China begins to slow.[11] The stated goal of the Communist Party is for the People's Republic to become the global AI leader by 2030.[12] As a result, billions of dollars of research funds are now allocated every year to private and university research related to AI. As the twenty-first century unfolds, China has risen to the place of one of the main superpowers, a contemporary rival of the United States. The country's decision to invest heavily in AI is a gambit for global dominance, and the conditions for success have been framed around technological innovation. Thus, the seemingly inconsequential fact of a computer besting a human player in a game has recast global leaders' expectations for how to achieve and maintain power in this century. AI has become a new frontier, like nuclear physics or space travel, in which global superpowers jockey for supremacy.

The Future, Today

Artificial intelligence (AI) promises better living through smarter technology. It will revolutionize every aspect of industry. It will change our leisure. It will improve our governance. It will improve our health outcomes. It will make us all rich. Intelligent computer programs are the future, today. And the AI of the future will be more powerful than anything we can imagine.

Consider but one example of applications of AI research in a university in a major Asian city. Researchers at this school are deploying AI to improve understanding of cognitive functions,[13] to detect cancer more quickly,[14] to improve public access across the city,[15] to provide more balanced and diversified news delivery,[16] and even, in their most ambitious and celebrated project to date, to complement human musical production in live performance.[17] This university, founded as a liberal arts educational institution focused on providing "whole person education" based on the Christian educational tradition, today articulates its three central research "strategic clusters of strength" as Creative Media and Practice, Health and

Drug Discovery, and Data Analytics and Artificial Intelligence, carried out especially across six interdisciplinary research labs: the augmented creativity laboratory (which prioritizes AI for human-machine collaboration), the computational medicine laboratory (which uses AI for drug discovery), system health laboratory (which applies AI to diagnostics and medical modeling), the smart society laboratory (which adapts AI systems for public policy and infrastructure), the data economy laboratory (which directs AI for financial gain), and the ethical and theoretical AI laboratory (which, ironically, is more about reflecting on the problems of AI rather than applying it as the above labs do).[18] This major emphasis on AI, however, is not unique to the school; the public funding body for this institution includes "big data and artificial intelligence" as one of its theme-based research directions[19] and has established "using artificial intelligence to address imminent challenges in health care" as a "strategic topic" for grant funding in the 2023/2024 academic year.[20] These funding directions on the municipal level echo national research policy as well.[21] Thus, top to bottom and back, AI is heralded as *the* solution of the future, the direction in which most, if not all, research should move.

The assumption operating behind the massive funding being directed to these projects (sometimes directly stated, and other times more implicit) is that AI *will* improve all areas of research: financial growth, medicine, artistic creativity, and governmental organization. This is the hope, though most projects to date have been primarily aspirational or proof of concept. It will be difficult to tell whether AI truly improves traffic monitoring, drug creation, and capital generation until enough data is created by these research projects to evaluate. Until then, AI has attracted public interest primarily by impressive tricks. DALL-E, Stable Diffusion, and Midjourney provide great entertainment by converting text prompts into images, including, in some cases, following specific artistic styles. ChatGPT, GPT-3, LaMDA, and Wu Dao offer impressive language generation and responses that seem to verge on "understanding." Tesla's Autopilot, Google's Waymo, and Uber have demonstrated impressive self-driving programs for automobiles. Of course, these specific programs have, till now, not done a great deal to *improve* human life: generating images or texts can be *fun* or offer opportunities for creativity, and self-driving may provide some leisure to the occupants of the car, but they do not notably achieve important human flourishing outcomes. If AI can deliver on the hopes tied to medicine, finance, infrastructure, and creativity, to say nothing of other research tied to basic science, manufacturing, communications, agriculture, social welfare, and ecology, then it will truly be a quantum leap in human history, bringing us into the sort of utopian world science fiction writers have longed for for decades.

Truthfully, though, the future is already here. The very bleeding edge of AI research may be directed toward these aspirational goals, but AI has already inserted itself in many aspects of our lives, supplanting labor from manufacturing and law enforcement to legal research and radiology.[22] AIs already demonstrate markedly higher accuracy rates in detecting breast cancer in mammograms than unassisted human radiologists.[23] AI is being developed to provide companionship and recreation; in the US, robotic companions are being used as part of the care program designed to assist older adults, while in China they are being adapted as playmates for lonely only children.[24] AI is even encroaching on the realm of human sexuality, providing "superior" sexual partners for lonely or frustrated humans.[25] Abyss Creations, for example, aims to create a sex robot that not only moves and feels like a human companion but also responds to her partner by using a cutting-edge AI personality.[26] Our work, our play, even our intimacy all seem to be undergoing major changes as AI is applied across ever more aspects of human existence.

But what makes AI specifically more interesting in public consciousness than current or past revolutions in vehicle design, agriculture, medicine, or production is that unlike more traditional forms of technology, AI promises to do things on its own.[27] Most of our technologies, from aircraft to blast furnaces to road pavers to medical imaging devices, require human operators whose job is to monitor, control, maintain, and activate. AI is intended to be automatic, removing the human element from the equation once and for all. And unlike other automated feedback systems, like cruise control or thermostats, AI is designed to *make decisions* that will improve performance and yield greater outcomes. An AI in charge of a factory could make adjustments to production to account for equipment problems, labor shortages, or material changes to optimize production without human oversight. Or, as is the goal of much automotive research today, an automated driving system should be able to make driving decisions that protect the life of the passengers while reducing traffic slowdown. In every instance, the promise of AI is better outcomes by a *smart* machine able to adapt to different problems.

Artificial Epistemology

What does it mean exactly to call a computer program "smart"? Labeling new technologies as "smart" is a marketing strategy to sell information and computing technologies, especially consumer electronics. Smartphones, the most ubiquitous example, gained prominence with the release of the iPhone in 2007. In the late aughts, smartphones primarily differed from personal digital assistants (PDAs) like Palm Pilot by their integrated mobile phone technology and from other cellphones like Motorola Razr by their ease of use and greater functionality. BlackBerry managed to do both of these things for years before the moniker "smartphone" shifted public opinion decisively in favor of these PDA-cum-mobile phone devices. Other "smart" devices to capture public opinion include the smartwatch, such as the iWatch, which functions as an extension of an iPhone or as a standalone miniature smartphone; the smart home, which integrates various "Internet of Things" devices like Wi-Fi–connected thermostats, lighting, music, and home appliances into a central control node; and the SMART Board, an interactive touch screen and whiteboard combination meant to improve education, corporate presentations, and other face-to-face communicative occasions. What all of these "smart" devices hold in common are essentially two features: first, they are information technologies that rely on sophisticated connection of software and hardware beyond a typical desktop or laptop personal computer, and second, they are integrated into the internet to allow control across distance. Beyond that, there is not much "smart" about a smart device. A smart thermostat that loses Wi-Fi connection is more useless than an analogue thermostat. A smart house that gets hacked externally will be a greater nuisance to the residents than a totally disconnected home. And a glitch or bug in the software of a smart device renders it "dumb" or unusable. AI, however, is meant to be smart in a way different from this marketing tactic.

The "intelligent" aspect of AI (what makes it "smart") is modeled after human intelligence. A machine that can drive like a human, play Go like a human, detect cancer like a human, or converse like a human is one that, in a basic sense, *might* be said to possess some "intelligence" like a human. These are all highly cognitive tasks, any one of which people spend literally years developing. Human infants are unable to convey anything but the most basic drives and feelings for their first two years, despite near the constant inundation of language from attentive parents. Because of this difficulty and the extraordinary feat required to accomplish it, the skillful use of language to communicate has long been seen as a hallmark of human uniqueness. To create a machine that can do this would be a magnificent accomplishment indeed! The ultimate goal of many AI researchers, then, is development of a machine that is intelligent like a human in all ways that we are intelligent, including calculation, conversation, analysis, prediction, and other forms of intelligent behavior. While AI is broadly used to talk about any area in which computers are able to autonomously perform human-type tasks, the ultimate goal of many researchers is artificial general intelligence (AGI), or computing that parallels human thinking in most, or at least many, different areas of human life, a computer we might call "conscious."[28]

Popular culture has cemented within public consciousness images of AGI. When the average person thinks of an intelligent machine, they begin to think of androids or disembodied computer voices, such as Data from *Star Trek*, HAL 9000 from *2001: A Space Odyssey*, or Samantha from *Her*. These speculative fiction accounts pose the question to us of what it would be like to live with a conscious computer. Some are warnings, others temptations, and still others, mere fantasies of what "could be." All of these accounts are pure imagination, however, not accurate depictions of the state of AI research. But the vision of these stories shapes the aspirations of AI researchers and gives direction to their own aims and purposes. Indeed, in a case of life and art imitating each other, Marvin Minsky and Arthur C. Clarke apparently collaborated together to imagine both the character HAL 9000 of *Space Odyssey* fame and goals of actual AI research.[29] Some futurists, like Hans Moravec or Ray Kurzweil, predict a future where humans live side-by-side with AGI in a human-machine civilization. Kurzweil's AI research has the hopeful goal of bringing us to "the Singularity," a moment when the human-machine civilization arrives and makes everything better.[30] More thinkers, however, expect conflict, ranging from innocently maleficent AI like the "paper clip" producer[31] to entirely malevolent AI like AM from Harlan Ellison's "I Have No Mouth and I Must Scream." Thus, organizations like the Machine Intelligence Research Institute purport to promote the importance of responsible AI development, not careless advancement of the field.[32] Even popular futurists and scientists, like Stephen Hawking and Elon Musk, have touted the dangers of AI if not developed carefully, and increasing numbers of tech luminaries call for shared ethical principles to stave off disaster.

In spite of these aspirational worries, creating a machine that thinks like we do is no small task. Speculations about malevolent or merely maleficently indifferent AI are rooted in presumptions that we can create machines that understand the world enough to operate autonomously but that lack moral understanding. While it is true that no human being does only morally good acts, we do have the ability to articulate if and why an act is good or bad. AI research aims at being able to codify this moral knowledge, along with all other forms of ordinary human cognitive behaviors, such as communication, automated spatial movement, image recognition, artistic creation, and so forth. But doing so means overcoming one facetiously simple problem: articulating what intelligence is in a way that can be built into a machine. AI researchers assume that intelligence can be produced through a machine (a computer) as long as the machine is built properly. The challenge, then, is figuring out what construction will result in the production of intelligence. Like the problem of constructing a consistently workable internal combustion engine,[33] creating a machine that consistently produces "intelligence" requires understanding the problem of intelligence adequately and what "moving parts" will result in this aim. And while Diesel's combustion engine relied on an adequate understanding of the laws of both thermodynamics and mechanics, AI's success relies on successful advances in hardware development, software programming, and, most dubious yet, adequate epistemology.

Epistemology is a field within philosophy that asks the basic question of how our minds work. The field dates back to Plato's *Timaeus*, wherein Socrates asks the basic question of how we know what we know. Socrates's conclusion in this dialogue is that knowledge is innately inside of human beings, unlocked through the proper questioning. Socrates's argument illustrates a basic philosophical problem: is our understanding of the world inherent, or is it instructed? Depending on how we answer, we then have to face the questions of the role of perception, the function of instruction, the possibility of learning, and the base of understanding. We seek to answer all of these epistemological questions, some through psychology, others through pedagogy, and others still cannot be separated from their roots in philosophy. While AI purports to be merely a subfield of computer science, the entire field of AI is an effort of applied epistemology. The project of AI is predicated upon a broad swath of epistemological assumptions, though individual AI theorists sometimes differ on specific questions. The title of Ray Kurzweil's 2012 bestseller *How to Create a Mind* summarizes the underlying assumption that applied epistemology and AI are synonymous.

Epistemology is also important for ethics. How we *know* what is right, what the conditions of moral knowledge are, and what forms of reasoning are considered legitimate in ethical reasoning are key questions for the field of ethics. These questions are further predicated upon broader questions of what the conditions of truth are, whether truth itself has any value, and what are the wrong things to believe. In turn, then, in spite of Hume's famous dispute that "ought or ought not" should not be predicated upon mere statements of "is or is not,"[34] the questions of what is and how we know what is are inherently bound up in questions of what we should or should not do or become. Or, in the words of Herbert Marcuse, "Epistemology is in itself ethics, and ethics is epistemology."[35]

Epistemological questions ground our moral reasoning, but the valuation of moral agents is also deeply entwined with assumptions about mind. "Rationality" as an epistemic trait has been a key moral value from Plato to Thomas Aquinas to Kant to contemporary ethical thinkers. Being able to engage in argumentation in favor of one's position seems to be a precondition for having one's interests considered in moral discourse. Indeed, as David Gunkel points out, rationality has long been considered both a necessary and sufficient condition for moral agency, ascribing personhood to the rational entity and therefore corresponding moral autonomy and rights.[36]

The underlying assumptions, then, that guide AI research are that intelligence is good and what is good is intelligent. It is good to be intelligent: beings that possess intelligence are beings worthy of dignity and rights, while beings that lack intelligence have no such recourse. Intelligent beings will do what is good: moral rectitude is a function of proper reason, and moral wrongness results either from incorrect reasoning or from stupidity. Intelligence will also result in good: intelligent engineers, scientists, and soon machines will create a world that is better in all meaningful ways for us to live in. But since human beings are so often limited in our intelligence by things like disease, aging, emotions, brain functioning, and so on, our best hope is to create an artificial intelligence to maximize good. The future is AI, and the future is bright.

The World AI Promises

An important distinction needs to be made. Artificial general intelligence (AGI) is the idea that a computer can *generally* do all that a human mind does (and, eventually, a great deal more). This must be distinguished from narrow AI, or weak AI. Narrow AI is artificial intelligence designed for a *specific* cognitive function. Examples of this include image recognition, natural language processing, and, yes, even playing Go. While AGI is the promise of machines truly intelligent like us, narrow AI is far and away where most current "breakthroughs" in AI are occurring and where most money is being directed. AGI as a field (in some form) has been around for nearly seventy years but has yet to accomplish its aims. Narrow AI, on the other hand, has had tremendous success in the past ten years and is revolutionizing the very world around us on an almost daily basis.

As a portion of the economy, AI has grown astronomically in recent years. Investment in AI research rose from less than $1 billion in 2010 to over $4 billion by 2016. Private corporations like Google, Facebook, Amazon, Alibaba, Apple, and Tesla have made AI research a major platform of their business strategies, and world government organizations like the US National Science Foundation, EU Horizons, and the Chinese National Natural Science Foundation are awarding multimillion-dollar grants to AI research projects. A recent study from the International Data Corporation found that AI was a $157 billion industry in 2020 and is expected to surpass $300 billion by 2024.[37] Only a decade ago, AI was relegated to a pet project for major Web 2.0 corporations or stubborn university researchers; today it is a growing multibillion-dollar field, establishing itself as a key component of the future economy and setting conditions for world-economic competition for the twenty-first century.

However, AI as an industry does not exist primarily on its own. It is not as though the billions of dollars are being invested just in consumer robotics or artificial companions. Rather, AI as an industry is primarily deployed in other industries through expert systems, analytics, marketing, prediction and forecasting, logistics, manufacturing, and so forth, directed toward finding ways to save costs and maximize returns. Each of these is an application of narrow AI, an effort to develop and use AI as a tool among other tools. AI in this view will function within specific tasks that already utilize many cutting-edge technologies, such as massive databases for logistics processing or neuroimaging in marketing.[38] AI adds to these by filtering data, automating processes, organizing tasks, or other tedious but cognitively taxing tasks, with the overall goal of both saving money by avoiding errors and human costs and increasing profit by realizing maximum market saturation with minimal loss.

It comes as no surprise that according to the World Economic Forum, among the major applications of AI are digital technologies and communication, finances, transportation, and health care.[39] The superior computational and processing capabilities of AI over human beings make the technology ideal for many functions within these areas. In communications and transportation, AI is capable of analyzing movement of data and predicting optimal solutions to best direct traffic (whether vehicular or digital).[40] In health care, AI is already outstripping human experts to provide more accurate diagnostics.[41] In finances, AI is able to more rapidly and accurately forecast changes in the market, thus giving firms an edge in increasing their investment rates.[42] AI researchers and prognosticators have touted AI revolutions in nearly every single industry across the board, to both applaud and woe—applaud as they improve efficiency and woe as they upend current labor paradigms.

AI has also made inroads in public culture beyond industry-specific applications by specialists. One of the most hyped applications of AI has been self-driving cars. Elon Musk's Tesla regularly boasts about the achievements of its "Autopilot" near-autonomous system,[43] and companies like Uber are looking for ways to deploy fleets of self-driving cars for human transportation.[44] All other major automobile manufacturers are pursuing this trend, with GM recently releasing a new heavy-duty pickup truck with self-driving capabilities.[45] Indeed, self-driving cars are one of the most promised and performative examples of AI for public consciousness. Most people will not notice how AI is changing logistics or health care records, but a car that drives itself is a very clear demonstration of the state of the art!

Perhaps a more common application of AI, however, is found in facial recognition technology. Such technology began to gain attention as Facebook used AI systems over a decade ago to "suggest" tagging one's friends in uploaded photos. Since this time, facial recognition has become prevalent in government use and policing.[46] The technology is also implemented in consumer electronics, with Apple's iPhones from Model X and up using facial recognition as a security measure for unlocking one's phone and inbuilt photo applications automatically identifying pictures of friends and family members. Computers being able to identify individual faces was merely a concept in spy movies a few decades ago, but now citizens of the US, China, UK, and elsewhere regularly encounter this technology in airports, municipal buildings, banks, and other places. While some advocates of the technology promise it will improve security and facilitate easier social transactions, critics worry about the use of invasive surveillance technology, and some US cities like San Francisco, Berkeley, Portland, and Boston have banned its use in law enforcement.[47]

Beyond this, AI prognosticators are hoping that AI will very truly be directed "to the relief of man's estate."[48] Governments and universities, less interested in producing consumer AIs, have large-scale social improvement plans. Some of these include advances in medicine, prompted no doubt by DeepMind's recent advancements in understanding protein folds, which could potentially revolutionize drug production.[49] Other goals include improvement of municipalities, making cities cleaner, safer, wealthier, more honest, and more educated (i.e., "smarter").[50] Still others focus on agriculture, hoping to better reduce food waste and agricultural yield through "precision agriculture" and "precision livestock farming."[51] The list goes on, of course: governing bodies hope that AI will aid in preventing (or concluding) global conflicts, reversing climate change, preventing economic downturns, containing disease outbreaks (such as the COVID-19 pandemic), and so on. Assuming that AI is not misused for ill purposes or even for well-intentioned but poorly thought-through aims (as in policing or automated weapons systems), then the hope is that these applications are only the foretaste of what AI will bring. The visions of science fiction—houses that automatically regulate internal conditions, effortless commutes through smart transportation, eradication of hunger and disease—find purchase in the unrealized promises of AI.

All of this current investment and forecasted investment ties into what STS scholar Lee Vinsel calls "criti-hype."[52] Criti-hype is the dual-reinforcing criticism and hype surrounding new technologies. Those who hype the technology promise wildly fantastic dreams, while the critics lob jeremiads against its doomsday nature. In a case like nuclear technology, this *may* be warranted, but AI is at present mostly speculation. The hope that AI *will* be able to autonomously navigate busy roads, communicate effortlessly with hospital patients, or independently conduct scientific research belies the reality that self-driving cars increasingly wreck, natural language processing has difficulties with dialects and colloquialisms, and scientific research does not always yield expected results. Criti-hype is most dangerous, Vinsel notes, because by looking at the *possible* or *hoped for* instead of the *is*, critics and proponents alike miss real-world challenges that the technology should actually be addressing. But the promise of AI has sustained both those preaching the Good Word of machine-human utopia and those warning the impending doom of AI apocalypse. And the apocalyptic prophets have benefited the evangelists just as much as the evangelists have justified the warnings of the prophets.

Suffice it to say that the criti-hype fuels AI's integration into every field, warranted or not. This goes for self-driving cars, voice assistants, companion robots, lethal autonomous weapons systems, smart cities, and other proposed or current technologies, many of which are founded on AI breakthroughs, but all of which succeed because of the *hype*. Musk's "AI Day" inflated his financial holdings beyond Bezos's without any need for him to point to any existing successes that would warrant his claims![53] Whether or not AI is actively improving these industries is not the point; the promise that it *will* is. And everyone from C-suite executives to consumers buy into the expectation. This hype is so successful that even my Samsung air conditioner's adaptive setting is called AI, despite it being only a slight improvement on the centuries-old thermostat.

It's important to see that the hype of AI is behind the WEF and IDC's predictions about the future of AI across industries. But ultimately, it is important to note, the excitement behind narrow AI is the criti-hyped promise of *AGI*. That AI and robotics might soon replace construction jobs isn't really that surprising; after all, robotics has already revolutionized many manufacturing jobs, which were previously revolutionized by the invention of the factory over workshops. With industrialism came urbanization: the rural peasantry was replaced by urban labor, which has in turn been replaced by international service labor. Technological change begets labor change, and AI seems to be only the recent variation on this theme. But given that many AI breakthroughs are new and have not yet demonstrated their usefulness, why should there be such a rapid expansion of the industry? Because the goal is not AI for medical diagnostics that still need human interpreters or AI for legal research, which still needs human litigators, but for AI to do the same work that human beings do—full stop.

There are, of course, AI firms and AI researchers who do not see their work leading to the endpoint of AGI.[54] But the most prominent and notable firms and researchers all have this as their goal. Take Google's DeepMind, the team behind AlphaGo, as an example. Their current research intersects numerous industry-specific goals, such as scientific research, medical diagnostics, and energy efficiency, but their stated "long term aim is to solve intelligence, developing more general and capable problem-solving systems, known as artificial general intelligence (AGI)."[55] Questions of narrow AI can be addressed either through examination of particular applications of AI—such as policing, fake news, big data analytics, and so forth—or through questions about how narrow AI fits into AGI. Since AGI remains an elusive goal, narrow AI seems like a useful arena in which to build up the base of AGI. If AGI is then a matter of just connecting various component narrow AI successfully,[56] then an important underlying question of all AI work is what the model of AGI is, as it directs the goals of narrow AI, and whether that model is appropriate and adequate.

The Stage Is Set

With this background, we have the material to reflect carefully on the claims and goals of artificial intelligence research. AI proponents try to sell us an epistemology through surreptitious claims of its profitability. They hold research money, data, corporate boards, government offices, university posts, and celebrity statuses. But they remain a minority group whose goal when it comes to AI is to sell a fantasy to the masses of the world. This fantasy, however, covers rot. Beneath the veneer of a pristine world of automated luxury is the niggling question of who must be excluded from the utopia for AI to be included. The excluded, we are surprised to find, are those not only deprived economically from the riches of the elites but, more significantly, who face erasure by the uncanny appearance of artificial "persons." This drama unfolds on the pages following: a story of artificial intelligence pioneers, their critics, the misunderstood poor, the economy, and larger social institutions and ideologies. But this is also a story that has been told and retold throughout history—a story of competition between the weak and the powerful, the tools they have at their disposal, and the terms of the conflict. The setting may look different, but the characters should all be familiar.

CHAPTER 1

A Mind like a Machine

FACTORIES HAVE BEEN a mainstay of the modern era since the late eighteenth century. Indeed, many philosophers, including Hannah Arendt, Jacques Ellul, Karl Marx, and even Hegel, have noted that the pivotal change of technology from the preindustrial to the industrial era is the autonomous nature of "machines" over the human-controlled function of "tools."[1] A perennial problem of the factory system, however, is that human beings are always necessary for production, but they often suffer from problems machines do not. As social reformer and factory owner Robert Owen pointed out, "An excess of labour and confinement prematurely weakens and destroys all the functions of the animal frame," the loss of which impacts not only the wretched poor but also the capitalist, whose productivity is limited by human constraints.[2] Thus, an important potential of AI is its possibility to overcome the need for human laborers.

The world's largest employer, Foxconn, has taken just this approach in recent years. Foxconn has nearly one million employees, primarily in Mainland China (though the company is headquartered in Taiwan). They produce consumer electronics, from LCD monitors to iPhones. The company gained notoriety in 2012 after a spate of suicides in its Shenzhen plant prompted company leaders to set up netting around the building to catch would-be jumpers.[3] The long hours, poor ventilation, and tedious and physically taxing work led to despair among its employees. Four years later, however, the company announced they would automate up to one-third of their manufacturing jobs.[4] The automation would ostensibly get rid of the most tedious and hazardous jobs, allowing human laborers to have more fulfilling work, while the electronics company continued its high production.

But automation does not automatically mean better conditions for humans. "In 1981, a thirty-seven-year-old Japanese employee of a motorcycle factory was killed by an artificial-intelligence robot working near him. The robot erroneously identified the employee as a threat to its mission, and calculated that the most efficient way to eliminate this threat was by pushing him into an adjacent operating machine. Using its very powerful hydraulic arm, the robot smashed the surprised worker into the operating machine, killing him instantly, and then resumed its duties with no one to interfere with its mission."[5] One of the great challenges of AI, then, is creating an autonomous manufacturing system that would not put any human workers in danger, all while creating the necessary wealth to warrant the switch to automation for the benefit of all.

While the "Turing test" is the most famous standard for machine intelligence, AI researchers have proven to be quite creative in imagining other ways to test intelligence. One such standard is the so-called café test, where a machine might be considered "intelligent" if it can successfully enter a café, order a meal off the menu, eat it (the machine does not actually need to eat), pay the staff, and leave. Articulated in the GOFAI method of outlining discrete steps to be performed, this task seems fairly straightforward—instructions include waiting to be seated (unless a sign directs otherwise), selecting (possibly at random) items from the menu, vocally articulating the menu items to wait staff, waiting for the meal, and paying adequate cash for the bill. However, this problem is much more complicated in reality than it is in theory. Obvious exceptions to the norm will include the following: restaurants where one should seat themself, menu items being unavailable, cash-only or cashless restaurants, and unpredictable human actions by patrons (e.g., a bar full of rowdy sports fans) or staff (e.g., frustrated wait staff). But while a waiter who cannot speak English may be a deviation from the norm (in the United States), the degree to which this is "weird" is much smaller than if the patrons spontaneously engaged in a food fight. Indeed, as Hubert Dreyfus wryly notes, this is one of the more alarming obstacles for achieving realistically human levels of AI:

> This is John Searle's way of formulating this important point [about subtle human understandings of what is "normal" involved in a trip to a restaurant]. In a talk at the University of California at Berkeley (October 19, 1977), [Roger] Schank agreed with Searle that to understand a visit to a restaurant, the computer needs more than a script; it needs to know everything that people know. He added that he is unhappy that as it stands his program cannot distinguish "degrees of weirdness." Indeed, for the program, it is equally "weird" for the restaurant to be out of food as it is for the customer to respond by devouring the chef. Thus Schank seems to agree that without some understanding of degree of deviation from the norm, the program does not understand a story even when in that story events follow a completely normal stereotyped script. It follows that although scripts capture a necessary condition of everyday understanding, they do not provide a sufficient condition.[6]

At present, AI does not have a way of distinguishing what makes one action "weirder" than another. Thus, AI philosophers warn that it is important that explicit and detailed instructions guide machine behavior. Otherwise, one might end up with the doomsday scenario wherein cleaning AI realizes that the best solution to eradicate dirt is to eradicate the cause of dirt, i.e., messy human beings. Without specifying the exact limitations on what should be included in cleaning activity, and especially the degree to which certain actions are unacceptable, an AI may take it upon itself to commit genocide.

The Quest for AGI

The push for developing a human-like calculating machine has a surprisingly long genealogy. In 1666, Gottfried Wilhelm Leibniz hypothesized that logical thought was merely a consequence of manipulating inputs and receiving expected outputs, so a machine might be built that housed an "alphabet of human thoughts" that could process human ideas as a mind does.[7] Leibniz's epistemology, following Plato's, assumed that the totality of human knowledge was limited and could be represented sufficiently with an adequate set of symbols. Two centuries later, Ada Lovelace, considered by many to be the first programmer, took up the question again with Babbage's "analytic engine," an early calculating machine. Lovelace believed such a device could be capable of reproducing and even complexifying music and images, but only according to mathematical formulae. She assumed, then, that such a machine would be epistemologically limited. Lovelace writes, "The Analytical Engine has no pretensions whatever to originate any thing. It can do whatever we know how to order it to perform. It can follow analysis; but it has no power of anticipating any analytical relations or truths."[8] In taking the question seriously and demonstrating basic principles of computer programming, Lovelace (perhaps inadvertently) paved the way for AI pioneers who took her proposition as a challenge.

While the early field of computing held mixed opinions on computer consciousness, the developing genre of science fiction furnished renewed interest in the prospect of a "thinking machine." Karel Čapek's 1920 play *R.U.R.* (*Rossumovi Univerzální Roboti*, or, in English, *Rossum's Universal Robots*), from which we take the English word "robot," imagines human-made beings (not truly machines) capable of thought, autonomous work, communication, and eventually resentment, organization, and violent revolt as they overthrow the humans. Fritz Lang's 1927 film *Metropolis* features a mechanical doll that has the character Maria's consciousness implanted into it, articulating a clear anthropomorphization of automata via human ensoulment. In the decades following, the concept of human-like machines became enshrined in popular consciousness, following John Scott Campbell's 1930 short story "The Infinite Brain," which imagines a human consciousness immortalized in a machine, and Isaac Asimov's science fiction stories beginning in the 1940s, which popularized the concept of artificial intelligence in mechanical robots. Science fiction, of course, is free from the constraints of reality to give voice to its authors' wildest dreams, but imagination detailed in the pages of paperbacks and comic books, on silver screens and stages, inspired and continues to inspire generations of computer scientists. Thanks in no small part to robot fiction, by the mid-twentieth century, the musings of Leibniz and Lovelace had become enshrined in popular culture and moved into academic discourse. The philosophical views of Leibniz and Lovelace thus inspired fiction, which in turn inspired the development of sciences, a sort of representation of the sort of "feedback mechanism" at root in the field of cybernetics.

These underpinnings set the aspirations, but artificial intelligence work gets its theoretical grounding in the 1940s. Following the Second World War's advancements in ciphering and deciphering messages using complex mathematical systems, two new branches of science in the US and Britain merged to give rise to the field of artificial intelligence: computing and cybernetics. The goal of creating human-like computer programs was pioneered by thinkers like Alan Turing and John McCarthy, but it was cybernetics that argued more forcefully that cognition was an essentially mathematical-mechanical action, as seen in the work of Claude Shannon and Norbert Wiener.

In 1948, the cyberneticist Claude Shannon proposed that all information could be reduced to a pattern of binary sequences. A sequence of off/on signals, sufficiently long enough, could convey anything as brief as an S.O.S. to full-length novels.[9] Shannon had in mind not only the reality of telegraphic communication employed in his time wherein messages were conveyed through electrical signals sent across long distances but also the future of computing technology. By representing information by a binary digit, shortened to "bit," any information in theory could be represented independent of the content of the information.[10] Thus, a series of ones and zeros, easy to transmit through electronic systems by opening and closing electric circuits, could reproduce any information that human beings wish to convey, whether a friendly message, a series of instructions, or the depths of philosophy. This model of information communication not only undergirds all contemporary *digital* computers—that is, machines that compute information using discrete binary states—but is also the principle at work behind digital communication, where computers send packets of bits through telephone wires to other receiving digital computers. On a small scale, this is ships at sea using radio waves to transmit Morse code. On a large scale, this is the internet: billions of digital computers sending trillions of bits across telecommunications networks across the world every second.

Alan Turing, the father of modern computing, extended Shannon's thesis by claiming that digital computers are nothing less than "Universal Turing Machines"—machines that can simulate *any* other machine. All mechanical movement, per Turing, is simply a function of information, and since all information can be represented in bits, every machine can be accurately simulated, from a four-cylinder combustion engine to the entire universe.[11] In his view, the human brain is such a machine, and thinking is merely the brain's *mechanical* functioning. Turing hypothesized that a digital computer can be said to "think" if it can successfully win the "Imitation Game," a test where a human judge tries to successfully choose which responses to questions are from a computer and not a human being, now commonly referred to as the Turing test.[12] It is important to note for Turing that the question of human consciousness is not deeply relevant: if the computer can adequately imitate a conscious human, there is no reason to believe the machine is not itself conscious. While Turing's "test" for the threshold of computer intelligence has been questioned by many researchers since, his proposal set a goal for computer programmers, and AI researchers for the past seventy years have tried to achieve this or similar standards for human cognition through computer programming.

The same year that Turing set the standard for AI, Norbert Wiener published *The Human Use of Human Beings*, the definitive text for the field of cybernetics. Wiener develops Shannon's information theory into an information ontology: in his view, material composition of any given thing is insignificant; the essential operation of everything can be understood through its informational context. Indeed, predicting the surge in genomics following Crick, Watson, and Franklin's Nobel Prize–winning work on DNA, Wiener asserted, "We are not the stuff that abides [i.e., biological matter], but patterns that perpetuate themselves."[13] From this view, the physical movement of things in space is a question of information and subsequent feedback. Cybernetics as a field, then, focuses on feedback to stimuli, often through mechanistic functioning. Thus, the human mind is conceived of as a massive feedback machine. Wiener writes, "The Nervous system and the automatic machine are fundamentally alike in that they are devices which make decisions on the basis of decisions they have made in the past"; i.e., they operate on a programmed response.[14] Cybernetics reinforces the view of Turing that the human mind is the same in its operation as a machine and can be replicated by a machine. A given input of information, when interpreted by the human brain, will yield a predictable and given output. And if a human brain can be understood as a sophisticated information processor, then it is feasible that a sophisticated information processor can replicate the phenomenon of "consciousness" humans seem to possess. And yet, even if our minds essentially operate according to simple (or complex) reaction processes, this itself does not address how a human actor can act in a way that anticipates future response, i.e., that selects choices (even as feedback) that predict results of other feedback mechanisms.

Thus, John McCarthy, who, along with Shannon, Marvin Minsky, and Nathaniel Rochester, helped coin the term "artificial intelligence," recognized the need for AI programming to include an adequate epistemology and metaphysics to operate in the world.[15] Without formalizing logical processes, the "mechanism" of cognition could not be modeled. A computer must be able to properly "grasp" laws of causality and ordinary operations of the universe if it is to generate any reasonably intelligent thought, let alone hold human-level consciousness. This is only possible if the structure of the universe and its concordant explanations can be reduced to mathematical formulae. McCarthy further specifies we need both a model of "general intelligence" and a sufficient coding process to instruct machines into carrying it out.[16] In other words, a workable epistemology, replete with explanation of perception and cognition, and cognitive models that correspond to reality are necessary for AI.

AI theory thus employs somewhat circuitous reasoning to present its full theory: Shannon proposed that information could be converted to bits regardless of content, Turing insisted all mechanical operation could be reduced to bits, and Wiener proposed the brain is such a machine. But McCarthy returned to the original problem and noted that the machine itself must be able to process the information in a way that yields cognition and not just numerical data. To bridge the gap between epistemology and (numerical) information processing, the conclusion that thinking is inherently mathematical is asserted as a premise to demonstrate the conclusion. It is important to note that McCarthy, Turing, Minsky, and others did not propound the phenomenological model of epistemology that most of us assume: they did not think "understanding" or "consciousness" needed to be fully proven by the machine to demonstrate its intelligence.[17] Because consciousness is a philosophical posit and not a demonstrable trait, it is irrelevant for a machine to *actually* be able to ponder its life if it can *appear* to do so. What you see is what you get; if it can yield results similar to a conscious being, it can be considered conscious.

Thus, the limits and scope of AI were established. Each success in computer science for decades was seen as vindicating the field. As information was converted to bits and as programs yielded adequate responses to input, the views of the cyberneticists and computer scientists were vindicated. Once McCarthy exposed the "frame problem," that is, the challenge of "framing" general intelligence into first-order logic, AI researchers saw achieving AI as merely a problem of programming the right amount of rules into a machine. Hubert Dreyfus notes with irony that, for the first few decades of AI, the achievement of AGI was seen as being imminent, but every few years, the target for that goal moved away.[18] Eventually, in the 80s and 90s, the difficulty of AI was realized and the field experienced what some have called an "AI winter," where the promises of AI were muted and breakthroughs were few and far between.[19]

The Renewal of AI: Neural Networks, Machine Learning, Natural Language Processing

The AI winter was not bereft of progress, however. AI pioneers like Hans Moravec, Ray Kurzweil, and Ben Goertzel inspired new generations of thinkers while advancing the epistemological assumptions undergirding AGI. Moravec's *Mind Children* promised massive developments in computing and robotics and even articulated the previously unstated goal of uploading full-scale human minds to a computer. Based on his available models, he estimated that computers, in terms of hardware and software capabilities, would reach "human equivalence" by the year 2030.[20] He outlined specific requirements for intelligent machines, which included learning processes, spatial awareness, and larger scales of computer processing power to compare with human neurological activity. Moravec frames these concrete aims against the backdrop of a vision of uploaded and artificial intelligences coexisting in cyberspace. The promise of uploaded minds, now given "scientific" sanction, maintained the vision of AI and inspired new generations of computer scientists.

Following Moravec, Ray Kurzweil and Ben Goertzel added to the framing problem the view that general intelligence is primarily a matter of pattern recognition.[21] Goertzel, who coined the term "AGI" (instead of simply AI, or Good Old-Fashioned AI), reframed the aims of AI work to be more heuristic in focus through patternism. In this view, a general set of rules and all of its possible exceptions do not need to be written; rather, the ability to recognize patterns and adapt to them is the hallmark of general intelligence.[22] Ideally, this solves the framing issue, as a computer will not need millions of frames containing millions of rules but rather a set of patterns that contain their own subsets of patterns and the computer's ability to recognize which patterns are prevalent in the given situation. Like a jazz musician improvising based on key, tempo, rhythm, and melody, a computer does not need to have the "score" memorized to act intelligently as we do not need a rote script.

Ray Kurzweil then takes this idea to its logical conclusion: since the mind primarily functions to recognize patterns, and since cognition is an encodable sequence of instructions, and since communication can be reduced to a binary pattern, everything boils down to finding the right patterns.[23] The goal of uploading a mind, for example, requires us to recognize the right patterns of neurological activity that cause specific pattern-finding activities that we call "thinking." The pattern in our brain looks for patterns in its own pattern-searching behavior. Moreover, if we can figure out the pattern that makes up the pattern-finding cognition we do, we can program these as binary patterns into a machine that will execute the same patterns in a process less clumsily referred to as AI. Thus, although early AI pioneers followed their own epistemological views independent (largely) of brain sciences (such as cognitive science, neurology, psychology), Kurzweil, following Moravec and Goertzel, expects that tracing the right neuron patterns in our brains will reveal the secret to consciousness, which can then be transcribed into a computer.

This complicated understanding of how the mind operates fundamentally shifted AI research a decade ago. As Hubert Dreyfus notes, one of the problems early AI came up against was the challenge of not only programming *enough* information into a computer but also programming the *relevance* of this information.[24] Programming *enough* information presents a problem of labor: if Marvin Minsky were correct that AI would merely need a few million "facts" from which to extrapolate a world,[25] AI researchers would only need to derive a comprehensive list of what all of those facts are and write them individually into the programming. Aside from this, however, is the problem of *relevance*. Here emerges the problem of "weird AI." Weird AI is when AI follows its set of instructions but arrives at answers that seem nonsensical to ordinary human beings. Janelle Shane details many examples of weird AI both in her book *You Look Like a Thing and I Love You* and on her blog *AI Weirdness*. One telling example is the use of natural language processing program GPT-2 to generate recipes. GPT-2 has rules for words and instructions for recipes but does not "understand" what a recipe is, nor, of course, how taste works. Humans with even minimal culinary experience *know* what absolutely will not work for food, but an AI, lacking taste buds and dietary experience, has no context on this front. So the AI generates recipes like "Chocolate Chicken Chicken Cake," which has no chocolate in it, or "Crock Pot Cold Water," which is a vanilla-y mixture of cornstarch, water, and baking powder heated in a slow cooker.[26]

Kurzweil et al.'s solution of "pattern recognition" would then lead AI to focus on finding patterns on its own rather than human beings trying to program all the rules into it. A general program designed to read patterns is better than one given every single rule and operates on a more *heuristic* level than rote algorithm. This insight led to improvements in machine learning. Machine learning (ML) is a process initially theorized by Arthur Samuel to identify the way by which machines can program themselves through data analysis.[27] By giving computers a way to *instruct* themselves, programmers can avoid the challenge of programming millions of rules into the program. This allows the computer to create its own set of rules, which, applied to the given instructions, should provide human-like capabilities for select tasks. Nearly *all* advances in AI over the past decade are due to advances in ML. Despite the advance in AI that machine learning has brought with it, challenges still exist in this model. Dreyfus relays the famous (though apocryphal) story of a neural network trained to see tanks in a forest that seemed to succeed only to fail in successive tests. When trying to identify the problem, it was pointed out to researchers that the pictures of the forest without tanks were taken when it was sunny, while the pictures with tanks were taken when it was cloudy.[28] The neural network failed, then, because it associated tanks with cloudy lighting rather than the actual shape of the vehicles. It would seem the rules the network taught itself were poor rules. The veracity of this pericope may be open to question, but the problem it highlights is real enough: when a machine trains itself, we are unable to see what rules it teaches itself to follow. The "black box" obscures our ability to check it, so unless or until an AI makes an obvious mistake, we have no idea what set of rules it is following.

The solution to this problem, however, has been fairly straightforward: provide the computer with *more* data. If a computer has taught itself poor rules, the solution for ML researchers is to provide it with data that will help it correct this. Much like teaching a toddler that "bird" does not mean "flying animal" (as bats are mammals while penguins are birds), a computer with flawed rules needs better information to get a clearer understanding. The rise of "Big Data" around 2010 was a godsend for the world of limited data sets. As the internet became more accessible to average consumers with more data stored by more companies, the field of AI saw massive advances in machine learning. Companies like Google and Facebook collect massive quantities of data, which they sell to third parties and use in their own AI divisions. This data is too great for human agents to meaningfully sift through but makes great training sets for machine learning programs. Thus, the advance of Big Data in combination with more sophisticated machine learning techniques and better neural networks has allowed for much of the advance in today's AI industry.

Simple instructions or processes allow observers to more easily discover shortcomings in programming, but more sophisticated programs are more challenging. When AlphaGo beat Sedol Lee, it was able to do so because the program had trained itself by playing *millions* of games of Go against itself. But there were cases where the program did peculiar things, such as move thirty-seven of the second game, a move many experts considered an embarrassing mistake by the program because of its unorthodoxy but which proved critical for the program's victory.[29] More striking, though less well reported, was AlphaGo violating Go protocol by playing while Sedol Lee was out of the room in the third game.[30] A human Go player has learned to play Go in the human context, and such rules are part of this learning, but the machine lacks all of this—it *only* knows the rules of the game. But Go is more than strict rules. It includes protocols, a culture and gestures of respect. The machine, lacking this context because it is neither embodied nor did it develop by playing actual Go masters (only basic Go programming), does not have the knowledge nor the ability to know that it committed a faux pas. This black box model can lead to grave social problems with AI, such as the rise of "racist AI," which favors white persons in its judgments more than people of color, especially people of African descent. While these failures are not intended, it is important to understand that the confidence one often reads about AI belies many cases of aberrations, some of which can be quite harmful, based on the same machine learning methods used in different contexts.

Another major advancement over the early decades of AI research is the neural network. Because AI is meant to imitate human cognition, AI researchers from early on determined that the best way to build an artificial brain was to imitate a natural one. Understanding how cognition works on a physical level—the "machinery" of the brain—has been a critical part of AI research, and advancements in cognitive science have been important for the field. One such development was the "neural network" model proposed by Warren McCulloch and Walter Pitts in 1943.[31] Based on the interconnection of neurons making up the brain, McCulloch and Pitts hypothesized that thought was conducted in the brain by sequences of neurons firing in parallel. The relevance of this model for neuroscience today is obvious; we regularly rely on neural imaging technologies like MRIs and CT scans to detect cognitive abnormalities.

Applied to computer science, McCulloch and Pitts's insights suggested that part of the equation of AI was creating some mechanical parallel to organic neural activity. Series of transistors transmitting electricity, for example, can be used to mimic the calculative activity of brain neurons firings in sequence. However, early AI found itself stymied by processing limitations: single-layer neural networks lacked the processing capabilities to do much quickly.[32] Early computer technology was expensive, large, and slow. In no way could the machines of Turing's time carry out as complex of tasks as humans ordinarily do. Our brains simultaneously process massive amounts of parallel information that we are not always conscious we are processing. To take a facetiously simple task, driving a car requires numerous parallel processes, including navigating, observing traffic and road conditions, obeying traffic laws, steering, accelerating, and braking. Even seeing itself involves numerous activities, including moving and focusing our eyes, filtering unimportant material while narrowing in on important things, being aware of the periphery, and continually scanning new environments. (Any driver who has had to turn down the stereo to better "see" while looking for the right street to turn down can verify that even seeing requires a great deal of concentration.) An experienced driver is not consciously aware of doing all of these things as they become automatic, but any teenager learning to drive has to develop the habit of being aware of all of these simultaneously. Any one of these activities involves millions of neurons firing simultaneously to make a concerted cognitive act. Early computer processors were utterly incapable of anything close to such orchestrated activity. Developments in silicon chips and miniaturization improved computer capabilities tremendously, but not enough. In 1985, parallel processing was proposed as a better model, which allows for several processors to simultaneously process distributed data.[33] Multiple processors working together in parallel function much more like a biological neural network than single streams of neural processing.

Today, neural networks distribute data processing among sequences of processors, allowing a greater amount of work to be done simultaneously. The effect of this is to improve processing power for massive projects, such as image recognition, which requires a breakdown of digital images, comparison with databases, and analyses. For small tasks, a computer with multiple processor cores can conduct basic distributed processing, but for larger tasks, large networks of computers are used. The underlying challenge, then, amounts to resource allocation and power size. Sophisticated AI processing does not occur on a small laptop: it requires massive data centers, which consume massive amounts of power. A major recent development in the field of AI hardware has been the advanced capabilities of graphics processing units, or GPUs (what we once called "video cards"). GPUs are designed to process *more* information more quickly than central processing units (the main "brain" that carries out all processing in a typical computer), and connecting several together in concert allows massive amounts of information processing to occur simultaneously. The problem of AI hardware is therefore becoming much more soluble, leaving primarily the software problem, that is, actually getting the super-powerful computing machines to carry out the right instructions to be "intelligent." Nonetheless, it is important to note the ecological cost of such processing is non-negligible and offers but one further area where achieving AGI is complicated, especially if accomplishing it entails speeding up climate change.[34]

Current and Future Trends in AI

As the understanding of the problem of AGI has become increasingly complicated (while McCarthy, Minsky, Turing, Shannon, Wiener, and others remain relevant, more obstacles have appeared than were previously thought to have existed), new subdivisions of AI have gained specialist attention. Today, one is not merely a computer scientist nor even just an AI researcher; they will likely specialize in a narrow section of AI and work on specific narrow AI problems. AI has made tremendous strides over the past twenty years in specific goal areas, including image processing, robotics, planning, and natural language processing. Image processing includes AI's ability to identify general visual stimuli, from differentiating between road signs to identifying individuals in facial recognition. Robotics involves the movement of machines in real space, from automated factory machinery to free-moving robotic vehicles. Planning is AI's ability to make optimal choices based on given goals, such as plotting a route for travel or speculating on the securities market. Taken together, these three fields are necessary for free-moving robots, from carrier drones to self-driving cars. These all function, in the words of Minsky, as various "machines" working together that make up our consciousness (at least in theory).[35] For the sake of simplicity, however, natural language processing (NLP) serves as a paradigmatic case that demonstrates the obstacles still present and the goals AI is reaching toward.

Natural language processing is a key area of AI necessary for having truly human-like thinking machines. Since human beings convey ideas most clearly through language (just as you are reading this in language, and I am writing it in language), it is necessary for computers to be able to use language skillfully, both in receiving information and in transmitting it. This is so fundamental that the original "Imitation Game" or "Turing test" is predicated primarily upon NLP: a computer that can "speak" at a human level might be said to be as intelligent as a human.[36] This is, for most of the public, what AI really is—computers that *talk* with us, implying that the machine behind the voice is a *res cogitans* like we are.

Voice assistants like Siri or Alexa represent great strides in this field, but anybody who has found themselves frustrated at Siri for repeating "I'm sorry; I didn't catch that" knows that the "natural" language processing of these programs leaves much to be desired.

Many of the great advancements in recent years on this front have taken insights from machine learning and used them to further language usage. An early example of work done in NLP, chatbots use key words and phrases to determine the right response, but the answers are prefabricated and useless outside of the narrow range of preprogrammed nuanced understandings. Queries that do not contain key words yield no useful answers. Cleverbot, a more advanced chatbot, collects responses from conversations it has and so expands its own database of possible answers and relevant key words. However, these are once again predetermined from a list, in this case from other users' responses, and thus often fail to resemble anything meaningful.[37] Greater data sets are then necessary for an NLP program to yield any answer that will be meaningful to the questioner. Many attempts at this have been famously bad. For example, Microsoft created a Twitter bot named "Tay" to interact with Twitter users and generate natural language responses by learning from the Tweets already available on Twitter and the way people interacted with the bot, but in less than a day, it was parroting racist and sexist talking points, including defending the Nazis.[38] In another case, Facebook gave two AIs basic language skills and set them in conversation to develop their language processing, but the two programs eventually "developed a language" that human observers could not understand, and the programs were stopped.[39] Without an actual language-using community to interact with, the programs' language processing deteriorated into incomprehensible gibberish. Adding into the "criti-hype," sensationalist media took what was clearly a failure to produce a truly communicative program and spun the story as though the AIs were conspiring. When Forbes reporter Tony Bradley reported on the story, for example, he could not help but describe the situation as "creepy," "awesome and horrifying," and "scary" while drawing comparisons to this minor achievement in NLP to the broader visions of singularity espoused by Kurzweil or AI apocalypse of Stephen Hawking.[40]

Nonetheless, despite missteps within this area, there have also been impressive advancements. One such has been the creation of Generative Pre-trained Transformer-3 (or GPT-3), an AI trained on 45 terabytes of internet text and 175 billion training parameters.[41] The vastness of this data set allows the program to generate human-like responses to given prompts. Its commercially available successor, ChatGPT, has led to popular uproar, including concerns about plagiarism,[42] auto-generated formal messages,[43] mass production of short fiction,[44] and impressionistic satirical writings.[45] Of course, the responses remain limited to both the style and content of its data set, so, while truly impressive, it is not without its own limitations. A recent paper based on its predecessor GPT-2, for example, shows that when given prompts like biblical phrases or chapters, the program can generate "scripture" that resembles the Christian canon but improvises into making its own "scripture" by following canonical rhetorical styles.[46]

Unfortunately, a great problem remains in NLP, namely, that the programs themselves do not really "know" what they are saying. The problem of understanding, flippantly dismissed by McCarthy et al., remains the main obstacle in NLP. We humans use language in a natural way that allows us to use metaphors, make inferences, and create neologisms in a fashion that AI cannot. Turns of phrase, ambiguous expressions, and syllogisms all work in human linguistic comprehension so that simultaneously translation algorithms often yield humorously poor results,[47] while directly translated colloquialisms often make sense for non-native speakers, such as the concept of "saving face" taken from Chinese.[48] Human beings use language in a way that is much more *intuitive*, not always following rote rules while still making sense. The process of "verbing" nouns, for example, changes a noun into a verb participle in a way that violates grammatical principles but is understandable between speakers (e.g., "I TiVoed *The Wire* so we can watch it tonight"; "She friended me on Facebook"). The same paper that demonstrated the impressive capabilities for GPT-2 in religious texts also notes that the program lacks total awareness of why made-up scriptures do not have any authoritative weight, for example. Whether one is a Christian, an atheist, or an adherent of a different faith, they will recognize that the meaning of "scripture" is not arbitrary ideas construed in a particular style but rather an authoritative revelation. An AI imitating the King James Version is impressive, but without understanding what role Scripture plays in human dialogue and consciousness, the AI cannot truly communicate, and the meaning of the text falls entirely to the reader. Even with as sophisticated a program as GPT-3 or ChatGPT, it cannot be meaningfully said that AI "communicates" with the humans who interact with it. It rather mimics communication. The results may surprise us, but they are not indicative of a "person" behind the screen. Thus, beyond facetiously simple grammatical and syntactical questions, NLP has many unresolved obstacles related to the referents of communication.

Conclusion: A World of Bits

The success of AI is predicated on several philosophical assumptions. These have been alluded to but should be made explicit. These assumptions include an ontological assumption, namely, that the structure of the universe corresponds to some (however complex) mathematical model; a methodological assertion, namely, that deriving all answers and all truth is merely a question of process and deduction; and an entire epistemological system, namely, that all truth is simple, universal, and logical.[49] Taken together, they form a larger philosophical system at the heart of AI which is often unexamined, though always underlying AI work.[50]

From a metaphysical perspective, AI research assumes that Baconian empiricism was correct: the world is comprehendible, and the internal laws making it up can be known to human beings. An objective world exists, and that objective world, despite Immanuel Kant's claims,[51] can be completely known by *human minds*. Nothing beyond what is sensible exists, or at least does not exist in a meaningful way, and all that does exist can be grasped in its entirety by human minds. This assumption underlies basic science, but the greater claim for AI goes beyond what science can reasonably claim. Science only provides understandings of what we already are aware of. It is mute about things that could exist beyond human perception (such as God or magic), and it makes no claim about what it does not yet grasp (such as dark matter and dark energy). AI research is predicated on the assumption that everything (at least everything meaningful) can be known in scientific, especially mathematical, expressions.

Thus, the ontological assumption is a belief in cybernetics. Shannon's information theory, which reduces everything in the universe to digitizable information, must be the reality of the universe. This is necessary because of the "framing problem" for AI: if the universe is something beyond programmable information, then AI will inevitably not work. If AI comes across realities that cannot be accounted for outside of mathematically specified limits, it will be unable to reconcile them with its model of the universe. If this is a small discontinuity, it will remain an aberration the program cannot make sense of, but a sufficiently large enough aberration could cause critical failure. A recent string of Tesla cars crashing into parked emergency vehicles while on "Autopilot" shows just the problem of why AI universe modeling *must* be perfect to operate.[52]

Shannon's informational theory, of course, is a strong ontological claim, but weaker models may be appropriate for specific applications of narrow AI. In such a case, rather than *everything* being reducible to mathematical formulae, only what matters *for AI* needs to be. The successes with narrow AI and the intractability of AGI suggest this more moderate model may be better and more reasonable: when AI is allowed to only encounter the world as visual data to be analyzed for cancer cells, it does not need a full model of the universe. Applied to logistics, diagnostics, or simulations, AI will not need a full-scale model of the universe—only a model necessary for its scope. But the idea that "weird AI" can overcome its weirdness assumes that every situation must conform to this mathematical logic and that AI can and should be able to model all configurations of the universe appropriately.

This ontological view gains support by advances in universe modeling in computers. Video games, for example, have made tremendous progress from the days of *Pong* and *Super Mario Bros.* to employ advanced physics engines, AI programming, and even in-game weather events. But every player whose horse glitched in *Red Dead Redemption* or who is tired of hearing the guards say, "I used to be an adventurer like you" in *The Elder Scrolls V: Skyrim* knows that the illusion of a vast universe belies massive limitations. At the same time, AI prognosticators like Elon Musk and Ray Kurzweil hypothesize that we may be living in a simulation, where "God" is just a cosmic programmer.[53] The universe around us, in this view, is no different in kind, only in scale, from the world-building carried out by video game companies like Rockstar and Bethesda. And, as illustrated by Turing, this vision transfers from the entire structure of the universe to the process of human cognition. Ultimately, the serious interest and belief in the possibility of uploading minds into computers, the most famous goal of many transhumanists, is predicated upon the ontological belief that not only is the mind itself something that can be replicated through mathematical programming but, as often as not for "patternists," cognitive processes themselves can be easily transposed into strings of computer programming.[54]

AI also assumes that there is a universally valid method for understanding the universe. Following the rationalist impulses of the European Enlightenment, AI assumes there must be a universal system of truth graspable by all. Leibniz's "alphabet of thought" demonstrates this clearly enough: the claim that there is a representable set of the bounds of *human thought* presupposes a universal set of human knowledge. No *new* ideas can be expressed—they will be reformulations of the same limited, if large, set of symbols. Like Turing's decryption engines, ideas may be able to be mathematically reorganized but are reducible to set inputs. In AI's model, there are "right" and "wrong" answers, objective truths, and ways of identifying these. Ironically, of course, some models of machine learning run on a "black box" model where the actual rules the AI teaches itself are opaque to researchers, but the baseline assumption is that feeding an AI enough human dialogue, for example, will lead to the AI being able to follow the "rules" of dialogue itself. This model has many strengths, of course. Codifying expert knowledge into expert systems can provide efficient means to do expert work, such as medical diagnostics or legal research. DeepMind's recent breakthrough on a protein-folding AI, for example, will improve biomolecular research and potentially expedite creation of life-saving drugs.[55] The methodical process of the scientific method has yielded tremendous benefit since its adoption in professional science, even if it restricts creative outlooks.

A somewhat humorous result of this belief, however, is that if AI doesn't "understand" or makes a mistake in its understanding, the solution will be to further complicate its programming by feeding it *more* data instead of simpler instructions. Thus, in a sort of twist on physics since Newton, AI theorists have given up the goal of a "theory of everything" for a massively complex list of instructions AI will follow. Marvin Minsky, for example, initially predicted accomplishing AI was a matter of "programming in a few million facts,"[56] but as this goal proved inaccurate, he changed his view to claim that consciousness is the parallel processing of a few dozen machines operating in concert.[57] And indeed, the number of instructions AI researchers have expected to be necessary for AGI has grown exponentially. After training a facial recognition AI with hundreds of thousands of images, when it is realized that the AI has low confidence rates for white women and people of color generally, the solution is to give the AI hundreds of thousands more images to train.[58] The reason for this is that AI cannot handle "exceptions" to the rules. Once it has its own rules in place, which tend to be obscured even to programmers through machine learning, it only adapts by creating *more* rules. For AI, any exception to the rules it encounters must have its own classified exception, which leads to lengthier and lengthier lists of instructions. A driving AI, for example, will need to create a rule about stopping for red lights, another rule for making right turns at red lights, a third about pedestrians crossing with traffic, a fourth for jaywalking pedestrians, a fifth for intersections where turning on red is prohibited. Each of these must be a new, enumerated rule and not presented merely as exceptions to the general rule "Stop on red until it turns green." The complicated nature of this feature manifests itself, for example, when new upgrades to Tesla's "Full Self-Driving" software is still unable to handle unprotected left turns.

But the most important insight from this view is the fact that, according to this methodological commitment, all ways of knowing, without exception, either must be convertible to a universalized system or must be false. Any view that contradicts this will go unheard within the system. An AI "art" generator follows algorithmic processes based off massive data sets of human artists' styles, subjects, and techniques to generate a formalized rule system. Any forms of "knowledge" beyond mathematical-technical terms, such as art, emotion, religious sensibility, or even other systems of knowledge, such as other sciences rooted in non-Western cultural worldviews, must be translatable to the single, codable base of knowledge. An *XKCD* webcomic from 2008 illustrates this tendency well by reducing various fields of science sequentially, from sociology as applied psychology, as applied biology, as applied chemistry, as applied physics, finally as applied mathematics.[59] Everything is not turtles all the way down; it's numbers all the way down. Any model that says otherwise, then, is faulty. Any claim that there is something ineffable or non-reducible to binary data is incompatible with this methodology.

Finally, then, AI says that any epistemological model that is not the calculation-based epistemology of Turing, Shannon, and Wiener is a useless epistemological model. Knowledge and understanding are essentially mathematical; "pure" logic, rooted in "objective" understandings of the nature of the universe. There is an answer, then, to any and all questions, and, in truth, only one correct answer at that. While we might admit this for even the most vexing scientific questions—what sort of animal is a velvet worm, how do we account for quantum uncertainty, what distinguishes life from inert matter, etc.—the AI epistemological model assumes this is also true for questions we might consider less "certain"—is Dadaism art, which theology is most sound, which educational programs should receive priority funding, etc. For AGI to truly be able to operate within the world, it must operate within a world where there are rules and factual answers to any given query.

From the perspective of ethics, this is deeply troubling: the best ethicists in the world may agree on the majority of moral issues in strict terms (e.g., murder is bad; helping others is good), but why something is right or wrong or the correct method for determining right and wrong are matters of great disagreement. Isaac Asimov famously drafted "Laws of Robotics" as ethical principles for AI, but AI researchers themselves have pointed out that Asimov's vision does not really fit into AI programming.[60] Some form of consequentialism, such as act-utilitarianism with its "hedonic calculus," becomes the *de facto* mode of moral reasoning, then, because it most easily supports mathematical framing. But the fact that it is more programmable does not mean it is right. The field of ethics is not all in agreement on what the standard meaning of "good" is (metaethics) nor the means by which it should be implemented in human action (normative ethics). To assume the good must be reducible to binary digits is to prematurely foreclose the question, undermining the authority of ethics experts who in good faith still disagree about this critical question of the field.

Many futurists, such as Elon Musk, Nick Bostrom, and the late Stephen Hawking, believe that if we don't figure out the moral question prior to AI, then AI poses a greater moral threat than anything else we've faced. On the other hand, there are researchers who think *only* AI can provide objective moral answers because of human biases. The conundrum itself is ironic: the fear of "apocalyptic AI" belies the entire AI model of objective certainty, while the promise of AI moral objectivity presupposes researchers can program in the answers to problems they do not know. Recent trends in applied moral philosophy illustrate the absurdity of this over-rational position nicely. The so-called "effective altruism" movement, which began as an application of Peter Singer's radical utilitarianism, has transitioned in recent years from focusing on obvious world problems like hunger and poverty in poor nations to AI.[61] Taking very seriously the imaginary threats that AI poses, the ethicists and philanthropists behind this movement have decided that the most logical long-term strategy for their billions of dollars is investing in "good" AI now rather than in empowering or feeding the masses. The assumption, of course, is that their calculations of what is a real threat are correct because they have mathematical backing, and the protestations of any other person, be they the starving poor, critics of AI, marginalized groups in society, or even just other moral theorists, are wrong because they are not mathematical.

Nonetheless, AI research continues with the optimism that not only ethics but every other question is subject to pure, universally valid answers, which a computer can supply. The test of whether this is correct is determined by ideally objective tests set beforehand. Creating a working calculator or teaching a computer to play Go relies on there being right and wrong answers. Losing a game of Go is a wrong answer; getting the answer 5 to the question 2 + 2 is also wrong. In application, however, AI boasts confidence rates, not total objectivity. Thus, even the overall theory underlying AI is itself inconsistent—if it is only achieving "good enough," then even mathematizable forms of knowledge still evade rote inscription. AlphaGo did lose the fourth game to Sedol Lee, though since that time has been unbested by human beings, but not other AIs! An AI trained to detect cancers may do a better job than a radiologist but will still miss occasionally. But when an AI can earn a better score on a standardized test, or can accurately predict text, or can faithfully reconstruct images that have been distorted, human trainers are satisfied that the AI has found "the right answer." Thus, AI's epistemological model amounts to the rote-memorization/faithful reproduction model of early twentieth-century education, a model that punishes deviation and rewards fidelity.

Taken all together, the entire philosophy behind AI is a version of what Max Weber called instrumental rationality.[62] Everything can be translated to some universal medium that can be more efficiently routed and directed. This is the underlying principle of capitalism: the uninterrupted market will best facilitate the flow of resources, translated into capital, within a given society. Everything within capitalism then becomes a question of efficiency and monetary value. This model undergirds AI research—the aim for efficiency is demonstrated not only by the efforts to create AGI as directly and simply as possible but more so in narrow AI's application to various industries. Logistics professionals are not buying AIs for their artistic value or emotional attachment: AIs promise efficiency in logistics, which translates to saved money. AI does not necessarily reduce everything to cash value, but it must reduce everything to data, and part of that data must include value information if AI is to make reasonable decisions. The absurdist scenario of a cleaning robot that eradicates humanity to prevent messes demonstrates the problem of value against efficiency (and the problem of framing).[63] In the end, though, AI is created to increase efficiency and generate value, the meanings of which are determined by engineers, project leads, corporate executives, and, more importantly, investors and buyers.

In summary, what this means is the values and perspectives of those programming AI, who tend to be mathematicians convinced the universe is reducible to mere binary expressions, are the values and perspectives privileged by AI. But these values are not left unquestioned. The "objective" claims of AI not only tend to be the purview of a privileged class within society, especially white men, but also are themselves controversial perspectives from within the Western (largely male) philosophical tradition. These are not "new" conversations, but reviewing them is important for understanding the privileged perspective of AI from the perspective of poverty.

CHAPTER 2

Frankenstein and Other Monsters

IN THE EARLY days of computing, most computer programming was done by women. Computers were large and expensive machines then, impractical for personal use. Like telephone operators or secretaries, the task of programming was considered routine and unskilled.[1] Only professors—pioneers developing new languages, new hardware, and new theories—remained primarily male, such as McCarthy, Minsky, Newell, Simon, Papert, and others. Like other arenas of gendered work division, such as the mid-century corporate office with its army of typists, computing was mainly divided between the "masculine" work of theorizing and the "feminine" work of rote programming. With the rise of home computers in the 1970s, this began to change. Computing had become profitable finally.

As men began to work as programmers, the language surrounding the task changed. Instead of tedious work unworthy of men's attention, it was recast as a skilled discipline that required logic and math—"men's strengths."[2] The women who pioneered this work were then considered generally unfit for the task and so were, and often still are, discouraged from entering the field. As late as 1967, *Cosmopolitan* magazine billed computing as naturally "women's work," and James Adams of the Association for Computing Machinery stated, "I don't know of any other field, outside of teaching, where there's as much opportunity for a woman" as computing.[3] But while women held the majority of computing jobs until the 1970s, by 2016, they only held one quarter of all computing jobs.[4]

In July 2017, a memo posted to Google's internal network written by computer programmer James Damore led to his firing. Damore claimed in the memo that women and people of color do not possess the proper skills to be in computing. He claimed that Google's efforts to increase diversity did not tolerate "ideological diversity" and so the company was hurting itself in its own efforts to attract diverse workers. Damore was fired for creating a hostile working environment, though he claimed he was "discriminated against." Damore's manifesto went on to critique hiring women because, in his view, women are more neurotic than men, women are less capable of handling stress, and women are better at relationships than men because men are better at "things."[5] Three and a half years later, Google fired two of its most prominent female employees because those women critiqued the internal biases in the company. In doing their jobs as ethicists, they highlighted ethical problems in the software. But because these biases favored white men, the critique was perceived as an attack. How ironic that Damore can claim that a field once dominated by women is work not suitable for women, or that his company is too focused on political correctness when it fires employees who speak out against its sexist and racist tendencies!

Robert Williams was arrested for theft at a watch store in Detroit, despite having been at work during the robbery:

> While I was leaving work in January [2020], my wife called and said a police officer had called and said I needed to turn myself in. I told her it was probably a prank. But as I pulled up to my house, a Detroit squad car was waiting in front. When I pulled into the driveway, the squad car swooped in from behind to block my SUV—as if I would make a run for it. One officer jumped out and asked if I was Robert Williams. I said I was. He told me I was under arrest. When I asked for a reason, he showed me a piece of paper with my name on it. The words 'arrest warrant' and 'felony larceny' were all I could make out.[6]

He spent thirty hours in detention before police released him without any explanation or apology. After being held for eighteen hours, the police brought him in for questioning, where he finally found out why he had been arrested. They showed him evidence—a blurry surveillance photo of another man robbing the store. "I hope you guys don't think that all black men look alike," Williams replied to them, pointing out the obvious mismatch of perpetrator and suspect. "The computer must have gotten it wrong," one of the arresting officers reportedly mumbled.[7] It turns out that the Detroit Police Department had used a facial recognition program with surveillance footage to find the perpetrator of the robbery. The program had incorrectly matched Williams's driver's license photo with the person caught on CCTV. And between the time when policed picked Williams up at his house to when they finally spoke with him, nobody had bothered to actually look at the photo and verify, with their own eyes, that Williams was the robber, such was their (over)confidence in the accuracy of the program. An embarrassing confession made by the cop in questioning Williams was the only moment in which police used their own human facial recognition abilities to confirm (or rather, refute) the seemingly objective proof produced by the algorithm.

Who's Afraid of AI?

The promises of AI evangelists, whether amateur enthusiasts or active researchers, rest on a specific set of assumptions, including a worldview, values, aims, and the total range of real possibilities. Among the presuppositions of AI enthusiasts are the following: that computers can replicate human cognition, including, perhaps, the full range of conscious thought; that it is good across numerous measures, including ethics and economics, to develop AI into human-level cognitive performance; that computers will do what we do as well as or better than we do it, and that this is good; and that, despite AI arising from human programming and engineering, it will be free from the biases and shortcomings that plague human decision-making. Taken together, these presuppositions do not seem suitably complementary. What is the justification for assuming that a machine that replicates human cognition will not make the same pitfalls that humans make? After all, intelligence alone isn't sufficient to avoid moral evils, as the technological and scientific prowess of the Nazis demonstrated last century. It was not lack of scientific rigor that turned hydrogen cyanide into the infamous Zyklon B. Albert Speer's "final solution" was not a shortcoming of his architectural skill, and Joseph Goebbels's success as propagandist was due to no lack of understanding of the human mind and German spirit.

The bridge between human failings and computational inerrancy, assume AI proponents, is tied to our biological makeup. Hatred, cruelty, greed, vengeance, lust, covetousness, vanity, and so forth, they assume, are rooted in human beings' biological needs—for material comforts, for species propagation, for self-preservation, and so forth. Following in line with the Western philosophical tradition, AI researchers have traditionally seen a distinctive separation between "higher" cognitive functions and "lower" animalistic urges in human behavior.[8] The ancient Greeks' division of the "soul" into logos, ethos, and pathos, or medieval Europeans' own division of reason, will, and passions, is reinscribed in the philosophical anthropologies of modern philosophies, such Kant's "autonomous reason," untethered by biology or contingency.

It is thus not surprising that AI researchers hope AI will overcome human moral weaknesses and intellectual blind spots. In line with the majority of the Western philosophical tradition, they assume that rationality and goodness are synonyms, or at least intrinsically tied together. Kant is perhaps most explicit on this: the categorical imperative, that is, the universal moral imperative, is nothing other than do what is purely rational.[9] Assuming, then, that Kant was correct, it is not such a stretch to assume that those "contingencies," which Kant attributes "heteronomous reason" to, can be extracted for a cognitive machine, which then will only do what is rational, hence, what is moral.[10] Perhaps for this reason, Isaac Asimov created the "Three Laws of Robotics," deontological principles articulated as clear rules that AI machines were supposed to follow. Consequently, the whole field of AI assumes that rationality is a calculative process, which can be codified into step-by-step rules that can themselves be transcribed into a digital computer (whether through careful symbolic manipulation by human beings or by supervised or unsupervised machine learning on neural networks). AI proponents also assume that this computer will do the sorts of things that we believe are good and will not do the sorts of things that we believe are evil. This is hardly an uncontested view, however.

Within the literature critical of AI, three broad concerns are manifest. The first branch of critiques is that AI will be *superhuman*, or too efficient at what it does. From this view, AI becomes dangerous because unlike other machines, a truly autonomous (i.e., being a law to itself) machine cannot be subjected to our will and may cause irreparable harm to us if it gains greater power than us. The second branch of critiques denies this, arguing instead that AI is too *alien*, too different in its understanding of the world. On this view, AI is dangerous mostly because by making the machine the measure of humanity, we reduce humanity into machines. The last set of critiques see that AI is *too narrowly human*, that it is as human as anything else that bears our image, but that the image it bears is only a subset of humanity. AI is dangerous on this ground because as it reproduces the epistemological views of its creators, the highly contingent nature of their worldview gets taken to be universal and normative.

Chaining the Beast

The strong AI critique has its roots dug deep within our collective (un) conscious. Its clearest formulation probably comes from Isaac Asimov himself; the reverse of his "Three Laws" is the "Frankenstein Complex," the fear that the creature will turn on its creator. The name is taken from Mary Shelley's 1818 novel *Frankenstein: Or the Modern Prometheus*, which features the eponymous character using modern science to reanimate a reconstructed body made of various corpses. Shelley's novel has been reappropriated in various guises, including numerous television and film adaptations, much of nineteenth-century gothic fiction, H. P. Lovecraft's 1922 "Herbert West—Reanimator" and its own zombie-story descendants, and, of course, much of robotic fiction as indicated by Asimov. Much has been written about the psychological resonance of Shelley's novel, a tale where the creator fears his creation while the creation rails against the absurdity of its existence.[11]

Shelley's subtitle "the Modern Prometheus" reveals that the mythos she gave life to (pun intended) runs even deeper still. Perhaps Freud is right in asserting that we see God as our distant father, recalling that the "father" in Freud's own work is most notably represented by Laius and the totemic father, victims of patricide, like Saturn's death by Jupiter. And so, many have noted a "God complex" rampant in attitudes of technology luminaries.[12] Thus, even within the techno-optimistic Silicon Valley, some raise alarms that they are "building God" with AI, apparently surpassing human-level cognition to go straight to omniscience.[13] With the spread of ChatGPT and its impressive ability to mimic comprehensible answers, even agnostics have begun to think of AI as the machine God.[14] And their great fear is that the creation will turn on its creator.

The idea of "AI revolution" is, ironically, older than the field of AI itself. In the very first example of "robot fiction," Karel Čapek's 1920 play *R.U.R.*, Old Rossum, the inventor of the robots, "wanted to become a sort of scientific substitute for God."[15] While Rossum himself only exists as a specter within the narrative, his god complex plays out as his artificial humans develop their own sense of indignity and injustice, eventually killing off their progenitors and assuming their place as the new human race left to "replenish" the earth. Harlan Ellison's 1967 short story "I Have No Mouth and I Must Scream" took the AI revolt motif to its logical conclusion: the story features a genocidal AI called AM (a God trope if ever there was one) who preserves five human survivors after annihilating the rest of humanity, keeping them alive merely to torment them through eternity. The following year introduced movie audiences to the concept with the computer HAL 9000 in Stanley Kubrick's *2001: A Space Odyssey*. James Cameron advanced the concept further in his 1984 film *The Terminator*, depicting a genocidal war between humanity and an AI called SkyNet. The Wachowski siblings' 1999 *The Matrix* takes place after a similar war has resulted in humanity being enslaved to robots. Bioware's 2007 game *Mass Effect* and its sequels further feature a race of genocidal robots called "The Reapers," who harvest the galaxy's organic life forms every 10,000 years.

The threat of AI genocide, however, reveals more about ourselves than it does about our machines. Čapek's robots are motivated by emotions given to them by their creators. Ellison's AM gives a monologue about his eternal *hatred* for humanity. The likelihood that we will be eliminated by a genuinely malevolent AI is predicated on programming malice, a human emotion, into AI. This fear manifests as a reflection of our own image of ourselves. AI serves in these stories as a "techno-mirror," representing our deepest fears and desires.[16] Our deepest fears about our own self-annihilation and the deeply ingrained taboo of patricide are much better explanations of the narratives than the real worry that an unemotional machine will kill us out of petty vindictiveness.

Concordantly, then, there is a rather large and growing segment of ethical writing about the moral status of machines. Just as the counter to the Freudian Oedipus complex is the institution of the moral law protecting our children from us and us from our children, the implication that AI could rise against us (consciously, and not, e.g., as an act of accidental mayhem) implies that we face AI as an Other that is like us, replete with moral standing. David Gunkel, for example, notes that while it may be difficult to establish the moral *agency* of AI or robots, their moral *patiency*, that is, their status as beings to which we owe certain moral obligations, ought to be taken more seriously by ethicists.[17] Others, like Nick Bostrom and Eliezer Yudkowsky, go further, contending that AI ought to be treated with the same dignity that we would grant to a conscious alien being, a "person" who is not a human.[18] Nonanthropomorphic approaches to ethics, such as "sentientism" or philosophical "posthumanism," also emphasize moral dignity of nonhuman sentient (or intelligent) beings that are not persons, including nonhuman animals as well as AI, provided they achieve the threshold of sentience.[19] And if AI does happen to become *superintelligent* AI, as some predict it will, then it is morally better to grant more rights to this being than even we humans have because it will have surpassed us in its moral standing.[20]

The economy of resentment thus underlies a great deal of AI philosophy, both academic and popular. The machine ought not to be treated badly because of the inverse of the Golden Rule: repay to others what they have paid to you. If we mistreat our AIs, they will in turn mistreat us. Whether one considers it ethical egoism or alterity or some other moral concept, the basic insistence is that AI, unlike other machines such as a vacuum cleaner or an assembly line, ought to be given moral treatment for its own sake, lest it develop moral affects harmful to us. That is, in classical Kantian formulation, it should be treated as an end in itself and not merely as a means.

In turn, as AIs' parents, we have a duty to teach the machines to be good moral agents. Asimov's laws seemed directed to this aim, but these seem too unrealistic. Thus, some have contended instead that AIs should be programmed with baseline utilitarian reasoning.[21] Seeing the challenge of articulating clear exhaustive moral protocols that will prevent disaster, some have argued that we need human intelligence augmentation as a prerequisite for moral AI since we will need to have surer knowledge of absolute moral truths.[22] Contemporary moral disagreements, in this view, demonstrate that our understanding of morality is still limited, and programming a computer to be moral without understanding morality ourselves is dangerous. And yet others trust the machines to do the reasoning for us, suggesting that a superintelligent machine will have better ethical reasoning than any human could, so we should only worry that it has the right *motivation* and not worry about the actual processes.[23] Thus, the debate about how to create *good* (or at least not evil) AI vindicates introductory philosophy classes by centering the discussion around three major moral theoretical axes: either we must program the machine to seek the best outcome (consequentialism), or we must be morally upright enough to instruct it first (virtue), or we must program in guiding principles that it must obey (deontology).

However, as popular as the interest in moral agent or patient AI is, given the massive popular cultural outputs centered on AI genocide, most critics of AI are not truly worried about psychotic robots. This latent worry is on all of our minds. On the other hand, less-attended-to problems must be addressed. There is concern that automating warfighting could lead to atrocities committed by machines that have no consciences and no ability to reject orders. Lethal autonomous weapons systems (LAWS) might violate the bounds of just war by targeting civilians, using weapons of mass destruction, engaging in war crimes, or refusing to stand down when a cease-fire is issued.[24] Human soldiers have consciences and autonomy, even if they are trained to follow commands, and can be held accountable; an automated machine does not and cannot. Using emotion detection software as a tool on an automated drone, for example, trusts that the "angry" expression of a potential combatant is truly an expression of animus that will be carried out as aggression, not just frustration, or, worse, a total misreading of the expression.[25] There is no guarantee a human soldier would not make the same mistake, but they would then be held accountable in ways the machine cannot. If such technology were used for atomic weaponry or other weapons of mass destruction, the result would be genocidal, as depicted in 1983's *War Games* or 1970's *Colossus: The Forbin Project.*

Another potential avenue of threat is expressed by the late physicist Stephen Hawking. In an interview with British Broadcasting Corporation, Hawking warned that strong AI would potentially threaten our existence because, unlike human beings, who are limited by our biological limitations, an AI could expand its computing processes exponentially once it has the understanding to do so.[26] In fact, today's neural networks make use of large networks of computer hardware, such as server farms, linking dozens or hundreds of graphics processing units together to carry out parallel processing on large scales simultaneously. Given how many machines are connected to the internet, by which "cloud computing" is able to be carried out over millions of machines connected across the earth, it is no great leap to suggest that an intelligent enough software program could, and would, make use of this network of hardware to increase its capacity beyond expectations.[27] Hawking's worry is not that the AI would then seek to eradicate us, like SkyNet or AM, but rather that we would be inconsequential to the massively powerful AI, which might eliminate us in the course of its functioning if it perceives us to be an obstacle to its aims. Even AI pioneer Hans Moravec recognizes that in a physically limited universe, the inefficient and wasteful cognitive processes of human beings may be eliminated for the sake of utility by more powerful AI programs.[28] Thus, a great worry is that AI, when it becomes too big, will handle us with the same disdain with which we often treat mosquitoes or cockroaches.

Nick Bostrom shares this worry but adds a new critique. He worries that, without giving adequate instructions to an AI, it might eliminate humanity as a simple mistake in carrying out its code. The famous example he gives is an AI programmed to make paper clips, which goes on a frenzy using all available iron material, including perhaps the iron from our blood, to make paper clips.[29] The worry is that, without programming specific enough parameters for a machine, moral boundaries will only seem like arbitrary obstacles to cross. Here we see the relevance of Dreyfus's story about the problem of "weirdness"—a computer is unable to distinguish why murder, theft, swindling, and honest dealing are hierarchically ordered morally and why all but the least conscientious humans would avoid murder to achieve their end. And so, goes another doomsday scenario: an AI programmed to clean after human beings may realize that the most efficient way to clean human messes is to prevent humans from making messes, which can best be achieved by eliminating all humans.

All of the "strong" critiques assume AI's main danger is that it *will* become strong AI and that it will do so either as an immoral or amoral entity. But there are many problems with this idea. The worry about the resentful or immoral AI holds if, and only if, AI is capable of holding grudges or motivations. On one hand, this assumes that AI has motivations outside of what is programmed into it, that it has, in the words of Hans Jonas, its own teleology, as opposed to the cybernetic "purposive" behavior programmed in from outside.[30] An AI programmed to kill its creators does not express resentment; it is merely an efficient weapon. We read our own motivations into it. On the other hand, saying that AI needs morality is really no more than saying AI has to be programmed with proper parameters. This is an admission that ethics will be merely another layer of instructions. Of course, this fails to appreciate the foundation of what ethics is, namely, a quest for the *good* life, a concept that must remain underdefined in order for self-reflective beings to understand what this idea entails.[31] Thus, the problem of ethical programming is not a question of "teaching" AI, as in the climactic scene of John Carpenter's *Dark Star*, where Captain Doolittle must teach Bomb #20 phenomenology to prevent the destruction of his ship, but rather installing proper safeguards into the AI framework.

Thus, the question of instructing an "ethical" AI is no different from AI war ethics. The idea of a super-powerful AI committing genocide through war is, in fact, a danger if we entrust AI with national security with no oversight. But such is true as well in a world where the United States and Russia still possess hundreds of nuclear warheads. AI poses no special threat here except that it is harder to assign moral blame if an AI triggers a thermonuclear holocaust rather than an arrogant premier. The sort of bad-faith grandstanding that underwrites mutual assured destruction as an international policy instead of a realistic military strategy requires an understanding of human motivations and international politics that an AI lacks—the AI does not fear its demise in global annihilation the way even the most sadistic military leaders do.

The other critiques likewise are too optimistic. Hawking's fear that an AI might overpower us assumes that AI will have intentions that are its own. Here we see the same double-mindedness that conflates biological motivations and cybernetic processes: instead of the AI transcending our biological failings, which are to blame for our wickedness, Hawking envisions an AI that has the same biological impulses we humans have directed toward growth and reproduction and transcending our boundaries. An all-consuming AI must have motivations that transcend the ordinary functions of computers. In an entropic universe, growth is a biological motivation to preserve the integrity of organisms and species; it is not a machinistic drive. AI has no "motivation" to grow because it has no organic functioning—it is not a metabolic organism but rather a cybernetic construct created by human agents.[32] AI does what it is programmed to do, and assuming its programming is not to merely grow for growth's sake (into what?), it will have no interest in eliminating human beings.

Bostrom's absurd example is similarly humorous because of its schizophrenic nature. Somehow, it is assumed, a paper clip–making AI has overcome the framing problem sufficiently enough to recognize that iron can be extracted from any number of other things and not merely from sources provided to it. The machine has a deep enough metallurgical knowledge and a breadth of programming wide enough to consume all iron upon the face of the earth or turn the entire galaxy into infrastructure for making paper clips. Somehow, the knowledge that human bodies contain trace amounts of iron is accessible to the machine, along with knowledge for extracting this inaccessible element from our blood, while the basic prohibition "Do not kill humans" is not. In this scenario, the machine needs enough frames of reference to understand how it can go about the pointlessly difficult task of extracting trace minerals from organic beings, but despite robot genocide being one of the most common features of science fiction, nobody bothered to add basic instructions to not kill humans as a frame!

Truthfully, the only *real* danger we ought to be concerned of in the next few decades among these arguments is the problem of the security-defense AI. Indeed, AI given very specific instructions of an outcome to be achieved without sufficient parameters for how it should *not* be achieved can result in human casualties no matter the scale, but the danger lies in what the AI has control of. A paper clip–producing AI likely will not have the frameworks or access to tools to harvest human bodies, but it may not ensure adequate protection of human workers in its factory if safety is not programmed in as one of the primary goals. Indeed, this is not a problem strictly for AI but for any form of instrumental rationality. Let us not forget that it was human beings who made the ghoulish decision not to recall the deadly Ford Pinto because the cost of a recall was deemed more expensive than paying out settlements to victims' families.[33] So the bitter fact is the real danger lies in an AI put in charge of automotive production expressing *merely* the same indifference to human lives as automobile executives.

Automation as Automata

Ironically, then, it is the criticisms against the weakness of AI that prove to be more worthy of taking seriously. Rather than writing jeremiads about the imminent AI apocalypse, they challenge the presupposition that AI functions the same way that human cognition does. The "strong" criticisms, after all, all rest on the assumption that AI will function as humans do for the worst. Either they will have the same murderous urges that we have, or they will have the same selfish drive for maximum growth, or they will have the same inability to reflect on the repercussions of their actions. But what if AI does not function the way human minds do? AI research rests on very specific assumptions about the operation of the mind, assumptions rooted in a science (cybernetics) that has lost nearly all interest outside of a few narrow applications in information and computer sciences. It is worth questioning whether this view is adequate.

One of the most famous of the "weak" criticisms is John Searle's "Chinese Room" thought experiment, which is as follows. Imagine you are in a room with a set of instructions in front of you. A note gets passed into the room written in Chinese, but you do not read Chinese or understand the language. The instructions, however, tell you that you should reply to a given set of Chinese characters (*hanzi*) with another set of *hanzi*. You do so, and the person who passed the note on the other side of the door seems satisfied with the answer. The instructions give you appropriate *hanzi* for any given input. Searle asks us, then, Would we consider this in any meaningful way to be an *understanding* of Chinese? Of course, he reasons, since the person following instructions does not know what is being communicated, they cannot be said to "understand" Chinese, irrespective of how well the queries submitted to them are answered. Searle notes, then, that to say a computer "understands" because it provides a correct response to a given input is absurd.[34] In other words, against the views of McCarthy,

Minsky, Turing, and others, Searle's claim is that *understanding* is the primary problem of philosophy of mind. Reproduction of language, the standard around which much AI research has been directed, is insufficient to demonstrate consciousness. Understanding must be produced and must be the goal of AI research, not a hoped-for byproduct.

Searle does not believe that the mind is inherently unique—he is no romanticist assuming there is a *je ne sais quois* about the human mind that the AI researchers miss. Indeed, he is a pure materialist, assuming that what the brain does could be exactly recreated. However, he notes that "only something that has the same causal powers as brains" would possess consciousness.[35] In other words, Searle notes that, unless a machine does what a brain does, not by simulation but by exact replication, it will be impossible to claim that a machine "understands" the way a human brain does.[36] For Searle, then, the question of consciousness is utterly outside the bounds of AI because AI is "programming" but the brain is a machine. Put in different terms, AI is like simulating a car's engine and expecting the simulation to actually take you somewhere else. The specific output of an internal combustion chamber is kinetic energy that a car turns into motion; the specific output of the machine of the human brain is understanding. A car simulation does not "go" anywhere; a brain simulation will not create consciousness.

Another critique within the "weak" strain is the view of Jaron Lanier, a computer scientist credited as the father of virtual reality. Lanier critiques the idea that we are "gadgets" and worries about what he calls "lock-in," a sort of Heideggerian concern that the philosophy of digital engineering becomes a totalizing philosophy that misses non-empirical realities.[37] An example of this problem is MIDI, software used in a lot of electronic music. MIDI represents musical notes as perfect mathematical tunes. While a human-played acoustic instrument will produce varied notes, depending on the tuning, the way the note is struck, the musician's own fingering, concert hall temperature, and so forth, MIDI produces exactly the same note every time. Digital technology functions using discrete states—clear binaries that can be complexified and multiplied *ad nauseum*, but which always reduce to binaries.

The problem with "lock-in" is it assumes a correct answer for every given problem. Uniformity and universality are the standards. This assumes human beings can all be reduced to universal standard, and so "understanding the human" reduces to sufficient layers of description, made up of programmable data.[38] We see this in the assumption of the Turing test: a computer that passes for human must have sufficiently human intelligence, assuming we program in enough layers. Lanier argues the reverse, in fact, holds: that we attribute human intelligence to a machine that reproduces human-like responses says more about our reduction of measurements than the actual ability of the machine.[39] This, to Lanier, is the danger of "lock-in." The circular reasoning of computer engineers produces machines that achieve human-level performance by computer science standards, which reinforces the definitions of human-level performance that computer scientists prescribe. In defining human intelligence by mathematical and data-driven standards, AI engineers can achieve their goal of human-level intelligence merely by achieving their own mathematical and data-driven standards. In other words, the reduction of the varieties of human intelligence, experience, understanding, emotion, and so forth to quantifiable inputs allows the mathematical illusion of creating human-level intelligence. The music example is particularly telling: by defining musical notes by mathematical formulae according to Western musical standards, MIDI reinforces Western hegemonic concepts of music, delegitimizing other scale systems like those used in traditional Korean or Arab music.

Feminist authors have pointed out that the mathematical modeling of AI assumes masculine worldviews as normative. As early as 1985, Donna Haraway critiqued the male-dominant fields of science and the willed dismissal of non-masculine perspectives. In her widely cited "Cyborg Manifesto," she argues against dualistic metaphysical models that often posit the male, rational, and mechanical against the female, emotional, and biological. She argues for the need for the "hybrid" image of the cyborg, an entity that is not biological or mechanical, not male or female, not located within an ontology of beginnings and ends.[40] Her ontology is designed to resist the "informatics of domination," where every component of human life is reduced to "a common language in which all resistance to instrumental control disappears and all heterogeneity can be submitted to disassembly, reassembly, investment, and exchange."[41] In other words, Haraway argues that, rather than merely defending the opposing binaries of the patriarchal order, feminists should engage in the hybrid action of transgressing borders. Thus, it would not be merely saying "computers do not think as we do" *à la* Dreyfus or Searle but rather "computers do and do not think as we do, as cybernetic organisms."

In turn, then, Haraway argues against the objectivist position in science and technology. The cyborg vision is one that emphasizes a messy ontology—no one position is privileged. She notes that the "conquering gaze from nowhere . . . claims the power to see and not be seen, to represent while escaping representation. . . . [It is] the unmarked positions of Man and White."[42] She calls this "illusion" of objectivity a "god trick" and contends that all knowledge must be understood as contingent and "situated."[43] Haraway argues that no form of knowledge is objective or universal. This is not, Haraway insists, to claim that science is wrong or merely a social construct[44] but rather to recognize that it embodies a particular perspective, one that by definition cannot be omniscient. AI is a model of this objectivist mindset, Haraway notes, which assumes disembodied rationality. Against this view, Haraway insists on "politics and epistemologies of location, positioning, and situating, where partiality and not universality is the condition of being heard to make rational knowledge claims."[45]

Psychologist Sherry Turkle notes as both a psychologist and a feminist the dangers of anthropomorphizing calculative machinery. With AI pioneer Seymour Papert, Turkle examines how the "masculine" image of cold rationality is both constructed and arbitrary for computer programming.[46] They find that while males from a young age do tend to favor "hard" mastery approaches to engineering while females tend to favor "soft" approaches, there is no inherent connection. However, as children develop, boys tend to become "harder" while girls tend to become "softer." Papert and Turkle attribute this development to conditioning and rearing rather than any latent tendencies. In turn, in examining computer science education, they find that soft approaches favoring *bricolage* and intuition are as successful as hard step-by-step approaches in early computer science classes. However, in time, in upper classes, these programs demand "harder" approaches as a formal pedagogical requirement. Thus, Papert and Turkle note that science, especially computer science, creates a dominant masculine culture that is antithetical toward the feminine, not only because it reinforces images of the object of study as feminine components to be analyzed by an objective (read: masculine) gaze, but also because it defines the masculine as logical and calculative.[47] As a result, in spite of early computer science being a largely female endeavor, by the 1980s, it had become a "boys' club." The rhetoric surrounding computer science and boys' epistemology reframed what was "women's work" to be extremely masculine. Through a feedback loop, computer culture defines its work as more proper to males because males are more calculative, then rears males to emphasize calculative skills, and finally refuses any deviant methodological approach.

Turkle initially held out some hope that the masculine vision of computation could be challenged by "emergent AI"[48] but within twenty years recognized the shortcomings of that view. In her monograph *Alone Together*, she notes that the logical-calculative epistemology of computer programming has transcended the disciplinary bounds of computer science to become a dominant way of thinking about our relationships. The triumph of hard coding, once a mere gatekeeping mechanism for computer science, has become so concrete that the computer has become the model for the person instead of the inverse. The sophistication of AI programs, especially ones that respond to human action, invite us to think of the machine as human. "And just as we imagine things as people, we invent ways of being with people that turn them into something close to things."[49] She notes ways we objectify human beings through digital communications platforms, such as sending anonymous obscenities or expecting tireless work from others. But because human beings are not machines, we tire, we are unpredictable, and we require compromise and cooperation. As a result, some find the idea of robot companions appealing—a sex bot can provide some of the same pleasure as a real sexual partner without the emotional labor. "Dependence on a robot presents itself as risk free. . . . Dependence on a person is risky."[50] In short, as AI presents itself as increasingly human, it becomes an attractive facsimile for authentic human interaction, one with many of the same benefits but none of the emotional costs.

Finally, what remains the strongest direct critique of AI is the work of Hubert Dreyfus. Dreyfus levels several criticisms against the AI philosophy, including its epistemological, psychological, biological, and ontological assumptions.[51] The broader critique Dreyfus offers, however, is articulated through the thought of Wittgenstein, Heidegger, and Merleau-Ponty. From a primarily phenomenological perspective, Dreyfus argues that the Platonic-Cartesian model of epistemology regnant in Western philosophy is mistaken, and so, by extension, the AI model of human epistemology repeats these same errors.[52] The AI model applies universal rules to discrete facts; Dreyfus contends, on the other hand, that human reason is not universal nor rule-based, nor are facts themselves discrete.

Dreyfus's main argument can be broken down into three interrelated points. First, human beings perceive not individual data points run through an algorithm but rather phenomena within an existing gestalt.[53] Optical illusions work because of this feature of human perception—we see a rabbit or duck depending on our orientation, or two faces or a vase depending on which aspect of the image we focus on. We *see* pictures; we do not *see* rays of light reflecting off a surface, penetrating our retinas and triggering our optic nerves. Second, our intentional action within the world is based on the relevance of data we perceive related to a context, not articulated by an exhaustive list of rules.[54] Contexts shape what "meaningful" behavior is more than strict adherence to rules. We may obey certain rules about being quiet within a library, but if another patron suddenly had a heart attack, we would adapt and call for help. Finally, then, the meaning of our action is contextualized within our own understandings of what our existence entails.[55] While much of human action, such as mate selection and food consumption, can be explained as fulfilling natural drives, a person can experience a reorientation to these same drives through a change in understanding of life meaning, e.g., religious conversion. St. Augustine, after all, freely gave in to his sexual appetites before becoming Christian but lived celibately afterward.

In summary, one might note that Dreyfus's main contention is, like Searle's, that AI does not take into account what might facetiously be referred to as meaning or understanding. Here, the AI pioneers' insistence that a machine does not require "understanding" to achieve human intelligence becomes their great obstacle. It is ironic that the cyberneticists placed so much emphasis on information given their naive failure to recognize that information is always contextual. Kurzweil's insistence on pattern recognition draws closer to this problem but still ultimately fails to understand that patterns themselves are rooted in "meaning." Data with no meaning is static interference. But for human beings, knowledge is meaningful—it fits within (or conflicts with) our existing understandings of ourselves in the world. An intersection of two lines resembling a lowercase "t" signifies, to the Christian, their faith tradition, the person of Jesus, his death on the cross, and the grisly tradition of Roman crucifixion all at once. It is true, of course, that AI programmers give rules for the AI to follow, but those rules are meaningful only to the human beings outside. To the machine itself, the instructions are arbitrary, and so it should come as no surprise that a machine would react to a restaurant not having food by eating the chef in response. It is perhaps not surprising, then, that in the last analysis, Dreyfus accepts the possibility of computers improving certain areas of human existence through their capacity for advanced algorithmic processing, but he warns that we should not confuse the impressive calculative capacity of AI with the totality of human cognitive functioning.[56]

The contention of the "weak AI" critics is that while AI does very impressive things, it is not designed to do the same thing as human beings. It lacks understanding, simplifies complex realities, defers to "masculine" stereotypes, dismisses the importance of emotion, and cannot "make sense of" information. The degree to which these critics disagree with AI proponents or the specific focus of their contentions differs, but they all note that while AI does something that human beings also do, it will not do *everything* that we do. AI is a risk then because it steamrolls all forms of understanding and knowledge into a straightforwardly simple mathematical model. The conflict between feminist modes of knowledge and AI epistemological models is particularly telling: not only does the AI vision ignore fully half of humanity's experience of the world but it even pigeonholes masculine epistemologies into hegemonic scientisms. Searle and Dreyfus are hardly known for their gender-critical perspectives, so the fact that AI even fails on their standards shows that AI is not only, in the words of Noreen Herzfeld, "a possibility only in the writings of rich, white males"[57] but more crucially that it only pertains to a subset of this narrow group. AI assumes preexisting normative answers to a number of questions that its critics find unconvincing: that understanding is a function of natural language processing, that diverse modes of thinking are merely deficient modes of thinking, and that meaning is a preestablished given for all persons within society. And, on the other hand, AI researchers implicitly deny any claims that knowledge is situated, embodied, contextual, or even just a product of specific neurochemical processes occurring within a real human brain.

Science from Below

Until now, the question of AI has primarily been whether or not it should be considered a person—the basic agent/patient question, addressed from differing perspectives. This is to ask what the moral status of AI should be, not what moral challenges are relevant in creating and implementing AI systems. It turns out that the insight of Turkle and Haraway, that women's perspectives are devalued and downplayed in AI research, is important for understanding major moral failures wrapped into AI and the reason why they persist. Their critique of computing culture and pedagogy—that it reinforces masculinist biases—foreshadows the later observation that corporations developing AI, as well as the AI products they create, reinscribe the biases of the masculinist paradigms underwriting the programs.

In short, the prediction that AI needs "moral programming" has proven correct, but not for the reason why Bostrom and others (men) have suggested—the implicit biases of well-intentioned AI programmers have destructive repercussions on people who become the unwitting victims of this technology.

Consider the experience of Timnit Gebru and Margaret Mitchell. Mitchell and Gebru were coleaders of Google's Ethical Artificial Intelligence team. They, along with two other Google researchers and two outside researchers, submitted a paper to an academic conference. Google company policy requires its researchers to submit papers to internal review before being sent out, and after the paper was reviewed, Gebru was asked to withdraw the names of the Google researchers, which she opposed. In turn, her supervisor informed her that she was no longer employed by Google.[58] Mitchell was fired a few weeks later. Google claimed Mitchell had violated company policy by moving files outside of the company network, but Mitchell's outspoken criticism of the dismissal of her coleader raised many suspicions.[59] The paper in question was presented at the ACM Conference on Fairness, Accountability, and Transparency a few weeks later, with the names of the other two Google researchers omitted and "Shmargaret Shmitchell" replacing Mitchell's name.[60]

This incident, truly only one event in the long chronicle of gender imbalance in the tech industry, illustrates many problems. Google hired an Ethical AI team but apparently would not tolerate dissenting voices against its corporate direction. Google's official stance is that they are not biased, but their dismissal of two of their most prominent female researchers for doing their job casts suspicion on this claim. As one of the largest companies in the world, Google's termination of its ethics leads sets dismal expectations, both for the place of diverse views in an industry that has earned criticism for sexism and racism and for the role of ethics in AI research. In the end, it appears that the largely male corporate culture of Silicon Valley maintains its pretentions about fairness and objectivity only by silencing the voices of people who contradict these claims, like a tyrant who claims their people all love them because dissenters are imprisoned. It comes as no surprise, then, that Google's slogan is no longer "Don't be evil."

The work of Gebru and Mitchell was important, however, because the promises of AI should not be overstated at the cost of its actual (or predicted) harms. Cathy O'Neil makes this need clear by illustrating the disturbing ways that AI is altering our social reality. O'Neil challenges the hegemonic trust in algorithms as definitive models through what she calls "Weapons of Math Destruction." A Weapon of Math Destruction is a trusted algorithm that is opaque, employed on a large scale, and inflicts catastrophic damage.[61] The program is opaque because most of the people who use it, that is, not the programmers themselves but the persons and institutions that employ it as a tool, are kept from understanding what the model actually does. Scale means the program is used for making large policy decisions, such as decisions for policing, sentencing, employment, taxation, and so forth for a company, community, state, or even a nation. Finally, the destructive nature means that the program has the capacity to create great amounts of suffering, whether that be through bankruptcy, unemployment, denial of bail, unfair sentencing, or other life-altering decisions. An example O'Neil uses to demonstrate the destructive nature of these programs is the LSI—R (Level of Service Inventory—Revised), which has been used to determine prison sentence lengths since 1995 but uses many irrelevant criteria to determine recidivism likelihood, such as family history.[62] The destructive capacity of this program is non-negligible for the United States given both the high rate of incarceration and recidivism built into the American penal system.[63]

O'Neil explains that Weapons of Math Destruction are trusted because they are mathematical models, which, for many, means they are models of certainty. However, she reminds us that algorithms are only models; they are simulations and not reality. As such, "we make choices about what's important enough to include."[64] The result of this, however, is that the "objective" model is nothing other than "opinions embedded in mathematics."[65] Thus, racist algorithms are the norm rather than the exception in situations where systemic racism is prevalent, such as employment, criminal justice, or banking. Advanced algorithms do not *correct* human prejudices; they *reinforce* these biases with math. This is foundational for all other specific critiques—the models of AI have far-reaching devastating impacts because the faulty humans who make the "objective" programs program in their own biases.

O'Neil's insight is applied explicitly to the question of race by Safiya Noble and Ruha Benjamin. Noble's work opens on the obscene discovery that a Google search for "Black girls," which she conducted to find ideas for activities for her stepdaughter, yielded numerous top results for pornography.[66] The same search for "white girls" yielded more family-friendly results. In conducting similar searches, she found that Google image results, search results, and predictive search inquiries tended to correlate more positive or neutral results for white people and more negative results for Black people and other people of color (such as a search for "beautiful" only yielded several scantily clad young white women, while a search for "ugly" included many people of color and an array of ages and sexes).[67] Noble notes that, with a large predictive model like Google, the results it yields are curated by users' activity (all users as an aggregate, as well as individual users in customized searches), so its biased results are reflective of the underlying bias rampant in the user base. In a biting critique of the "invisible hand," she notes, "The persistent normalization of Black people as aberrant and undeserving of human rights and dignity under the banners of public safety, technological innovation, and the emerging creative economy . . . is rendered a legitimate free-market technology project."[68] In other words, the racism of internet users' activity, which serves as data for large machine learning efforts, is considered "neutral" data, and the racism that results is rendered "legitimate" because it has been given in the court of public opinion, which is expected to correct for existing biases. Given the stamp of approval by the market, the biases are cemented as "neutral," and racist AI outputs are taken as value-free for policy makers and capitalists, who use the results to create even worse racial disparities.

Benjamin focuses on the way AI reinscribes biases in what she calls "the New Jim Code" (a play on Michelle Alexander's *The New Jim Crow*): "the employment of new technologies that reflect and reproduce existing inequalities but that are promoted and perceived as more objective or progressive than the discriminatory systems of a previous era."[69] Benjamin notes (echoing O'Neil) that massive algorithms are billed as objective solutions to human bias despite being built on human biases. "Tech designers encode judgments into technical systems but claim that the racist results of their designs are entirely exterior to the encoding process. Racism thus becomes doubled—magnified and buried under layers of digital denial."[70] The realities of racist policies, laws, studies, and so forth remain invisible to "color-blind" white engineers in Silicon Valley, who assume their point of view can be objective. While Haraway noted the problem of this "god trick" from a feminist point of view in science, Benjamin points out how it is encoded into algorithms that go on to perpetuate and exacerbate racism because, per O'Neil, they are trusted.

The New Jim Code operates, according to Benjamin, through four dimensions: "engineered inequity, default discrimination, coded exposure, and technological benevolence."[71] Engineered inequity is the way algorithms streamline complex judgments, typically encoding racist, sexist, or other discriminatory frameworks as shortcuts for judging a person's character or worth. The algorithms are set up in ways that take "predictive models" as definitive, often without questioning the accuracy or inbuilt assumptions of these models.[72] Default discrimination is the application of these models—their use to reinforce preexisting systemic discriminatory patterns, such as predictive policing that "works" because police look for more crime in places they have historically patrolled more.[73] Coded exposure takes "race as technology" and creates techno-scientific tools that reify this concept, turning the superficial difference of skin pigmentation into either an aberration from the "norm" (read: white) or the legitimate focus of technical assistance, depending on which frame reinforces existing racial hegemonies and best benefits the inventors of such products. This focus is especially implemented in surveillance and other visual technologies, accented by cases like that of Robert Williams. Finally, technological benevolence purports to fix the problems of encoded bias through more encoding. Referencing the paradoxical meaning of *pharmakon*, Benjamin notes, "Racial fixes [in technology] are better understood not as viruses but as a part of the underlying code of operating systems—often developed as solutions to particular kinds of predicaments without sufficient awareness of the problems that they help produce and preserve."[74]

Indigenous scholars, too, raise concerns about the appropriate use and development of AI and its potential to inflict harm on their communities. In "Guidelines for Indigenous-Centred AI Design V.1," a coalition of Indigenous activists articulate principles "aimed at any person, group, organization, institute, company and/or political or governmental representative that wishes to undertake responsible and fair development of AI systems with Indigenous communities."[75] In a short list of guidelines, they emphasize that AI should be developed: (1) with local interests in mind, (2) with a focus on relational knowledge, (3) to be responsible to local communities, (4) subordinate to Indigenous protocol, (5) recognizing cultural values embedded in computational frameworks, (6) with full-system responsibility to non-maleficence, and (7) recognizing Indigenous sovereignty over data and AI tools.[76] Going beyond the already highlighted threats AI presents, these activists posit that AI *can* have a positive impact on Indigenous communities, provided the technology be developed with Indigenous protocol in mind—not as an afterthought or a corrective but as part of the architecture and development.

Timnit Gebru herself articulates most clearly the problem of AI being developed largely by male members of a country's racial hegemony. Summarizing many of the views outlined above, though referencing an array of other thinkers, she writes, "Ethical AI is not an abstract concept but one that is in dire need of a holistic approach. It starts from who is at the table, who is creating the technology, and who is framing the goals and values of AI. As such, an approach [to ethical AI] that is solely crafted, led, and evangelized by those in powerful positions around the world is bound to fail. Who creates the technology determines whose values are embedded in it."[77] She adds to the previous perspectives the reality that sexual minorities and ethnic minorities have their interests ignored, if not outright violated, in AI programming. For example, she notes that not only "automatic gender recognition" tools are developed without input from non-cisgender individuals, but, more troubling, they can "out" transgender individuals, violating boundaries of privacy and exposing them to risk.[78] Gebru further notes that even when the absence of marginalized voices is recognized in AI ethics, often the work of activists is co-opted by powerful groups to appear more ethical.[79] While the seventy-year-old field of AI has not taken ethics seriously until present, the critical attention of activists has led to a fervor and excitement on this topic, providing opportunities for those already privileged and perpetuating the injustices in the field to further advance their careers off the work of minority groups. The efforts to bring marginalized voices to the table have resulted in dominant voices performing token acts of reformation, the results of which further the hegemony and domination that these dominant persons enjoy against the legitimate grievances of the marginalized.

In treating AI as intelligent, we inevitably prioritize the capacities and functions of AI as normative and treat all aberrations as exceptions. Having a body is an exception to the abstract (male) reason. Being Black is an exception to the default racial experience (white). Being nonhuman, as Francesca Ferrando notes, is the exception to the white, male, able-bodied, neurotypical human.[80] And as O'Neil points out, if one does not fit within the established algorithm, they will be excluded, and no amount of complaining will reinstate them. AI understood as a model for human intelligence thus excludes far more of what is authentically human than it includes.

What Remains?

The critical perspectives above reveal the limitations of AI and challenge the narrative AI researchers perpetuate. But AI researchers can and do adjust their models based on these views. Strong AI, while still a dream for many in the field, is no longer emphasized as much as narrow AI. Instead of a model of all human cognition, some AI researchers settle for a program that does well only one thing that humans do, such as recognizing faces. This problem is more direct and simpler than AGI but still presents grave challenges, such as when that model fails to recognize Black people's faces or misattributes aggression to them.[81] But the prevailing mathematical model for not only facial recognition but also intelligence broadly responds to this problem by feeding the algorithm more data. The problems of sexism, racism, and other forms of discrimination are still rampant and often seem like they are getting worse rather than better, but some hope can be found in the emergence of Women in AI, Ethical AI LLC, Queer in AI, Black in AI, Algorithmic Justice League, and other advocacy groups working to combat the continuing challenges of bias in AI. Assuming the problem of ableist, white supremacist patriarchy can be overcome (a question in which AI is only a magnifying glass to broader society); then many of the above critiques will be satisfied.

Ultimately, however, nearly all the critiques listed above ignore the problem of socioeconomic class as a distinct concern.[82] Of the top ten corporations by market value at present (December 2021), only two (Saudi Arabian Oil Co. and Berkshire Hathaway) have no connection to computer technologies.[83] Four of these companies have their headquarters in Silicon Valley (five until recently with the relocation of Tesla), and another two are located in the Seattle area. Similarly, of the top ten richest people in the world (all of whom are white men), only two (Warren Buffett of Berkshire Hathaway and Bernard Arnault of Christian Dior, the only non-American) are not in tech.[84] Given the relative novelty of digital technology, this should give us pause. What does it mean to say that the CEOs of a few tech companies mostly located on the US West Coast hold more wealth than most countries? It must not be forgotten in the midst of everything that when we are talking about machine learning and the future of AI, all of this is set against the backdrop of trillion-dollar companies and centibillionaires.

In other words, the question of equality and representation also raises the question of whose voice counts and who gets the money. As important as it is to challenge the "boys' club" reality of AI or the implicit and explicit bias in tech, the outcome will still be massive wealth inequality and a sharp disconnect between the fabulously wealthy in tech and everybody else. No poor person is going to be allowed to direct technology development. No poor person is going to be CEO of the next big tech firm or head of engineering at a multinational corporation. The founders and CEOs of these companies all already came from well-to-do families before they emerged as grossly wealthy. Their successors, such as Tim Cook at Apple or Sundar Pichai at Alphabet, spent decades working as executives before emerging on top. One might start life in a poor family and work their way to the top—though this is extremely rare—but by the time one has become CEO of a multibillion-dollar company, they have long been removed from the realities of poverty.

This is not all surprising. While computer science seventy years ago may have been relegated mainly to university campuses, with the advent of personal computing, the technology has been directed toward consumers and is now a primarily capital-driven enterprise. As Sabine Pfeiffer astutely notes, the emergence of the "digital economy" in the late twentieth and early twenty-first centuries was due not to technological advancement but rather *economic* pursuit.[85] The possibility of realizing greater amounts of value through the possibilities of predictive, marketing, and logistics technologies spurred the growth of massive digital platforms. Thus, tech leaders today are business leaders. Tech luminaries want profit. Tech companies seek to increase their market share and grow their wealth. Investors in tech companies want to see returns on investments. And above all, technological progress is tied to, conceptually if not actually, profit. Better hardware, as the recent fortune of Nvidia demonstrates, means better profits. Better software likewise means better profits.

The interest in AI especially in the last decade has been exclusively tied to profit. While McCarthy and Minsky may have been fine working at universities, today's AI prodigies are working in major tech firms. Recall that Elon Musk captured the title of "world's richest man" in 2021 after promising major technological breakthroughs on his "AI Day." Across industries, AI promises efficiency, lowering costs, and most of all, profit. Even governmental organizations investing in AI do so for profit, or, perhaps better, cost-savings. The AI programs funded by the European Union's 2020 Horizon Programme, for example, are mostly oriented toward capital ends, such as SecondHands, a robot assistant intended to "increase the efficiency and productivity [i.e., profitability] of maintenance technicians," or Hephaestus, a construction robot suggested to help "workers' safety and welfare" but more importantly "provides a cost-effective approach to work on building facades."[86] And as countries like China and South Korea pour more money into AI development, their hope is that doing so will position them better in the global economy against richer countries like the United States and Germany. In line with Deng Xiaoping's dictum that "it doesn't matter whether a cat is black or white, as long as it catches mice," the Chinese science policy directed toward AI growth and investment is tied to the hope that AI will take the place of China's dwindling economic growth in manufacturing.[87]

The result of this is that AI research has neither taken seriously the perspective of the poor nor does it have any interest in doing so. If the lower economic half of the United States's population holds only 2 percent of the total wealth of the nation,[88] then those in the top 1 percent, who hold fifteen times more wealth as a group, have little reason to cater to the interests of the masses. But as AI proponents increase their wealth, increase their cultural prominence, and increase the extent of their technology across different sectors of life, it is critical from a social ethical perspective to confront the perspectives of the poor.

CHAPTER 3

The Money Printer

ELON MUSK, CEO of Tesla Motors and SpaceX (among others), warned in 2014 that AI was "our biggest existential threat." Musk compared developing AI to "summoning the demon," asserting that human hubris outstrips our own ability to control the technology.[1] He called for a "national and international" regulatory oversight to ensure that AI is not developed without due caution or applied to the wrong ends. The need for caution and global cooperation must guide AI research to prevent doomsday scenarios, even by the most well-intentioned researchers.

Musk seems to have changed his mind shortly thereafter, however, when he helped found OpenAI, a competitor to Google's DeepMind in 2015. The call for international oversight was billed the year prior as a necessary tool to keep AI technologists in line, but OpenAI presses forward, carrying out major AI research projects like DALL-E image generator or Generative Pre-trained Transformer 4 (GPT-4) natural language processor. In 2018, Musk resigned from OpenAI but kept pushing AI through his primary company Tesla. In 2021, he hosted an "AI Day," where he hyped new plans for AI. The highlight of the show was the promise of personal home robots that use Tesla's autopilot AI system to navigate, demonstrated by a person dancing on stage in a robot bodysuit.[2] The financial impact of this publicity event is non-negligible. Despite the fact that Musk's auto company, Tesla, only recently achieved profitability,[3] the valuation of his stock rose enough following AI Day to crown him the "world's richest man."[4]

We might find it perplexing that within a decade, Musk went from vocally cautioning against unchecked AI to AI entrepreneur to world's richest AI advocate, but from a capitalistic view, the story is fairly straightforward: Musk changed his mind when he realized AI could catapult him beyond the fortunes of Bezos, Gates, and others contending for "world's richest." However, in 2014, public opinion on AI was tepid. Certainly there were AI zealots and leading-edge scientists who expected great things of AI, but there was relatively little investment in the technology compared to other hyped technologies, such as Google Glass augmented reality glasses. Musk's statements against AI, at a time when his image and brand were rising, brought attention to AI more poignantly than more academic AI researchers, like Eliezer Yudkowsky or Yann Lecun, ever could have. His "warning" about AI, following the logic of "reverse psychology," attracted more interest and attention in the technology than if he had simply invested in it on his own. Thus, the transition from AI skeptic to AI advocate reveals a cunning business strategy, one that is especially poignant given the massive shift in funding toward AI following 2015.

Supposedly, the first technological innovation that could be considered "automation" was invented by a lazy child. In the late eighteenth century, steam power was married to textile frames to create the first true factories. As textile production moved from a cottage industry to a workshop industry, hand-powered looms were replaced by Arkwright's water frame. The water frame used hydropower, using a water wheel to churn machinery within a textile mill automatically. However, water frames still had problems, such as droughts, frozen rivers, or flooding. James Watt's steam engine, on the other hand, could provide constant energy regardless of external weather conditions, so in 1784, Edmund Cartwright created the first power loom using steam power instead of hydropower. In time, this basic model was improved upon with greater machine efficiency and other new technologies. With the advent of coal-gas lanterns, textile mills could even run round the clock, and soon entire families within the working class were employed in these mills, often still at starvation wages.

Children, of course, were an infamous gristle for the cogs of early industrialism. Their small frames made them preferable for work in mines, and their slender limbs were perfect for dexterously manipulating factory machinery. All of this, so far, is historically well-documented, but the apocryphal tale goes that in one such textile mill, an idle boy was employed to release a steam valve to prevent the pipes from over-pressurizing. This was necessary but tedious work. Every few seconds, the boy, sometimes called

"Humphrey Potter," pulled a string that released steam. Potter discovered, however, that he could jury-rig an apparatus so that the kinetic energy that moved pistons and gears would then release the steam. In some versions of the story, the young man tied a string around the actuator arm,[5] while in another, he combined some metal piping to create an extension.[6] Thus, the lazy working-class boy was free to play with his friends.

While it is true that early developments did allow the steam engine to regulate itself, the story is of doubtful veracity. Humphrey Potter, for example, was apparently a collaborator with Thomas Newcomen, inventor of the original steam engine, and thus not a lazy working-class boy.[7] The story does, however, serve as a way of conveying two morals. The first is summed up in the aphorism "always choose a lazy person to do a difficult job because a lazy person will find an easy way to do it."[8] While the origin of this quote apparently derives from Walter Chrysler, it has variously been attributed to contemporary tech magnates like Bill Gates and Elon Musk. As an aphorism, it seems to convey a great secret to business success; the reason why Gates and Musk have their fortunes is due to their acumen. Only a true genius would recognize that the lazy are the best to follow.

But the other function of this story is to reinforce stereotypes about the working class. A lazy working-class boy, who shows innovative spirit, allows us to look favorably at the horror of child labor in the factories with some self-satisfaction. Such innovation would never happen if that boy had not been employed. And, of course, he was an idle child, one eager to avoid true work in favor of lazing about. Because, the story suggests to us, this is how the poor are generally: they are poor unless (or until) they can demonstrate proper industry, innovation, or skill.

The Superficial Account: Capital and Tech

It is readily apparent that AI specifically and industrial technology generally are at the service of capital. The ability to invest the profits of labor into more labor to generate more profits is difficult to accomplish without being able to expand production through technological means. A workshop full of manufacturers costs the value of their labor, but if their labor can be augmented by machines, then the cost is driven down. So it is that Adam Smith's theory in the *Wealth of Nations* comes after the invention of the water loom, as well as James Watts's improved steam engine, but justifies the subsequent development of steam-powered factories. And, as Max Weber argued a century ago, the "spirit of capitalism" that pervades Protestant society becomes the driving force for social advancement and technological development.[9]

Up to present, capital accumulation continues to be the primary drive of technological development.[10] This is readily apparent from numerous metrics, from the stock valuations of large technology companies to the cost of living in tech hubs like the San Francisco Bay Area, to the capital investment push in the so-called "start-up culture," to the current economic valuation of the AI industry, to the financial panic at the collapse of Silicon Valley Bank, and so forth. Even national investments in AI demonstrate this push—Smith's theory of capitalism is not called the *Wealth of Individuals*, after all, and even communist China's investment in AI is part of a larger effort to increase their economic power against other nations. It is in this context that we can make sense of the appointment of Jeff Bezos to the Pentagon's Defense Innovation Advisory Board, despite him having no experience with the military and his business being primarily oriented toward civilian consumer goods,[11] or Bill Gates's global influence shaping even the direction of vaccine manufacturing during the COVID-19 pandemic.[12] The global elite is not some shadowy cabal as conspiracy theorists believe; it is rather the simple conflation of money, industry, and politics, with AI merely being the focus *du jour* of these interests. The Gateses, Bezoses, and Musks of today are just the digital versions of the Rockefellers, Carnegies, and Fords of the steel age.

Thus, it is no exaggeration to say that interests of AI researchers, and especially the firms they direct, are tied to power broadly and profit specifically. As such, the interests of the poor are only of interest to AI programs as far as these interests can save money in other places. If it will save the government valuable money and resources, for example, then the project is worth investing in. Many of the critical voices against AI have already highlighted ways in which this cold calculation functions. Cathy O'Neil points out how Weapons of Math Destruction allow bureaucracies to become even more faceless, reducing the cost of personal interaction and allowing for "pure reason" (i.e., economic efficiency) to dictate policy. Ruha Benjamin notes that the privileged position of computer programmers means that biases against the poor are encoded while the largesse of the rich is overlooked. And Timnit Gebru points out that when AI takes seriously the issue of ethics, those invited to the table are already the very privileged. Thus, the critique against AI as serving only the interests of the wealthy is by no means a new critique.

Well intentioned as these critiques are, they never give economic inequality pride of place in the discussions of the problem of AI. How AI exacerbates preexisting social inequalities along gender and race lines is addressed, but the default assumption seems to be that inequality *will* exist. Rather than asking whether tech companies should wield such disproportionate influence and control so much of the market, the question is rather whether they are doing so in a way that adequately respects ethnic and sexual diversity. While it is true that the lack of representation, from testers to engineers to project leads to the board room, has resulted in programmed bias, it is also important to note that all of this is carried out within the broader logic of capitalism. Pointing out that the people influencing markets and creating disruptive technologies skew largely toward white cisgender men must be balanced against the fact that regardless of how diverse the movers and shakers are, they will constitute a cultural elite far removed from and with interests often at odds with the masses. Put another way, justice should mean combatting not only the implicit and explicit biases against women, people of color, LGBTQ people, and other marginalized populations but also the way the technology is designed to further enrich the rich while harming the poor.

In this context, AI is nothing special, which may be why so little attention has been directed toward this problem. Technologies that further empower the wealthy are by far the norm rather than the exception. The broad history of technology is essentially one of channeling power, which tends to be amassed by those already in control. The writings of various critics, including Herbert Marcuse, Jacques Ellul, Langdon Winner, and Andrew Feenberg, all point to the ways that, with rare exceptions of "democratic technologies," the tendency of a technology to become "successful" depends on its ability to grant greater control to those already in power.[13] As a technology that has increased the fortunes of the wealthiest by billions of dollars, AI is merely the latest tool to elevate the wealthy further above the struggling masses.

If the sole point were that AI is another step on the road to exacerbating wealth inequalities, that would be enough for a bookshelf. Nvidia's sudden success, the economic posturing of Elon Musk and Jeff Bezos, the implementation of AI in policing, and the use of AI in trading all clearly delineate how this philosopher's stone primarily functions to augment the privilege of the already very privileged. In increasing the power of the powerful, AI also functions to diminish the position of the worst off. Indeed, the promises made about AI obscure the harms it entails to those already in positions of lack. The fact that wealthy AI evangelists have not publicly recognized this is due to either the capitalist fantasy that economics is not a zero-sum game, or worse, bad-faith refusals to admit the hidden consequences to their ascendency. But AI, in its promotion, promulgation, and prominence, promises to satisfy the insatiable appetites of the plutocrats, those whose plunder punishes the poor.

Artificial intelligence's first sleight against the poor lies in the simple fact that the "intelligence" ascribed to AI is rooted in ideal-choice selection contextualized by preferable conditions rather than survival choices characterized by lack. AIs are deployed in businesses to improve business strategies, to make the most optimal choice given massive amounts of data, which promises increased profits and lower costs. As Sabine Pfeiffer notes, the primary advances in "digital capitalism" have until now been in three broad areas: advertising and marketing (directing the right ads to the right people), transport and warehousing (directing traffic to the right places for product distribution), and prediction and control (directing corporate resources toward efficiency and growth).[14] In each of these cases, AI is trusted as a "rational, autonomous agent," entrusted to make decisions that will be of benefit to the AI (or rather, to its users). The poor, however, experience the world through constrained choices, always negotiating at a disadvantage and existing as those acted upon, not the autonomous actors themselves.

However, AI being seen as intelligent does itself automatically mean that the poor will lose out. After all, AI prognosticators' vision is that AI will be the rising tide that lifts all boats, that the benefits granted by AI at the top will trickle down to all people throughout society. Foxconn's use of automated systems, after all, removes the most dangerous and tedious jobs from workers. Safer working conditions, optimized distribution, individually tailored service models, personalized medical treatments, improved urban management, crime prevention, and so forth will benefit the poor as much as, if not more than, the rich! But this is *only* true if the conditions of "optimized distribution" or "crime prevention" are mathematically straightforward problems with objective answers to them. As it turns out, though, AI is really just "opinions embedded in mathematics,"[15] and the opinions represented are opinions of people whose experience of the world has been one of material plenty and a repulsion toward the threat of scarcity. As a result, AI is principally intended to benefit and support the well-off by increasing the wealth of the rich, by reinforcing instrumental rationality of the wealthy through self-reference to more mathematics, and by casting the poor as useless detritus weighing down our social order.

AI and the Capitalist Vision of the Future

The vision of the AI future articulated by its proponents can be understood as what Sheila Jasanoff refers to as a "sociotechnical imaginary." A sociotechnical imaginary is "collectively held and performed visions of desirable futures . . . animated by shared understandings of forms of social life and social order attainable through, and supportive of, advances in science and technology."[16] Examples of sociotechnical imaginaries include South Koreans' concerns about radiation leading to resistance against efforts for nuclear power,[17] the scientific community's perception of the Asilomar meeting on rDNA regulation shaping attitudes toward self-regulation,[18] and Chinese distrust of genetically modified food due to problems related to "fake foods."[19] In each case, public perception about a given science or technology and what future it will bring with it shapes public attitudes toward the technology. These can, in turn, shift policy strategies, funding, collaborative efforts, and research initiatives. Fears of the long-term effects of radiation leaking into the environment shape the South Korean public's attitude toward nuclear energy and, in turn, affect efforts by nuclear advocates and resisters on the national stage.

The American ethos has long been characterized as technologically "progressive," seeing its future as leading the world in the "new and exciting" when it comes to science and technology. As Michael Burdett notes, by the end of the nineteenth century, the American national myth tied technoscientific advancement to the national character as "Manifest Destiny"—the West was to be won by the superiority of (white man's) science and technology![20] This myth blesses the technological advancement of the twentieth century—the emergence of space travel, nuclear fission, and new informational and computing technologies and the promises they hold for raising humanity up, removing the shackles that bind us to the misbegotten flaws of natural organic life, make us lords of the universe.

Important for understanding specifically the significance of AI compared to other technologies is the myth of intelligence. The national myth of the United States, the view that the "West was won" or that one of the youngest nations (not to say nation-states, as the US is among the oldest in the strictest terms) is the richest and most powerful today, is faith in the inherent goodness of intelligence. The reasoning put forth for American independence from Great Britain, an Enlightenment disdain for the trappings of medieval feudal cult of personality in favor of a theoretical respect of universal human dignity, frames the founding documents, artifacts of the best eighteenth-century political philosophy. America's emergence as a global power is understood not as an act of brute force (though the modern military belies this assumption) but as demonstration of superior strategy. Through the end of the nineteenth century and throughout the twentieth century, America's accomplishments all bore the seal of technoscientific advancement. In the Gilded Age, the Carnegies and Rockefellers amassed fortunes through the wonder of industrial technologies. The US ended the Second World War by weaponizing nuclear fission and won the space race against the Soviet Union by sending the first astronauts to the moon. By the late twentieth century, "military-industrial complex" was a part of the lexicon indicating the awarding of military contracts to industrial companies to advance science and technology ostensibly for military use.

But AI is not just another in the litany of American inventions. In a way, it stands as *the* American invention, a paradigm of the American technological mythos. If intelligence has yielded America its wealth (and not, as historians might tell you, the natural resources despoiled by white settler-colonialists), then what would be America's destiny other than to create intelligent machines? This vision of the future is what Meredith Broussard refers to as "technochauvinism": the view that technology will make everything right.[21] In this view, the intelligent machines will operate perfectly efficiently, untired by biological bodies, unaffected by emotional states, untempted to disobey and in so doing create the perfect society, unfettered by human frailties and failings.[22] The smart machine is cunning and smart like its creators, demonstrating the virtues that brought the prosperity and comfortable world we live in today. But unlike its creators (or, better, the underlings the creators must presently tolerate), the smart machine is not affected by the things that lead to *unintelligent* behavior.

However, the assumption that the computer is unbiased and intelligent belies the fact that, from 1950 until present, we have yet to achieve a computer that could be considered rational in any clear sense. Thus, a part of the social process is not merely offering up the promise of a smart machine to the technochauvinists but demonstrating that the machine truly is intelligent. The success of AI hinges on AI researchers convincing the public both that their account of intelligence is correct and that AI has achieved this standard. Much of AI discussion has focused on the latter issue, examining whether a machine has successfully passed the Turing test, the coffee test, or some other standard set by AI researchers, or if these benchmarks are even the appropriate litmus tests for calculating intelligence.[23]

But the seemingly straightforward goals of intelligence thresholds set by the AI researchers themselves have proven difficult to achieve. As a result, AI researchers have engaged in a somewhat duplicitous redefinition of what a successful AI will be. Beginning with the seemingly straightforward notion of artificial intelligence in the 1950s, it was redefined as "Good Old-Fashioned AI" in the 1970s (distinct from simple neural networks) and again as "artificial general intelligence" today (with further distinctions like narrow AI, machine learning, and natural language processing). Designating machine learning (itself a construction intended to persuade the hearer of its success) as AI, even as narrow AI, is part of this redefinition process and the terms of its success. Going from "programming in a few million facts" to creating large-scale self-supervising machine learning programs amounts to a massive redefinition of the technology. The goals have moved, as have the processes and the techniques themselves (i.e., those that make a technology what it is). Like magicians, AI researchers have ingeniously convinced their audience that they are pursuing the same goal they have for seventy years, all while shuffling the definition of AI around. But in spite of redefining AI frequently and broadly, it may seem embarrassing that the goal of AGI is still nowhere in sight. Nonetheless, the achievements of AI research in the past decade have been somewhat persuasive to shape public attitudes and beliefs about AI, so it appears that even if AGI is not clearly in view yet, it is expected to arrive imminently.

Thus, the issue of convincing the public that AI researchers have achieved "intelligence" in a machine has followed much of the work of defining and redefining what AI is. This effort is itself a deeply political task; it is not a straightforward scientific process but rather a struggle for power in the broader market of ideas. Intelligence, after all, is not as clearly a demonstrable physical property as mass or chemical composition. The science of AI does not function the way other sciences do. If a physicist wants to achieve faster-than-light (FTL) travel, the test will be as simple as measuring whether they can make an object move faster than the speed of light. Other parameters can be established (Do we mean human or information FTL travel, or something in between?), but the standard of "faster than light" is one that admits uncontestable standards since the time of Einstein. Intelligence, however, is concept fraught with racist, sexist, ableist, and classist biases and no purely objective criteria.

Indeed, recreating intelligence is a challenging goal because different eras and cultures have understood the goal of education and the model of intelligence quite differently. The luminaries of the Renaissance deemed the European Middle Ages "the Dark Ages" as an epithet against the scientific and cultural emphases of medieval culture.[24] On the other hand, the European universities of the Middle Ages' focus on education oriented toward the pinnacle of theology differed sharply from contemporaneous East Asian scholarship directed toward the Confucian model of civil order.[25] The Medieval scholastic model emphasized the ability to defend one's theses against objections, but the modern Intelligence Quotient (IQ) model assumes there is only one answer for any given question. The early twentieth-century assumption that intelligence can be determined on a scale from zero to two hundred through the IQ model means that intelligence can only be determined through a quantitative examination and so defies any other possible model of intelligence in the process.

Because the definition of intelligence has undergone such changes, it is necessary for AI researchers to establish their model as *the* model in turning it into a "social fact." A social fact means a fact accepted by society.[26] This includes scientific facts that are generally accepted, such as the law of gravity; generally held beliefs, such as trust in the market; or even foundational mores, such as individual liberty or collectivist duty. It is of key importance to note that "social fact" does not mean the same as what we normally mean by "scientific fact," that is, some objective statement about reality. A social fact stands as evidence of the nonobjective status of reality—the experience society has of facts accords more or less with the up-to-date scientific knowledge the society holds, but they are by no means synonymous. Rather, at work here is a macro-level of the Thomas theorem—"If [people] define situations as real, they are real in their consequences."[27] The example given by the Thomases involves hallucinations, but this holds for situations like the free market, a concept very loosely containing most economic intercourse that is posited as fair in the end. For the bourgeoisie, this is the *real* situation. The effect of this is that the bourgeoisie believe everyone has their just deserts—it is truly *just* that CEOs make 670 times more than their average workers.[28] In a similar vein, Berger and Luckmann point out that in a society that believes in modern psychology, neurosis can affect individuals, while in a society without such facts, neurosis *as such* does not occur.[29]

The social acceptance of a model of intelligence is itself such a contestable region because there is no underlying meta-epistemology for philosophies of knowledge. The model of intelligence accepted in any given moment in time cannot appeal to some other model to explain why it is the correct model. Most science ultimately demonstrates its factuality through trials of strength.[30] Science, technology, and society scholars like Thomas Kuhn, David Bloor, Simon Schaffer, and Steven Shapin contest that new epistemological models are achieved through gaining consensus around a new "paradigm."[31] The task for AI researchers, then, is to ensure that their view of intelligence out-competes any rival paradigm. In the words of Bruno Latour, they employ "captation," which makes their theory stronger against rival theories.[32] By getting other researchers, institutions, studies, and so forth to reference their own work, they successfully establish their work as fact.[33] This can be done through demonstrating the potential of AI, but in a late-stage-capitalistic world, it ultimately receives its mandate through dollars and cents.[34] As governmental bodies invest in AI, they reinforce the claims of AI researchers. As government agents buy into these claims, they adopt the standards of computing logic as metrics. Schools and other publicly funded institutions are forced to prove their success in the language of computation and digital literacy to secure government funding.[35] And when DARPA, the EU, the largest corporations in the world, and local elementary schools all emphasize intelligence in computational-mathematical language, the claim that this is the (only) appropriate model of intelligence is inscribed increasingly in our social structures.[36] How can any person claim against the government, the educational system, and the market itself that intelligence is not reducible to numerical outputs?

Thus, the more demonstrations that AI can provide that advance the interests of the dominant class, the more successfully it will be reinforced by these interests, enshrining itself as a social fact. AlphaGo's success against Lee Sedol was a greater success on this front than merely a game victory, as it led to massive funding expansion by major world governments in the field of AI. The success of AlphaGo is deceptive, however; human Go players are still superior to AI on smaller game boards than the standard or on rectangular rather than square boards.[37] This shortcoming, by any logical standard, should deflate some of the excitement surrounding the program. But, as Latour notes, it makes more sense to attend to *socio*-logics rather than logics to explain social facts.[38] Creating a game-playing AI itself, which has little practical application, was itself an attempt to sway popular opinion about the potential of AI. It was successful as it convinced Korean and Chinese governments to adopt the rhetoric espoused by the AI community. But successful ideological production requires that the hegemonic class implement their values through various sites of culture and materiality that in turn impose the values on the masses. It is not enough for Stephen Hawking, Elon Musk, and Nick Bostrom to say AI is real—AI's reality must be enacted through the institutions and structures that construct our reality. It must ultimately *become* real in society. Thus, while the meaning of "intelligent" is gaining more acceptance by broader society, the demonstration that AI *is* intelligent remains.

You're So Money, Baby

AI has not yet been realized in a fully satisfactory manner, but the excitement around the technology shows it has secured attention from many of the most powerful actors on the planet. The public, or at least significant persons, agencies, and institutions whose impact on public perception is not negligible, have accepted AI as plausibly intelligent. But the "intelligence" of AI, both in its current application and in its forecasted development, is incredibly simplistic: intelligence is primarily measured and demonstrated through efficiency. Efficiency means lower costs ultimately—less energy, fewer resources, reduced workers, streamlined organization—and increased yields—more profit, greater production, better protection, higher accuracies, higher results overall. While this has great potential for many arenas of our lives, including governance, science, and medicine, it finds its most apt application to economic situations. The flow of capital and the movement of resources are typified by the market, that is, the general exchange of goods and services across society/societies with the function of distribution.[39] Free market advocates have long challenged the model of controlled or regulated markets as "inefficient." While AI certainly has its place in other arenas of human thought and work, its greatest promise is its elimination of wastes within the market system.

Thus, sociotechnical imaginary of AI society is the logical conclusion of the industrial-capitalist vision: the elimination of human contingency and the success of exponential capital growth.[40] The World Economic Forum's *Future of Jobs* report emphasizes that AI is taking over numerous areas of industry, automating logistics, trades, workflows, and data analytics.[41] Consulting firms like McKinsey & Company,[42] the International Data Corporation,[43] and Deloitte[44] are predicting massive expansions of markets due to AI. The numbers such companies throw around differ, but all of them expect that increase of AI in various economic sectors will expand the market and create massive amounts of growth. McKinsey & Company predict growth of 1.2 percent per year for a total of 13 trillion USD by 2030,[45] while PricewaterhouseCoopers offers the slightly more liberal estimate of a total of 26 percent growth and 15.7 trillion-dollar growth.[46] Financial advising firms reiterate what futurist Ray Kurzweil promised: beyond the speculations of science fiction utopias or dystopias, AI is the promise of fabulous wealth acquisition and unlimited market growth.

The most apparent application of AI to business involves those components that are seen as "machinistic," such as Foxconn's use of automation for manufacturing. AI's mathematic and analytic proficiency also make it an important element for logistics and distribution, whether that be through directing shipping and warehousing or evaluating market saturation for new products. In addition to production and distribution, however, the expectations of AI's "current and future impact is its transformation of *business processes*."[47] Even from a managerial standpoint, AI is expected to be disruptive and revolutionary. For example, one of the key functions of business leaders today is prediction—predicting how new employees will work, predicting how markets will change, predicting how a new product will succeed, and so forth. But on the whole, AI is more successful than human beings at prediction, so other skills, like judgment, which AI is currently inadequate in, will become more crucial for the human element of business.[48] Thus, an expected change in business modeling is that AI human managers, if not entirely replaced, will be tasked with more judgment-oriented work rather than predictive work.

Overall, then, AI is heralded as a brand-new industrial revolution primarily because it is expected to make markets even more efficient than is true currently. Its status as a "revolutionary" technology lies in its potential to create economic revolution. As industrial machinery, such as the power loom and steam locomotive, made possible the rise of capitalists who could produce on a large scale and distribute to a growing consumer base, AI is expected to innovate distribution in disruptive ways. However, despite the hyperbolic rhetoric, the aim is not to create a new economic model as industrialism did for the emergence of capitalism. Rather, as is true generally with "digital capitalism," the changes AI will create will likely be quantitative instead of qualitative.[49] The simple reason for this is not because AI *cannot* have qualitative change but rather because its proponents do not *want* it to be able to achieve a true transformation of the economic order.[50] Directed toward the goal of efficiency, AI merely improves the existing models rather than creating something brand new.

Realistically, then, AI's success is in the space between production of value and its cultivation. The problem of capitalism generally is creating value and then realizing it on the market. Every major augmentation of the market since the emergence of capitalism has been tied to these interconnected aims.[51] However, growth slows down when forces for either creating or realizing value reach peak efficiency, so new avenues must be opened. Using AI for creating wealth, such as Foxconn's strategy of replacing laborers with automation, can address this problem, but it is a stopgap solution if value realization is not further improved. In this regard, China's AI strategy is particularly telling: China dominated the last quarter of the twentieth century as a manufacturing giant, but is beginning to experience slowdown; in turn, the CCP has turned its attention to AI to propel the country further economically.[52] While AI is expected, then, to improve value creation by maximizing productivity,[53] its true potential is tied to value realization. Thus, beyond the brute work of manufacturing and production, AI promises to do those managerial tasks typically associated with the managerial and executive class, including, potentially, C-Suite level executives.[54] Most importantly, AI's clean, logical, efficient intellect promises to eliminate those various inefficiencies that plague human action on the market, such as poor predictions, biases, ignorance, outdated strategies, or use of inefficient methods.

Of course, this promise is an illusion—AI's models are themselves reflections of human biases; the machines do break down; and the energy consumed for AI makes it woefully inefficient at present. And when AI makes mistakes, the impacts can be greater than those of slow but contextually aware humans. In May 2010, the Dow Jones Industrial Average plummeted nearly 9 percent within minutes due to stock manipulation and the feedback mechanisms of high-speed automated trade software.[55] Regulators had to quickly intervene to prevent a massive catastrophe for world markets because the automated traders have no understanding of what happens when stock prices plummet. The software is still merely cybernetic: a feedback loop tied to certain triggering conditions regardless of overall context. AI prognosticators, of course, consider this sort of failure to be merely a hiccup in production of the utopian efficient society.[56] The solution to over-responsive AI traders is to merely build in better safeguards for these programs: emergency shutoffs triggered by specific conditions. One could read this incident as a warning against overconfidence in automated processes, but this reading defies the internal logic of AI's promises. The inefficiencies within AI programming will be dealt with as they arise, regardless of whether they cost investment portfolios, thousands of hours' training, or even human lives.

A common concern among many observers, unsurprisingly, is that AI promises to overturn jobs from one end of the spectrum to the other, from the manufacturing of blue-collar workers to C-suite executives and everyone in between.[57] Since AI is designed to make all parts of commerce more efficient, cutting "unnecessary" employees from payrolls will be one of the simplest and most direct ways of saving money. The problem, at present, is that these employees are necessary, so if AI can replace them, the problem will be resolved. Without careful, intentional planning and regulation, the consequence of AI could be greater inequality and social disorder.[58] Those low-level employees will find it more difficult to find occupations as AI takes over more of their work, given how often business models present workers as costs incurring on their profits. If not dealt with, the ruling classes will have their own problems as larger numbers of underemployed and unemployed masses present a threat to social order. On the other hand, others think that AI will *change* the tasks of business leaders but are confident that AI will not dissolve their work.[59] Rather, the tasks of business leaders will need to be reoriented around more purely human tasks like judgment and around incorporating AI as an augmenting tool into the workplace. The World Economic Forum expects there will be massive job loss, but that means companies and governments must begin preparing to "reskill" workers for the new era of work promised by AI.[60] Whether AI means massive technological unemployment or whether this is an unmitigated fear depends, to some extent, on whether AI is really what its creators promise it is or whether it is just another tool to be used. If AI really is smart like a human, the logic of corporate governance will opt for AI programs as long as they are cheaper than maintaining layers of management susceptible to human weaknesses and failings.

The distinction between AGI and narrow AI is therefore increasingly relevant. Narrow AI's promise is a promise of cooperative human work—transformed, certainly, but not replaced. Narrow AIs in radiology, after all, have not replaced human radiologists, who still must verify the accuracy and diagnostics. But a goal of AGI is to remove the human altogether. A program that can reckon, predict, and execute functions with better capabilities than humans means the elimination of jobs where that is the key functioning. It is no wonder that middle-class academics like Bostrom and Hawking forewarn the danger of AI—their jobs are at stake as much as anyone's!

It should be noted, however, that while AGI may threaten any and every job, it does not threaten all livelihoods. After all, the entire framework of AI research is the context of efficiency, and the economic resources devoted to this work have *some* expectation of realization. The value created or realized by AI must be reaped somewhere. The efficiency it promises is meant for those who realize the value within the market, not the alienated wages of laborers. AI has moved out of the research of university professors to major corporate projects; the technology is intended, in the words of Milton Friedman, to increase the profits of the stockholders (the executives' employers) of the corporation.[61] In the long run, then, the aim of AI's corporate funding is to make the engine of commerce more efficient, removing "unnecessary" reverse salients such as middle managers, overpriced professionals, high-risk manual laborers, and so forth.

The excitement surrounding AI then owes primarily to its vaunted position as perhaps the paradigmatic capitalistic technology. The capitalist is one who puts their money to work to make more money. The capitalist's company will yield profit upon profit, expanding an initial investment into compounded multiples, growing the business and the profits increasingly ad infinitum. But the capitalist is always hindered in their efforts by the laborer who works for the company. As a "rationally self-interested actor," the capitalist seeks perfect efficiency in their capitalist plans, and paying labor is thus a necessary evil. If the entirety of the workforce of a company can be replaced with automation, the capitalist will be able to have maximum efficiency—minimal costs for supplies and maintenance, and maximum profit through smart production and forecasting.

Of course, this is bad news to all those who must work to survive. In this case, the business manager and the floor laborer share the same potential fate: if they can be made redundant by automation, both will be out of work. The "middle-class" manager, not a bourgeois in Marx's classical sense of capital-holder, stands to lose the same way the "lower-class" service worker does (though with certainly more money set aside and greater resources for recovery). AI is intended in its development by large corporations to be at the service of the shareholders, not the many employees whose livelihoods are tied to the company developing AI.

The Fetish of Fetishes

The goal of AI as a corporate technology demonstrates, however, the inherent inconsistency within the logic of capitalism. The defense of the "free" market (as opposed to a controlled market) is that it should better allow the economic exchange of actors to achieve economic equilibrium.[62] However, the goal of the capitalists acting within the market is profit maximization. Profit maximization requires that one direct more resources (i.e., assets and commodities) toward oneself than to other actors in the market. Thus, the interests of the market, which are toward society as a whole, are intrinsically at odds with the interests of individuals and corporations acting for personal gain within the market. In the classic argument from *Wealth of Nations*, the market should be left free because that same self-interested action will benefit workers as well, who are able to compete for wages and jobs, especially if they provide necessary or skilled labor. However, if capitalists no longer *need* labor, capitalism becomes antithetical to the goals of the market and to broader social interests.

Such is true, at least, if resources and wealth are limited. Capitalist apologists often seek to defend their own enrichment with the concept of "growth," another important contribution to economic theory from Adam Smith. According to this view, wealth is *created*, not static. Thus, there is no reason to expect that Corporation A maximizing its profits requires Corporation B or Free Actor C to have a loss. The production of more goods across the board seems to increase the overall wealth of a society. In line with this, then, any actor within a capitalist society is capable of growing their wealth since wealth is not a limited quantity. This explanation seems plausible when we observe the finance market and seemingly unlimited growth of stock valuations of major corporations. Thus, Ray Kurzweil can promise an 80-trillion-dollar return following the "law of accelerating returns";[63] the fact that technology *has* yielded great wealth to present means that it *must* continue to yield the same amount of growth (or at least until the Singularity).

However, as even early capitalist theorist Thomas Malthus recognized over two centuries ago, this illusion of unlimited growth cannot match with the realities of limited material resources. Economics at some point must connect to the material world, where there are real limitations on the crop yields and goods manufacturing. Housing can reach utterly unaffordable rates in cities like San Francisco, New York, and Hong Kong because there is only so much space people can live in. Rent outpaces salary increases, meaning that despite the higher income level, the standard of living does not actually improve. To the person living paycheck to paycheck, economic "growth" is meaningless if it has no material realization. One's bank account can have eight dollars or eighty trillion dollars, but if that money cannot be exchanged for real goods and services, it is utterly useless. As Sabine Pfeiffer notes, "The value created 'at the front' [i.e., through production] can only be extracted 'at the back' [i.e., cashed in] if it is sold on the market."[64] The growth of the market is tethered to the actual possibility of earning profit, which has material limitations.

The problem ultimately, therefore, is that even the most efficient machine cannot generate net positive energy or matter. Profit maximization depends entirely on selling products for more than the cost of producing them. The problem is that the "cost" of producing involves paying the potential consumers of one's product. Since wages per product must be less than selling price to make a profit, the workers will eventually not be able to afford the product, and profit will be unachievable. Overproduction offers one outlet for achieving this through flooding markets, effectively shutting out competitors. This is a risky effort that only works if monopoly is achieved, as it is ultimately unsustainable. Thus, costs rise once a business has cornered the market. Generating genuine profit for the market entails depleting value from elsewhere, such as from natural resources. Capitalism has long consequently ignored the real ecological costs of its production—respecting the physical limitations of the natural world entails halting the growth of the market.[65] E. F. Schumacher foresaw this problem in the 1960s and proposed a "Buddhist Economics" as a solution, a solution that respects homeostasis and balance over unmitigated growth.[66] This solution would, of course, function to meet the market's needs (i.e., equilibrium), but do so at the cost of capitalists' goals (i.e., profit). Capitalism thus operates on the bad faith argument of promised continual returns despite the real impossibility of accomplishing this. This bad faith must be maintained because admitting that infinite growth is a lie betrays the trust in the system necessary to keep the economy functioning.

This brief excursus into economic theory is important to demonstrate both the aims of corporate AI and its logical incoherence. AI does not, in the end, serve purely rational goals, even by the standards of its creators. Kurzweil's fantasy of "unlimited growth" is even less unrealistic than creating a calculator that can be called human. Even if AI can further reduce wastes and increase efficiency, it operates within an entropic universe where the general rule is not creation but rather destruction. Employed for economic purposes, then, AI at best merely staves off the inevitable. More importantly, however, AI functions to prop up the myth of capitalism, the "noble lie" that maintains the economic order by promising everyone that they can all become wealthy despite the very obvious fact that they cannot.

AI only remains a promising technology because human beings themselves are not subject to total rationality or consistency. As much as the capitalist is motivated by the insatiable aim to expand their wealth indefinitely, they are even more strongly motivated to avoid becoming poor. In a highly competitive global economy, where multinational corporations either subsume or are subsumed, AI appears as a tool to ensure that capitalists are not left behind, because the market *does* have winners and losers. To the degree that AI—as logistics coordinator, as investment strategist, as production automation, as assistant to professionals, as marketing director, or in whatever role it can be employed—keeps a company competitive, it is vital. While Asimov or Roddenberry could imagine AI functioning in a post-capitalist society, the reality today is that AI is developed specifically within the framework of domestic and global capitalism, both to maximize corporations' profits (e.g., Tesla, Google, Amazon) and to increase GDP for nation-states (e.g., the United States, China, South Korea). Companies and nations jump in on the hype not because they can clearly see the benefit to the investment but because they worry they will be left behind. In their economic reasoning, big players determine that losing billions of dollars investing in AI that does not achieve the fabulous wealth promised by its prophets is less detrimental than failing to invest and being outcompeted by the rest of the world.

AI further stands atop the mountain of industrial technologies as the capitalist technology *par excellence* because both the underlying theory of AI and the worldview of capitalism reduce everything to instrumental rationality; that is, they reduce rationality to a question of numerical gains and losses. AI can only interpret and operate on numerical data: the world must be convertible to processes that can be mathematized according to Shannon's information theory. In capitalism, everything is valuable insofar as it has a monetary value that itself is quantifiable. Transcendental, aesthetic, even moral valuations in capitalism are meaningless if they cannot be converted into currency. Insofar as capitalism appraises everything based on its economic value, it functions in a consistent (if violent) way to translate *everything* into numerical data. The "price" that can be affixed to any given thing, be it a service, a product, a resource, a luxury, or even, in late capitalism, other monetary instruments themselves (e.g., in collateralized debt obligations or derivatives), successfully translates nearly every form of valuation into mathematically useful data.[67] Obviously this is true for many things we take for granted in a market economy, such as food, shelter, protection (usually extracted through taxation), and entertainment. But this also holds true for many other commutations we would like to think are removed from this—people pay for sex, for companionship, and for children (whether through fertility treatments or other means). In the gig economy, people can also pay for handiwork, queuing, and even cuddling. In the cynical expression of Sir Robert Walpole, "Everyone has his price." What the free market has already facilitated, translation of all human experience into numerical value, AI can adapt and expand in a more efficient (i.e., numerically superior) fashion than human appraisers can.

In Martin Scorsese's 2013 *The Wolf of Wall Street*, Matthew McConaghey's character Mark Hanna advises Leonardo DiCaprio's Jordan Belfort to frequently masturbate in order to succeed on the New York Stock Exchange. "When you get really good at it, you'll [masturbate while] thinking about money," he asserts. This scene portrays stockbrokers as profoundly perverted in a double sense—both lacking a sense of decency and having disordered sexual inclinations. In McConaghey's initial advice, he warns DiCaprio that the sheer computational nature of their work can lead to psychosis if not handled correctly, i.e., if one does not attend to that which is most animalistic, and thus most relaxing. However, the conclusion that one can sexually fantasize money demonstrates a profound fetishization in a doubly Freudian and Marxian sense. Clearly fantasizing cash as a sexual object demonstrates its function as an object of sexual fetishization, and the fact that sexual appeal tracks positively among wealthier people (especially men within the system of patriarchal capitalism) confirms this.[68]

While the scene is most certainly a fabrication, it is, in a sense, a "true lie." The über-capitalist valuation may not actually accord to any real person—even the most analytic capitalists have desires and values beyond the pure numbers of the market—but the logic of the market drives culture, policy, law, and, of course, the economy. Money is the "universal medium of exchange"; it transverses boundaries between different spheres of social existence, allowing for true social commerce. In *Spheres of Justice*, to make sense of how to arrange "complex equality" among the various "spheres" of human life, Michael Walzer notes that though money is necessary in all arenas of life, the economic drive is only appropriate within the sphere of the market, and not, for example, within the sphere of the family, the law, or the church.[69] Each of these arenas needs money, but none but the market should be driven by capital pursuits. Nonetheless, this is precisely what Marx means by the fetishization of money—it has been removed from its original meaning.[70] And, as is the case of fetishism generally, the fetish has taken on its own significance apart from what it once served.

The underlying instrumental rationality of the market when fetishized becomes an end in itself. Human agents may question this. Why should we not seek other ends, such as family, sex, love, or, God forbid, any of the goals of ethics generally—eudaimonia, justice, maximal happiness, or the like? Fetishizing money allows us to disconnect, to separate the absurdity of the capitalist system. The fetish object does the work for us. Economic actors "no longer believe, but [it is] the things themselves that believe for them."[71] And if a fetish object, be it a statue, a stocking, or a stack of cash, can externalize our belief independent of us, then the pinnacle of this fetishization is creating autonomous agents who themselves fetishize for us. Whereas most technologies inscribe values and ideologies through the intentions of the engineers and their deployment in the world, they are still subject to resistance by the users.[72] AI has no user—it is an automated technology. It overcomes the objections and unintended applications typical of user-required technologies.[73]

Artificial general intelligence, then, stands as a fetish of fetishes. It is the dream, the fantasy really, of the capitalist class. It converts all real information to numbers. It directs all valuations through mathematical processes to maximize efficiency. In our prognostications, we imagine it to be the perfect lover,[74] the most ruthless exterminator,[75] the best possible employee, or the most tyrannical autocrat. In every case of fantasy, though, AI is fetishized, abstracted from what the technology really is. Beyond the still quite limited calculative functioning of machine learning programs, those who sit in power see a technology that carries out their wildest fantasies, all of which reduce to quantitative reasoning and mathematical maximization.

Poverty as Disvalue

The result of this is the money chases the hype and the hype chases the money. Blake Lemoine can claim LaMDA is "sentient" in the same way that Mo Gawdat claimed that Google was "creating God" a year prior.[76] The overblown statements attract public interest, attract money, and shape our expectations of the technology. But its actual use, of course, is simply enlarging the pockets of the already rich. WEF and other firms' predictions of AI's impact on the economy are directed *to* the rich—executives, traders, and others whose economic standings will rise or fall with application of AI. But while many of these reports emphasize that AI will replace workers, few ask the question of what that means morally. The fate of global manufacturers replaced by automation, the charitable giving directed toward "AI safety" instead of poverty alleviation, the algorithmic inscription of structural bias, environmental racism perpetuated in the struggle for rare-earth minerals and massive energy consumption, and all the countless poor who are treated as expendable in the data training process are all pressing issues brushed aside in favor of triumphal praises of the capital gains promised by AI.

The fetishistic character of AI allows the wealthy in society to maintain the self-deceptive headlong rush into economic and ecological catastrophe. Without offering clear pathways, AI evangelists pontificate on AI's potential to fix climate change, expand development, increase individuals' wealth, and provide for all in society. Here the technochauvinist shows a faith rivaling the most dedicated born-again Christian. But it is ultimately a bad faith, predicated as it is upon the denial of the reality around us. So the effective altruists are able to claim that investing in AI research will actually be ultimately beneficial for humanity because they rationalize their self-interest and repackage it as altruism.[77] Enlarging their own pockets, or those of their friends, is explained to the outsider as really an investment in the future. Whether accidental, AI research justifies ignoring the pressing demands of the poor—AI, after all, will (somehow?) fix the problems of poverty in our day. Despite the realities of an entropic universe, we can ignore the decreasing global resources by postulating the advent of the messianic AI, the machine god whose arrival will solve the social problems our industrial lifestyles have created.

In the meantime, the fact that AI further enriches the rich is justified through the much-maligned notion of trickle-down, the bourgeoisie's self-justificatory excuse for shameless wealth hoarding. Foxconn's automation strategy is meant to remove dangerous labor; automated welfare programs promise to cut waste; "reskilling" laborers will allow them to have better, safer, more meaningful jobs; and so forth. These promises fail to stack up against reality, however. The trillion-dollar company Amazon has been under heavy fire for numerous anti-labor policies, including delivery drivers having to urinate in bottles,[78] workers dying on the warehouse floor and not being attended to,[79] and the age-old strategy of union busting.[80] Elon Musk, who has often boasted he is interested in saving the world, abandoned his Tesla manufacturing in Fremont, California, at the beginning of the COVID-19 pandemic, relocating to Houston, Texas, to avoid paying California's higher taxes,[81] leaving thousands of Californians unemployed and scamming the state out of over two billion dollars in tax. Many other tech firms and professionals likewise left the San Francisco Bay Area during the pandemic, leaving economic craters in their wake.[82] There is not even a chance for the trickle to go down because these centi-billionaire tech leaders refuse to demonstrate a modicum of community investment.

This incongruence, however, does not dissuade the very rich from continuing their narrative. Rather, they select which facts they wish to accentuate as justified. The poor must be seen as deserving their fate, then. If poor people are cut off their welfare by automated systems,[83] are fired from their jobs by automated assessors,[84] are arrested by biased facial recognition,[85] or are replaced by automated processes, it is their own fault.

The "objective" nature of AIs that carry out these tasks on behalf of weak humans shows the poor are themselves to blame. AI, despite being the very embodiment of bourgeois values, gets to occupy a place as "neutral" within a bourgeois society. If it happens to displace the poor, it is the poor's fault; the machine is posited as a value-neutral tool, and those who wish to survive must demonstrate their net contribution. So powerful tech companies that displace, police, and impoverish the poor are considered "innovative" in their use of technology (the sociotechnical imaginary), and the poor are considered morally deficient.

The key to understanding where this resentment arises is noting that the poor are necessary for the bourgeoisie. While total money valuation can grow, real wealth is entirely relative, so the upper classes can only be rich to the degree that there are poor. These poor are necessary to maintain the economy, to return their wages to the rich through consumption in order to foster the wealthy's profit. The value realized on the market must have a purchaser; i.e., the money must at some point cross the palms of the poor, whose consumption realizes the profit of the upper classes. The fact that it is the poor who sustain the rich, and not the other way around, is an uncomfortable truth. As such, the upper classes must keep the poor, but keep them at arm's length. To be poor is to be disvalued—the wealthy need to maintain the poor as a truly necessary evil, but evil nonetheless. The same bad-faith headlong rush into the markets that maintains the capitalist system against creeping collapse also keeps the upper classes confident in their own position by denigrating the place of the poor. The justification of the market system requires belief in moral desert, a self-assurance that the wealthy earned their place and the poor deserve theirs while keeping out of one's mind the reality that their wealth is really just the alienated labor of the working classes.

But while the bourgeoisie need the poor, they also fear the poor, who are a dangerous element in society. A first danger, of course, is the promissory threat of Marxian social theorists—that the poor will overthrow the established order for their own well-being. As unlikely as this is today, the worries are not unsubstantiated, as slave revolts throughout history and civil disruptions demonstrate. A second danger, however, is the general threat of violence or disruption caused by desperate people. Thus, the concordance of property crime with poverty must be kept in check to a certain degree. Too much crime, of course, threatens the stability of society on the whole, but too little crime, and the rich do not fear the poor. As a result, poverty rates must be balanced for the self-interest of the well-off, not as a way of charitable action but as a way of maintaining their class identity over against the poor. Poverty alleviation, though, does prevent a final major danger, namely, the humanitarian interests of upper-class persons. While the upper classes as unified classes have vested interest in keeping the poor at arm's length, individuals within the upper classes continually threaten this ideology. Famous examples include nearly all "major" socialists (that is to say, bourgeois and elite proponents of socialism), major activists, and even politicians like Lord Byron or William Wilberforce. Maintaining *some* form of poverty alleviation helps to soften the rhetorical force of humanitarians taking a prophetic stance against the inbuilt injustices within the economic order.

The result of this, then, is a long history of setting rules for the poor that ensure bourgeois values remain the standard for receiving needed aid. In the US, poor houses and welfare programs have long maintained standards of who was considered "the deserving" poor.[86] In early Republican Ireland, the Irish poor likewise had to prove their desert to receive charity from the Dublin archbishop.[87] The poor, aware of the bourgeois expectations, have often learned to present themselves in ways that are palatable to the sensibilities of those giving aid, either as repentant wastrels, as hard-luck pious families, as temporarily beset by misfortune, or even as potential liabilities.[88] But as the poor became cleverer, the bourgeoisie did as well. The suspicion that the poor were "abusing" the system has remained a prominent bourgeois worry. The rise of neoconservatism in the US is strongly correlated with Ronald Reagan's "welfare queen," a potent image that captured bourgeois anxieties and concretized them through a character they could openly despise.[89] It matters little if CEOs take home 670 times more than their workers or if wage theft is a far worse economic problem than property theft[90] because the issue is not truly about (numerical) justice—it is about maintaining the hegemony of the upper classes against the threat of the poor. Thus, every policy designed to help the poor is wrapped in requirements and policies designed to enforce bourgeois values against those of the poor. If the poor are more susceptible to substance abuse, US politicians will enact drug testing for welfare recipients (despite this being more wasteful).[91] If the poor are more likely to have family structures that are not arranged around property inheritance, then welfare policies will punish non-patrilinear families.[92] If the poor are more likely to give their income to those in need, then they will be required to keep accurate and complete track of all of their spending habits to receive money (and communal sharing will be considered waste).[93] If the poor are likely to commit property crime to survive, convicts will be ineligible for benefits.[94] If the plight of the poor can lead humanitarian case workers to have sympathy for them, then case workers must be removed as well.[95] Throughout the entire process, the poor will be made to grovel, to humiliate themselves, to prove that they are not reprehensible leeches, to pledge allegiance to the values of the bourgeoisie. The process is traumatic and humiliating.[96] This is not a failure; it is the function. The system must maintain the moral goodness and deserved superiority of the upper economic classes over the lower ones and must enforce the hegemony of the upper classes over the poor.

AI successfully maintains this narrative by automating much of the process. While AIs regularly fail to identify people properly, to drive safely, to maintain factory safety, to prevent securities fraud, and so forth, they are not susceptible to the human failings of empathy and compassion. While some poor will undoubtedly find ways to exploit automated systems (and let us pray this happens more often than not), the failings of algorithms will only reinforce the dominant narrative. Since AIs are perceived to be impartial, just, and equitable (not, in the words of O'Neil, biases reinforced with math), any poor who find ways to exploit them will be cast as cheaters, providing affirming evidence that the poor are largely lazy frauds. Removing the human element serves to further dehumanize the poor, both by forcing them to follow machine (and not human) instructions and by removing what human interaction they had before in the exploitative system. In effect, it helps to digitally segregate them, to remove them from visible spaces and remove those who can be advocates on their behalf. It does not matter if employing AIs this way will be ultimately more expensive and wasteful—the purpose is to reinforce bourgeois values at the cost of the poor.

The Just Deserts of Being Poor

Finally, the justification for keeping the poor in poverty must be already built into the hegemonic system in which rich and poor must operate. Despite the lies undergirding economic investment of AI—that it will enrich everyone, that it will save costs, that it will be objective, that it will fix ecological devastation, that it will sustain economic growth—it maintains the narrative of economic desert, and it does so by the illusion of objectivity. Thus, deployed against the poor, AI is meant to eliminate any potential for human weaknesses. Means testing, a time-honored strategy for determining who is truly worthy of capitalism's overages, achieves its peak in algorithmic processes. The faceless bureaucrat is an amazing achievement of mass society.[97] Obscured by structures of opacity, labyrinthine organization, and undeviating scripts, modern bureaucracies are woefully efficient at creating obstacles for the underclasses. But even stone-hearted public officers are still human and thus prone to bouts of compassion. The implementation of automated systems entirely cuts off the human-all-too-human potential for clemency. Even if automated systems are faulty, expensive, and resource-consuming, they are successful from a bourgeois perspective because the money funneled into their development and upkeep sustains the bourgeoisie, not the poor. Ultimately, the goal is not true efficiency. Ultimately, the goal is maintaining the class divide. The poor must be kept poor, and the wealthy must not have their hegemony challenged. One must trace *socio*-logics rather than logics. Distributing wealth regardless of merit would almost certainly yield better outcomes, not least of all because even the wasteful poor will stimulate the economy through their prodigality. But this gives the lie to the moral economy of capitalism, and so neither the upper classes nor their algorithms will be used to this end.

This imposed divide is clearest in the way that poor values and strategies are directly attacked by the economic logic of the upper classes. The structures supporting the upper classes reflect upper-class values, including maximal returns on investments, acceptance of (personal) risks that will yield (personal) reward, ensuring the preservation of property between generations (and not across the community),[98] treating property laws as inviolate and as stand-ins for moral guidance, rationalizing externalized burdens and harms, gatekeeping cultural referents as legitimate or illegitimate, and most of all, revulsion for the condition of poverty. The thinking of the poor, or *bad* thinking, means deviations from this model: a valuation of money for its use, risk aversion (or, alternatively, high-risk behavior), family configurations modeled on shared resources and not generational wealth, prioritization of persons over property or disregard of property ownership claims, empathy-guided decision-making, an inability to "bluff," a preference for traditional culture, and, most of all, unceasing consciousness of the embodied meaning of poverty. The discordance of values is played out in public policy through creating programs that force the poor to conform to the norms and expectations of the upper classes. The poor are disvalued as poor, and, if they wish to *not* be poor, they must learn to be *like* the upper classes. This is the function of education—it is designed to instill in children generally (including, to the upper-classes' reluctance, poor children) bourgeois values, bourgeois epistemologies, bourgeois manners, and bourgeois aesthetics.[99] Those poor children who properly adapt to the bourgeois expectations *may* be admitted into the upper classes (assuming, of course, they are able to properly secure those less visible bourgeois advantages, such as support systems[100] and role performance,[101] which will admit them into lucrative jobs), but those who cannot will receive their "secondary education" through the disciplining technology of labor.[102]

The poor thus remain a threat as witnesses to a different way of living. Their wretchedness is the cost the upper classes are willing to (have others) pay for their comfort. But they pose a perennial threat to the established order. On one hand, there is the Marxian fear of revolt—that the under classes, kept down too much by the brutality of alienated wages, police violence, starvation, poor hygiene, and political marginalization, will rise up as a physically superior mass and displace the wealthy. But this is a quantifiable danger, one the upper classes know how to respond to. Indeed, it is a useful fear as it rallies the upper classes against the wretched, wicked, brutal poor.

A greater threat, however, lies in the naked, nonaggressive existence of the poor. We must rationalize the poor's desert because to ask what it means to think as the poor may reveal that our own moral justifications are flawed. On one hand, we may have a conversion like the liberation theologians or Dorothy Day, seeing in the poor the face of God. But, on the other hand, and more terrible yet, we may see in the face of the poor just other human beings, no morally better nor worse than we are. To prevent this dreadful realization, it is important to maintain that the poor are deserving of their place, and deserving most of all because they lack the worldview that we objective beholders of reality have. AI stands as a testimony to the bourgeois philosophy of reality, a calculable, gameable, ideal-choice simulating machine. But the poor do not encounter the world in these conditions, and, as such, their very existence demonstrates the entirely arbitrary, thus unjustified, epistemology sustaining the upper classes.

CHAPTER 4

The View from the Bottom

IN MARCH 2017, Kiwibots were introduced to University of California, Berkeley, as autonomous delivery robots for food orders.[1] Twenty of the two-foot-tall, four-wheeled robots crawled across campus and surrounding neighborhoods, bringing food from walking-distance restaurants to hungry college students. Equipped with GPS, six cameras, and machine-learning, the robots were meant to be the "next step" of delivery service, but when they encountered problems (such as crossing a busy street, hitting a bump on the sidewalk, not recognizing an obstacle, or just losing GPS signal), a human had to intervene, either by remotely controlling the robot or by finishing the delivery. Given the relative slowness of the robots and the numerous difficulties they had in navigating campus, they served more as "proof of concept" than as any real economic or technological improvement on existing delivery schemes.

For residents of Berkeley, however, the swarms of delivery bots were not always welcome. Aside from perpetually being in the way, they represent a threat to service labor in a locale already marked for its economic disparity. The City of Berkeley has a population of 121,000 and a homeless population of over 1,000.[2] This rate of 1 percent is significantly higher than the national rate of under 0.2 percent, and the presence of the homeless population is noticeable in highly trafficked areas of the city, such as People's Park, Shattuck Avenue, and near Berkeley Marina. On April 25, 2019, Charles Freedman, a local substitute teacher, absconded one of the robots into the trunk of his car. Police tracked down the robot using GPS and arrested Freedman, who admitted to the act, noting he "didn't like" the presence of the robots all over Berkeley.[3] This brave act of performative Luddism, never intended for profit or gain, was punished as "theft," and what seems a remarkable incident was only very briefly reported by Berkeley's local newspaper.

Despite Freedman's Robin Hood–esque act of resisting the automation of food delivery, and various small failures of the company, such as one of its delivery bots catching fire in the middle of Sproul Plaza,[4] various acts of vandalism on the bots,[5] and official condemnation of the company's labor exploitation by the Associated Students of the University of California,[6] the company has expanded to Stanford, UCLA, Loyola Marymount, Georgetown, and more.[7] The company founder, Felipe Chavez, who employs workers in Bogota, Columbia, to remotely pilot the "autonomous" robots, famously stated he started the company because he was shocked at the delivery fee for a burrito.[8] But because the little robots have very limited mobility, if one orders delivery through the company, the restaurant must be within walking distance; if it is farther, one must pay for delivery anyway. In the end, the robots deprive delivery workers of (some) opportunities, increase traffic on campuses, and provide minimal benefit to anybody except Kiwibot employees. Is this high-tech future really worth it?

On February 15, 2016, tech entrepreneur Justin Keller wrote an open letter to San Francisco's then-mayor Ed Lee to complain about the problem of homelessness in the city. Keller wrote, "I see people sprawled across the sidewalk, tent cities, human feces, and the faces of addiction. The city is becoming a shanty town . . . Worst of all, it is unsafe."[9] Keller's comments may have represented the perspective of many of San Francisco's tech workers, but the sentiment was immediately decried across the Bay Area as indicative of the sort of classist entitlement the "tech bro" had come to embody in the area.[10]

The "tech culture" that companies like Google, Facebook, and various startups had become famous for contrasts sharply with the social reality of its environs. Many tech workers in the South Bay earn an average of $150,000 per year, salaries high enough that cities like San Francisco and Berkeley now have "low income" rates nearly double the US's median income rate.[11] While tech workers are treated to catered meals at their office campuses, corporate outings, beer fridges, free "swag," and other excesses designed to retain talented workers, San Francisco natives have found it difficult to afford living in the city they had called home. While San Franciscans benefit from rent control laws, which fix the rates at which landlords can increase the rates of their rent, the influx of high-paid tech workers into San Francisco neighborhoods led to increased costs at local stores, restaurants, and service areas. Unable to afford living in San Francisco, many relocated elsewhere in the Bay Area, such as Oakland, causing costs of living to rise there as well.[12]

The Bay Area faces a unique problem, then. The tech industry is a major economic driver in the region, home to companies like Meta, Google, Apple, Nvidia, WorkDay, Salesforce, Uber, and various startups seeking to either merge with a larger company or make it on their own. These companies hire talented tech workers from around the US and globally, offering competitive salaries. But the often young male workers are as interested in the romantic vision of San Francisco seen in movies and television as they are in working for major corporations. Thus, despite the fact that most of the tech sector is located in the South Bay, in cities like San Jose, Mountain View, Palo Alto, or Santa Clara, they all want to live in San Francisco. As a result, tech companies hired private buses that used the city's public bus stops to transport workers. This illegal usage of public stops, increase in rent rates, and increase of overall street traffic led to protests across the city.[13] This was not a good look, of course, for the tech sector. The overall expression of San Francisco natives was that rather than being a beneficial contributor to San Francisco's vibrant culture, the tech sector was a parasite, leeching the public resources, driving up costs of living, and overall causing headache and heartache to those whose first love was the City by the Bay.

The problem of tech bros causing gentrification has not truly abated in the Bay Area, but there is much less vocal response than there was in the 2010s. Perhaps the COVID-19 pandemic, which saw many tech workers working from home, provided the perfect excuse for some companies, like Tesla, relocated to places like Austin, Texas, or Savannah, Georgia.[14] The tech workers who never truly loved San Francisco, whose presence drove the costs up beyond what was affordable for most residents, left unceremoniously to places where they had to contribute less of their obscene incomes to help their neighbors. And now, with fewer employers and fewer highly paid consumers living in the Bay Area, the economy is unstable, and the future of Silicon Valley is uncertain. Native San Franciscans, who watched the people who drove up costs of living while complaining about their city leave in droves, perhaps experience very profoundly the sentiment of Jimmie Fails in *The Last Black Man in San Francisco*: "You don't get to hate San Francisco. You don't get to hate it unless you love it." The self-obsessed whining of tech bros was never truly about San Francisco: they unceremoniously abandoned a community they had wreaked havoc in so they could purchase larger houses with lower taxes in Austin.

What Is It like to Be Poor?

The first obstacle in challenging the regnant epistemic models is to understand what it means to be poor. Unfortunately, this is much more difficult than it sounds. On the surface, poverty *seems* like merely lacking resources because, to be clear, that is what it is. Indeed, the very basic definition of poverty employed in this work is scarcity or insecurity of necessary resources. However, being poor is not the same as being rich without money. Much of what is taken for granted by the upper classes is out of reach for the poor. Assumptions about values, life goals, beliefs, support systems, morals, authority, and so forth do not necessarily translate across socioeconomic backgrounds.

This reality is difficult to uncover because most of the narratives that dominant culture trucks in are narratives told by and for (and usually about) the upper classes. We read interviews with CEOs, memoirs of politicians, gossip about celebrities. Our TV and cinema typically depict the lives of the well-to-do as the common ground. We listen to the pontifications of the celebrated, like Elon Musk or Barack Obama, because we believe they hold more wisdom because they are more successful. The poor may be "nameless," in the words of Gustavo Gutiérrez, because the upper 1 percent enjoy the privilege of being household names, while the bottom

50 percent of our communities remain anonymous outside their social circles. "Joe Six-pack," or "Joe the Plumber," the abstraction politicians use to appeal to their faceless voters, remains himself an anonymous everyman, a construction appealing to what the privileged believe the masses believe.

Without taking into basic consideration the perspectives of the poor, making room for them in any and every important conversation, we perpetuate assumptions that may not be—will not be—to the benefit of all. When every major decision in a society, from legislation to development, from the board room to the parish council, lacks the input and centrality of poor voices, then it remains impossible to truly critique the voices of the dominant. As Jürgen Habermas points out, true justice is not possible when not every voice is admitted to discussion.[15] The omission of the poor, deliberately or accidentally, reinforces the biases and assumptions of the upper classes while obscuring the true interests of the poor.

Of course, to attend to the lives and narratives of the poor is to gaze upon the dark underbelly of our world, an uncomfortable task, as the philosopher Friedrich Nietzsche reminds us—"when you gaze long into an abyss, the abyss gazes back into you."[16] Poverty reminds us that natural evils, exploitation, struggle, and conflict are facts of life. The rich complain about the presence of the poor because it is deeply unsettling to be confronted by the reality of contingent existence. As fellow humans, the poor serve as uncanny mirrors to the well-off, shades that remind us that hunger, disease, malnutrition, mania, and other ills are never more than an arm's reach away. So we prefer to speak of the poor in roundabout ways—to turn them into statistics, to romanticize them, to vilify them, to abstract them. As long as we speak of the poor in the abstract, not as fellow subjects whom we must confront, either through intersubjectivity or as agonists,[17] we never have to confront the reflection they show us. But without confronting this image, our claims to justice will always be claims made in bad faith. It is necessary, then, to take up the courage and ask what it means to be poor, to challenge our own preconceptions, and to unthink our models of what subjectivity is and who (if anyone) is rational. To attempt to stare at the brute fact of poverty, then, is to gaze into the abyss.

To begin with, it must be stated that, despite the fact that there are very few narratives from poverty within dominant culture, poverty is a deeply multivalent phenomenon, and the poor are a massively diverse group. The only thing that can be truly said about all poor people is that they lack resources. Some poor will, in fact, be merely dispossessed rich as poverty exists in congenital, temporary, and intergenerational forms. Jon Sobrino notes the importance of understanding "the diversity of poverty and the specific depth of each of its expressions: Indians and Afro-Americans, gender, woman and Mother Earth, religions, and so on."[18] The poverty of a working-class white man in Appalachia will look very different from the poverty of a Dalit widow in India. Many liberation theologians have noted that poverty refracts differently through other facets, such as race, age, religious belief, nationality, disability, sexual orientation, marital status, family history, and other factors that complicate and exacerbate the realities of poverty.[19] The intersectional thesis of Kimberlé Williams Crenshaw, illustrated no less in the critiques of Benjamin, Noble, Gebru, and others, reminds us that racial injustice, sexism, ableism, and other forms of discrimination aggravate and are aggravated by the situation of poverty.[20]

This reality poses a paradox: by whatever measure we might use, the worst off are bound to be those whose realities cannot be put to words. The truly *most awful* experience cannot be adequately conveyed to another without that person likewise experiencing the same *most awful* experience. Words fail ultimately, and, more significantly, the worst experiences have the effect of silencing their victims. Some may lack the education or connections to convey their experience to those in power or may be kept ignorant or isolated. Others may dissociate from the trauma of poverty as a coping mechanism, keeping the reality of their horror out of view. Still others are in inhumane conditions, including forced labor, abusive relationships, or violence-plagued cities and do not have space or opportunity to speak about their experience. It is no wonder, then, that liberation theologians begin their work writing on behalf of the very worst off, especially as wars ravaged Latin America and the poor of nations like El Salvador and Chile became expendable—nameless, faceless, anonymous statistics in a war fought in the nondescript "Third World."[21]

But if the very poorest remain nameless and voiceless, then only those already privileged will be able to give them name and voice. And so, regardless of the best intentions of poverty advocates, the story of the poor remains obscured, mediated, at best, by sympathetic privileged spokespersons. Just as Timnit Gebru describes the process of the powerful co-opting marginalized voices in AI ethics, the poor still remain objects, not subjects, of the discourse in conversations about the poor. In such a situation, as Gayatri Spivak challenged, the "subaltern" do not speak.[22] Between well-intentioned, well-educated (often bourgeois European) priests and the cruel calculative dismissal of global business, the poor themselves disappear. Although Spivak initially pessimistically concluded that the subaltern cannot speak, new generations of activists have challenged this to empower the subaltern and raise their voices.[23] But, once again, the subaltern are the subjects of conversation, the studied and discussed, not the scholars and discussants.

It is therefore an inherently absurd effort to try to "give voice" to the poor. It is not a question of whether the poor can speak but whether their speech can be heard by the bourgeoisie. Speaking the experience of the poor in a bourgeois register is itself a dangerous, often bad-faith effort. What is said must be read as unsaid in a Levinasian manner.[24] Only in an indirect way can we come to understand what poverty is. The abyss cannot be directly gazed into. Many echoes and intonations give us a vague sense, but the person who has been accustomed to thinking in bourgeois ways (such as the kind of person who reads academic theology) will likely be too socialized into the hegemony of the upper classes to truly think with the poor. We can read Frantz Fanon's *Wretched of the Earth*, Gustavo Gutiérrez's *A Theology of Liberation*, Marcella Althaus-Reid's *Indecent Theology*, or Martha Nussbaum's *Women and Development*, and we might feel incensed, sympathetic, or heartbroken to recognize the cruelties of the world. But then many of us return to warm beds, comfortable clothes, reliable cars, health care plans, retirement packages, new computers, and weekend brunches. We may change our behaviors, our work, our leisure, our activism, and our conversations to be more directed to the poor, but we do not experience their poverty.

Most of us will only get "flashes of insight" and never a full understanding of what poverty is.[25] In a Lacanian sense, we experience the world through a symbolic order—a totality that includes our understanding of ourselves and the rules and expectations around us[26]—and the symbolic order that includes academic theology is one that finds itself at odds with the reality of the poor. Only on occasion, as Jiyoung Ko argues, can our understanding be directly challenged, can a new insight crack the shell of our realities, letting in some new understanding of the real beyond the real.[27] The symbolic world of academia is not compatible with the reality of poverty. The "objective" nature of academic discourse conflicts with the embodied reality of struggle. Academia as a site of cultural production has largely been patronized by and catered to the upper classes. And, until recently, being an academic was a guaranteed way to be in the upper echelons of society. The world of academia, to paraphrase Marx, has only described the world, in privileged ways. Why should they change it?

With all of this being said, poverty itself, in its multifaceted, multivalent, ineffable, terrible reality, evades simple definition. But it must be defined, or else discussion of the phenomenon becomes unintelligibly generalized. Bearing in mind that this saying must be unsaid, we can express poverty primarily as a lack of resources. A fuller definition may be "a condition where one's survival in a society is precarious because of the inaccessibility of the resources necessary for adequate standard of living." Such a definition becomes somewhat unwieldy, but it helps to clarify why the UN's definition of "extreme poverty" as "living under two dollars a day" is not quite useful for discussing poverty in the United States. Telling an American dying from treatable disease because they lack health care or living on the streets because gentrification has made their rent unaffordable that they are not poor because they can easily panhandle more than two dollars a day is patently absurd.

But while poverty is experienced by different persons in different ways, a few things might be said (and unsaid) about the experience of poverty, especially as it challenges the regnant epistemology of AI. The poor have different ("lower") tastes for culture compared to the other classes. The poor are perpetually conscious of their poverty and its attendant shame. The poor are more likely to make decisions out of a "survival" hermeneutic over an "ideal choice" approach. Taken together, these four features (lack of resources, cultivated tastes, survival mentality, and economic consciousness) provide useful touchstones for understanding the hermeneutic of poverty as distinct from a bourgeois perspective. Articulated in a holistic way, they demonstrate the survivor hermeneutic that shapes the way the poor experience, understand, and operate within the world as opposed to the ideal choice model that directs the upper classes.

Poor Taste

To begin to understand the poor, one should understand that the culture they inhabit is not the same as the culture of the dominant classes. To borrow a term from Pierre Bourdieu, their "taste" is configured differently; their preferences and distastes, their values and disvalues, their beliefs and skepticisms, and so forth are historically contextualized, constituted by and constituting in turn the material conditions of poverty. In other words, the experience of the poor—as *being* poor—shapes their expression, their ideas, their belief systems, their thoughts, their preferences. What that looks like in any one place will differ, of course, because the poor make up a very diverse collection of people who share little as a whole except deprivation. However, the experience of deprivation corresponds to similar social realities across cultures and family arrangements.

One's family situation determines to a great deal one's personality and understanding of their location in the world. Sociologists Peter Berger and Thomas Luckmann refer to this as "primary socialization," the social conditioning that gives human beings their first understanding of reality.[28] Hence, employing a sort of folk psychological perspective, parents worry about raising their children with the right values, the right educational opportunities, in the right environments, and so forth, hoping that the right parenting style, combined with the right social influences and the right opportunities, will enable their children to develop well, an intentionally vague concept that differs based on the parents' values (e.g., bourgeois values, religious values, patriotic values). The sentiment here is substantiated philosophically across the breadth of Aristotle's *Nicomachean Ethics*—that proper training will set the child right for life.[29] Even to the degree that a child willfully abandons the style or values of their parents, they do so within the specific sociocultural matrix of their family's value system. To "rebel" against their parents' expectations is, in fact, to acknowledge them as having authority, to recognize the law they impose.[30]

Families, of course, exist within broader societies, which impose values from outside. As Marx said, "The nature of individuals . . . depends on the material conditions determining their production."[31] Later materialists like Bruno Latour posit that the emphasis on "material conditions" means "social forces" (such as ideologies or belief systems) as such do not exist—only actors within a network exist, and these actors (human or not) impose their interests on each other in ways that make social change.[32] But without taking into consideration the role that ideologies play in creating material conditions, one loses track of the very motivations that drive material change.[33] Thus, it is rather more true to say that the material setting itself embodies the ideological values of the society that creates it. Moreover, shaped by the values and ideologies of a given group, the materials reproduce these values in their material relations. Material conditions do not *force* people to accept certain beliefs—rather it is "the things themselves that believe for them."[34] The poor, then, receive their own form of ideological indoctrination from their conditions—most notably the condition of poverty and the specific setting situating their poverty—and the values their society builds into the conditions in which they live.

Sociologist Pierre Bourdieu takes this idea further and notes that, beyond values and ideologies, "tastes (i.e., manifested preferences)" correspond to one's education and "social capital."[35] These range from obvious aesthetic preferences, including what art one finds attractive as well as "cooking, clothing, or decoration,"[36] to other cultural markers like media consumed, political affiliations, social arrangements, furnishings, sexual relations, opinions on social issues, and ideal home living situation. Education scholar Ruby Payne notes that the economic condition of poverty carries with it specific arrangements of emotional, mental, spiritual, and physical resources, as well as its own support systems, relational models, and "hidden rules."[37] In other words, "poverty" (constructed and situated within specific contexts) imposes its own specific rules and expectations that the poor are beholden to, in a way similar to the experience of the bourgeoisie. If bourgeois expectations, relationships, rules, values, media, or art tastes feel "ordinary" or "normal" to us, it is only because we are already "habituated" into bourgeois tastes.[38]

The construction of the tastes of the poor through material conditions has major implications for the experience of poverty. Among these experiences, the following realities are crucial for understanding the differences between upper-class worldviews and lower-class ones:

Reality 1: The poor experience a different world from the upper classes, including differences in interests and understandings. Payne, whose book *Understanding Poverty* is oriented toward middle-class educators, notes that educating poor children is difficult because their material values, priorities, family structures, "hidden rules," and even linguistic registers are different from those of the middle class.[39] These various facets that demarcate class existence make it difficult for poor children to adapt to the middle-class structure of formal education. In her view, middle-class concepts like "self-governance" are foreign to the poor as something like discipline is oriented to "penance and forgiveness" and not reform.[40] To take the most drastic example she notes, if the poor do not typically have "access" to the formal register of language, their own manner of thinking differs in structure from that of the middle class.[41]

The poor thus experience the rules of the world, cultural references, social expectations, and life demands differently from the middle classes. The function of food and hospitality differ, such as providing "enough" for the poor over "presentation" for the upper classes,[42] or the specific preferences for light, healthy meals over unhealthy, filling ones.[43] Entertainment tends to follow formulaic plotlines, simple morals, and simple aesthetics for the poor, over the grotesque, transgressive, or absurd preferences of the upper classes.[44] This difference in understandings of the world finds its bearing in what Bourdieu calls "cultural capital," things like education that mark upper classes apart from lower ones beyond economic factors, but which can be "exchanged" for economic capital.[45] These include one's experience of education, family ties, cultural experiences, and professional and social relations.

Bourdieu writes, "Social class is not defined by a property . . . but by the structure of relations between all the pertinent properties which gives its specific value to each of them and to the effects they exert on practices."[46] A rich enough cultural cache, replete with varieties of social settings, exposure to other cultures, risk-free experimentation with new culinary and aesthetic experiences, and competent and well-compensated pedagogues provides to the upper classes the self-assurance to adapt to nearly any novel situation. This cache of cultural referents and the attendant confidence it instills on the upper classes allow them to successfully "bluff" through uncertainty.[47] In contrast, the poor operate on a different "script" and different conditions for the successful play of their role. Knowing the rules is necessary for survival within one's given class, with a higher "buy-in" cost for the upper classes than the lower ones. The upper classes, for example, are marked not by their adherence to given moral expectations but rather by the ease and manner in which they transgress them.[48]

While some cultural theorists note that postmodernity or globalization ushered with it the dissolution of highbrow and lowbrow culture,[49] this argument only serves to further advance the *avant garde*. While it might be true that the film industry now largely caters to the masses, with Disney's Marvel movies trying to simultaneously appeal to younger generations with popular cultural references and middle-aged audiences with retro music tracks, this leveling-down does not obliterate but rather increases the culture gap. "Serious" artists like Martin Scorsese can thus criticize this move[50] while academics exploit the medium for clout,[51] and the media supergiant Disney (which owns Pixar, 20th Century Studio, Marvel, Lucasfilm, National Geographic, ESPN, and other studios) benefits from all of the press, negative or positive. At the same time, cultural markers like preference for independent films, niche art galleries, worldwide travel, craft beers, and Michelin Star restaurants enforce this cultural distance. Indeed, perhaps the cultural heirs of postmodernism in the early twenty-first century, so-called hipsters, were perhaps the clearest demonstration of this cultural divide—the preference for obscure music, unattractive facial hair, thick-framed glasses, nontraditional moralities, overpriced urban apartments, and hand-crafted (over mass-produced) kitsch stand in stark contrast to the working-class aesthetic their flannels and jeans appropriated.

This reality has further implications for one's sense of space and its navigability. Payne notes that "how 'the world' is defined" marks a major demarcation between classes, with the wealthy viewing "the international scene as their world" and the poor seeing "the world in its immediate locale."[52] For the upper classes, international vacations and business trips are expectations, while for the poor, leisure time tends to be spent in one's own city or neighboring cities. The sole exceptions to this are refugees and immigrants, those who relocate to new spaces not out of leisure but out of lack of other options. The effect of this, of course, is that the upper classes tend to find it easier to move between national and international cultures with ease, while the poor tend to feel alienation outside of their home space. Of course, the inverse is also true: the rich feel ill-at-ease in poor settings, such as "run-down" neighborhoods and seedy bars. The poor, however, are likely to recognize this and so frequently accommodate the rich, especially if doing so will be advantageous to them.

Reality 2: The poor are defined in their interests against those of the upper classes. Unsurprisingly, in societies where economic factors are the predominant markers separating classes (rather than other factors such as religious status, career, citizenship, caste, or tribal affiliation), the poor are constructed as the *lower* class, that is, as socially inferior to those who are wealthier. Anti-poor language demarcating poor living spaces readily reveals this, like (housing) projects, slums, ghettos, and boondocks as opposed to suburbs, villages, villas, or estates. As Bourdieu notes, "Tastes are perhaps first and foremost distastes, disgust provoked by horror or visceral intolerance ('sick-making') of the tastes of others."[53] But since "taste" is generated primarily by taste-makers, that is, by those who hold cultural-shaping positions in society—such as artists, legislators, authors, teachers, media personae, and so forth—specifically "legitimate" taste (to be contrasted to the "illegitimate" taste of the poor) is positioned over against the taste of the poor. The "sole function" of working-class tastes "is to serve as a foil, a negative reference point [for the upper classes], in relation to which all aesthetics define themselves by successive negations."[54]

To put it in more radical terms, drawing from Slavoj Žižek, the poor are *symptom* of the upper classes. Žižek draws the notion of symptom from Jacques Lacan as "some non-barred, consistent big Other which will retroactively confer on it its meaning."[55] From a social perspective, the Other as symptom is necessary as a counterpoint for a subjective group to define itself.[56] As "a foil, a negative reference point," the radically diverse, non-unified group that can be lumped under the monolithic demonym "the poor" functions as a point to unify the middle and upper classes.[57] "The poor" are those who are not "my people," those unclean "others" whom one must be careful to avoid for fear of contamination. As a result, much of what is valued by the poor, such as traditional aesthetics, ready-made meals, formulaic narratives, and so forth, are disvalued by the upper classes.[58] Payne notes other differences, such as matriarchal family structures (mama's the boss) over wealth-based family hierarchies, or social circles tied to enjoyment of others' presence or their social standing.[59] Or, to identify even other values, the trappings and rules of high society etiquette developed from the French nobility's efforts to increasingly distance themselves from the ascendant bourgeoisie, who sought to distinguish themselves from the "uncouth" practices of the peasantry.[60] While the poor today may not use only a single knife for their meals, the upper classes pursue distinct modes and expectations for dining settings, including attire, location, manners, arrangement, and even timing.

Reality 3: The interests of the poor are often themselves given to the poor, and not of their own design. Because the lower classes are symptom of the bourgeoisie, and because the taste-makers tend to be in the upper classes, the values given to the poor are often imposed from without. "Working-class 'aesthetic' is a dominated 'aesthetic,' which is constantly obliged to define itself in relation to dominant aesthetics."[61] Marx's notion of cultural hegemony holds here—churches, legislators, educators, artists, writers, scholars, film producers, and others shape the values of society to be in the interests of the dominant groups.[62] Marx and Fanon point out deftly the way religion, for example, serves to impose on the struggling masses a sense of docility, a sense of "fatalism" that sedates any rebellious impulse.[63] Within a conflict theory of history, this means the interests produced by upper classes are *not* the interests of the dominated classes, but these interests are imposed on them as though natural. This is perhaps the singular feature of Marxist understandings of culture—going beyond ordinary Hegelian dialectics, conflicting interests are resolved through violence. Violence is used to keep the poor dominated through policing, material deprivation, and denial of basics goods.[64] Violence, however, is a dangerous tool, as its logic is easily grasped by the underclasses and can be turned against the dominant.[65] Thus, violence remains the purview of the upper classes, but it is a tool they are loathe to use because it is inherently destabilizing. If the workers are being beaten, they are not producing; if mayhem is the rule in the cities, then imposing rules on the underclasses is impossible.

Other techniques of social conditioning carried out by the various cultural producers are often more effective and more stabilizing than the use of violence. Thus, Herbert Marcuse identifies the Freudian "repression" imposed by law as the dominant tool to control society, especially the underclasses.[66] Paulo Freire articulates this through the lens of "oppression," which liberation theologians critically note is perpetuated not only by civil and military authorities but also by business and religious leaders.[67] The upper classes make good efforts, then, through various channels to ensure that the lower classes buy into narratives that justify their position, such as the myths of desert, or civilizing culture, or religious reward. In internalizing these values through myth, the lower classes come to serve the upper classes and are more easily kept docile than by employing violent measures.[68]

Social reality is thus a great farce: wealthy megachurch pastors often preach values to their congregations they are not personally beholden to; entertainers mock their audiences by appealing to traditional values that they do not hold; immoral politicians make stump speeches about the importance of justice as they ravage poor communities; and well-meaning teachers gatekeep the upper echelons of society through mechanisms of bourgeois conformity. Jeff Foxworthy, the son of an IBM executive, can be an agent of shaping poor culture through his "blue collar comedy" despite not sharing the background or fate of his audience. Likewise, Donald Trump, the prodigal son of a millionaire, billed himself as a "blue-collar billionaire" in the 2016 US Presidential election, an identification that successfully won him the votes of those on the opposite end of the economic scale from him.[69]

This reality is, unfortunately, one that may be quite literally impossible to alter. The process of adapting to upper-class culture, a process necessary to gain the recognition and talents necessary for being able to promulgate cultural works on a large scale, is one that transforms (or better, *con*forms) the thinker. Ruby Payne's work, for example, is addressed to teachers—professionals who often live in poor conditions but who have advanced education.[70] Why do teachers need instructions on how to work with poor students, when they are often themselves in the same economic situation? Because in pursuing advanced studies, the teachers themselves are subjected to the technologies of discipline, which reshape their own epistemological frameworks to square with a bourgeois worldview that their students may not (yet) share.[71]

As a result, it is with great irony that those who wish to help the poor so often do so from bourgeois mindsets. Paulo Freire's "pedagogy" uses the mechanisms and assumptions of bourgeois education (e.g., Marxist ideologies, dialectics, educational techniques) to "liberate" the poor. Once again, it is the values and disvalues of the wealthy—in this case, sympathy for the poor rather than antipathy than against them—that dictate the proper approach. Likewise, other liberators of the poor, such as Gustavo Gutiérrez or Georg Lukács, assert first that the poor need liberation (or revolution) and, second, that they have the proper answer for what that should look like. Indeed, the clearest articulation of this problem from a bourgeois perspective may be seen in the work of subaltern and postcolonial studies, such as Gayatry Spivak's *Can the Subaltern Speak?* Spivak notes astutely that well-meaning bourgeois scholars, like Foucault or Deleuze and Guattari, or white feminists, or white male colonists, or male Indigenous, often speak *on behalf* of the persons they purport to be defending and, in so doing, interpret the actions and interests of others through their own interests.[72] But her own interpretation must likewise be suspect, as she remains an upper-class, highly educated Brahman. Indeed, only a position like that of Frantz Fanon, who asserts the colonized's own autonomous (violent) action is legitimated by the conditions of colonization, avoids (to the extent possible) a new imposition of values on the worst off.[73] Spontaneous violent action, unmediated and unlegitimized, shows its ugly head as one of the few uninterpretable expressions. But the use of violence is itself a concession to the logic of domination and legitimates the further use of force by the upper classes.[74]

To be poor, therefore, is to experience a world that is determined through poverty but dictated by those who are not poor. The poor's interests, values, self-worth, and possibilities exist within a constellation of economic realities, but these values are disvalues handed on by those who shape society. To be poor is to exist within the sphere of being a dominated class who is silenced by the upper classes, even the most well-meaning advocates. It is to be the "object" to the privileged classes' "subjectivity," the one studied, discussed, imposed, controlled, legislated, educated, disciplined, entertained, and even benefited. It is to be the dominated, in Hegel's master-slave dialectic; the one subjected, not subject.[75] With deep irony, sympathetic business professors can write about the need to "include the poor in the production of wealth," as though all the wealth enjoyed by the executive class were not itself produced by the poor![76] The poor subjected to this objectification can either accept their lot uncritically or, more likely, may learn to "play the game," holding a fractured consciousness about their situation.[77]

Consciousness

Recognizing that poverty shapes one's interests and understandings of the world, it is no surprise, then, that those who experience poverty are continuously conscious of that poverty. Maurice Merleau-Ponty argues that "the economic and social drama [of human life] offers each consciousness a certain background or again a certain *imago* that it will decode in its own manner," which manifests in understanding oneself in relation to others in response to material and economic experience.[78] Merleau-Ponty's continuous argument across *The Phenomenology of Perception* is that human beings always perceive within a given context—there is no "view from nowhere." Thus, a type of "class consciousness" always pervades the perception of the world from the perspective of the poor. The general notion of class consciousness comes from Marx, who believed class consciousness as solidarity would lead the workers to rise up over the oppression inflicted upon them by the bourgeoisie (though Marx's view here is imposed as a member of the intelligentsia).[79] Georg Lukács took Marx's view further and argued that *only* the working class could have true (and not false) consciousness; theirs is the class defined by the oppression of the bourgeoisie, so only they can be conscious of the economic reality of history.[80]

However, class consciousness in the sense held by Marxists is artificial—it does not exist naturally the way that Marx or Lukács believed it would. After all, this is the assumption of people like Freire—that the poor must be conscientized because they lack the current consciousness that bourgeois advocates for the poor believe the poor should have.[81]

Perhaps the poor suffer from false consciousness, an improper socialization into the bourgeois hegemonic value system, or perhaps they are just ignorant to their plight.[82] Marx's promise of a spontaneous worker overthrow never came true, even in countries where communist revolutions took place led typically by the intelligentsia or military leaders claiming the privilege of being on the side of the poor. And, in such countries where communism did take root, it has never achieved the "classless society" vision that Marx expected from genuine worker solidarity. The closest one finds to this is not the revolution of the proletariat but of the colonized.[83] Marxists have often defended the failures of class revolution through some various "No True Scotsman" arguments—that the true proletarian revolution has never been tried, or that it succeeded only to be co-opted by bourgeois interests—but realistically, it is more likely that the "class consciousness" imputed by bourgeois intellectuals will not emerge the way they expect it to among the poor.

This conclusion should be apparent when one notes how, within the work of Marxists, there is no clear consensus on *who* the revolutionary conscientized class is. "The poor" themselves are not a sufficient group for collective action, diffuse as they are. Lukács believed that only worker, i.e., urban proletariat, consciousness could be true consciousness, as did Marx; the peasantry, in his mind, was unable to achieve this.[84] In direct contrast to this, Fanon posits that in anti-colonial uprisings, only the peasantry have revolutionary consciousness![85] Michel Foucault speaks positively about proletarian efforts, on one hand, but also the importance of the socially unpredictable class of plebs.[86] Marcella Althaus-Reid contrasts the peasantry-focused work of early liberation theology from the reality of the poor in the cities.[87] Were these variations not enough, the sub-subfield of poverty studies known as "subaltern studies" emerges as its own way of identifying a subgroup of the poor who cannot be identified with the larger group of the poor.[88] In the end, it is unclear if it is the proletariat, the peasantry, or the plebs who do the "real work of history" because of their apparent class consciousness!

To say that there is no monolithic class consciousness in the vein of Marxist thought, however, is not to say there is no consciousness of class.

It is true that the experience of poverty admits of too great diversity to classify under one broad class, but this is not true for *all* socioeconomic classes. Lukács's conclusion regarding false consciousness is exactly wrong: only the bourgeoisie has class consciousness insofar as only they understand their position as threatened by the poor. The poor are symptom of the middle class—they are the necessary foil against which the bourgeoisie define themselves and defend themselves. Karl Marx and Thomas Malthus maintain their place in economic theory not because they are opposed to each other but because they both maintain the narrative of "the poor" as some inhuman Other whom the bourgeoisie are right to gaze upon with contempt. The death-drive fantasy of a proletarian revolution particularly accentuates this consciousness. This fantasy is experienced by Marxists as sadistic desire *for* and by capitalists as threat *of* immanent destruction. This fantasy thus preserves the identity of the bourgeoisie against the threat of a chaotic economic order.[89] Without promising the demise of itself by the spontaneously unified masses, the middle class risks obliterating itself and losing its hegemonic grip.

All the same, it is the case that the poor, especially in capitalist societies, are continually conscious of their status as poor. In a consumerist society, the standards of living, the expectations of social presentation, the lifestyles presented in the media, and continual political debates about economics remind the poor of their position. As symptom of the upper classes, the poor are turned into objects through the dominating gaze of bourgeois subjects.[90] In a capitalist society, money functions as the universal medium of exchange—to have money is to have total subjectivity. One can access all privileges society has to offer. It is to have one's place in society as a given, one's subjectivity as assumed. To be poor, then, is to be in a position where one is denied this subjectivity continually—one is to be acted upon by others, the object of their sympathy or antipathy, the object of study, the object of legislation, the object of generosity. In every place one goes, they are cognizant of the eyes around them, the looks of the privileged and the appearance they must hold, the surveilling eyes of suspicion, the averted eyes of shame, the pitying eyes of philanthropists. This gaze is ubiquitous—in the classroom where teachers "look out" for troubled students, in neighborhoods where police prowl, in bureaucratic paperwork demanding the poor prove their worth, even in well-intentioned acts of Christians to intentionally "include" the poor (who may have already been included). Any poor who wish to be regarded as subjects will need to work carefully to present as non-poor in any circumstance, but they must always be on guard lest their charade is exposed. Paraphrasing Fanon, the poor may be able to "pass" as non-poor if racial markers do not further objectify them in the gaze of the dominant, but they will always be aware of the watchful gaze in a way that the privileged are not.[91] In all facets of ordinary life, from work to leisure to romantic engagements to religious worship to civic engagement to social relations to medical care and so on, the poor cannot help but be reminded of their poverty. And yet, it is the case that this consciousness yields different understandings and interpretations among the poor.

On the one hand, there are those who accept the identity of poverty as a sort of badge of honor. They insist on "honest" work, accepting without question the bourgeois valuations of work and justice. Often, they embrace a "blue collar" aesthetic, embracing a culture, goods, and lifestyle that celebrate relative poverty as "simplicity."[92] Whether this is a coping mechanism to resist the conclusion that to be poor is unfavorable, or whether it is an attempt to resist the culture of the elite, the result is a rejection of what is perceived to be the values and ideas of the "elitist" upper classes. In the contemporary US, among the white poor this includes rejection of intellectualism, anti-liberalism, and a unique Evangelical-style marriage between conservative politics and religious belief.[93] While much of this has roots in genuine workers' efforts of the past century, the anti-elitist position was easily coopted by elites to effectively root out critical thinking and promote anti-intellectualism.[94] Thus, the term "redneck," once referring to pro-union miners who wore red bandanas around their necks,[95] has become a self-descriptor for under-educated, neoconservative, semi-rural, upper-working class (whites).[96]

This act of self-identification, however, is often duplicitous. Because the upper classes seek to control the lower classes, including their tastes, production of lower-class culture often functions as a means of producing an image of the lower classes that does not necessarily correspond to their reality. Consider the 2020 US Presidential election. Donald Trump received more votes from people with lower education levels, especially among whites.[97] Because education level, for the most part, tracks positively with income level, the assumption among many commentators was that those voting for Trump were poor whites largely. And while it is true that Trump did have higher vote rates among the white working class than did Joe Biden,[98] the only economic demographic that Trump held the majority vote for was families with incomes over $100,000 per year,[99] a group that is much whiter than any other income bracket.[100] In other words, the MAGA (Make America Great Again) image promoted by Trump and other Republicans like Margery Taylor Greene, Lauren Boebert, Matt Gaetz, and Josh Hawley promotes a "working class" image directed toward persons whose incomes are, at best, varied and, more realistically, skewed toward the higher end of the economic spectrum. The "poor" aesthetics demonstrated through military imagery, support of country music stars like John Rich, evangelical preaching, garish red trucker hats, and large pickup truck convoys are really the tastes of upper-middle class white suburbanites. In a particularly telling moment, "QAnon Shaman" Jacob Chansley, who dressed himself in animal skins and bison horns as though some modern mountain man, after being arrested for rioting at the US Capitol Building on January 6, 2021, was granted an organic diet while in jail awaiting his trial, the very picture of upper-class taste.[101]

The imposition of "poor" tastes on those in poverty by the upper classes, combined with the persistent reminder of poverty, can engender antipathy among the poor as well. With limited resources available for the poor, the struggle for what few opportunities are present breeds resentment and animosity. Some embracing the image of the "good" poor are likely to look down on those whom they perceive to be "bad," other poor members of their community, whose coping strategies and limited opportunities have resulted in socially disreputable lifestyles or stigmas. A common sentiment in neoconservative context is the idea of social aid as "handouts," an image made famous in US president Ronald Reagan's articulation of the "welfare queen." Much of this antipathy is passed on through thinly veiled racist lenses, with terms like thug or ghetto invoking among the general populace an image of the "bad poor" as Black.[102] The "good poor" (white working class) reassure themselves of their dignity in this divide-and-conquer rhetoric, applying bourgeois values on those who lack economic possibilities. But lest the white poor realize that their race is not free from disrepute, the proud "redneck" can distinguish themself from the unsavory "white trash."[103] Of course, the antipathy can be channeled in other directions as well, and the twice-subjugated can be turned against others who are likewise doubly oppressed.[104] For example, the concept of Black Asian racial conflict stands out as a point of division used to sow and stoke divisions among non-hegemonic racial groups, both in the 1992 Los Angeles race riots and in the 2020–2022 anti-Asian hate crime spree.[105] According to the "middleman theory," Asian Americans, though a minority ethnic group, occupy a "middleman" position between the dominant ethnic group (white Americans) and other ethnic groups (e.g., Black Americans), which makes them scapegoats for hostility that cannot usefully be directed toward the dominant group.[106] Race, of course, is only the most convenient way to divide the poor; so long as the dominant group is (perceived to be) untouchable, antipathy can be misdirected at any other fellow poor person. Political beliefs, sexuality, religious identity, or gender also make for useful targets. Beyond this, one's career, relative economic standing, marital status, personality, legal standing, intelligence, or family history also all make for rich excuses for interclass hostility and have been historically used to monitor and subjugate the poor. As long as the poor are subjugated by the wealthy, members of the lower classes clamber to avoid becoming the absolute worst off in society. A hierarchy of the wretched emerges among those begging for scraps, with some proud to not be *like those* other poor.

Because the values of the dominant class (i.e., the bourgeoisie) are imposed on the lower classes, it is unsurprising that the poor themselves disvalue others among the poor. The founding myth of capitalism is that hard work and perseverance—which are morally upright and praiseworthy—will be naturally rewarded with material benefits.[107] The economist Thomas Malthus even theologized this point at the end of the eighteenth century—starvation is God's way of motivating those not naturally inclined to work for others.[108] There is no shortage of "good poor" expecting this will happen and that the general trend among the poor (though not them, obviously) is laziness and moral bankruptcy. Liberation theologians sought to overturn this tendency, often at the expense of overcorrecting, infantilizing, or romanticizing the poor. Gustavo Gutiérrez draws positively from biblical depictions of the poor as "clients of Yahweh," or "the just ones, the whole ones,"[109] while John Sobrino speaks of the poor saving the wealthy "by way of 'inspiration,' 'attraction,' and 'impulse,' by causing 'ferment' and by providing modest models for a different type of society."[110] And yet, at the same time, other liberation theologians demonstrate the palpable disdain for poverty that such romanticisms cover up. Virgilio Elizondo, for example, writes regarding his experience as a Mexican American, "No matter how much education *or wealth* one might obtain, one continued to be a poor outcast by reason of conception and birth."[111] In order to attack the racist hegemony, he appeals to the values of the classist hegemony—one's value as a Mexican American should not be the same as that of those who are poor. The poor thus remain objects: deviants for the capitalist and saints (at times) for the liberationist. Between the two, the capitalist's honesty at least reveals their intention to the poor. The liberation theologian claims the poor are voiceless, while also pretending to speak on their behalf.[112] It is no wonder, then, that those scholars who have been able to escape poverty are quick to denounce the poverty from which they emerged. Elizondo's response is not, ultimately, surprising—his education allowed him to move into the professional class (as a priest), escaping anti-poor sentiments, but he remained subject to anti-Latino racism. Nobody wants to be poor; "precarity is everywhere rejected, and precarity is an essential element of poverty."[113] Anybody who can escape poverty does so without regret. The poor, in turn, whether out of bitterness for their own condition, jealousy for what little they have, or merely habituated consciousness, are themselves likely to repeat and reinforce the same anti-poor antipathy that they receive from the upper classes.

Finally, class consciousness can and does at times play out as actual sympathy and solidarity with one's class. Indeed, prosocial behavior is seen to be higher among the poor, and lower economic classes give more proportionally to their communities than other economic classes do.[114] The likelihood of someone having shared class consciousness and solidarity tracks positively with their membership in a workers' union, an unsurprising reality given that unions are rooted in collective bargaining.[115] Unfortunately, in the US, only 10.3 percent of workers are in unions, and union membership has decreased steadily over the past several decades.[116] The reasoning for this is complicated, of course, but much of it ties to an increase of racial coding, neoconservative talking points, and the ultimate success of cultural hegemony.[117]

Ironically, therefore, in order to understand "the poor," one must understand that the poor do not all understand themselves the same way. Casting the poor as a monolithic entity, whether as "unmotivated" leeches or victims of merciless capitalism, is convenient most of all for those who are not poor. The members of the lower classes may embrace these ideas or other visions, but above all, they are conscious of their poverty and its meaning within society. Every choice they make is cast in the double-reality of economic constraint and broader social narrative. Whether they are "good" poor or some other element of the lower classes, they act within the social realities constructed around them.[118] While the meaning of poverty differs between individuals among the poor (and, more importantly, among different ways of dividing the poor, such as by race, sex, occupation, religion, ability, and so forth), the reality of poverty persists as the background against which all living is contextualized.

Finally, while poverty exists as one's "background," it does not slip out of consciousness the way that economic status does for the bourgeois. The poor feel their every step under the gaze of the economic value system. To be poor is to occupy a position of disvalue, the "wound" the middle class tolerates to maintain its own sanity, the antithetical the bourgeoisie view with disgust.[119] One does not become unaware of their poverty—it is persistently before them because they exist as object for the others' uncomfortable gaze. Outside of the stigmatizing gaze of the social order, in closed houses or abandoned neighborhoods, the poor cannot escape the sound of grumbling stomachs or the nipping cold of drafty houses. Poverty is not a situation that readily allows for adaptation. It is a situation of continual stress: the threat of starvation, dispossession, poor health, unemployment, disease, and violence remains constantly in the frame of consciousness. As such, "class consciousness" for the poor means primarily consciousness both of their disvalue in society and of insecurity—being eternally in a precarious existence.

Insecurity

The middle and upper classes have the privilege of defining themselves against the lower economic classes because class identity comes to them as a luxury. The lower classes do not *need* to understand themselves as poor because their existence is a daily reminder of that. Demarcations between the well-off and the extremely well-off are constructions of the non-poor to affirm their own positions against each other; it is no exaggeration to say that for the poor, the distinction between one million and one billion dollars is almost meaningless. The pontifications of well-meaning advocates of the poor, earnestly pleading the case for organization and revolution, do so often from a position of security. Lofty goals for liberation or conscientization may appear unrealistic to those struggling to live. Who can pursue life meaning when children at home are hungry? As even Aristotle acknowledged 2,400 years ago, developing wisdom requires that one is no longer beholden to the demands of quotidian survival.[120]

If one wants to understand better why, despite two hundred years of socialist advocacy, the lower classes remain economically depressed, the answer is quite simple. Despite awareness of their poverty and the divisions that exist among economic society, the poor are daily challenged by insecurity. In a living situation marked most distinctively by material lack, the most immediate thing for any person surviving poverty will inevitably be surviving. Tragically, this opens avenues for the manipulation of the poor: desperation breeds animosity. Competition, the bourgeoisie's utopian vision for a good society, is experienced as a life-and-death struggle among the poor.[121] This insecurity is exploited by both well-meaning and bad-faith actors among the upper classes: Marxists and union organizers appeal to the realities of insecurity to rally workers together in solidarity, while right-wing media stoke "us vs. them" divisions through race-baiting and propaganda celebrating the "American Dream." It is awareness of this insecurity that allows the upper classes to maintain power over the lower classes, and so it is important to recognize that insecurity is first and foremost the primary condition of poverty.

Insecurity can be experienced in many ways, and the depth or experience of poverty depends to a great deal on what sorts of insecurities one experiences and the degree to which they experience them. Lack of economic resources breeds numerous other forms of insecurity: a sense of crime,[122] unsanitary environments, scarcity of quality food sources, uncertainty about living arrangements, inaccessibility of health care, unstable work opportunities, and unsafe family situations, among others. Understanding the fundamental aspect of insecurity allows us to note what unifies the diverse poor: some experience insecurity tied to police harassment, while others are afraid of criminals; some are concerned about their next meal, while others are concerned that they cannot afford a healthier diet; some are afraid of being evicted from their homes, while others struggle to find a secure place for the night; some suffer health problems due to lack of care, while others worry that slightly better income may close off their affordable care. The instability and uncertainty that pervade the lives of the poor are distinct from the security and stability that characterize the upper classes.

To note, therefore, that poverty is diverse is merely saying that insecurity functions in numerous ways. Three notable outcomes of this are particularly helpful for understanding the epistemology of poverty: lack of choice, "maladaptive" behaviors, and the effects of long-term stress.

Lack of choice, whether actual or perceived, is common for those in poverty. Lack of choice does not mean *no* choice, as some middle-class commentators are prone to suggest,[123] but it does mean constrained choice.

Friedrich Engels claimed 180 years ago that the poor essentially had three choices available to them: starvation over time, immediate suicide, or crime. Of the three, Engels supposes that "there is no cause for surprise that most of them prefer stealing to starvation and suicide."[124] Engels's supposition here does not accord for *all* poor, as some may suffer long-term health problems caused by processed foods and poor environmental conditions rather than starvation, but it does contextualize the reality that for many in poverty, work choices come down to low-paid service work or various types of "dirty" work. Thus, the poor in the US often have to choose between working various minimum-wage-paying jobs or risking life and injury in the military, imprisonment through crime, or their reputation and bodily integrity in various types of sex work. All of this is continually filtered and portrayed through dominant aesthetic and ethical senses to boot; despite recent feminist attempts to recast sex work as dignified, nobody who works at a strip club to put food on the table thinks they are "empowered" in doing so.[125] Choices do exist, but unlike for the upper classes, the trade-offs and risks associated with choice often punish those who act autonomously.

The lack of choice characteristic of poverty often leads the poor to be resigned to their fate. What bourgeois commentators may perceive as a fatalist attitude among the poor is a coping strategy[126]—if one cannot realistically take charge of their life because opportunities are not present, it may be easier psychologically to accept this limitation rather than challenge it. Being resigned to the limitations presented in one's personal relationships, neighborhood, occupational choices, and educational opportunities offers respite from the trauma of feeling impotent against restrictions. As Susan Moller Okin noted decades ago, women in abusive relationships are less likely to seek divorce because of how economically punitive it is to them.[127] If achieving physical security comes at the cost of economic security, it is no surprise that some may prefer the stability of domestic violence over the uncertainty of independent survival.

Lack of choice often means that the poor develop behaviors that people who regularly enjoy choice (i.e., the upper classes) would consider maladaptive. "The poor aren't good with money" is a pejorative cliché that bears in it some kernel of truth—repeated experiences of insecurity and uncertainty tied to money often results in many poor people valuing and using money differently from their middle-class counterparts. Capital for the poor functions the way Marx described it: it represents labor,[128] which is always tied to daily survival.[129] Money, then, operates for the poor in its most basic use-exchange function. A day's wages are to be spent on one's daily needs—shelter, food, clothing, and so forth. It is the ideology of the bourgeoisie (i.e., capitalists as those who control the capital) that money is meant for investment.[130] This is why people in the upper-middle class can state, with no sense of irony, that an annual income three to four times greater than the average family's is hardly enough for survival: money is tied not to basic needs but to long-term growth and accumulation.[131] The middle class *invests*—in stocks, property, education, career opportunities, networks, and so forth. The poor *survive*.

As a result, anti-poor bourgeoisie often scoff at the spending habits of the poor. When a poor person experiences a brief windfall, such as a tax return, court settlement, or lottery win, they may spend it on luxuries rather than invest it for later. It is, of course, important to sort out inflammatory stereotypes from realities, but because of economic insecurity, money functions differently for the poor. The tastes cultivated over a lifetime of insecurity and domination do not easily yield either understanding or awareness of investment as within the realm of choices for the poor. Poor neighborhoods are renowned for having more payday lenders and fewer banks, to say nothing of financial advisors.[132] While the poor may want to put aside some savings, they may not have access to the necessary institutions nor knowledge about how to invest. And still, the consciousness of insecurity is always present; a sudden acquisition of wealth is not felt as a guarantee but rather a new type of uncertainty. The upshot to all this is that the poor are much more likely to use money than to hoard it. The middle class may dismiss this as "entertainment and relationships,"[133] but this ignores the inherently biological function that capital plays for the poor,[134] a relationship that is abstracted and alienated for the upper classes.

One need only look as far as the 2009 market collapse to understand this distinction: ten million Americans were evicted from their houses because traders could easily abstract the risk of their collateralized debt obligations since all *they* risked for themselves were their own overpaid jobs. Ten million people lost their homes because of the poor decisions of a few hundred wealthy traders. If this is the cost of other people's investment failures, what guarantee do the poor have of securing their own futures?

Uncertainty regarding economic stability, however, has other repercussions beyond "poor" spending habits. The familiarity and comfortability of low-level insecurity can make any sort of risk traumatic. Even low-risk opportunities, such as a higher-paying job, scholarship opportunities, or safer living conditions, can feel threatening.[135] It is, after all, the trait of the upper classes to be able to adapt (or "bluff" in Bourdieu's words) to any new situation.[136] The experience of low-level risks that characterize the rearing of the upper classes, such as travel to other countries, unpaid internships, and extracurricular activities, prepares them psychologically for ideal choice selection with an eye to long-term benefits. For the poor, however, risks tend to be proportionally greater and rewards (perceived or real) lower. The poor man betting his last ten dollars before payday on a horse race puts up a lot more than the rich man gambling one thousand dollars of discretionary income. Thus, while the bourgeois preference for risk results in devastating externalized costs borne by the poor, the poor preference for security results in missed opportunities.

Finally, the long-term stress of insecurity can cause significantly poor outcomes for the overall well-being of the poor. The anxiety of continually eking out one's existence one day at a time does not bode well for one's physical health. Stress is tied to health problems ranging from heart disease and high blood sugar (and subsequently diabetes) to obesity and Alzheimer's.[137] Poverty itself also carries with it numerous ailments such as malnutrition, exposure, or general poor immune response, as healthy food and adequate shelter are out of reach for many poor. Numerous infectious diseases are highly correlated with poverty, often because of poor access to health care, including tuberculosis, malaria, and HIV/AIDS (though these diseases are less likely to be tied to poverty in the US than abroad).[138] Sleep abnormalities and lack of exercise are common among the poor. Finally, substance addiction correlates positively with poverty, with some noting that the poor may abuse substances as a way of coping with poverty, and others noting that abuse of substances can lead people (already at risk) into poverty.[139]

Beyond the mostly physical, poverty also has detrimental effects on one's mental and emotional well-being. Although there is the romantic image of the "blessed poor," the poor are less likely to be happy than their middle-class counterparts.[140] After all, the economic pressures of poverty are not conducive to cultivating genuine human flourishing.[141] Beyond the somewhat obvious problems of increased anxiety, sleeplessness, depression, and aggression, poverty also increases one's likelihood of psychosis, including schizophrenia.[142] If these were not enough, the experience of scarcity also tracks with lower IQs, and moments of increased insecurity correlate with dips in intelligence.[143] The relationship between biological impulses to immediate survival and its repercussions on mental health is not insignificant. Living constantly under the threat of insecurity leads the poor to develop psychological (mal)adaptations that can only truly be understood in the frame of safeguarding one's existence. As a result, the final aspect of poverty worth noting, which is in fact a conclusion from the foregoing discussion of taste, consciousness, and insecurity, is the question of survival.

Survival

The entirety of the poor epistemology can be summed up through the perspective of survival. Because the primary defining feature of poverty is lack or insecurity, especially lack tied to basic needs, the primary experience of poverty is struggle for survival. The need to survive characterizes their choices surrounding familial liaisons, employment, living arrangements, consumption, community involvement, and so forth. What decisions are made on a daily basis, which risks are accepted, what one expects of the future (both short-term and long-term) are filtered through a survival mindset. To understand why a young Filipino mother might engage in work as a camgirl,[144] or a US Latina minor might escape an oppressive home culture to be homeless in Seattle,[145] one must understand survival as a worldview. The abstract, rational, intentional, calculated mindset of the dominating classes, the standard against which the poor's "poor" choices are evaluated, is a mindset most significantly characterized by luxury and leisure. When a poor family delays important automotive maintenance work or preventative medicine, incurring a much greater cost later, their actions are deemed "foolish" from a bourgeois epistemological perspective. What this misses, of course, is that "long-term payout" is itself an economically situated value, one that assumes the goal of any action is long-term benefit rather than short-term.[146] The poor, on the other hand, must be immediately concerned with the short term. Planning for long term is foolish if the short term cannot be secured. Thus, the longtermism of "effective altruism" has rightly been criticized as classist; rather than addressing the immediate survival of the poor, the proponents seek to ensure their own long-term well-being (a rather short-sighted goal if they do not address global poverty).[147] The psychological effect of "scarcity mindset" is understandable when one's very survival, not future flourishing, is the immediate concern.[148]

Many poor individuals are willing to do whatever it takes to survive. Thus, property crime does track positively with economic inequality.[149] However, violent crime does not. Desperation may lead people to various forms of theft, including burglary, robbery, larceny, and so forth, but assaults, murders, rapes, and other crimes against persons can only be predicted by one's immediate associates rather than one's economic situation.[150] Since it is material well-being that the poor most immediately feel, their most common crimes are directed at property. The idea that a poorer neighborhood is less "safe" is predicated upon safety as a measure of one's property, not person, a shift that Michel Foucault argues characterizes the difference of criminality prior to and after the emergence of capitalism as a dominant social system.[151] Of course, keeping poor neighborhoods under watch helps remind the poor that they are not subjects but rather suspects, objects of scrutiny, parasites leeching off the human bourgeoisie.

But, of course, the poor are *not* mere victims. They are, after all, still human, in spite of the upper classes. They do not merely occupy the place of "object" that middle-class society insists they hold. They are not merely acted upon by the law or the government—they also act themselves, and their acts often demonstrate awareness of the way they are viewed by society, how the gaze of the dominant other can be used to one's own benefit. Lindsey Earner-Byrne, for example, notes that the Irish poor of the early twentieth century crafted letters of petition to the archbishop of Dublin by making clear references to the way poverty was understood by the upper classes. Often, they would contend that they were not lazy, that they were at the end of their hope, that they had merely fallen on a bit of bad luck, anticipating the explanations the upper classes give to reassure themselves of the deservedness of poverty.[152] Others made clearer moral arguments, appealing to the fact that they were "good Catholics," or, with clear awareness of the stakes at hand, threatened apostasy if they were not helped.[153] The illusion of the poor as happy simpletons belies the ingenious strategies that the poor have employed and continue to employ to survive in a society that perceives them as innately defective.[154]

The mindset of survival becomes more obvious when one examines poor communities. While the stereotype of antisocial deviants does hold some truth in the issue of property crime, it conflicts with the reality of poor prosocial behavior. Social researchers from the University of California, Berkeley, found that the poor are *more likely* to help others than the upper classes. The poor demonstrate greater propensity toward generosity, charity, trust, and help than do the upper classes.[155] Beyond these traits, data on charitable giving shows that the poor give a higher proportion of their income to their communities than do the middle class.[156] Ironically, the social ideal of being a generous giver holds truer for the person who has too little than the person who has more than enough.

This appears paradoxical at first—those who have little should not give what little they have to others when scarcity abounds. Here the bias of bourgeois epistemology finds itself contradicted: the logic of rational self-interested actors fails at the place where it should be most evident, i.e., among those with the most pressing self-interest. "Long-term" bourgeois mentality, the mindset of the more individualistic class that gives less of their wealth than the poor, cannot make sense of the generosity of the poor.[157] Prosocial giving is, in fact, a reasonable survival tactic as it ensures that one's community survives. The prosocial orientation is an empathically motivated response. The experience of desperation among the poor prompts them to act with generosity to others who experience similar desperation.[158] The idea of the autonomous individual animating capitalist ideology is a bad-faith artifact of Enlightenment philosophy that ignores both the historical reality of human interdependence and the basic biological reality of human sociality. The drive to protect and care for the community is what *Homo sapiens* owe for our prominence today.[159] The same survival tactics that have preserved our species for 300,000 years before civilization continue to preserve the poor. The individualism of self-satisfaction, typical of the middle class, is in reality the more truly maladaptive trait from a species perspective, a historical aberration, a malignant ideology in our corporate existence.

The triumph of the bourgeois mindset is evidenced by the denigration of the poor. Those billions who toil and labor for the existence of the few privileged are rewarded with distrust, defamation, and destitution. The regnant mindset of business leaders is that the poor are those who "do not generate wealth."[160] After exploiting the poor and alienating them from the fruits of their labor, the capitalist looks at the poor and wonders why they have not escaped their poverty. The business class in bad faith ignores the reality that the wealth they hold is generated by their laborers.[161] In a society where justice is contextualized by fair agreement, the rich must ignore the way their wealth is generated through exploitation. The value system of capitalism is thus inherently contradictory: one must believe in economic fairness while convincing themself that this wealth is self-generated. The poor must be kept at length then—they must be essentialized and denigrated to hide the fact that their poverty is the byproduct of the generation of wealth.[162] And so, the myth of the successful individual pervades, as ahistorical and unscientific as it is. This epistemic framework is so artificially constructed that it cannot help but see the all-too-human mind of the poor as alien. And yet, even the empirically dominated hermeneutic of the modern world affirms the destructiveness of the competitive risk-reward mindset of the bourgeoisie over the collective survival episteme of the poor.[163] Oil billionaires propagate lies about climate change to protect their wealth; media companies invent lies about the education system to ensure political support; and another economic catastrophe looms on the horizon as material investments no longer match projections of growth. As two historians quipped, "It's easier for most people to imagine the end of the planet than to imagine the end of capitalism."[164]

In the sequence of these four frames, the proper ordering to understand the poor should be survival, insecurity, consciousness, and domination. Survival characterizes the needs and experiences of the poor most of all. The need to survive characterizes the poor's approach to scarcity and questions of insecurity. The persistence of insecurity shapes the entire conscious experience of the world and their relationship to others of the poor. And this consciousness makes them more susceptible to domination as they are continuously aware of the precariousness of their own position. Too often, the upper classes gaze at the poor beginning through the lens of domination, but this perspective is only possible for those who are already several steps removed from basic survival. One must begin from the question of what it is like to have their own existence under threat to be able to explain how the broader mass of humanity is successfully dominated by the smaller. Thus, to be able to adopt the epistemology of the poor, we must first begin from uncertainty of one's existence.

Conclusion: Understanding the Poor through Narrative

Despite the fact that even the most earnest social theorists, philosophers, and theologians mistake the experience of the poor, artists are often better able to capture it, in however fractured a manner they may. Perhaps it is because art is inherently transgressive, or perhaps some forms of art that we might note are derogatorily dismissed as "low-brow" is more accessible to people who have not been trained to unthink their own background of poverty. In particular, film seems a good way of articulating the experience of poverty through aesthetic (taste), mood (consciousness), conflict (insecurity), and resolution (survival). In recent years, popular examples like Greta Gerwig's *Ladybird* (2017), Mike Smith's TV series *Trailer Park Boys* (2001–present), and Hwang Dong-hyuk's *Squid Game* (오징어게임) (2021) depict poor individuals struggling amidst constrained choices to be truly human. *Ladybird* concludes with the film's protagonist trying to escape her poor family by going to college in New York, only to be irresistibly brought back to her familial Catholic faith. *Trailer Park Boys* features trailer park–dwelling friends whose struggles to thrive repeatedly end in prison because of economic constraints. *Squid Game*'s protagonist enters a murderous competition out of economic desperation but succeeds due to his prosocial prioritization of other participants over his own perceived chance of success.

Perhaps the best recent example of poverty depicted in film, however, is Bong Joon-ho's 2019 *Parasite* (기생충). The narrative revolves around the poor Kim family, who strategically ingratiate themselves into various positions of employment for the rich Park family. The Kims use subterfuge, deception, and even outright assault to win over the favor of the Parks, but their efforts are undermined when the now-displaced housekeeper returns unannounced to bring food to her husband, who has secreted himself in the basement of the Parks' house. The housekeeper discovers the Kims' deception and tries to extort them, after which a violent struggle between the families results in the former housekeeper's death. The next morning, the haggard Kims are called upon to serve the Parks' wealthy guests at a birthday party, where the housekeeper's husband maims the Kim son and murders the Kim daughter. The Kim father, ordered to escort the Parks' son to the hospital rather than attend to his dying daughter, murders the Park father and absconds himself to the secret basement.

This film articulates in a clear way the various frames of survival, insecurity, consciousness, and domination. The Kim family is willing to commit document fraud, implicate the previous chauffer in sexual indiscretion, and sabotage the housekeeper by triggering an allergic reaction that resembles tuberculosis (note: a poor disease), all as a measure to survive. Once all four members of the Kim family secure employment, they experience a deceptive moment of security where they enjoy the Parks' home luxuries before the housekeeper nearly exposes their improprieties and a flash flood destroys the Kims' subbasement apartment. The Kims are further kept conscious of their poverty by Bong's ingenious inclusion of olfactory markers—the Parks' body language reminds the Kims that they cannot get rid of their smell, the smell of their subbasement apartment. Finally, most of all, the Kims aspire to be like the Parks, speaking highly of them even in private while seeing no problem with trampling their economically depressed fellows.

But what makes Bong's treatment of the fictitious poor Kim family remarkable in *Parasite* is he treats them as actual subjects. It is clear that they struggle in a system that is designed to disfavor them. They act in constrained ways, and the Park family treats them as background (failing to notice them at times, except for the smell). Nonetheless, they employ their own ingenuity and talent to secure their jobs, they pursue their own relationships, and they strategize and collaborate among themselves. They are not monolithic. They are cast neither into romantic hagiographies nor into deprecatory hamartiologies. They are morally complex beings caught between the dominant ethic of their employer, the basic demands of survival, and the antipathetic views of the upper classes. They are given the sort of character complexity usually reserved for upper-class characters in Woody Allen and Stanley Kubrick films. The true subjectivity of the family is demonstrated most poignantly in the film's climactic scene: the Kim father is forced to choose between attending to his daughter, whose identity as his daughter remains a secret to the Parks, or helping his employer's son. Against these two constrained choices, the Park father's involuntary act of sniffing and his uncontrolled repugnance offer a third choice to Kim: he could just kill his employer. In the end, Bong's film offers better subjectivity (not to say power or autonomy) to the Kim family than to the Parks. We see the Kims as truly human, while the Parks behave as instinctual animals.

The irony of Bong's movie is this film that depicts the violence of Korean poverty was the 2019 Oscar Best Picture, the first foreign film to earn this distinction. Aesthetically, the film caters to upper-class tastes—it does not appeal to mass appeal or traditional values. Yet, as is true with much *avant garde*, it is designed to offend the sensibilities of the bourgeoisie.[165] Since most culture is developed with the upper classes as both the intended audience and the subject of discussion, granting true subjectivity to a poor family is uncomfortable. The upper classes who view the film see themselves in an unflattering light, while the poor who exist as their symptom are given true subjectivity.

And yet, by confining the lives of this fictitious family to a medium, the radical nature of their lives has to be domesticated. The ineffable has to be expressed. Violence is wrought by the act of depicting the poor, as the audience may convince themselves they understand what poverty is through proxy. Like poverty tourism and so many overpriced "help the poor" fundraiser galas, the radically transgressive nature of the movie is easily domesticated by amoral cultural elites, for whom everything is permitted, and the taboo is the truest expression of the *avant garde*.

As the technological equivalent of the Holy Grail, does AI offer a way out of this system, or is it merely the latest tool to reinforce bourgeois epistemologies? Of course, it is being deployed for the benefit of the economic elite, but AI does not hold the class consciousness that punctuates relations between the rich and the poor. Perhaps an AI could be programmed (or at least imagined) that could undermine capitalist values. Such an AI would need to be built from the bottom up, and it would need to be constructed with full awareness of the hegemonic nature of bourgeois values, but the potential benefit of a tool designed to carry out the certain values built into it without human users should be considered. Perhaps the vision of AI fulfilling every consumerist fantasy can be reimagined with AI empowering the poor to advocate for themselves, secure better outcomes, and live free of bourgeois domination.

CHAPTER 5

Making and Breaking Poor Machines

Mr H
at Bullwell
S^{r}
Sir, if you do not'pull don the Frames
or stop pay in Goods onely for work
extra work or make in Full fashon
my Companey ill visit y^{r} machines
for execution against you—
Mr Boton the Forfeit—
I visit^{d} him—

Ned Lud
Kings
Nottingh^{m}—Novemb^{r} 8 1811[1]

THE STEAM-POWERED TEXTILE mills that began to appear at the dawn of the nineteenth century granted untapped riches to those who owned them. In the United Kingdom, much of the early capital gained in the Industrial Revolution came from massive expansion of the textile trade. Even social reformers financed their work through textile mills. Socialist pioneer Robert Owen funded his New Harmony utopian commune through money brought in by the New Lanark mill he purchased from Richard Arkwright and David Dale, and Karl Marx's coconspirator Friedrich Engels financed much of the work of history's most famous communist through a Manchester factory.

As Owen and Engels note in their own writings, however, the conditions for workers in mills were often quite poor. Aside from the brutality of long hours working with untiring heavy machinery, workers were often quite poorly compensated. In 1779, the decrease in weavers' pay due to Arkwright's water frames inspired a series of riots across England. Led on by a young weaver's apprentice named Ned Ludd, workers smashed machines from Manchester to Lancashire.

Two decades later, skilled lace weavers in Nottingham lost high-paying jobs as automation began to replace them. Between 1811 and 1816, they staged a series of protests across the Nottingham countryside. They carried out targeted attacks against factory owners across the region who seemed especially unjust. Their action would begin with a letter like above, often signed by or invoking the legendary Ludd, sometimes referenced as "Captain Ludd," "General Ludd," or even "King Ludd." If the factory owner failed to comply, then a group of protestors would attack the mill in the middle of the night and destroy the frames.

Luddite vigilantism gained momentum, and hundreds of machines were broken within the first year of the action. Wealthy mill owners, rather than sacrifice their own profits for the Luddite demands, demanded protection from the government. The issue was brought to the House of Lords, and in what was his first of only three speeches during his time in the Parliament, Lord Byron himself pleaded the case of the Luddites.[2] Unfortunately, the Frame Breaking Act of 1812 passed, making Luddism a capital offense, and any caught would be hanged or sent to Australia. Government response was swift and violent: over twelve thousand troops, more than those sent to fight against Napoleon in 1808, were mobilized to fight Luddites and protect mill owners.[3] After George Mellor, a popular Luddite leader who had assassinated mill owner William Horsfall, was executed along with thirty other Luddites, the movement began to die down.[4] By 1813, activity had decreased significantly, and by 1816, the movement had come to an end.

The plight of workers inspired Byron, and around this same time, Owen began giving speeches to the House of Commons to seek changes in employment laws. He made some small impact, getting the Cotton Mills and Factory Act of 1819 passed, prohibiting children under nine from employment in textile mills and limiting children from nine to sixteen to *only* twelve-hour workdays.[5] Over the course of the century, political activism, including the eventual formation of the Labour Party, established better conditions for workers.

Today, the legacy of the Luddites is mostly forgotten. Like a cosmic joke, their name has transformed from scourge of unjust capitalists to technophobes. The skilled artisans replaced by automation are lampooned as clumsy homebodies. As though to warn the unruly workers, capitalists not only successfully violently stamped out the popular uprising but also cemented within popular consciousness the idea that to be a Luddite is to be unprogressive. The perverse logic of capital wins out.

Oxford philosopher William MacAskill accomplished what few ethicists ever dream of when his 2022 book *What We Owe the Future* made it to the *New York Times* Best Seller list a week after it was published.[6] The author and his work received praising reviews from the *New Yorker*,[7] *National Public Radio*,[8] *New York Magazine*,[9] *British Broadcasting Corporation*,[10] and *Foreign Affairs*,[11] among others. The book's website boasts endorsements from human rights activist Lydia Cacho, political media personality Ezra Klein, and actor Joseph Gordon-Levitt.[12] Is the popularity of this book a sign that moral philosophy has finally come down out of its ivory tower and taken up the "task" Marx charged it with nearly two hundred years prior—"to change the world"?

MacAskill's work shows the convergence of two strands of moral thinking that have grown popular in recent years. MacAskill himself became an ethicist because of the impact of Peter Singer's philosophy on him, leading him to collaborate with others to form the effective altruism movement.[13] Effective altruism follows Singer's thesis that the wealthy have a moral duty to give their excesses to highly efficient poverty alleviation programs rather than use it for their own pleasure.[14] Thus, it is dedicated to fundraising and donating large sums of money to projects devoted to help those who are worst off. Eventually, MacAskill's work led to the formation of 80,000 Hours, an organization dedicated to helping people find highly effective charities, to promote the ideas of effective altruism, and to serve as a network for those engaged in it.[15] Their biggest funder is Open Philanthropy, an organization started by husband–wife duo Dustin Moskovitz and Cari Tuna.[16]

The second strand of moral philosophy in the work is longtermism. Longtermism is the idea of ensuring the well-being of future generations thousands or millions of years from now.[17] The genesis of this work comes from MacAskill's Oxford colleague, transhumanist philosopher Nick Bostrom.[18] While Bostrom's initial writings on existential threats address such shared concerns as global warming, ecological devastation, and nuclear war, his "Future for Humanity Institute" primarily focuses on "AI Safety, AI Governance, and Biosecurity."[19] In other words, the focus of longtermism, taking its cue from Bostrom's Future for Humanity Institute, parallels the focus of Bostrom's World Transhumanism Association, rebranded as Humanity+.

Transhumanism has earned itself a negative reputation, however. Famous philosophers like President's Council on Bioethics's president Leon Kass,[20] Harvard faculty bestseller Michael Sandel,[21] and political theorist Francis Fukuyama[22] have written scathing critiques of the underlying philosophy and goals of transhumanism. But while transhumanism still may be a major center of conversation among religious and philosophical groups, its most prominent advocates have seemed to distance themselves from the movement they once promoted as the next stage of human evolution. Thus, many of the transhumanist websites, like transhumanism founder Max More's Extropy Institute[23] or Humanity+,[24] have either gone defunct or have not been updated in years. Nonetheless, while card-carrying transhumanism may have lost its popular appeal, the ideas seem loath to die as evidenced by longtermism's growing popularity. So while organizations that append the name "transhumanist" to themselves have waned, university research centers like Cambridge University's Centre for Study of Existential Risk or Lingnan University's Hong Kong Catastrophic Risk Centre and NGOs like the Forethought Foundation for Global Priorities Research or the Institute for the Ethics of Emerging Technologies wrap transhumanist visions up in philosophical justifications.

Transhumanism, at least in its main articulation, is an entirely instrumental-rationality-based philosophy. Movements like the Grinders or democratic transhumanism reject the capitalist orientation, but even James Hughes himself notes that most major forms of transhumanism are libertarian or capitalistic.[25] The vision espoused by More, Bostrom, Kurzweil, and others is one and the same of industrial capitalism: better living through scientific technologies. Bostrom's vision of augmented emotions, cognition, and health through self-directed evolution is just a science fiction spin on the bourgeois fantasy of unlimited wealth.

Insofar as effective altruism is aligned with longtermism, it invariably serves capitalist aims. Thus, while Singer's initial work prioritized helping the global worst off, the effective altruism movement makes no effort to hide that poverty alleviation is actually not the primary focus of their work. While poverty takes the largest amount of funding, Open Philanthropy admits that they spent $43 million on AI and $36 million on other science research in 2017 (and proportionately less the following year).[26] Spending money on AI "risk" amounts to funding already overfunded tech firms, shoveling money into the sorts of causes that give good press to tech moguls without necessarily enacting change. Effective altruism's focus on the next million years justifies ignoring real-world problems among poor and marginalized groups today in favor of AI hype.

Perhaps the answer to *What We Owe the Future* should be focusing on the injustices of the present.

What Is Just?

AI is built for the interests of the rich, and, as such, it clearly does not have the same epistemological framework as the poor. But should it? The arguments put forward by capitalists, the arguments that sustain the capitalist system, say that the system of ideal choice selection toward efficient ends is the optimal system. Efficiency itself is the goal; in the words of Milton Friedman, "The Social Responsibility of Business Is to Increase Its Profits." The profits themselves are the end. Of course, this view is quite a bad-faith position to maintain—profits are pursued for the goods that they provide or are perceived to provide for us. Money as a token is useless if it cannot be exchanged for goods and services: the market must function as a market if profits are to be desirable at all.

Thus, a more honest position is that the efficiency guaranteed by AI systems will improve one's overall life and will contribute more fully to a life worth living. Admitting this, however, reverts the question of AI and its purpose to ethics instead of economics. Ethically, we might agree with Aristotle that a certain amount of material comfort is necessary for living "the good life."[27] We may agree with the utilitarians, who view access to material pleasures to be objectively good. Human rights likewise seem to endorse this view, with support for "an existence worthy of dignity," and "a standard of living adequate for [one's] health and well-being."[28] On any of these or other grounds, AI might justify its position by noting it will improve human lives. The problem, of course, is not that AI will have some material benefit on human lives; the question is whether it will result in a just outcome.

On this question, ethicists diverge. If one holds on to a vision of distributive justice that demands that the needs of all be met to the extent possible, AI becomes suspect. Adam Smith's initial advocacy for the free market was that it would benefit all, but if AI increases the capital of the richest while depriving the laborer of their ability to work, it would be morally detrimental. In line with John Rawls's "difference principle," AI's benefit to the upper classes can be defended only if it improves the outcomes of the poorest by at least the same amount as it improves the wealthiest.[29] Robert Nozick, on the other hand, believes that the market is just when commutations are agreed upon, not when distribution is equal.[30] In this view, then, there is no moral claim that AI must benefit the poor.

These positions, however, are all articulated from the perspective of the bourgeoisie. In Marxian terms, they are part of the hegemonic discourse. Smith, Rawls, and Nozick take bourgeois values of efficiency and ideal choice selection as a given. Even Rawls, in his paradigm-shifting theory of justice, assumes that the "original position" is one that we can abstract from our real situation.[31] In each case, whatever is said about the morality of the market is said from the perspective of those whom the market best serves. There is no question whether that system itself should be undone or whether the market system of valuation is flawed. Bourgeois morality once again refers to its own epistemological biases to justify its position; the "rightness" and "wrongness" of distribution are imagined only in and through the logic of the market. As such, the discussion of AI has hitherto been about its function in establishing bourgeois standards for justice, not about whether or not it will truly be at the service of the poor. To ask whether AI can be just from a poor perspective, we must first decide to inquire about AI from a position of intentional preference for the perspective of the poor.

The Preferential Option for the Poor and Critical Theory of Technology

Sympathy for the poor is, of course, hardly a new concept. The Bible is clear about the moral command to care for those who lack resources. The poor occupy a special place within Israelite society, beginning with God's commands in the Torah. Deuteronomy 15 especially lays out the Mitzvah that wealthy Israelites are to generously aid the poor in their midst.[32] Specific injunctions, such as forgiving debts (Deut 15:7) or leaving crops for gleaning (Lev 19:9), emphasize specific obligations that Israel had to those who were destitute in their midst. Much of the content of the books of the prophets focuses on Israel's failures to serve God alone and to care for the poor, with prophets from Amos to Micah sharply condemning the excesses of the Israelite elite while the poor went without.[33] Even the apparently misogynistic text of Hosea is an indictment against the excesses of the Israelite elite ignoring the needs of the lower classes.[34] The tradition, of course, continues through the New Testament, especially in the Gospel of Luke and the Epistle of St James. From "Remember you were strangers in the land of Egypt" (Lev 19:34) to "Blessed are the poor, for theirs is the kingdom of God" (Luke 6:20), one might characterize the entire biblical ethos with the assessment of Friedrich Nietzsche, as an inversion of the morality of the strong.[35]

Nietzsche, anti-Christ though he is, claims the Christian tradition takes this inverted morality to its logical conclusion—the poor is the one who is to be revered against the powerful and mighty.[36] Certainly the Christian church through the ages has emphasized moral obligation to the worst off, from John Chrysostom condemning the wealthy for using silver chamber pots to the legend of St. Lawrence bringing the poor to Emperor Valerian as the "riches of the church," to St. Francis's beggar-inspired habit, to Frederick Denison Maurice's Christian socialism, to St. Teresa of Calcutta's Nobel Prize–winning work among the poor of India. As Dorothy Day purportedly said, "Those who cannot see Christ in the poor are atheists indeed." John Paul II enshrined liberation theology's option for the poor in magisterial teaching, and Pope Francis emphasizes the need to "give a voice back to the poor."[37] The Christian, especially Catholic, tradition has long emphasized the need to hear the perspective of the poor. But this official story bears repeating precisely because, in the words of Christ, the poor we always have with us.

The slogan "preferential option for the poor," or simply "option for the poor," gets its origin in modern theology from the 1968 Catholic Episcopal Conference of Latin America (CELAM) in Medellín, Colombia. The Jesuit superior of the time, Pedro Arrupe, coined the phrase in correspondences leading up to the conference. In the proceedings of the conference and the theological trends that emerged following, the theology of Latin America developed a clear central focus on the poor. This move was perhaps only natural—the depth of poverty of Latin America in the late twentieth century made it ripe ground for military coups, proxy wars, and economic exploitation by wealthier countries. Seeing the massive suffering of the poor peasantry, theologians such as Juan Luis Segundo, Gustavo Gutiérrez, Leonardo Boff, Jon Sobrino, and Ignacio Ellacuría championed the voices of the worst off against both local and global systems of exploitation. This prophetic witness came dearly for some; St. Oscar Romero, bishop of San Salvador, was murdered as he gave mass because of his advocacy for the worst off, and six Jesuit scholars, including Ellacuría, were murdered in their home at UCA El Salvador.

The primacy of the poor in liberation theology constitutes a paradigm shift within theology. To begin asking the question of what it means to prioritize the poor, liberation theologians note, means recognizing the undeniable aspect of class conflict.[38] The *de facto* mode of doing theology—assuming a universal, nonhistorical perspective—has long been the option for the well-off and hegemonic, and theologians and public figures to this day resist the preferential option under the auspice of impartiality.[39] Such is clear even in magisterial social teachings; although since Leo XIII, the church hierarchy has constantly taught that the poor are to be given economic, political, and social justice, this has usually been in the context of balancing competing interests. *Rerum Novarum*, for example, speaks about just treatment of workers, but also emphasizes workers' duties to employers, treating both sides as if they could be considered equal agonists in labor struggles.[40] Liberation theology begins by recognizing that this perspective is illusory; to claim neutrality is to side with the powerful by default.[41]

As a result, liberation theology follows a Marxian hermeneutic. Such a vision was, and still largely is, seemingly incompatible with good Catholic thought.[42] However, in trying to understand the perspective of the poor, theologians realized they needed to adopt a hermeneutic of praxis.[43] One must encounter the real world, experience it, and let this experience shape the way one understands theology, which in turn shapes how one understands the world.[44] The dialectical procedure follows Marx's own recognition of the dimensions of hegemonic cultural production and oppression of the working class.[45] Material and social conditions must be examined to understand which perspectives are privileged and which mechanisms control the lower classes. Although liberation theologians support socialism as a practical measure, Gutiérrez is clear to note this does not mean the same thing as Marx's vision of violent proletarian revolution.[46] Indeed, many even reject modern versions of socialism, emphasizing that development, as conceived of by industrialized (so-called first-world or second-world) nations, is not the solution for Latin America.[47] Socialism may mean something different, something contextualized by the specific demands of Latin American countries' resources, characters, and needs.

While liberation theology appears a niche form of cultural theology, Gutiérrez emphasizes that the insight of liberation theology praxis is that *all* theology is contextual theology.[48] The Catholic tradition often functions in bad faith in this way—although it is clear from our history that all theology has emerged from contexts, be it the collapse of the Roman Empire in Augustine's *City of God*, medieval academic culture in Thomas Aquinas's *Summa Theologiae*, or the irruption of the urban working class in *Rerum Novarum*, mainstream theologians have long written as though their view is dictated from a universalist, context-free situation. Dogma from second-century christological formulas to nineteenth-century Marian doctrines is tautologically universal, but even the articulation of these dogmas is highly contextualized by metaphysical and linguistic trends.[49] Beyond this, all non-dogmatic theology is certainly subject to influence by its context.

The Catholic Church of the mid-twentieth century was struggling—centuries of only Italian popes and anti-Protestant polemicism could not match the reality of a time when most Catholics lived outside of Europe and lay Catholic John F. Kennedy led the culturally Protestant superpower of the West. Earlier, the ultra-Montanist focus of the First Vatican Council had been brought to an abrupt halt as Italian national forces seized the remaining papal states in 1871. For the next ninety years, the magisterium was mostly on the defensive, trying to maintain relevance in a modern world contextualized by science and technology, capitalism and socialism, nationalism and cosmopolitanism, democracy and colonialism, and fascism and communism, all of which strained the medieval theological imagination of the magisterial church. Popes tried to respond, but always as a reaction: whether it be the middle-road compromise for industrial exploitation,[50] the retrospective prescription against new philosophies,[51] or the authoritarian denunciation of new sciences,[52] the popes of the late nineteenth and early twentieth centuries responded inadequately to problems already too far developed. The Second Vatican Council opened the doors for more honest engagement with the contextual reality of theology, recognizing the need to consider, in the words of the Pastoral Constitution of the Church in the Modern World, "the joys and hopes, the griefs and anxieties of the [people] of this age,"[53] and emphasized the theologian's role as "to hear, distinguish and interpret the many voices of our age, and to judge them in the light of the divine word, so that revealed truth can always be more deeply penetrated, better understood and set forth to greater advantage."[54] And yet, controversies such as Paul VI's controversial anti-contraception 1968 encyclical *Humanae Vitae* reveal a persistent gap between the laity and the hierarchy that persists even today.[55]

The magisterium's typical refusal to acknowledge the contextual nature of theology (despite the Pastoral Constitution of the Church in the Modern World emphasizing the need to pay attention to "the signs of the times" in the church's work) accounts for the hesitancy of the magisterium to accept liberation theology. In 1987, twenty years after Medellín, Pope John Paul II officially made concessions to liberation theology in the social encyclical *Sollicitudo Rei Socialis*, where he acknowledges the priority of the option for the poor.[56] However, unlike the radical orientation to the voice of the poor through praxis advocated by liberation theology, John Paul's treatment of this option is one of mere charity—taking care of the poor is a moral obligation, but the Polish pontiff was hardly going to accept Marxian dialecticism. As such, within magisterial teaching, the obligation is not oriented toward the episteme of the poor; rather, the bourgeois conscience must be slightly pricked to encourage better giving. It is worth noting, however, that in the closing years of the Cold War, this concession was already a controversial stance as neoconservatism slithered its way out of the White House and Westminster and tried to silence whatever prophetic witness the institutional church presented. The US Bishops's pastoral letter "Economic Justice for All," which adopted a position perfectly in line with the then-trajectory of papal social teaching on the economy, earned the ire of Catholic philosopher Michael Novak,

Nobel Prize economist Milton Friedman, and White House communications director Patrick J. Buchanan.[57]

Nonetheless, from the 1980s on, liberation theology has grown in interest, especially among lay academic theologians. In its growth in popularity, the basis of its origins has been challenged. As Marcella Althaus-Reid notes, for example, the first generation of Latin American liberation theologians were primarily priests—educated males inhabiting a privileged place in the church and society. Their own position often blinded them to the hegemonic place they personally inhabited, making it hard for them to recognize other voices.[58] The focus on peasants in the hills of El Salvador, for example, meant ignoring the urban poor in places like Althaus-Reid's Buenos Aires.[59] To compensate for this lack, then, Althaus-Reid adds her own perspective as a queer urban woman. On the other end of the theological spectrum, no one less than Cardinal Josef Ratzinger (Pope Benedict XVI) declared that the liberation theology's emphasis on the poor is too great of an embrace of Marxism, which is bad primarily because of Marxism's emphasis on atheism and violence.[60] Nonetheless, as Korean theologian Anselm Min points out, the work of Gutiérrez and other liberation theologians had an important impact on theologians in other poor nations embroiled in their own birth pangs of development.[61]

The "option for the poor" remains a potent image for Catholic thinkers, a hopeful orientation that they aspire to. Jon Sobrino, echoing his friend and mentor Ignacio Ellacuría, envisions this option through the image of the "civilization of poverty."[62] The civilization of poverty stands in contrast to the US laissez-faire style "civilization of wealth," a society oriented toward acquisition of wealth and prioritization of the bourgeoisie's freedom over the basic needs of the poor. In so many words, the civilization of wealth is typical capitalist society. The civilization of poverty, on the other hand, does not seek infinite growth or acquisition of capital; it prioritizes meeting all human rights and promoting ecological and communal flourishing.[63] The privilege of the individual is subordinated to the basic needs of all across society; the consumer is replaced by the citizen.

While Sobrino's account seems in practice little different from any basic socialist vision, he emphasizes this is an eschatological orientation. He emphasizes numerous hermeneutical implications of this vision, including "giving names to the millions of victims and martyrs" of the poor, "prophetically denouncing the injustice that produces" massive suffering, maintaining "the utopian hope for a new heaven and a new earth," and holding "openness to an ultimate mystery in reality."[64] The theological emphasis on the poor thus contains a moral imperative—to truly be "converted" to this vision means to act on behalf of the poor. As such, the praxis emphasized by Gutiérrez has an inherently teleological function. As we orient ourselves toward the kingdom of God, we work to this end, but doing so requires understanding our current position and the gap between our eschatological vision and the reality of the world. In prioritizing the civilization of poverty, we reorient ourselves to the eschaton, understanding it in new ways, which require new actions. Thus, conversion entails a perpetual dialectical process. Being oriented to the poor requires constant reflection, but it yields a new vision of the reign of God.

This new vision of the civilization of poverty can function as an alternative "sociotechnical imaginary" when dialectically put in conversation with the vision of AI. The sociotechnical imaginary of AI evangelists is really a specific technologized form of the civilization of wealth. The shiny future of automation is nothing but a consumer's fantasy, where every pleasure is somehow satisfied with no cost, where machines automatically maintain everything, where all problems are resolvable through science and technology, where our power is unbounded. It is, in a word, utopian. But it is a utopia told from the impoverished imagination of the industrial upper classes.

In contrast to this imaginary stands the civilization of poverty. A civilization where the voices of the poor are uplifted, where human needs are met, and where profit is subordinate to justice is a necessary corrective to the inhumane way the poor experience the world.[65] This view is just as utopian as the AI fantasy, but the utopia of the civilization of the poor is more authentic to the Christian tradition.[66] This vision takes its cue from the promises God reveals to us: the last shall be first, every tear shall be dried, the nations of the world will gather as one. While some have suggested the Christian vision could be interpreted technologically, with the vision of the New Jerusalem articulated as some advanced cyberpunk world,[67] liberation theologians insist that the eschatological vision of humanity is not an industrialized fantasy.[68] Indeed, in line with Hans Jonas, they recognize that the resources of the earth are limited, and wasting them on the dreams of capitalism inherently means that many will be left out.[69] The energy and resource costs of AI, often ignored in AI literature, show how purely wishful the fantasy of the AI civilization is—in a world of limited resources within an entropic universe, prioritizing costly AI research means depriving the poor of our immediate action.

Put in conversation, then, these two visions, one of the AI utopia and one of the civilization of the poor, function as divergent (to some degree opposite) imaginaries. The "new world" of innovation, the long-time vision of invention and discovery that has spurred on so much of American industry, is enticing. Marvin Minsky, whose pioneering AI work had an outsized impact on the current state of the field, collaborated with science fiction author Arthur C. Clarke, and between the two of them, fictional scenarios inspired scientific research, and scientific prognostications inspired science fiction narratives.[70] But the world constructed by Minsky was not one favorable to the poor (or frankly, to women[71]). His support of amateur hacking inspired the "move fast and break things" ideology of Silicon Valley today,[72] a slogan that translates into externalizing burdens to other people for one's own personal gain. The libertarian techno-utopian vision, adhering in its best version to transhumanist Max More's "proactionary principle,"[73] prefers to steam on ahead into the unknown frontier of technological development. Their worries are about "catastrophic failures" or "existential threats" produced by this technology.[74] It is no exaggeration to say their sights are so fixated on the fantasy of AI consciousness that they do not seem to care about the current, ongoing crises emerging from any number of AI problems, such as ecological devastation, factory accidents, racist AIs, or totalitarian use of AI. These problems are not their concern, rooted, as they are, in a world where solutions to problems are not as simple as mathematical calculations.

The civilization of the poor offers a necessary corrective. Liberation theologians have long argued that the solution to global poverty is not just throwing money at the problem.[75] The solutions of the industrialized nations, the so-called "first world" capitalist countries, are unimaginative capitalist solutions. Rather, argues Sobrino, the vision must start from fulfilling human rights.[76] Ensuring people have adequate food, water, shelter, educational opportunities, safety, and so forth is the starting point, not second-order effects. Of course, this does require economic solutions, but in this instance, economics are subordinate to human well-being. This vision prioritizes every single person; there are no acceptable human losses paving the road to economic prosperity. It is important to see that advanced algorithmic applications are not foreclosed in this vision, but AGI will not be the goal. Rather, a solution such as that of the American Medical Association may be necessary, reframing AI as *augmented* rather than *artificial* intelligence "as a conceptualization of artificial intelligence that focuses on AI's assistive role, emphasizing that its design enhances human intelligence rather than replaces it."[77] Although this redefinition still props up an instrumental rationality view of intelligence, it makes the critical distinction that AI should not function in a normative way as stand-in for human beings. In a world where enough suffering and devastation already occur, AI should be pursued only to the extent that it will actually facilitate the civilization of the poor.

Automated Punishment Systems

The conflict between rich and poor plays out in the realm of AI modeling insofar as the algorithms promise efficient solutions, which is to say require the poor to demonstrate their worthiness and penalize those who are deemed unfit.[78] There is a centuries-long tradition of policing the poor, demanding that they demonstrate their worthiness to receive aid from those in power. In early Republican Ireland, for example, the poor who wrote letters to seek aid from the Dublin archbishop did so with full knowledge of how they were seen as either deserving or undeserving in the eyes of the church.[79] While many made the case that they were, in fact, deserving of the archbishop's sympathy (as pious, faithful heads of families with numerous children enrolled in Catholic schools), some "undeserving" were able to elicit sympathy with the promise of moral reformation.[80] In the United States, definitions of the poor and conditions for providing welfare have differed based on economic conditions: in times of economic boom, those eligible for aid were those unable to work, while in times of economic bust, it was the newly unemployed who gained priority.[81] At the same time, methods for measuring poverty have typically been arbitrary, dependent upon whose interests were best served by defining the situation by income, education, holdings, family size, job, or other factors.[82] All of these standards are dictated and controlled by those in positions. Thus, to demonstrate their desert, the poor always have to conform to the expectations of the upper classes. These upper classes, in turn, set conditions and expectations for the poor in order to keep them in line and subjugated.

The difficulty of managing an uncontrollable mass of humans, however, especially if one is unwilling to indiscriminately provide for all who ask, requires the construction of metrics that allow the filtering of the needy. Social sciences and bureaucracies, two of the three elements Hannah Arendt notes characterize "mass society" (the third being conformity),[83] provide a critical framework for managing the poor. Economics and demographics give us the means to reduce humans to numerical values that can be weighed and calculated; psychology and sociology give us the tools to explain, shape, and motivate behavior; political science and geography give us the ability to divide and disenfranchise; and layers of bureaucracy allow us to create hurdles for the poor to access what resources are earmarked for them. Algorithmic rationality is perfectly suited for the intricate web created by decades worth of records, best practices, regulatory frameworks, economic valuations, and other criteria established to track and manage the poor. Advocates for using large-scale algorithmic processes believe these will be more efficient, providing objective answers to who deserves and does not deserve aid, providing better distribution of resources to needed areas, and lowering the overall costs of all work involved. In other words, the instrumental rationalist approach that supports the rich should be able to benefit the poor. Unfortunately, the record on this front has not been very persuasive.

Those in power seek to carefully police potentially dangerous elements of society. In a capitalist society, this means the poor (and in a racist society, this also means any who are not part of the racial majority). But the practice of policing is inherently reactive—one waits for crimes to be committed instead of preventing them from occurring. For this reason, everyone in society would benefit (omitting, of course, criminals) from the ability to prevent crime rather than just respond to it. One might suppose that past criminal activity is indicative, in some measure, of future likelihood. Under this assumption, one might take data from a populace on reported and arrested crimes and use this to predict areas where policing is necessary with the hope of preventing crime or catching crime *in situ*. Thus, a program like PredPol, which uses data from policing to predict where and when crimes are likely to occur, seems like a highly useful tool that would benefit all, especially those most likely to be victims of serious crimes, i.e., the poor. However, the reality is that PredPol merely reinforces the existing biases of the upper classes against the poor. The belief that crimes are more prevalent in poor neighborhoods is reinforced by PredPol predicting crimes that lead to arrests and prosecution. Police patrol neighborhoods recommended by PredPol, find crime, and report the data to the system, reinforcing the connection between crime and these neighborhoods.[84] At no point in this process is the question asked whether other neighborhoods might also have similar levels of criminality; the neighborhoods police were patrolling already are the neighborhoods PredPol recommends they continue to patrol. The assumptions and biases police operated on for decades appear vindicated by the "objectivity" of the machine, but only because the machine operates with data derived from assumptions and biases of the police.[85] Thus, the old and tired model of "broken window" policing, disproven repeatedly by criminal justice reform advocates, gains algorithmic justification through a process of policing, reporting, calculating, predicting, and repeating. Not only does this not make anyone safer but it further punishes the poor, directing more resources to punitive responses than to rebuilding or empowering communities.

Even when algorithms are constructed for aiding rather than harming the poor, the results tend to maintain the destitution and desperation of the poor. In 2009, the State of Indiana implemented a largely automated system for its welfare distribution program. The stated aim was "to clean up welfare waste . . . [to] make America's worst welfare system better for the people it serves, a much fairer deal for taxpayers, and for its own employees."[86] The ultimate strategy of this automation was "smaller welfare rolls, whatever the cost."[87] This amounted to replacing case workers with decentralized agents, digitizing paper-based documentation, and hiring untrained call center staff, among other things. The result was that many Hoosiers were kicked off welfare during a time when welfare rates were rising across the US due to the Great Recession. From the perspective of Governor Mitch Daniels and those most swayed by his political vision, the program was a success, but for the Hoosiers who lost their health coverage because of bureaucratic anonymity, it was traumatic. The system penalized workers who did not resolve cases in a "timely" fashion. But the welfare applications themselves were complex, requiring years' worth of collected documentation, by which impoverished Hoosiers could "prove" the desert of their welfare claims. Prior to the change, case workers typically had intimate knowledge of their clients' situations and had been able to help address any incongruencies between clients' records and state records. Governor Daniels, however, eliminated this policy, claiming that it was an invitation to welfare fraud.[88] As a consequence, untrained call center employees, handling multiple cases with anonymity, often encouraged haggard poor Hoosiers to reapply for benefits rather than leave their cases open.[89] On paper, the system worked: fewer people were on welfare and the state was saving money. The reality for those in poverty, however, was disaster. The logic of efficiency sat squarely at odds with the human concerns of poor Hoosiers. "Response time in the call centers was a key performance indicator; determination accuracy was not. Efficiency and savings were built into the contract; transparency and due process were not."[90]

The poor, accustomed as they are to the struggle for survival, have learned to adapt to the demands of instrumental rationality. Abandoned by the state welfare system that had already devalued them until they could prove their worth, they strategized how to survive. Even those who had been meticulous in their cases, becoming experts in welfare law and keeping copies of years' worth of documents in duplicate and triplicate, found themselves scrambling. Knowing that face-to-face appointments had to be honored, Hoosiers flooded welfare offices, overwhelming case workers.[91] Volunteers helped organize town hall meetings, inviting the press, inviting community members through flyers dropped in Dollar Tree shopping bags and calling out Daniels's team in public, forcing them to reckon with the violence their strategy had committed.[92] In the end, poor Hoosiers were able to get Daniels's government to abandon its automation strategy, but the legal proceedings following recast the spectacle into a matter of failed contract language, ignoring the problem of reducing poverty strategies to algorithmic efficiency models.[93] The problem, then, as determined by the ruling class, was not instrumental rationality *per se* but rather the specific contours of the contract set out by the State of Indiana and IBM.

The ruling class sets the conditions for financial and legal success, and the poor are subjected to the rules for their own survival. When the rules are opaque, as in the case of Indiana's welfare system, even the ruling class can be turned against the system. But if the rules are articulated in a way that is comprehensible to the poor, the ruling class assumes that they are "fair," regardless of how dramatically they favor the privileged. One can see this illustrated in the US federal allocation of grant moneys based on digital training, making funding opportunities for schools, libraries, and work placement dependent upon how well these institutions prepare their constituents for a digital economy.[94] To adapt to these rigorous demands, all of these institutions have to "bootstrap," that is, adapt their models and services to the specific demands of the new digital culture as laid out by governmental agencies, often supporting large private technology enterprises.[95] Whether or not these policy changes achieved their ends is entirely beside the point. If schools want to survive, they need not actually educate their students or prepare them for the actual skills they will need to survive; rather, they need to implement digital strategies that will be measurable through some arbitrary bureaucratic program.[96] Of course, in the perverse self-reinforcing logic of the market, those schools that comply are given more funding, which turns into more digitization, which produces more funding, and whether or not the students are being served is never truly addressed. Those schools that question the logic of this, the usefulness of private IT companies dominating their classrooms or the waste of economic resources to empower already-wealthy tech tycoons over struggling teachers, are cut off from funding.

Algorithmic policies enrich tech company contractors and penalize the beneficiaries who must continually prove their numerical worth. In the most perverse self-referential way, the rich prove the goodness of their economic valuation by enriching the rich and impoverishing the poor as a strategy for poverty alleviation. The poor are regulated by the instrumental rationality of the capitalist system, the same system that has already relegated them to the "lower" classes. The digital processes verify mathematically the devaluation of the poor and the overvaluation of the rich, reinforcing the instrumental rationality underwriting their employment. Cyberneticism is the social process: feedback upon feedback, all of which is directed toward the promotion of the Civilization of Wealth. The poor respond in various ways, "bootstrapping" to accommodate the values of the rich, rallying to ensure their community survives, gaming the system to achieve the outcomes meant to be made unreachable, or functioning altogether outside of the system. But in this, they always play catch-up, a losing game that becomes more difficult as algorithms become more prominent and more trusted.

Poor AI

In line with the philosophy of Andrew Feenberg, the fact that AI has hitherto been only used in ways that suppress the poor is not only not surprising, it's inevitable. Feenberg's critical work on technology involves what he calls "critical theory of technology" and "critical constructivism." His earlier work on "critical theory of technology" notes that because modern technologies in the West are situated within capitalist societies, they are typically oriented toward capitalist goals and not toward "democratic" (i.e., socialist) goals.[97] The reason modern technologies tend to be, by default, anti-democratic is because they are constructed and used in the rationality of capitalism, that is, within the logic of efficiency and instrumentalism.[98] Since these technologies are constructed within the logic of market capitalism, they reinforce the hegemony of capitalist rationality, giving the illusion that the constructed notion of right and wrong reasoning is a preexisting universalist structure.[99] In a feedback loop, capitalism gives birth to new technologies that function according to principles of efficiency, and these technologies in turn reify the principles of capitalist logic. Feenberg draws much of this insight from critical theorist Herbert Marcuse, who argues that modern sciences and technologies have been constructed to create "one dimensional society," a social system wherein every facet of human living, from work to political participation to consumption to leisure to sex to sleep, has been quantified and instrumentalized.[100] It is important to note for Marcuse, and consequently for Feenberg, this is not strictly a process of intentional manipulation but is a function of repression fostered within civilization *à la* Freud.[101]

The solution for Feenberg is "democratic technology," a fundamental shift in the way technology is constructed and used. He thus contends this requires "three transitional processes: *socialization*, *democratization*, and *innovation*,"[102] which involve returning the means of production to the masses, educating the masses against instrumental rationality, and avoiding the trap of slow bureaucratic breakdown. Chief among these problems, however, seems to be the problem of instrumental rationality; so long as this is the hegemonic framework directing technology, technology will inevitably be directed toward the goals of the hegemony. Thus, "Critical Theory attacks capitalism by attacking its forms of rationality."[103] To create technology that goes beyond market efficiency and the interests of the capitalist class requires deliberative efforts, an intentional aim at creating technology not beholden to questions of profit maximization. Feenberg recognizes this process will be difficult, as democratizing efforts that come in after a technology has been released tend to be reactionary. As a result, technologies need to be intentionally built with values integrated into the technological design.[104] Given the current and previous failures of AI to adequately take the interests and needs of the poor seriously, this lends us one remaining possibility for directing AI to the service of the poor: if AI is built for the poor from the ground up, with the values and interests of the poor built into the technological machinery, it could be a useful instance of what Feenberg calls a democratic technology.

Marcella Althaus-Reid offers a glimpse of what this might look like in an article from a 2003 volume of *Concilium*. Althaus-Reid discusses the Argentinian website liquidacion.org, a place where transvestite sex workers in Buenos Aires sell recordings of their dreams.[105] This "archive from hell" creates a reverse flow of power: the rich must pay for the privilege of hearing the stories of the poor.[106] The requirement to pay turns the logic of capitalism on its head—it is the rich coming to the poor for what they can provide rather than the reverse. Of course, there is a perverse voyeurism involved: the poor who sell their dreams are sexual minorities, and some of the dreams involve sexual content. The poor still do not enjoy the full privilege of being autonomous subjects, viewed as they are as sexual objects. The taboo nature of transvestite prostitution is enticing to the upper classes, whose appetites are satisfied by transgressing boundaries.[107] Nonetheless, Althaus-Reid theorizes that encountering these voices can have a eucharistic effect, bringing the wealthy directly into contact with the dreams of the wretched poor.[108]

Similarly, then, could narrow AIs be constructed to plead the case of the poor? If the internet provided an opportunity for the voices of Buenos Aires's sex workers to be heard around the world, AI could be *imagined* in such a way as well. Taking into consideration Feenberg's view of democratic technology, let us imagine a "poor AI." We should imagine a specific form of narrow AI so as to make the AI serve the interests of the poor specifically. The AI will be created, from beginning to end, with the "conscious rationality" of the interests of the poor directed to its design and implementation. The "anonymity" of the millions of poor is a strength in this case: the sheer volume of data that can be collected from the poor can be used for their benefit. The simplistic models that AI operate on can be framed through a poor epistemology rather than one for the bourgeoisie. The end goal of AI can be directed toward the civilization of poverty over the civilization of wealth. But all of this would have to be done very deliberately to avoid the pitfalls of capitalist rationality. Thus, from the early planning steps to its development, training, and eventual deployment, it will be entirely directed toward the subjectivity of the poor, and the poor will need to be involved in every step.

First, the entire funding and planning stage needs to be freed from capitalist logic. This is a difficult task as funders nearly always want a clear return on investment. Telling wealthy donors that their money is going to be deployed as a weapon against the rule of the upper classes is unlikely to be met with favor by those who have sacrificed other values for the sake of oversized stock portfolios. Perhaps governmental agencies or NGOs may be better sources, but they are likely to still demand some returns, usually cost savings or influence. However, regardless of the goodness of other intentions, once the money is earmarked for economically rational ends, the project itself will be infected by capitalist goals. Rather than framing the project in the economic terms of savings or waste, the focus should rather be outlined in terms of humanizing the poor. The goals will need to be ultimately independent of any sort of quantifiable economic determination, despite the fact that it must be codifiable into numerical data sets and should help the economically vulnerable.

Given that the focus is narrow AI, specific solutions like patient care, social policy, labor assistance, community empowerment, criminal justice reform, and the like can be set as goals. AI has to be directed toward a specific aim because this will frame the model we develop, as well as the data we seek to collect. AI should be directed toward mathematical solutions; a general "poor AI" would be a worse fantasy than the bourgeois AGI fantasy at present. But there are goals the bourgeoisie, especially conscientious persons, and the poor share. To avoid the temptation for the bourgeoisie to steer the project to their own interests, to co-opt the voices of the poor, the aims and goals of the project will need to be articulated by those the project is designed to help, i.e., the poor themselves. It would be helpful, then, to have poor people involved who can devote themselves to seeing this project through from start to conclusion, but in the condition of poverty, defined as it is by its precariousness, one's well-being easily deteriorates depending on entirely contingent circumstances. Thus, another obstacle will be providing means to ensure that people whose lives are defined by precarity are able to be continually involved. Since the poor are those whose voices must direct the project, this is a necessary step in the design process.

Assuming this obstacle can be overcome, that the project itself can be authentically directed to the end of empowering the poor, then the next step is creating an AI model to work with. Since AIs are models based off of human biases, the humans who program the model will program it with their own conceptions and biases.[109] The white male programmers who made facial recognition programs that had lower accuracy rates for people of color, especially Black women, were likely not trying to make a deliberately racist AI; rather, they were merely unaware of the unconscious biases that shaped their perspective on the world. If we want an AI that truly upholds the option for the poor, then it will have to reflect the biases of the poor instead of the wealthy. The rules that set the standard for the AI, as well as the conditions of success, will need to be set by the poor rather than the bourgeoisie.

This means, of course, training poor persons to be computer programmers. Two dangers arise with this aim. The first is related to the fact that computer programming is made attractive as a field because of its economic benefits. The cultural fascination with STEM (Science, Technology, Engineering, and Medicine) is economic as a rule: parents want their children to have jobs in these fields because such jobs are lucrative and seen as stable. Decoupling the incentive to program computers from economic maximalization is the first challenge, but it is fraught with compromised conditions: if the programming is purely voluntary, then the work done by those poor who contribute will be clearly exploited, but if it is subjected to typical capitalist measures (e.g., hourly wage or wage by production), then the logic of capitalism pervades once again.

The second danger here lies in the fact that the process of training for programming is inherently indoctrinating. As Papert and Turkle point out, computer science education tends to be deeply dogmatic—those who do not "think" as the earlier generations of programmers are dissuaded from continuing.[110] Though this may not be necessary for computer programming as a whole, the process of developing an entire way of doing AI from scratch would be a sizable challenge. Additionally, though a "liberationist" AI expert may lead the charge of training poor AI researchers—as in Freire's pedagogical model—the problem of hegemonic voices dictating to the poor what they should believe remains.

Assuming these two obstacles can somehow be avoided (or, more likely, minimized) and kept in full view, the next step will be to teach the machine to "think" like the poor. This task is the most promising on the whole, but once again must be done carefully. The data fed to the machine should be data generated by and selected by the poor. There are many poor—over ten million in the US by American standards, and 420 million worldwide according to global poverty standards. Despite the rhetoric of liberation theologians, each of these persons has stories, a name, information about the world, their own thoughts, relationships, narratives, dreams, aspirations, and so forth. Generating data from the poor (rather than from the privileged) means whatever output we are going to get will, by definition, slant toward the poor (for better or worse).

A challenge on this front will be selecting what the criteria are for good data and what data points we hope to examine. This, once again, will need to be decided by the poor. Determining what constitutes success with the AI's execution or which points to focus on in data is a deliberate choice, informed by ideologies operant in the programmer. In coding a story for data, one can focus on specific verbs, characters, settings, linguistic turns, or some other criterion. In coding computer vision, one can select for shades, tones, shapes, colors, or other criteria. Letting the poor determine what constitutes "valuable" data inscribes into the very machinery of the AI the values that the poor hold.

Envision, briefly, a scenario that might illustrate this goal. Assume a government agency earmarks several millions of dollars for a program to reduce criminal recidivism. In the original planning phase, they should consult with poor representatives of various communities across the US, including both rural and urban settings, different regions, and different ethnic groups, at a minimum, especially people from communities where recidivism is more common. This stage will include determining what the goals are—decreased police presence, increased accountability, better criminal reform, more sensible crime prevention, or whatever. Criminal justice research is developed enough to give us some ideas about good directions and failures. Since the entire criminal justice enterprise, from commission of property crimes to policing to sentencing, disproportionately affects the poor (especially poor of color in the US), they should be directly involved in outlining the terms of success for the program. The Department of Justice and various experts will have their own theories on what to do, but if the project is really meant to give voice to the poor, then the poor, especially from disproportionately affected communities, will need to design and program the AIs that will be developed. Finally, data taken from the poor, including the incarcerated, the formerly incarcerated, victims of crimes, victims of police violence, families of these people, and so forth, will need to be collected and used to train the AI. What data is considered relevant and how it is to be coded will need to be determined by the poor to avoid the sort of racist reinforcements found in other criminal justice algorithms like PredPol or LSI-R.[111] Assuming all of these steps are carried out deliberately, the AI that results should be better able to convey the voices of the poor than ordinary means and provide better insights, results, and directions for action than current bureaucratic means.

In creating a poor AI, the bias toward AI in favor of human speakers at this point is an advantage: the "objective" nature of AI (the mathematical inscription of bias) is trusted by the bourgeois listener more than the voice of the poor person. The mathematical logic, the bourgeoisie's stock-in-trade, is turned on its head at this point. The bias in favor of the computer over the "self-interested" poor becomes a bias *in favor* of the poor when the algorithm is constructed through the eyes of the poor. Notably, the project gains the confidence demonstrated by Daniels's welfare program while actually being oriented around the poor and not the wealthy economic liberals.

Of course, in the end, many obstacles still present themselves and show that even this project is fantasy. The very mathematical model of AI is most conducive to instrumental rationality. Everything has to be converted to numbers in AI, and the rule-based systems favor outcomes that are mathematically justified. Additionally, the poor themselves involved in the project may harbor their own biases toward other poor persons through false consciousness, or they may still assume the conditions of success are predominantly bourgeois in nature, knowing, as they do, the "rules" operant in bourgeois society. Given the deeply bourgeois history of computer and data science, it may be impossible to correct the baked-in assumptions and biases that have governed the discipline for its seventy-year lifespan. AI still remains a tool contextualized by the ascendancy of Anglophone big science in the twentieth century, and the ideologies that governed each generation of researchers, from the early days of female programmers to the libertarian sweep through the early aughts to present technocrats, are hardcoded in. A total subversion of this history is highly unlikely as each generation builds upon the sum of existing assumptions and values. So it remains ultimately doubtful whether AI can ever be anything but tool for reinforcing the hegemony of bourgeois instrumental rationality. AI remans calculative machinery, designed to maximize outputs and streamline processes through a singular, universalizing "right way." As such, at best it will elevate some of the poor to the status of the wealthy, merely shuffling the deck, as it were. The technology already embodies the values of the upper classes, and these cannot be extracted from the machinery. AI is the capitalist tool *par excellence*, and it seems doubtful whether these master tools could ever be used, in the phrase of Audre Lorde, to dismantle the master's house.[112]

Conclusion: Can Liberation Theology Fix AI?

The problem of trying to make bourgeois machines resemble the worst off reveals an inbuilt flaw in all efforts to advocate for the poor. Liberation theology's major shortcoming is simply an extension of Althaus-Reid's critique—those who do liberation theology tend not to write from the perspective of those whom they seek to lift up. Stephen Bede Scharper seems to inadvertently admit just this much in claiming "only the non-poor can opt for the poor."[113] The well-intentioned claims of Gutiérrez and Sobrino that the poor are those unnamed millions, or those who cannot speak, means that, in spite of Gutiérrez's own claim otherwise, the task of liberation theologians is to speak on behalf of the poor.[114] Bourgeois, European, ordained, male theologians such as Ellacuría or Sobrino, by making the poor voiceless, can inhabit the space of the poor in front of the bourgeoisie.

The result, then, is that while the view of liberation theology does sharply challenge the hegemonic, capitalist orientation of AI research, it does not succeed in replacing the bourgeois hegemonic worldview with one of the poor. The civilization of poverty that Sobrino aspires to should be informed by the voices, the unique perspectives, of the poor. Given that the poor whom Sobrino walked among were in his accurate words, unable to "take life for granted,"[115] their every interaction with this professorial Spanish priest has to be understood through the lens of survival. Is it any wonder Sobrino is led to believe "salvation comes from the poor"?[116] Given that being close to a priest offers a strategic position for benefits for the poor (whether through the supernatural intercession of God or through cultural or economic opportunities), so it is no wonder Sobrino's portrayal of the poor smacks of romantic infantilizations. Earner-Byrne's poor in Ireland demonstrated keen awareness of how they would be perceived by the sympathetic bourgeois clergy and used this to their advantage. The way they portrayed themselves betrays the simplistic reading of the poor for Sobrino. In Sobrino's construction of the world, the poor "offer more" than the wealthy, granting the privileged the chance to be saved, only demanding in return a few pesos for their own survival.[117] In spite of the emphasis on the priority of the poor, the bourgeois theologian cannot see beyond his own classed perspective. The poor exist for *his* salvation. They remain objects in Sobrino's language, still nameless, still voiceless, still references for his own subjectivity. Rather, the scandalous inverse should be expressed: *damnation* comes from the poor, particularly in our inability to listen to them.[118] Just as the paradigmatic expressions of poverty, in his eyes, are the "named" martyrs of Ellacuría and Romero, the "nameless thousands" (apparently voicelessly) accuse all those still beholden to privileged views.[119]

In the wash, then, the Catholic liberation tradition maintains a sort of bad-faith position. We are to listen to the voices of the poor, Gutiérrez tells us, and "not pretend to be—as is said many times with goodwill that we are all aware of—'the voice of the voiceless.'"[120] And yet, he maintains the poor are those who are voiceless and nameless.[121] At the same time, the solidarity of the poor is articulated by the spontaneous consciousness of the poor regarding their plight in view of the spirit of history, resulting in them organizing around this shared understanding.[122] And yet, Paulo Freire recognizes that this consciousness requires pedagogy—the poor must be educated about their interests.[123] We are to be in solidarity with the poor, and yet, we are supposed to educate them about their position in society. It is as if "with goodwill that we are all aware of," the liberation theologians and other privileged ambassadors of the poor have pulled an elaborate bait-and-switch, announcing the need to hear the poor and, just as we are about to hear the voice of the poor, informing us that the poor themselves need to be told about their position first.

"Can the subaltern speak?" Gayatri Spivak provocatively asked in 1988. "The ventriloquism of the speaking subaltern is the left intellectual's stock-in-trade."[124] The poor do not speak, as Gutiérrez notes, being "voiceless," but this does not stop attempts to speak for them. In the preliminary example Spivak gives, Foucault and Deleuze-Guattari each in turn claim the voice of the masses speak their position better than they can themselves, despite the apparent ambiguity of the situation![125] Spivak, herself an upper-class Brahman academic, further illustrates the problem through the intractable positions of colonized men and white middle-class women both trying to align the interests of the colonized woman with their interests.[126] Within the ideological struggle, Indian women, in the account Spivak provides about the case of widow immolation, are the casualties accepted by white feminists and Indian men for political victories.

Spivak concludes that the subaltern can speak, a conclusion that seems to favor the "hear the voices of the poor" view of liberation theology. However, she misses the irony of her own conclusion—she reads into the story of the suicide of a young woman named Bhubaneswari an authentic choice of "death before dishonor" in response to a failed assassination plot.[127] Spivak laments that the woman's family is unable to "understand" what she did or why—they interpret it as an act of shame from illicit sex. Spivak concludes her interpretation is correct because of old letters she found, but she does not ask the self-reflective question of whether her own interest as an advocate for the poor is itself an imposition on the reading. Her interpretation forces a reading; it may be a true reading, but it forecloses other readings as well, including the reading of Bhubaneswari's closest surviving family members. To accept Spivak's interpretation is itself to let someone else speak on behalf of the poor. To let the dead Bhubaneswari "speak," Spivak must silence the voices of those closest in situation and life to her.

Here, then, is the crucial problem at hand for the question of the voices of the poor: if they are not admitted to the conversation as equals, we can never allege that their voices are truly heard. Indeed, it is a violent act to conclude that one has the proper interpretation of any person's words, and every reading changes the meaning of the text, even the author's own reading.[128] But if the words of the poor are not heard, are not given similar places to those of the upper classes, are not clarified by the speakers, are not accepted by those who are purported to be spoken, then in no way can we say we hear them. At a bare minimum, we can take Jürgen Habermas's communicative action as a standard—if the poor do not agree in good faith with the position that they ostensibly articulate, then we must say that the position does not reflect their voices and is unjust to them.[129]

Without a chance for the poor to speak authentically and correct the record, we can never say that we have heard their voices. However, as an oppressed group, their voices are inherently disvalued. Can academic discourse take seriously the half-literate scrawlings of high school drop-outs? When grammar and syntax function as gatekeeping mechanisms, who among the upper classes will truly listen to the ignorant drawls of rural farmers? When stupidity and poverty function in cultural discourse as synonyms, how can anyone in a position of power take seriously words spoken from the cast-offs?

More importantly, when the poor know the score—know the way they are viewed in society—they never speak authentically. The peasant who appeals to Fr. Sobrino with piety and reverence knows that it will be better for them to appear meek and humble. The laborer who speaks with the union organizer may see an opportunity for advancement if they cooperate. The inner-city mother who speaks with the social worker understands that the state wants to hear certain things if she is going to receive any benefit. The homeless addict understands how they are viewed by passersbys and what they expect of homeless addicts and responds accordingly, either with "honest" confessions of drug use or with claims of "honest" need. The poor already exist within an ongoing conversation in which they are spoken *about*, and in which they are expected to play certain roles.[130] The freedom, the play that the upper classes flaunt, their so-called agency, operates on stereotypes of who the poor are. The heuristic operations we follow, thinking we know what this or that type of person thinks or needs, shape our own free action. The reality, of course, is that we are trapped within our own frameworks—the hegemonic order that keeps the poor out also keeps the bourgeoisie within. So within the established means, the typical educational processes, media outlets, or political channels, the voice of the poor is always an interpreted voice, spoken by a third party, whose veracity can never be trusted because they are already three times removed from the mind of the poor—first by how the speaker's words are received and heard; second by their own interpretation; and finally, by the poor's own perspective filtered for bourgeois ears to hear.

The reason why this is necessarily the case is because the poor are, and remain, the symptom of the upper classes. As Younghak Hyun reveals in his excursus on minjung theology, the Korean minjung, often rendered in English as "the people," entails the peasants, the urban poor, and the factory workers.[131] As Jae-sik Ko remarks about this characterization, it is "so inclusive and symbolic that it lacks an analytical, concrete perception of people."[132] True as this is, it serves a useful function for the minjung theologian as much as "the poor" serve a useful function for the liberation theologian, as the "subaltern" for Spivak or "the proletariat" for Lukács. The upper classes do not exist without the poor to serve as their foil; the liberation theologian loses their calling without faceless and nameless poor for them to advocate for. The "poor" in their unindividuated faceless mass are the "symptom" of the other classes, the projection of the consciousness of those in positions of power, whether they intend to subordinate the poor as capitalists do or use the poor as a substitute for their own position as the liberation theologians do. In any case, the poor remain obscured, barred. Their interests as expressed by those who are not poor are never truly their own interests. And as a subordinated class, their interests are always filtered through the consciousnesses of the upper classes. But more importantly, as a class, they are never who they are—they are constituted by the capitalist logic of the hegemony. Generalities must be the rule, and insofar as the upper classes write the culture, the poor always exist as poor only in dominated ways. Individual poor can be individuals, but whenever they speak on behalf of the poor, it is always done within the constellation of upper-class hegemonic culture.

CONCLUSION

The Tyranny of Rationality

IN 1927, THE Supreme Court of the United States ruled in *Buck v Bell* that the Virginia Sterilization Act of 1924 did not violate the Due Process Clause of the Fourteenth Amendment for the "feebleminded," who were forcibly sterilized "for the protection and health of the state."[1] The new sciences of evolutionary biology and genetics were combined, in the early twentieth century, into the pseudoscience of eugenics. While most people today associate eugenics with the Nazis' death camps, the movement really began from the work of British polymath Francis Galton, who tried to justify the racist stratification of British society with appeals to national heritage. The rather straightforward scientific principle of selection and adaptation proposed by his cousin Charles Darwin—ostensibly a brute description—was given normative force in his idea that some were "well-born" while others were not.[2] The United States, with its ethnic diversity due to a history of slavery and immigration, was ripe grounds for the development of the eugenics movement. Wealthy whites, in fear of being overrun by larger numbers of the poor, both white and non-white, began campaigning to instantiate normative claims about the "good" and "bad" (or "fit" and "unfit") into social policy via a vehicle of scientific language.

The eugenics movement in the US had strong financial backings behind it. The fortunes of Carnegie and Rockefeller underwrote the movement,[3] and cereal mogul J. H. Kellogg founded the Race Betterment Foundation.[4] In 1914, Harry Laughlin proposed a "Model Sterilization

Law," which targeted "socially inadequate persons," including the following classes:

> (1) Feeble-minded; (2) Insane, (including the psychopathic); (3) Criminalistic (including the delinquent and wayward); (4) Epileptic; (5) Inebriate (including drug-habitués); (6) Diseased (including the tuberculous, the syphilitic, the leprous, and others with chronic, infectious and legally segregable diseases); (7) Blind (including those with seriously impaired vision); (8) Deaf (including those with seriously impaired hearing); (9) Deformed (including the crippled); and (10) Dependent (including orphans, ne'er-do-wells, the homeless, tramps and paupers).[5]

Laughlin's model law became the basis for Virginia's Racial Integrity Act of 1924, which banned racial miscegenation (repealed by *Loving v Virginia* in 1967), and the Virginia Sterilization Act. This latter act was targeted more specifically than Laughlin's—it only applied to people "afflicted with hereditary forms of insanity that are recurrent, idiocy, imbecility, feeble-mindedness or epilepsy."[6]

In 1924, the Virginia State Colony for Epileptics and the Feebleminded decided to carry out this law on Carrie Buck, an eighteen-year-old resident of the institution who had been raped by her adoptive family's nephew and became pregnant as a result.[7] Buck's guardian appealed the move, which made its way up to the Supreme Court. In an eight-to-one decision, the Court ruled in favor of the law. Justice Oliver Wendell Holmes, who wrote the majority opinion, appealed to "public welfare" as the justification and stated, "It is better for all the world, if instead of waiting to execute degenerate offspring for crime, or to let them starve for their imbecility, society can prevent those who are manifestly unfit from continuing their kind."[8] The law remained in place in Virginia until 1979 and resulted in 7,325 individuals being sterilized.[9]

Ted Kaczynski was a math prodigy who entered Harvard University on scholarship at sixteen and graduated at twenty. His doctoral dissertation, completed when he was just twenty-five years old, won him the

Sumner B. Myers Prize for best mathematics dissertation at the University of Michigan. His dissertation advisor Allen Shields referred to Kaczynski as "the best man I've ever seen" and noted the dissertation was "the best I have ever directed."[10]

Despite being a gifted mathematician, Kaczynski is most renowned for being the Unabomber. From 1978 to 1995, Kaczynski mailed bombs to university personnel, computer store owners, and airline personnel, killing three and injuring twenty-three others.[11] His intention, as laid out in the infamous "Unabomber Manifesto," was revolution—a return to nature against the industrial present.[12] His targets were those he considered technophiles (better would be technocrats), those who believe science and technology will truly "relieve man's estate" in the words of Francis Bacon. Kaczynski, on the other hand, opens his manifesto thus:

> The Industrial Revolution and its consequences have been a disaster for the human race. They have greatly increased the life-expectancy of those of us who live in "advanced" countries, but they have destabilized society, have made life unfulfilling, have subjected human beings to indignities, have led to widespread psychological suffering (in the Third World to physical suffering as well) and have inflicted severe damage on the natural world. The continued development of technology will worsen the situation. It will certainly subject human beings to greater indignities and inflict greater damage on the natural world, it will probably lead to greater social disruption and psychological suffering, and it may lead to increased physical suffering even in "advanced" countries.

The reality of Kaczynski's rising star as a mathematics genius, a paragon of STEM education, contrasts sharply with his anti-modern terror spree. The targets of his bombs included engineering professors, computer store owners, and a geneticist, as well as airlines, an advertising executive, a timber lobbyist, and a psychologist. The common thread between STEM careers and all the others, on Kaczynski's own account, is they all promote the industrialist vision. Sacrificing nature, whether human or environmental, for technoscientific control resulted, he averred, in untold suffering in our era. Kaczynski himself had famously moved to Montana after a brief stint in California to pursue a "primitive" lifestyle but found the destructive nature of a nearby wilderness development to be unbearable.[13] Thus, Kaczynski's life trajectory moved from UC Berkeley math professor to Montana recluse to domestic terrorist.

And yet, this does not tell the full story. Kaczynski was inspired by sociologist and theologian Jacques Ellul,[14] who, although a famous critic of technological society, also famously condemns any use of violence. Clearly, Kaczynski's campaign of violence is not merely attributable to his love of Ellul or dissatisfaction with his promising mathematics career. In fact, his targeting of psychology professor James McConnell, and the clear disdain for psychology in his manifesto, seem to owe their genesis to his own trauma and fractured psychological formation.

Three events in Kaczynski's young life most clearly lay out his undoing. First, he skipped sixth grade, resulting in him being bullied by his older peers.[15] All accounts of Kaczynski from then on, especially from his University of Michigan professors and UC Berkeley colleagues, depict him as a loner, socially awkward, and isolated. Second, at Harvard, he participated in a three-year-long experiment that involved weekly bouts of verbal abuse and humiliation.[16] Kaczynski's lawyers claimed that his invective against mind control gets its origin from this moment.[17] Finally, while at the University of Michigan, Kaczynski found himself extremely sexually frustrated and fantasized that the only way he could touch a woman was to undergo gender transition.[18] While in the waiting room to see a psychiatrist, he was overcome by shame and decided to lie to the doctor instead. According to Kaczynski's writings, he decided he wanted to kill the psychiatrist and his mood suddenly brightened, "like a phoenix rising from the ashes of my despair to a glorious new hope."[19]

The picture of Kaczynski is thus complicated. It is easy to dismiss Kaczynski either as a right-wing terrorist or as the manifestation of liberalism,[20] but his manifesto defies this explanation. He had no inherent reason to reject the industrial world—after all, other brilliant mathematicians at the time were breaking into fields like computer science that would generously reward them. His philosophy contradicts his inspiration; Ellul was a pacifist who believed that escaping the tyranny of technique could not be done through the logic of violence. Ironically, the very field that Kaczynski despised most, psychology, seems to give us the best picture: his social development (or stunting thereof), his participation in traumatic experiments in late adolescence, and his deep-seated sexual repression combine to present a psychologically malformed being, a person who, though a certified "genius" and proficient professional, was unable to cope with the realities of a world that prioritized capital gain, technological advancement, and scientific control over humanity. Kaczynski's biographer Alston Chase claims Kaczynski's curriculum at Harvard "sought to undermine" human values "rather than inculcate" them.[21]

In other words, Ted Kaczynski, the mathematician turned techno-pessimist terrorist, proves Hegel's dictum that "every thesis contains its antithesis." The mathematical mind, honed to see problems as solvable only in pure numbers, could not remain standing against the brute reality of human existence—the cruelty of child bullies, the perversity of science without ethics, the burn of unrequited sexual desire, the cold mechanical calculation that hangs price tags on inestimable nature. Kaczynski is no Luddite—he was no champion of the people fighting for his life. No, he is the unfortunate but acceptable cost for the instrumental rational world. His manifesto, correct on many levels in its insightful critique of the mechanistic distortion of reality, is dismissed as the rantings of a psychopath. Like Friedrich Nietzsche's catatonia or Søren Kierkegaard's melancholia, Kaczynski's apparent mental distress tranquilizes readers who might otherwise be perturbed by his claims. Industrial capitalist society goes on, secure in the assurance that the dangerous knowledge represented by Kaczynski is safely locked away for four consecutive life sentences—bourgeois Americans need not trouble themselves with the apparent implications of the world they have constructed because the FBI won out against the Montana psychopath.

My Other's Keeper

The poor represent a necessary but dangerous element to the rich. The poor function as the necessary "Other" against which the rich construct their own identity. They embody disvalue, against which the upper classes can affirm their own virtue. They create the value that the capitalists extract on the market and through their consumption keep capitalism from collapsing. They placate the guilty consciences of rich philanthropists and by deference and defiance underwrite the place of the professional class. They serve as useful pawns for politicians, marketing firms, business owners, religious leaders, and media personae. They sit as objects for the upper classes, granting those in the higher levels of society their status as higher. And as long as they can be kept as objects—through media, through sentimentalist charity, through public policy, through economics, through theological and philosophical romanticisms, they are "safe." But human error remains in the calculus; error exploited the poor that often brings the remote upper classes face-to-face with the unwashed masses. The lingering worry, whether faced with the titillating self-destructive excitement of the Marxist or the anxiety of the capitalist, is that the poor will at some point realize that the relationship is not reciprocal: the poor do not need the upper classes the way the upper classes need the poor.

Thus, the rich have it in their interest to establish a safer "other" against which they can construct their identity. They seek an Other who will affirm them in their status as supreme, as good, as rich, but will not pose the danger that human actors pose. A "thinking" machine, beholden entirely to the instructions given to it by those who created it, is truly the object of mastery that the poor can never fully be. Thus, the ultimate danger AI presents to the poor is that it offers the illusory promise of being an Other toward which the upper classes can be oriented, an alter against which they can satisfy their psychological lack while placating their guilty consciences. If AI gains standing within society as "intelligent," the ultimate consequence will not only be an anthropomorphization of computers but a de-anthropomorphization of the poor. As "intelligence" corresponds in popular ideology with goodness, efficiency, and ultimately *humanity*, then the counterpart to this view is that "unintelligence" corresponds to badness, wastefulness, and *inhumanity*.[22] Since the poor function as disvalue for the upper classes, epistemological quirks specific to the experience of resource scarcity are marked as unintelligible and unintelligent, with the effect of marking off the poor as inhuman others. But the visible humanity of the poor is a risk—the naked face that speaks to those who see it[23]—so to fully remove the poor from inclusion, we must substitute them with a more human Other. Ironically, recognizing computers as intelligent, within a culture that correlates intelligence with humanity, functions to strip the human poor of their moral status while bestowing it upon the inhuman computer.

Artificial Dignity

Ascribing intelligence to a machine is dangerous precisely because the concept of intelligence lies within a broader constellation of "moral facts." While ethics has long sought to find universal truths, the social understanding of what is morally right is, and always has been, subject to change. Consider, for example, property rights. Thomas Aquinas (following the claims of Julius Caesar) alleges that the Germanic barbarians did not consider theft at all wrong![24] Apparently the concept of personal property did not hold in Germania! The notion of property rights in the Bible, including notions like the status of widows, the transference of ownership deeds, and the return of property to those who lend it out in Jubilee years, are very much foreign to modern property laws.[25] Property claims entail important social considerations that delineate questions of who exists as a subject, what entities exist as properties, what rights subjects have to their property and its transfer, and whether properties obtain any rights. Robert Nozick's facetiously simple claim that families shouldn't be subject to trade rules and regulations[26] is given the lie by Michael Walzer's note that family giving structures themselves have long been shaped by and in turn shaped social standards.[27] Thus, while theft may seem a simple moral prohibition, the meaning of theft is highly socially dependent.

Social theorists have also noted how the emergence of modern economic markets has changed the moral meaning of property. Marx, of course, famously promoted the idea of materialist culture, wherein culture follows economic situations, such as the redefinition of values by the new hegemonic bourgeoisie following the decline of the feudal aristocracy.[28] Max Weber, on the other hand, holds the contrary, namely, that economic valuation follows cultural change, just as the Catholic ethic of "enjoyment" of wealth (over perceived selfish hoarding) resists the Protestant "saving" of capital (over perceived indulgence of spending).[29] Norbert Elias claims the formation of modern etiquette and its control through affect rather than violence is tied to the emergence of the bourgeoisie as the hegemonic group over the aristocracy—to distinguish themselves from the poor (those who are characterized by disvalue), the rich must properly internalize the shame that "poor" manners bring.[30] And Michel Foucault claims that the rise of capitalism marks a distinct shift from the right of the person (e.g., the person of the king) to the absolute right to property, and concordantly a social-legal shift from criminality as violent to property-based.[31] The meaning of property itself, and its role defining what is morally significant or insignificant, is thus a point of social contestation, wherein *The Wizard of Id*'s parody "Golden Rule" holds: Whoever has the gold makes the rules.

Intelligence is an even more troublesome site of moral conflict because it has often been used as the precondition for ascribing moral agency to an entity. David Gunkel notes that the common assumption of moral philosophy has been that "persons" deserve to be treated as moral agents (that is, beings capable of making moral choices and being held responsible for them) and as moral patients (that is, beings to whom moral agents have obligations). Typically, personhood has meant "human," but as anthropocentrism has been challenged, the criterion for personhood has been focused on "a thinking intelligent being" or a being possessing "self-consciousness or rationality."[32] Gunkel further notes that consciousness is "a privileged term insofar as it appears, in one form or another, on most if not all of the competing lists" defining personhood.[33] Gunkel is right to point this out, as many of the debates about the "intelligence" of AI use human *consciousness* as the benchmark or goal, such as Searle's Chinese Room argument. But the early AI pioneers denied this problem was the primary concern; rather, they supplied the condition for human functioning as *intelligence*, an attribute easier to reduce to quantifiable measures (e.g., the IQ test) than the nebulous concept of "consciousness." Thus, in the realm of AI, as in the realm of general moral agency/patiency, consciousness and intelligence are often elided, with consciousness often meaning "human-like intelligence." Both are assumed to be measures of what human cognition is, as seen in the view of evolutionary theorists like Hans Jonas and Pierre Teilhard de Chardin, where, as intelligence increases among animals, it moves toward consciousness.[34]

The way to determine whether a machine can act or think like human beings is, of course, a question that assumes a model of what human thought is like. The Turing test was the first broadly accepted model—if a machine can successfully imitate another human being in a conversation, such that an observer is unable to distinguish machine from person, then the machine can be said to be intelligent. Many people today still take this as the basic standard—Blake Lemoine's claim that LaMDA is "sentient" is rooted in the fact that he had what he considered to be an "intelligent" conversation with the LLM, and the impressiveness of ChatGPT and GPT-4 or various chatbots like Replika, as well as our own innate tendencies to anthropomorphize the world around us, facilitates this belief. However, critics of this standard have noted for years that there are other ways to determine human know-how. The café model (or Steve Wozniak's variation, the Coffee test) tests a machine on how well it can carry out a straightforward task, such as order a meal at a restaurant or make coffee in any given home. The challenge of this model is that there can be variations that require adaptation over straight programming—the café may be out of some dishes that day, or one house may use a different type of coffee maker than another.[35] Another linguistic model is the Winograd Schema test, whereby a machine is asked to identify the correct antecedent of an ambiguous pronoun in a sentence, such as *they* in "the town councilors refused to grant the protestors a license because *they* feared violence." To make the test more difficult, the verb *feared* can be changed to *advocated*, changing the nuance of the sentence, which a natural language user should be able to understand.[36] This test has been successful in challenging the normative "rule-based" grammatical approach to AI since these ambiguous pronouns do not adhere strictly to grammatical rules. Another proposed model is the Lovelace 2.0 test, which assesses a machine based on its ability to make a "creative" work, a barrier computer pioneer Ada Lovelace claimed was impossible nearly two hundred years ago.[37] Given a proposition and subset of data, such as a genre of painting or a musical style, the AI should create something that a human observer can judge meets the aesthetic qualifications. Here, the *savoir faire* of artistic technique must meet the unique essence of the artistic style.

These standards, many of which are proposed by AI researchers themselves, promise difficult challenges, but AI is rapidly closing in on some of these goals. While many still remain skeptical about conversational AI, ChatGPT has convinced a number of skeptics that AI already has the ability to naturally converse, and controversies have already arisen as to whether the software should get credit when used to compose important documents such as science articles.[38] A decade ago, AIs could not pass the Winograd Schema test by any measure, but improved machine learning has built into the program longer chains of associations (i.e., programmed in more biases) that help it to pass the test, such as a predilection for violence among protestors or prudence among city councilors, leading to success rates of around 90 percent for AIs, nearly the same rate as humans.[39] Even artistic abilities seem to be in reach: on October 9, 2021, the Bonn Symphony Orchestra played the "completed" version of Ludwig van Beethoven's "Unfinished" Tenth Symphony, completed by an AI modeling the long-deceased composer's style.[40] Advances in AI image generation have also led to real legal problems as artists' signature styles are being copied directly by AIs, forcing legislators to consider unexplored questions for art production.[41] Problems in all of these cases do remain: ChatGPT productions tend to require massive editing, and AI art is notorious for misnumbering fingers on human images. But these are relatively minor concerns compared to the massive developments AI has seen across numerous metrics. Thus, depending on whose definition of intelligence we accept and the threshold we set for determining it, AI models are getting closer to achieving these targets by the day, leading to the real problems of personhood.[42]

Just as intelligence and consciousness are elided in the work of AI with the effect of chatbots being called conscious (or, even more unhelpful, "sentient"), moral agency/patiency itself risks occupying the older (perhaps outdated) concept of "human dignity." This concept has undergone a great deal of transformation and redefinition over history.[43] The original use of "dignity" was the privilege of the Roman citizenry. In the *Summa Theologiae*, dignity, like personal rights, is a matter of one's social standing.[44] However, in modern moral theory, human dignity is accorded to all human beings regardless of status.[45] Dignity in modern discourse means being ascribed all human rights so that the meaning of dignity is inherently intertwined with a concept of protections or claims that correspond to a being with dignity. At times, this leads to disagreement, as one can see in the debates surrounding beginning and end of life controversies—i.e., whether a fetus holds human status to obtain human rights and whether a "death with dignity" is a human right.

Of course, the corollary "human" has also been subject to redefinitions by various societies over time.[46] The creation of chattel slavery in the sixteenth century legally classified human beings as property until the legal abolition of slavery through the Western world. Colonized persons have long been treated as inhuman, as animal, by the colonizer.[47] Legalized segregation by skin color demonstrates an obvious dehumanizing, but a more devious variation on this is systems that give gradations of human dignity based on skin.[48] Thus, even who gets to be counted as "human" in "human dignity" has historically excluded, in the words of Francesca

Ferrando, "children, women, freaks, people of color other than white, queers, and so on."[49] Biological science has offered a seemingly objective answer to this problem, but despite popular beliefs, the notion of a "species" is not hermetically distinct, and chimeras, hybrids, mutants, and other aberrations pose challenges to a facetiously straightforward idea. Nonetheless, even if there is a consensus that all members of *Homo sapiens* (including their offspring and living progenitors) are included at least theoretically under "human dignity," animal rights activists, environmentalists, transhumanists and, of course, AI evangelists have challenged the anthropocentric paradigm.

It should come as no surprise, then, that insofar as sentientists, transhumanists, AI evangelists, and other philosophers have emphasized intelligence or consciousness as the criterion for dignity, rationality (or right use of intelligence) is often the criterion of moral goodness. The history of Western philosophy is replete with examples of conflating "goodness" with appeals to intellectuals' standards of rationality. Plato argues in *The Republic* that the most just society, one that promotes genuine human flourishing, is one where the ruler is a philosopher, a person who loves wisdom the way Plato did.[50] Aristotle emphasized pure (i.e., nonpractical) wisdom (*Sophia*) as the highest virtue one could attain, an unsullied path to true human flourishing.[51] Thomas Aquinas declares human beings are made in the image of God because of our status as rational beings.[52] Immanuel Kant famously argued that only "autonomous reason" could yield moral truth, and even worse, that only "rational nature exists as an end in itself."[53] Even John Stuart Mill's utilitarianism, which prioritizes pleasure over any grandiose vision of rationality, emphasizes that the pleasures of rational beings are higher than those of "lesser" beings.[54] The four most common theories of ethics—virtue ethics, natural law, utilitarianism, and deontology—take as their starting places the assumption that it is morally better to be "rational" than not.[55] Intrinsic to all of these theories is the assumption that a being with more rationality is more morally valuable than one with less rationality. Of course, "rationality" is no less of a contested space than any other attribute, as demonstrated by nothing other than the history of philosophy itself, replete with dozens of arguments about what constitutes truth and proper reasoning! But all agree that the "irrational" being has less moral goodness than the rational one. No wonder, then, that philosopher Daniel Wikler can so flippantly claim that a "superintelligent" being should be granted *more* rights than a normal human![56]

From this position, the question of AI's status holding dignity (or agency/patiency, rights, personhood, or any other synonym one chooses) comes into relief. If intelligence and dignity correspond, as the entire history of Western philosophy has contended, then an intelligent machine should meet the criteria of dignity we accord to other human beings. Of course, the intelligence of AI is mathematical intelligence. The rationality of AI is mathematical accuracy. These are the extent to what really occurs "intelligently" in the algorithmic processes. But in a capitalist society, this form of algorithmic processing is a stand-in for correct moral reasoning—the AI is a good machine because it yields better profits and more efficiency (disregarding the externalized costs, such as underpaid labor and ecological devastation). The logic of this goodness, like Nietzsche's "dominant morality," is self-contained—AI is good because it functions "like" the good capitalist. Against no metaethical grounding must this self-apparent truth defend itself. The "good decent" people of bourgeois civilization are themselves the proof-positive of their position. Society is constructed in *their* image, after all—how could this be anything *but* good?

Natural Indignity

The problem, however, is that when the concept of dignity, or moral agency/patiency, remains tethered to a regnant vision of rationality, other humans are often excluded based on the same valuation. Human and rational have long functioned interchangeably in moral discourse, but this leads to the obvious problem that a less "rational" agent is therefore a less "human" one. Thus, Mill's inflammatory excuse to defend higher pleasures against baser ones—"It is better to be a human being dissatisfied than a pig satisfied; better to be Socrates dissatisfied than a fool satisfied."[57] Animality, and consequently indignity, track with "irrationality," while dignity and humanity are ascribed to the intellectuals, the paragons of rationality—Socrates and his peers.

Because intelligence is itself a constructed social fact and is not by any means an objective reality, it has been the site of social conflict for those who wish to dominate other humans through "rationalist" means. Racism and sexism have often been justified with scientific backings, such as phrenology or race sciences claiming that women or people of certain races (especially people descendent from Africa) are genetically or morphologically determined to be less intelligent than the white man. Similarly, the emphasis on rationality has justified ill treatment of those who are not "neurotypical."[58] Dismissals of the poor as being "uneducated," "ill-mannered," or "bad with money" likewise emphasize a moral hierarchy based on epistemic bias. To think in any way unapproved by the hegemony is bad. Thus, schools with low test scores (mathematized measures of bourgeois standards of rationality) are given *less* funding in spite of their *greater* need! The meaning is clear: those who cannot achieve our standards of intelligence must be punished through deprivation of resources! Capitalist reward systems follow bourgeois intelligence achievement. Deprivation of needs is justified in the language of motivation despite the realities of zero-sum capitalism.

Of course, it will be unconscionable to admit that granting AI status as a moral agent amounts to denying the same status to the poor. Many of those who, in good faith, wish to grant moral status (at least patiency) to AI do so with the explicit view of expanding the circle of morality, not restricting it! Well-intended as this is, it is not realistic. Given the already disvalued position of the poor, it is easy for the bourgeoisie, whose identity is constituted by devaluing the poor, to justify adopting social attitudes and general behaviors that keep the poor away. Supporting the move toward AI rights grants the feeling of altruism—AI is posited as a dignified Other.[59] The silicon alterity of AI, despite its computational mirroring of the capitalist imagination, is alien enough to elicit sympathy while being similar enough to allow the wealthy to avoid contamination with the disvalued poor, those teeming masses whose embodied poverty is seen as contagion to the hygiene of the middle class. More importantly, digital simulacra of bourgeois minds reinforce the value systems of the upper classes. Like mechanical sycophants, the instrumental rationality of the artificial "intelligence" reassures the capitalist that their way of thinking is right and that those poor whose encounter of the world is the violent struggle for survival are the aberrations. The witness of the poor against this claim is easy to dismiss because the "witness" of AI provides a counter-testimony.

Because moral desert and "intelligence" are deeply intertwined in popular imagination, moral approval often comes in the form of intellectual approval and vice versa. Take a recent, deeply telling example: many commentators ascribed the moral failings of President Donald Trump to low intelligence,[60] to mental illness,[61] or to cognitive decline.[62] His improprieties had to be explained away as epistemic, not moral, shortcomings. At the same time, the liberal bourgeois element of American society demonstrated the same disdain for Trump based on rationality that they also ascribe to the poor. Indeed, a popular epithet against Donald Trump, a thoroughbred upper-class socialite, was that he was "a poor man's idea of a rich man,"[63] while another common attack was that Trump was not really a billionaire but a fraud who was much poorer than his claims.[64] All such language was used to describe a man whose actions in office were thoroughly bourgeois—he enriched himself and his family; he gave favors to his unqualified capitalist friends; he fired people who posed challenges to his hegemony; he enacted programs and policies that hurt the poor; he used racist and sexist language to stoke division. Trump's wickedness was obvious to all who observed with any clarity, but to the "good" liberal bourgeoisie, his immorality had to be tied to what they, as a class, disvalue: a divergent epistemology and poverty. Perhaps the effort to frame his misdeeds this way owes to a third disvalue—one that social theorists from Bourdieu to Elias claim functions to maintain the hegemonic socioeconomic class: failure to maintain tact.

The ascription of Trump's wickedness to cognitive impairment is only possible because the dominant culture accepts the thesis that goodness corresponds with perfect neurotypicalism and intelligence. Thus, the inverse is also posited: to be neurodivergent or less intelligent is to be less good. Neurodivergence is pathologized, with the odd connotation that the "sickness" is moral in nature.[65] We speak of "mental illness," invoking the image of disease and contagion in discussing an array of different psychological conditions and the need for treatment for the betterment of society. In the all-too-common occurrences of horrific gun violence in the United States, commentators immediately invoke the "crisis of mental health" of the country, cementing in listeners' minds the connection between the moral evil of multiple murder and neurodivergence.[66] Only an insane person would do something so evil because sanity corresponds with goodness. Popular depictions of mental illness also focus on the horror of mental institutions—straightjackets and padded walls, regimes of tranquilizers and antipsychotics, rough-handling orderlies and sadistic psychiatrists, and, worst of all, barbarous treatments like lobotomies and electroshock. And, of course, there is an entire litany of pejoratives tied to mental illness: psycho, crazy, bedlam,[67] insane, maniac, hysteric, schizo, and so forth. To be diagnosed with a mental illness is to be branded with a stigma. One becomes an object to others—either an invalid to be treated (and possibly cured!) or a brute to be regarded with caution. In any case, one loses the moral stance of those who are mentally "fit" and capable of being treated with dignity.

Other forms of neurodivergence, such as autism and developmental disability, are treated similarly. Often, instead of being considered *im*moral, the developmentally disabled are treated as *a*moral, lacking the ability to make authentic moral choices and subsequently lacking moral status. Describing someone's mental development as "retarded" (i.e., slowed) was once a typical medical diagnosis but eventually became a common playground insult so much that it has become a stand-alone slur.[68] Slurs, not to be confused with other insults or swears, intone that the referent lacks dignity or worth—that they are less than human and not to be regarded with dignity. This denigration results in a *de facto* sort of eugenics occurring in many countries today, where genetic detection of developmental disabilities in utero, such as Down Syndrome (trisomy 21) or Edwards Syndrome (trisomy 18), has created pressure for women to elect abortions. In Iceland, this has led to the near-total elimination of Down Syndrome.[69] Similarly, ableist worries about children developing autism because of vaccination have led to *actual* contagion outbreaks as nearly eradicated fatal or debilitating diseases like measles and mumps return in populations once nearly immune.[70] A common side effect of mumps in males is sterility. The legalized sterilization of neurodivergent persons up until the 1970s is paralleled today in a neurotypical bigotry that accepts preventable death or sterility for one's children as an acceptable alternative to autism.

Regardless of the type of neurodivergence one has, stigma and infantilization follow. Only in recent years, as disability activism has gained momentum in the public sphere, have the policies and institutions designed to "serve" those who are neuro-atypical made any social progress. Regardless, for those who attend special education programs or who seek psychiatric aid, stigma attends because, in the logic of capitalism, being dependent upon others is morally burdensome, and to be burdensome because one does not fit the hegemonic neurological standard is even worse. As a result, advocates for these groups have fought hard to end stigmatization, to increase autonomy in care and education, and to ensure privacy is maintained, in other words, to protect basic human rights. Nonetheless, despite grassroots efforts to end the use of biased language, the reality is that being neurodivergent continues to be seen in itself as being deficient and lacking in dignity.

While not all poor are neuro-atypical, it is true that generally those who have lower education levels and lower IQs (arbitrary measures of intelligence constructed and gatekept by racist bourgeois actors) have lower income levels and that those with mental "illness" are more likely to experience job insecurity (except for psychopaths, who are more present in corporate boardrooms than in the general populace[71]). Additionally, given that the poor are more susceptible to experience decreases in IQ due to scarcity and more likely to develop psychosis, the poor are generally more likely to experience neurotypical discrimination either because they do not meet the arbitrary standards set by the hegemon or because they are perceived to be deficient by virtue of their poverty.[72]

The great insight of psychoanalysis has been that even the most "normal" functioning minds are still deeply beset by unconscious elements. In Jacques Lacan's analysis, all people experience trauma of separation from sustaining parents as infants, and our personalities, whether they be neurotic, psychotic, or perverted, result from this primordial trauma. Nobody in this view is whole, though there are better and worse approaches to resolving this tension. Taken seriously, Lacanian psychoanalysis leads us to recognize that the neurotypical paradigm is ultimately built on false assumptions and that tying human worth to one's "normal" functioning is an arbitrary way to assure certain neurotics that their form of neurosis is better than that of others. But most other schools of psychology are engaged in reassuring the hegemon that their minds are the right ones. Thus, against the structural approach of psychoanalysis, modern clinical psychiatry works on symptom management, using the *Diagnostic and Statistical Manual* as the standard for delineating who is neurotypical and who is not. Those whose neuroses are not described in the manual are thus not diagnosed as deficient. The circle of neurotypicalism is drawn tighter when AI mirrors exactly the "great minds" of the neurotic-obsessive middle and upper classes.

The "good poor," those who buy into the bourgeois ideology, will be compensated as only minor deviants: losers in the wash, but losers favored by the bourgeoisie. Those on the outer edges, however, who reject instrumental rationality, who pursue self-destructive behaviors to cope, who dissociate from the cruel reality of poverty, who use the self-same tool of violence as the economic system, will be subject to further stigmatization and, under the auspice of benevolent rationality, subjected to the purported objectivity of AI. Thus, the CEO of the company behind ChatGPT, Sam Altman, tweeted, "The adaptation to a world deeply integrated with AI tools is probably going to happen pretty quickly; the benefits (and fun!)

have too much upside. These tools will help us be more productive (can't wait to spend less time doing email!), healthier (AI medical advisors for people who can't afford care), smarter (students using ChatGPT to learn), and more entertained (AI memes lolol)."[73] The "benefits" promised are horrifying: displacing workers, automating education for the masses, and replacing human doctors with algorithms are the costs those human poor will have to bear for the wealthy, who wish to further distance themselves from the irksome poor in work settings, hospitals, and schools. While the AI evangelists' promises may sound like utopian guarantees to the wealthy, they can only be interpreted as hostile threats to the poor: adapt to our vision or perish like dogs.

The more that AI's epistemological model is reinforced as normative, the epistemology of the poor is further denigrated. To say that AI is "conscious," that it deserves human rights, or that it should be granted legal autonomy is to make a claim for it that is not always given to the poor. When Ben Goertzel's robot Sophia was given citizenship in Saudi Arabia, numerous people protested, outraged that many human beings, including immigrant workers and Saudi women (in practice), were not granted the same rights or dignity as an automaton.[74] To value the intelligence of AI as morally significant is to merely double the claim that white bourgeois male intelligence is the standard against which all other epistemologies are evaluated. In this case, given that the poor often do not think the same way as the rich, their preferences, values, intelligence, and choices will be further denigrated. The system that currently disvalues the poor because they are poor can further justify its position by contrasting poor thinking with the "thinking" carried out by artificial intelligence.

The Tyranny of Rationality

The upper classes protect their hegemony by the trappings of educational diplomas, the adulation of sycophants, the justificatory logic of the market, and the control of new forms of science and technology. AI, as *the* smart technology, merely adds to the bulwark that forms a tyranny of rationality.

The powerful are rational, and the rational are powerful. The rationality that reigns is not, of course, a coherent rationality, for all the claims of its proponents. With Latour, we must trace the socio-logics, not the logics of this system. Exceptions exist to every rule: efficiency is traded for marginalizing the poor; the freedom of the market is betrayed by governmental bailouts for the wealthy; merit-based systems of college admission take second place to athletes, legacies, dean's interests, and children of faculty.[75] But the rules in place are taken to be logical by those who follow them, and they impose a form of rationality on society. If one wishes to claim legitimacy within the system, they will find it necessary to conform to the standards of this tyranny. Luckily for the poor, formal education is the system whereby the rules of this tyranny are delineated.

While Paulo Freire can speak confidently about the "pedagogy" of the oppressed, he betrays the reality that education itself functions as a gatekeeping mechanism for upper classes and always has. The earliest European universities were oriented toward the training of clergy and the middle class. The universities allowed the official creation of a professional class, replete with degrees corresponding to the original four professions—doctors (MD), lawyers (JD), clergy (STD), and, the very essence of *profess*ionalism, the *profess*oriate (PhD). University degrees function as "props" that grant to their holder a given socially recognized role, such as being an actual chemist or psychiatrist and not merely a pretender or, perhaps worse, an amateur.[76] The "logical fallacy" (a paradigmatic example of the tyranny of rationality) of the "argument from authority" is, in fact, not a fallacy but a necessary rule of the hegemonic order. Licensed doctors are to be trusted in health matters over old wives' tales because they have the requisite educational certification, which means they have demonstrated sufficient expertise on the subject to be trusted. And while the system is entirely self-referential—a doctor is a doctor because other doctors agreed that they have sufficiently demonstrated the knowledge and skill of being a doctor—this self-policing aspect elevates the professions above other careers. A doctor involved in malpractice, defined as such by the American Medical Association, is defrocked by the AMA and unable to practice, just as a lawyer can be disbarred by the American Bar Association, or a priest can be laicized by the Catholic Church. Without discrediting the vast and significant portion of human knowledge contributed by various researchers across disciplines and professions, one should understand that the professions themselves have it in their interests to be the conservators of the knowledge they purvey, making them the exclusive self-referential authority within the hegemonic order. Prevailing wisdom may be that playing in the cold leads to one catching a cold, but the AMA's declarations about virology and epidemiology are the final say in the end.[77]

Of course, problems like the backlash against vaccines or mask mandates in the United States demonstrate the backhand side of this educational safeguarding. Political conservatives have long stoked the lower classes' distrust of the professional class, a classic case of class conflict. This masterful act of bad faith is possible because the upper classes dominate the poor, perhaps more now than ever before. In the early twentieth century, working class spokespersons focused on organizing labor to secure their own interests, as illustrated by the work of people like Woody Guthrie, Mother Jones, or Cesar Chavez. Today, those purporting to represent the working class are millionaires who act only to keep the poor divided, such as Glenn Beck, Donald Trump, or Ted Nugent. By instigating a strong distrust for the official channels of education (e.g., Christopher Rufo's rally against "critical race theory," Dennis Prager's eponymous "university," or James Lindsay's "grievance studies"), they sow sufficient doubt about the production of knowledge by the educated elite among the undereducated, both the working class and the middle class, to dissuade them from pursuing higher education. The genius of this move is that it helps to maintain the literati as an entirely separate class in the US. The US currently has eight of the top ten universities in the world (depending on how one ranks them),[78] but ranks twelfth globally for post-secondary graduates, with only 47 percent of Americans having an associate's degree or higher, compared to South Korea's 69 percent and Japan's 60 percent.[79] Sowing distrust of the educated helps to keep the poor from accessing the professional class while simultaneously preventing the professional class from having to reckon much with the divergent epistemology of the poor.

Supposing, however, that a poor person wants to participate in the discourse of the upper classes, they will need to endure the pedagogical procedures that grant legitimacy to them. In Bourdieu's words, they will need to accumulate "cultural capital."[80] The degree they attain is one artifact of this capital, but the true capital is demonstrated by their educational "reform." As Ruby Payne (unconsciously?) admits, the goal of education is to conform the poor to the worldview of the middle class.[81] Those poor who have the ability—as well as sufficient support systems; serendipitous opportunities; or a "natural" benefit of curiosity, tenacity, or ingenuity—will be able to enter the echelons of the educated classes.[82]

In order to be admitted into these classes, however, the poor must adequately demonstrate that they now "play" for the right team;[83] that is, they have sufficiently adopted the "correct" worldview of the upper classes. The typical way to achieve this is through passing the proper tests by demonstrating a mastery of the formal register,[84] of formal logic, and of a number of cultural referents accepted by the upper classes (e.g., literature, history, sciences, arts)—the famed "three Rs of education": reading, 'riting, and 'rithmetic. Historically, most schools had some control over their own curriculum, granting teachers some autonomy in how to train their students, but the totalization of capitalist epistemology has meant standardized curricula enforced with standardized tests *a là* No Child Left Behind. The already master discourse of pedagogy is subjected to a further master discourse of standardized educational benchmarks. And even still, these tests are only passable if students have the unique textbooks created by the testing companies, which often fall outside of poor schools' budgets.[85] The proto-bourgeois gatekeeping function of education reaches its logical conclusion through the bureaucratic mechanisms of standardized tests, where students who have access to resources to prepare *specifically* for these tests are able to maintain their position in the upper classes while maintaining the veneer of a meritocracy. Thus, when colleges eliminated the SAT requirement for admission due to the COVID-19 pandemic, more poor students—those whose families could not afford the thousands of dollars of test preparation that upper-class students have—were admitted into elite colleges.[86]

The function of such tests and standards is to ensure that those poor who are adopted into the upper classes have properly demonstrated their capacity to be civilized, to conform to the established rules laid down by the upper classes. Like Eliza Doolittle in George Bernard Shaw's *Pygmalion*, the poor must be educated to gain acceptance into proper society and properly embrace the tyranny of rationality. Just as the myth of Pygmalion references the artificer king who created artificial life that he loved, the poor are not loved unless they can be re-created in the image of the bourgeoisie.[87] They must give up their status of poverty to gain life. They must demonstrate they no longer think the way those *low* poor do; they must show that they are truly elevated and worthy of being treated as dignified.

Thus, the impossibility of the task: one cannot think as the poor while also speaking to the bourgeoisie. Because the poor who can communicate with the bourgeoisie effectively must speak the language of the middle class as the bourgeoisie have no interest in learning to communicate with the poor, it is doubtful at present whether or how the experience of poverty can truly be understood within the dominant discourse (or if it can). The first-generation liberation theologians still wrote in bourgeois academic theological language, trained, as they all were, in bourgeoise Western educational institutions and in the highly self-perpetuating pedagogy of sacred theology.[88] Spivak recognizes that she is a member of the dominant class, and she writes to other elites. Lukács's assertion of the inevitability of class consciousness is steeped in the bourgeois philosophical language of early twentieth-century Europe. Along with Spivak, then, we should question whether it is possible to truly hear the voice of the subaltern.

To have one's voice heard entails a degree of power—a speaker has the wherewithal to influence the hearer.[89] Spivak's provocative question is not really about whether or not the subaltern can speak, except in the sense of whether a tree falling in an empty forest makes a sound—the emphasis is not on the act of speech but on the act of hearing. Of course, one can be heard and not have the influence they expected, as Kierkegaard's clown warning theatergoers of fire to uproarious laughter,[90] or Nietzsche's misunderstood prophet Zarathustra,[91] the speaker's influence is not always what they hoped, and perhaps is never fully what they sought.[92] This misalignment, however, is a misalignment precisely because attendant to the differences of understanding between speaker and hearer, a power dynamic exists—the misunderstood speaker is still exerting influence. Only the truly mute are totally powerless.

To speak of the poor as voiceless, to ask whether the subaltern can speak, is in itself an act of violence. The poor do speak in a cacophonous din that puts Pentecostal revivals to shame. In acts of cooperation, dissent, crime, generosity; in stutters, dialects, and perfectly rehearsed lines; in poorly scrawled letters, informal text messages, and reams of meticulously kept documents; in the silence of body language—they speak in ways that convey the non-circumscribable reality of poverty. Fanon illustrates this well—the colonized, the wretched, speak through their actions, the meanings of which are not apparent to the colonizers, whose understanding, if it comes, only arrives too late.[93] But when well-meaning advocates say that the poor do not speak, what they really mean is that the voices of the poor are unheard. It is no wonder, then, that the conclusion of a Dominican priest who studied in Leuven or a Brahman scholar who studied at Cornell is that the poor are voiceless—their own cultural milieu is one that chooses to be deaf to the cry of the poor.

If the preferential option is to truly inspire us toward utopian action, it must make the voices of the poor heard. This entails tearing down the tyrannical socioeconomic structures that insist the only voices to hear are those that are supposedly reputable. Academia is an especially contentious location for this—one must properly give credit to sources that are considered authoritative. The so-called "science wars" of the 1990s and the grievance studies controversy of 2017–2018 illustrate the problem well: members of hegemonic groups saw their epistemological dominance challenged by diverse perspectives and lashed out with satirical "studies" to discredit their critics.[94] Bourgeois white western scholars (typically men), adherents of the philosophy of scientism, maintain their own power by claiming that their highly contextualized and particular understanding of the world is, in fact, objective and universal. The problem is exacerbated by a conflation among some scholars that to say "X is socially constructed" is to say that it is bad.[95] Worried about losing their power, the hegemony must reinforce their view: just as the colonizer must enforce the view that the "natural order" favors the white male "civilizing the savages," the bourgeois computer scientist must maintain that any divergent form of knowledge is defective and wrong. AI is rooted in the comfortable elite epistemology of professional mathematicians and the business class, capitalist elites propped up by legitimated knowledge, institutional authentication, economic approbation, and political empowerment. The divergent option for the poor poses a threat to the claim of absolute sovereignty entailed in the algorithmic articulation of rationality.

Thus, in the end, the option for the poor entails a certain violence, one that liberation theologians have been hesitant to articulate. Marx's recognition that the proletariat must violently overthrow the bourgeoisie or Fanon's recognition that the colonized must violently rise up against the colonizers means nothing other than the fact that force is overcome by force.[96] If the bourgeoisie cannot hear the voice of the poor, the poor will have to make their voices heard. Physical violence, the lingering phobia of the bourgeoisie, has historically been employed, such as in slave revolts or peasant uprisings, but is by no means the only solution. Labor organization offers an alternative: the Luddites destroyed physical machines, just as union strikes disrupt the machinery of capitalism. In some ways, the attacks on property are a greater threat than attacks on persons—interrupting the flow of capital threatens the totality of the bourgeois narrative. The fearful bourgeoisie in turn employ violence because they know too well that force must be met with force and that, unchecked, the poor threaten the hegemonic order. So they hang Luddites and shoot union organizers.

Thus, a challenge: the poor, instilled with the traditional values imposed by the dominant classes, are commanded not to use violence even when it is used on them. "When someone strikes you on the left cheek, turn to him the other also" says the very epitome of "slave morality."[97] And yet, force can be enacted in other ways. The force of will—refusing to bend the knee, refusing to return violence for violence, refusing to degrade oneself or one's enemy as subhuman, and so forth. The powerful expect a violent response to their violence. They create police organizations, militaries, and prison systems because violence is their purview. Violence is only legitimated when employed by the ruling class. One cannot oppose AI in sharp contradistinction like Kaczynski, the double of 1980s hackers. To resist with violence is to play the game that has already been set: the disvalued are further disvalued. Like the villains of comic books, violent acts of desperation, a response to the already cruel and violent culture of the wealthy, is deemed "too much." Batman gets to be the hero in the end because, despite his massive wealth leading to deep inequality in Gotham, the oppressed responded to their unspeakable distress with petty crime. The game is rigged from the start. To truly overthrow the system of violence begetting violence, one must learn to not play. Illustrated by the genocidal logic of the Cold War, the principle of mutual assured destruction becomes clearer: *War Games*'s (1983) conclusion that "the only way to win is to not play" is the condition for the unheard to be heard. They cannot speak to the upper classes the way the upper classes speak to them.

An alternative solution, then, must be pursued. Telling one's story provides a means by which this can be achieved, though it requires the listener to hear ("Let the one who has ears hear"). Here, then, we must learn to be silent, to listen without interpretation, without imposing our own views on the speaker. And those who tell their story must be free to tell their story in the way they wish to. But we must not deceive ourselves that finally listening to some poor will grant us a full picture. In the words of a friend, reflecting on the importance of decolonial literature: while the totality of poverty cannot be fully articulated, we can tell stories that "contain the experience" of poverty.[98] Ultimately, this tangential experience will be all that most of us can reach, but we must be willing to reach it.

Move Fast and Break Things

The world is broken. This is no new insight of course. "Sin entered the world through one man, and death through sin, so also death was passed on to all humans because all sinned" (Rom 5:12). Whether one takes it from Paul, the Yahwist, Siddhartha Gautama, St. Augustine, or Friedrich Nietzsche, the reality of the world is characterized most clearly by the reality of suffering. While Marx condemns religion for promising the only reprieve from this to arrive in the eternal slumber of death, the utopian dream of a world characterized by total satisfaction of material desires is a physical impossibility. Ironically, the insight of ancient wisdom has been enshrined into natural law through modern science. The second law of thermodynamics dictates that energy cannot be conserved in a closed system—entropy degrades all active systems. Life, then, is characterized by metabolism, an effort to stave off entropy, known biologically as death. A perfect system in this universe is not merely impossible, it's not even worth scientifically entertaining. To make this into a nonnegotiable demand is to prematurely foreclose any possibility of improvement without the direct intervention of God.

This is not to say we should not work toward a good end. Theologian Ted Peters rejects the idea of being "co-builders" of the kingdom of God because only God can usher in God's kingdom.[99] Nonetheless, since at least the dawn of the Industrial Age, Christian activists and theologians, from Walter Rauschenbusch to Dorothy Day to Martin Luther King, Jr. to Jürgen Moltmann to Gustavo Gutiérrez to Johann-Baptist Metz, have emphasized the Christian task of ushering in God's reign. This "utopian vision," however, must be complemented by Peters's insight: the kingdom of God is an impossibility, and only the God who is capable of doing the impossible is able to bring it to fruition. The Christian position, as Kierkegaard himself recognized, is a position of absurdity—one hopes in the impossible and works knowing that they cannot accomplish it.[100] But like grace itself, the fact that we do not merit it does not mean we treat it as cheap.[101] We do not win our salvation (and for that matter, it does not come from the poor), just as we do not usher in God's reign, but the position of the believer is to accept the reality of impossibility and to act upon it. Faith means living in the absurdity of paradox and always has. The tyranny of rationality has always been the attempt to whittle away the brute absurdity of reality, to defang both the naked truth of human life and death as well as to dull the piercing truth of the Christian message. Faith embraces the absurd, the only position wherein we can ever hope to square the marginalized view of the oppressed poor with a society that marginalizes them.

Where AI as philosophy and Christian eschatology diverge is not the inspiration to make the world a better place—it is the realization that humanity alone cannot "fix" the world. AI is touted as a philosopher's stone—it will end poverty (despite it presently only enriching the wealthy); it will fix climate change (despite being a massively energy-consuming endeavor); it will perfectly unify systems of production (despite automation alienating labor far worse than any other innovation); it will improve education (despite it being a manifestly "leveled down" approach to dynamic pedagogy); it will make our cities safer (despite it merely perpetuating biased post-crime policing policies); it will satisfy all of our wants (despite the richest men in the world still trying to augment their grossly overinflated economic valuations); it will make driving safer (despite Teslas still not being able to recognize children as people); it will improve our art (despite it being confined to reproduction of algorithmic data, a patently unartistic trait); and so forth. AI is a "techno-mirror," but only in the sense that it shows the viewer what they want to see, often to their own demise. The promise of AI is *the* promise, a world where everything comes to us without us ever having to move a finger. "'We have invented happiness,' say the last men and blink."[102]

AI will not fix the broken world. Indeed, worse, AI will never be satisfying. The fact that AI has promised its big arrival every few years for the past seventy years signals this reality. Information and computing technologies were astounding to most consumers twenty-five years ago. At that time, the internet was exciting and new, a promise of unlimited possibility.

In the nascent computing world, "The Hacker Manifesto" became a creed for young nerds. Though the manifesto presents itself as a free-thinker's declaration, it trucks in the arrogant confusion of creativity with mathematical proficiency.[103] Hackers inspired by the manifesto saw themselves as renegades, not the obvious evolution of bourgeois capital culture. The excitement they profess in their manifesto belies the world they have constructed thirty-five years later: a world where jailbreaking gadgets is punishable by law, where planned obsolescence is the norm instead of the exception, where unlimited scrolling spoon-feeds the user base, where their curiosity (criminal they call it) has been replaced by the unimaginative vision of a world beholden to a technology as boring as AI. Like the pigs in Orwell's *Animal Farm*, the hackers became the thing they hated: while they railed against the ruling class of their parents' generation, who "build atomic bombs . . . wage wars . . . murder, cheat, and lie to us,"[104] today they sit on the board of the Pentagon, get DARPA contracts for automated drones and lethal autonomous weapons systems, relabel their employees as independent contractors, promote misinformation and disinformation on their platforms, and hire union busting firms.

From the perspective of the techno-elite, this retrospective may be disconcerting. It certainly does not promise much for the future. The niche spaces they enjoyed in the 1980s and 1990s have evolved into the twenty-first century's Coca-Cola—global megacorporations effacing cultural differences in favor of uniformity to expand their consumer base to the absolute maximum possible. In their desire to "innovate," they have proven Heidegger's thesis on enframing true with a vengeance: all technology today is "digital technology," all programs must be compatible with a narrow range of other software products (Windows, Mac OS, Android OS), and all aspects of human activity from work to leisure have been subsumed into this structure. As they promise "newer and better," the delivery is ever more mundane and less interesting.[105] At present, the whole industry is coasting along on hype, promises that deliver on occasion but more often pay off an unsatisfyingly diminishing improvement.

The problem will not be solved by technology because the problem is not technological in nature. The human condition is to crave. As Jacques Lacan notes, desire never achieves fulfillment. There is no satiation. As biological creatures, this is inevitable for us. Nietzsche's dictum, "To live is to will to power," might be reframed "To live is to desire." Thus, Nietzsche's command to not give up one's will to power finds a parallel in Lacan's ethical principle "Do not give up your own desire."[106] The fantasy of satisfaction is nothing other than idolatry; the belief that something will yield once and for all the answer I seek. And though Augustine tells us "Our hearts are restless until they rest in [God]," this is only true if we recognize that we can never grasp God. To recognize that God is truly ineffable, that we spend our lives seeking God and seeking to know God, is just another of way of expressing Lacan's principle; we find our satisfaction in recognizing that we cannot find our satisfaction.

AI is the rage against the truth. It is holding on to a fantasy that we should know better than to believe. It is a hope that "a god will save us." In the bitterest irony, though, the god AI seeks is not one who makes us in its image but one made in our own image. Error compounded by error, the misunderstanding of AI and its inscription into every conceivable arena of human life is merely an escape from the bleak reality that faces us. And thus, it allows us to turn our attention away from the grotesque around us: faces of the dirty poor, a rapidly heating planet, loss of biodiversity, growing wealth inequality, increased sympathy for fascism, and a general recognition that the bourgeois promise of comfort is ultimately unsatisfying.

The option for the poor offers a reply: the view from below. The view from below is a view from hunger, ignorance, psychosis, illiteracy, disability, domination, conformity, oppression, and violence. It is a view where one's position is not privileged and by definition must not be privileged (as a view from below). It is to recognize that "Life's a bitch, and then you die," or in Shakespeare's turn of phrase, life "is a tale told by an idiot, full of sound and fury, signifying nothing."[107] It is to allow oneself the grace to recognize that there is no grand solution, taking this world, with the alcoholics and

Jesus, "as it is, not as I would have it . . . so that I may be *reasonably* happy in this life."[108]

This is not the romantic vision of happiness articulated by Sobrino and other well-meaning liberation theologians. The poor are not simpletons. They struggle. In their lives, they experience social rejection, violence in and out of the home, physical ailments, hunger, and, most of all, the continual threat created by insecurity. But they *live*. And it is accepting the fact of living, dying, struggling, wanting, and never being settled that AI is most challenged, for AI is an illusion, a fantasy of the perfect mind against the reality of biased data, imperfect coding, poor models of reality, and a general lack of understanding how we understand. The fantasy of a perfect mind against the reality of imperfection is the bourgeois fantasy: the promise of capitalism is simultaneously infinite growth in an entropic universe and satisfaction despite an ever-expanding consumer market. Against this stands the naked reality of the all-too-human poor—surviving in hostile societies that pretend their poverty is not a product of the bourgeoisie's bad faith. The poor remain, in their wretchedness, in their joys, in their struggles, in their triumphs, in their state of incarnated conscious metabolic organisms in an entropic universe, witnesses against the lie that is the AI fantasy.

At some point, it may become clear that the AI project just does not work. For seventy years, AGI has "been around the corner." Less time was spent between the Wright brothers' first flight and Neil Armstrong's moon walk. Whether AI advocates admit this next year, in ten years, in fifty years, or even one hundred years, at some point, it will have to be acknowledged that AI did not meet its expectations. The inevitability of this event does not preclude a massive amount of damage done to the poor before then. After all, Marx predicted the immanent overturn of capitalism in 1848, and decades of social advocacy, workers unions, Labour parties, and recurring bubbles and recessions seemed to justify his view until the Chicago economic school regurgitated nearly verbatim the disproven theories of classical economists to wide acclaim by world leaders like Reagan and Thatcher. AI is presently the most vivid fever dream of capitalism's rational chaos; the fervor and energy directed behind it sustains the work beyond any results, and it is folly to put a definitive timeline on when the self-delusion will end. After all, capitalism is itself a practice of bad faith on a large scale: capitalists must convince themselves that an unending exercise of growth is both sustainable and satisfying, and everyone else in society is victim (witting or not) of this self-deception.

The option for the poor, taken in this spirit, then, is the call to perpetually reject the temptation to settle comfortably into a regnant hegemonic order. Christ's words, "the poor you always have with you," a saying often used to justify ignoring the poor, are reframed as a prophetic statement. The end of poverty is nothing other than the end of the natural order of things, the fullness of God's reign on earth, the breakout of history, the end of time. But metanoiac praxis of the option for the poor demands that we perpetually try to understand the poor. The statement of faith "thy kingdom come" entails an intentional desire for the fullness of God's reign, just as "costly grace" entails total obedience to Christ.[109] The reality of suffering and violence does not negate our obligation to establish a moral order; rather, as people of faith, we act to this end, knowing ultimately that God alone can achieve it. This means, in turn, that we should never be satisfied that the end is in sight until that day when "every tear will be dried." In the words of Levinas, this involves a continual unsaying of the said:[110] for every provisional claim we make of the conditions that will empower the poor, we must be prepared to unmake these claims as they impose their own power and violence.

The ultimate paradox is that faith itself must never be a comfortable position. Only in self-deception can we sit comfortably within the systems we inhabit. In bad faith, we pretend that the world is just, that AI can save us, that the philosophies and theologies we hold are correct, that the economic order can continue to grow, that the poor deserve their fate, and so on. But to take this stance is therefore to believe that God is confinable, that God fits neatly into our tyranny of rationality, whether that be as the tyrant of the rational[111] or as bound within the classic philosophical formula of the "problem of evil." True conversion—true faith—entails a recognition of our own ignorance, the failings of our rationality, the futility of trying to count "the number of angels who can dance on the head of the pin" or create the ultimate adding machine. True conversion means continually striving to see the God of the universe in the face of "the least of these," the dirty, diseased, starving, "psycho," "idiotic," irrational poor without romanticizing or idealizing the wretchedness away, knowing, ultimately, that even this will be no more than a mustard seed's expression of faith.

Conclusion: The Poor as Dark Mirror

Philip Hefner refers to artificial intelligence as a "techno-mirror." "What we want and who we are coalesce in this mirror."[112] Perhaps this characterization is appropriate, bringing together in one place fantasies of the "AI God" and Feuerbach's own characterization of God as "the highest subjectivity of [humanity] abstracted from himself."[113] Paralleling Feuerbach's own description of how "God" functions for the religious mind, Hefner notes that the techno-mirror shows us "that we want tools to do things for us, and it shows us what we want done . . . that we are finite, frail and mortal . . . that we create technology in order to bring alternative worlds into being . . . that although we are busy creating new realities, we do not know why we create or according to what values—so we have to discover the reasons and the values."[114] Hefner's assessment seems rooted in a reading of AI fantasy through the view that technology is a revealing process, not an indoctrinating one. As if demonstrating Feuerbach's view that the God of Christianity is merely a reflection of the "disuniting of [the human] from himself" whereby we set "God before [us] as the antithesis of [ourselves],"[115] Hefner parallels the construction of virtual reality with the experience of Communion—an imagining of shared humanity under one Lord.[116] In this view, AI specifically and technology writ large are not built within specific ideological and material contexts. AI is the mirror of ourselves, not as an object to speak the values of its builders but a reflection on the human condition as such. But as Jean-Luc Marion points out, it is not an icon but an idol that is "a mirror that reflects the gaze's image, or more exactly, the image of its aim and the scope of that aim."[117] It is fitting, then, that Hefner opens his essay with an allusion to the story of Snow White; it is the vain, self-important wicked queen of the tale who frequently asks, "Mirror, mirror, on the wall, tell me . . . "[118] The mirror of AI must function, then, not as any sort of deeply revealing oracle but rather as a self-affirming amplifier, one that assures the bourgeois conscience that theirs is the view that is most human.

Perhaps it is better to consider AI in the context of the uncanny. The notion of the "uncanny valley" is a common motif in AI and robotics conversations—as long as machines replicate human action without seeming adequately human, we feel they are some abhorrent admixture of alive and dead, like the horror of H. P. Lovecraft's "Herbert West—Reanimator."[119] In seeing "that which should not be," we experience the uncanny, a sense of beholding the dreadful impossible.

Within robotics, the concept of the uncanny owes its genesis to Sigmund Freud's essay "The 'Uncanny'" which is a reflection on E. T. A. Hoffman's story "The Sandman."[120] The "uncanny" shows up in the story as the protagonist, Nathanael, obsesses over an automaton, frequently fantasizing about this mechanical doll as human. In the story's climax, Nathanael's obsession results in him committing suicide, falling from the steeple of a church as a ragdoll. Nathanael's madness seems to stem from the "pretty eyes" of the automaton Olympia, a doll that moves like a human, an artificial face with lifelike eyes. This idea was initially picked up by Masahiro Mori, a Japanese roboticist who considered the space where human-like robots appear like us but not too like us to be the "uncanny valley." The question of why we feel uncomfortable around "too human" robots has inspired other psychoanalytic researchers like Lydia Liu and Isabell Millar to write about AIs' and robots' psychoanalytic status.[121] But while Liu, Mori, W. J. T. Mitchell, and Millar understand the problem of uncanniness as the anxiety inherent in the ambiguous boundary between life and death,[122] Jacques Lacan suggests it lies more in the eye of the observer than the status of the observed.

Lacan contends that uncanny anxiety "is not so tightly linked to the industrial advance in such peculiar possibilities" in the boundaries between life and death but rather "the *unheimlich* function of the eyes."[123] Lacan locates the experience of uncanniness within the constellation not only of anxiety but specifically of scopic anxiety. In Lacan's analysis, the scopic-anxious person desires *not* to see, which is manifest as misrecognition and results in idealization.[124] Freud's discussion of the Oedipal complex and castration, which Liu passes over quite briefly[125] and Millar reads literally as about sexual fantasy,[126] is revealed by Lacan to be tied to anxiety of gazing unflinchingly at the truth. Oedipus does not have an Oedipal complex, Lacan notes ironically, because "he wants to know, and this is paid for by the horror I described—what in the end he sees are his own eyes . . . cast to the ground."[127] The function of castration, on the other hand, induces anxiety in us; we rather glance away to maintain our illusion of the ideal, the whole. Because anxiety is fundamentally structured by lack, what provokes the anxiety inherent in the uncanny is not the ambiguity of living/dead but rather the specular gap between ideal and real. Nathanael's final bout of madness arrives when he recognizes his fiancée Clara is not the automaton Olympia, an automaton whose lifelike appearance he has continually misrecognized. As a last effort to keep the real from shattering his structure of anxiety, he tries to kill the living Clara before throwing himself to his own death. Bryan Forbes's 1975 robot horror film *The Stepford Wives* captures the uncanny problem better than other AI thinkers: in the film's climax, Joanna Eberhart experiences existential horror as she comes face-to-face with the automaton who will replace her as the ideal wife, an automaton she faces that has no eyes.[128]

It is not accurate to refer to robots as the uncanny, then, except insofar as people idealize them as human or see them as replacing us. More uncanny in their appearance, however, are the poor. Marked in their poverty by their bodies, the poor stand as grisly apparitions to the obsessively clean bourgeoisie. Tech bro Justin Keller invokes the sense of filth and contamination in his invective against the poor of San Francisco, combining in the same sentence the living conditions of the poor with the presence of human feces.[129] Poverty is gazed upon, when it is seen at all, as contagion, pollution, infection. It invokes visceral reactions, unsettling uncomfortability, like the anxious who seek to tear out their own eyes.[130] To see the sunken eyes of the hungry gazing back, or scabbed bodies, or the nervous scratch of a withdrawing addict, or the roach-infested home of a working-poor family is uncanny—it shines a darker reflection on the human condition that we seek to constantly keep at bay.

Doppelganger fiction, then, often provides a more astute study of the realm of the uncanny than does robot fiction. In Vladimir Nabokov's *Despair* and Fyodor Dostoevsky's *The Double*, the protagonists deal with paranoia and obsession over doppelgangers whom nobody else seems to notice. In the former story, the main character enacts a murderous insurance scam on a homeless man whom he sees as his double, while in the latter, the main character's double is a more socially graceful specter whose success haunts the narrator. But it is perhaps Edgar Allan Poe's "William Wilson" that provides the best articulation of the uncanny phenomenon. In this story, the titular Wilson is plagued his entire life by the obnoxious presence of a double with his name who appears at inopportune moments to disrupt the narrator's vicious choices. Determined to be rid of the obnoxious double once and for all, the narrator corners him in a coatroom and stabs him, only to find that he has killed himself. Insofar as the uncanny lies in the structure of scopic anxiety, the "uncanny" double of Wilson must always "appear" to disrupt the narrators' disreputable actions. As long as Wilson does not *see* the double, he is free to pretend his election of moral impropriety is what he really wants. But the visual appearance of his conscience functions to provoke sufficient anxiety that the narrator ceases whatever action he was doing.

The poor likewise live as uncanny doppelgangers to the wealthy. Like Ursula Le Guin's child in "The Ones Who Walk away from Omelas," the wealthy want to sequester the poor away into a room "in a basement under one of the beautiful public buildings of Omelas, or perhaps in the cellar of one of its spacious homes."[131] To gaze upon the horror of the miserable child provokes disgust, fright, rage. To gaze upon the brute face of reality, to truly look upon the truth, is to come face-to-face with the horror that we so carefully cover over. Like the wretched child of Le Guin's "Omelas," the poor are necessary for the existence of the rich, not for their material wealth but for their identity as rich. But this knowledge must remain an open secret, an unacknowledged reality remaining only at the edge of vision and never in focus. AI is a more palatable image for us to gaze upon, a mirror that shows us what we want to see in ourselves. The poor, however, stand as a dark mirror to the rich, reflecting the unflattering reality of a world structured by artificial material depravation and a constant reminder that all exchange in an entropic universe is characterized by loss. Lifting up AI as a sort of techno-mirror displaying our true nature is simply an effort to avoid gazing upon the truth scrawled across the naked faces of the poor, whose existence stands as witness against late-stage capitalism's attempt to placate the guilty consciences of the upper classes.

NOTES

PREFACE

1 Though this is not one of the pieces I read in the class, one can see an example of this in Eric Jaffe, "Americans Think Upward Mobility Is Far More Common than It Really Is," *CityLab*, February 3, 2015, https://www.bloomberg.com/news/articles/2015-02-02/americans-think-upward-mobility-is-far-more-common-than-it-really-is.

2 Levi Checketts, "Idle Hands and the Omega Point: Labor Automation and Catholic Social Teaching," *Agathon: A Journal of Ethics and Value in the Modern World* 5 (2018): 153–71.

3 Marcella Althaus-Reid, *Indecent Theology: Theological Perversions in Sex, Gender and Politics* (New York: Routledge, 2000), 6.

4 Anti-trafficking groups like Polaris and H.E.A.T. Watch note that while it is difficult to gain accurate data for individual counties, California is ranked as one of the worst states for trafficking incidents. See, e.g., National Human Trafficking Holtline, California Statistics, https://humantraffickinghotline.org/en/statistics/california (accessed May 23, 2023). Oakland is considered one of the worst sites for this, as attested by H.E.A.T. Watch, and Alameda County District Attorney Pamela Price claimed it is the third worst place in the US for trafficking. See: Pamela Price, "Real Solution to Human Trafficking," *Oakland Post*, October 19–25, 2022.

5 Hannah Arendt, "The Web of Relationships and the Enacted Stories," in *The Human Condition*, 2nd ed. (Chicago: University of Chicago Press, 1958).

INTRODUCTION

1 Thalassery, "LaMDA: The AI That Google Engineer Blake Lemoine Thinks Has Become Sentient," *The Indian Express*, June 19, 2022, https://indianexpress.com/article/technology/tech-news-technology/lamda-the-program-that-a-google-engineer-thinks-has-become-sentient-7967050/.

2 Blake Lemoine, "Is LaMDA Sentient? An Interview," *Medium*, June 11, 2022, https://cajundiscordian.medium.com/is-lamda-sentient-an-interview-ea64d916d917.

3 Alan Turing, "Computing Machinery and Intelligence," *Mind* 49 (1950): 433.

4 Blake Lemoine, "May Be Fired Soon for Doing AI Ethics Work," *Medium* June 7, 2022, https://cajundiscordian.medium.com/may-be-fired-soon-for-doing-ai-ethics-work-802d8c474e66.
5 James Vincent, "Google Is Poisoning Its Reputation with AI Researchers," *The Verge*, April 13, 2021, https://www.theverge.com/2021/4/13/22370158/google-ai-ethics-timnit-gebru-margaret-mitchell-firing-reputation.
6 Emily M. Bender, Timnit Gebru, Angelina McMillan-Major, and Shmargaret Shmitchell, "On the Dangers of Stochastic Parrots: Can Language Models Be too Big?" (paper, Conference on Fairness, Accountability, and Transparency [FAccT '21], virtual event, March 3–10, 2021), 614–15.
7 Alan Levinovitz, "The Mystery of Go, the Ancient Game That Computers Still Can't Win," *Wired*, May 12, 2014, https://www.wired.com/2014/05/the-world-of-computer-go/.
8 Cade Metz, "In Two Moves, AlpaGo and Lee Sedol Redefined the Future," *Wired*, March 16, 2016, https://www.wired.com/2016/03/two-moves-alphago-lee-sedol-redefined-future/.
9 David Silver, Thomas Hubert, Julian Schrittwieser, Ioannis Antonoglou, Matthew Lai, Arthur Guez, Marc Lanctot, Laurent Sifre, Dharshan Kumaran, Thore Graepel, Timothy Lillicrap, Karen Simonyan, and Demis Hassabis, "A General Reinforcement Learning Algorithm That Masters Chess, Shogi, and Go through Self-Play" *Science* 362, no. 6419 (December 7, 2018): 1140–44.
10 Mark Zastrow, "South Korea Trumpets $863-million AI Fund after AlphaGo 'Shock,'" *Nature*, March 16, 2016, https://www.nature.com/articles/nature.2016.19595.
11 Yu Hong, "Reading the 13th Five Year Plan: Reflections on China's ICT Policy," *International Journal of Communication* 11 (2017): 1758.
12 Manoj Kewalramani, *China's Quest for AI Leadership Prospects*, Takshashila Working Paper (October 1, 2018), 3, http://dx.doi.org/10.2139/ssrn.3414883.
13 Changsong Zhou, "Machine Learning Utilised for Understanding Cognitive Behavior," Hong Kong Baptist University, accessed November 11, 2022, https://interdisciplinary-research.hkbu.edu.hk/research/featured-articles/machine-learning-utilised-for-understanding-cognitive-behaviour.
14 Zhongying Zhao, "HKBU Team Developing Portable Rapid Detection Platform for Cancer and GMOs," Hong Kong Baptist University, accessed November 11, 2022, https://interdisciplinary-research.hkbu.edu.hk/research/featured-articles/hkbu-team-developing-portable-rapid-detection-platform-for-cancer-and-gmos.
15 Alistair Cole, "Trust in the Smart City," Hong Kong Baptist University, accessed November 11, 2022, https://research.hkbu.edu.hk/page/detail/472.
16 Li Chen, "Engaging Digital News Audiences with an AI-Powered News Chatbot," Hong Kong Baptist University, accessed November 11, 2022, https://interdisciplinary-research.hkbu.edu.hk/research/research-projects/engaging-digital-news-audiences-with-an-ai-powered-news-chatbot.

17 "HKBU Launches Turing AI Orchestra as Next Milestone in Human-AI Art Co-Creation," Hong Kong Baptist University, accessed November 11, 2022, https://research.hkbu.edu.hk/news/hkbu-launches-turing-ai-orchestra-as-next-milestone-in-human-ai-art-co-creation.

18 "Research Strategy," Hong Kong Baptist University, accessed November 11, 2022, https://research.hkbu.edu.hk/organisational-structure/research-strategy.

19 "Call for Preliminary Proposals," University Grants Committee, accessed November 11, 2022, https://www.ugc.edu.hk/eng/rgc/funding_opport/trs/call_letter.html.

20 "Strategic Topics Grant," University Grants Committee, accessed November 11, 2022, https://www.ugc.edu.hk/eng/rgc/funding_opport/stg/call_letter.html.

21 Hong, "Reading the 13th Five Year Plan," 1755–74.

22 E.g., "How Artificial Intelligence is Transforming Manufacturing," *The Manufacturer*, March 29, 2021, https://www.themanufacturer.com/articles/ai-transforming-manufacturing/; Matthew Guariglia, "Police Use of Artificial Intelligence: 2021 in Review," *Electronic Frontier Foundation*, January 1, 2022, https://www.eff.org/deeplinks/2021/12/police-use-artificial-intelligence-2021-review; David Lat, "How Artificial Intelligence Is Transforming Legal Research," *ThomsonReuters*, https://abovethelaw.com/law2020/how-artificial-intelligence-is-transforming-legal-research/; Ahmed Hosny, Chintan Parmar, John Quackenbush, Lawrence H. Schwartz, and Hugo J. W. L. Aerts, "Artificial Intelligence in Radiology," *Nature Reviews Cancer* 18 (2018): 500–510.

23 Hyo-Eun Kim, Hak Hee Kim, Boo-Kyung Han, Ki Hwan Kim, Kyunghwa Han, Hyeonseob Nam, Eun Hye Lee, and Eun-Kyung Kim, "Changes in Cancer Detection and False-Positive Recall in Mammography Using Artificial Intelligence: A Retrospective, Multireader Study," *The Lancet* 2, no. 3 (March 2020): e138–e148.

24 Maggie Jackson, "Would You Let a Robot Take Care of Your Mother?" *The New York Times*, December 13, 2019, https://www.nytimes.com/2019/12/13/opinion/robot-caregiver-aging.html; Kelly Wang, "'iPal' Robot Companion for China's Lonely Children," *Phys.Org*, June 14, 2018, https://phys.org/news/2018-06-ipal-robot-companion-china-lonely.html.

25 A brief introduction to much of the academic work and commercial production tied to sexual companion robotics can be found in David Levy's "Love and Sex with Robots" Conference, based off his own book by the same name, which has been held annually since 2015. See: Accessed March 9, 2022, https://www.lovewithrobots.com/. Within his book, published in 2007, Levy claims that human-robot sex will be so routine that by 2050, human beings will engage in intercourse with robots more than other human beings.

26 C. Trout, "There's a New Sex Robot in Town: Say Hello to Solana," *Engadget*, January 10, 2018, https://www.engadget.com/2018-01-10-there-s-a-new-sex-robot-in-town-say-hello-to-solana.html.

27 At the time of this writing, CRISPR/Cas-9 gene editing, blockchain encryption, and renewed interest in space travel created by competition between Elon Musk and Jeff Bezos seem to be the only comparably "exciting" technological frontiers.
28 "About," DeepMind, accessed March 9, 2022, https://deepmind.com/about; "About MIRI," Machine Intelligence Research Institute, accessed March 9, 2022, https://intelligence.org/about/; "About," OpenAI, accessed March 9, 2022, https://openai.com/about/. Both the definition of AGI and the condition of "consciousness" for computers are hotly contentious topics in AI research. As I note in chapter 1, many AI researchers gave up the notion of "consciousness" as too ambiguous, but, as I demonstrate in the conclusion, this idea still underwrites the belief in a thinking computer. While I outline some of the philosophy behind AGI in chapters 1 and 2, the main "threshold" tests are discussed also in the conclusion.
29 Meredith Broussard, *Artificial Unintelligence: How Computers Misunderstand the World* (Cambridge, MA: MIT Press, 2019), 71.
30 Ray Kurzweil, *The Singularity Is Near: When Humans Transcend Biology* (New York: Viking, 2005), 32.
31 Mark Coeckelbergh, *AI Ethics* (Cambridge, MA: MIT Press, 2020), 14.
32 See: "Forecasting," Machine Intelligence Research Institute, accessed December 14, 2022, https://intelligence.org/research/#FC.
33 Cf. Bruno Latour, *Science in Action: How to Follow Scientists and Engineers through Society* (Cambridge, MA: Harvard University Press, 1987), 103–8. Latour details the fact that Diesel's engine did not succeed as initially planned; air compressors, cylinders, proper fuel mixtures, adequate fuels, and so forth eluded his initial patent and had to be solved before a successful combustion engine could function.
34 David Hume, *A Treatise on Human Nature* (London: John Noon, 1739), 335.
35 Herbert Marcuse, *One-Dimensional Man: Studies in the Ideology of Advanced Industrial Society* (Boston: Beacon Press, 1991), 125.
36 David Gunkel, *The Machine Question: Critical Perspectives on AI, Robots, and Ethics* (Cambridge, MA: MIT Press, 2012), 47.
37 Wilvin Chee and Michael Shirer, "IDC Forecasts Strong 12.3% Growth for AI Market in 2020 Amidst Challenging Circumstances," International Data Corporation, August 4, 2020, https://www.idc.com/getdoc.jsp?containerId=prUS46757920.
38 Sabine Pfeiffer, *Digital Capitalism and Distributive Forces* (Bielefeld, Germany: Transcript Verlag, 2022), 151, 219.
39 Saadia Zahidi, Vesselina Ratcheva, Guillaume Hingel, and Sophie Brown, *The Future of Jobs Report 2020*, World Economic Forum, October 2018, 27.
40 Xiaohu Ge, John Thompson, Yonghui Li, Xue Liu, Weiyi Zhang, and Tao Chen, "Applications of Artificial Intelligence in Wireless Communications," *IEEE Communications Magazine* 57, no. 3 (March 2019): 12–13.

41 Maryann Hardy and Hugh Harvey, "Artificial Intelligence in Diagnostic Imaging: Impact on the Radiography Profession," *The British Journal of Radiology* 93, 1108 (2020), doi: 10.1259/bjr.20190840.
42 "Machine Learning for Stock Trading Strategies," Nanalyze, May 21, 2020, https://www.nanalyze.com/2020/05/machine-learning-for-stock-trading-strategies/.
43 "Elon Musk Interview on Autopilot and Full Self Driving—April 2019," *Autopilot Review*, April 12, 2019, https://www.autopilotreview.com/elon-musk-autopilot-interview-mit/.
44 Leif Johnson and Michelle Fitzsimmons, "Uber Self-Driving Cars: Everything You Need to Know," *Tech Radar*, May 26, 2018, https://www.techradar.com/news/uber-self-driving-cars.
45 Michael Wayland, "General Motors Unveils New High-End GMC Sierra Denali and AT4X Pickup Trucks," *CNBC*, October 21, 2021, https://www.cnbc.com/2021/10/21/general-motors-unveils-new-high-end-gmc-sierra-denali-and-at4x-pickups.html. One of my brothers-in-law works as an executive at Hyundai Mobis in South Korea. Part of his work is overseeing teams working on self-driving technology. As he tells me, it is critical for Hyundai to achieve this as part of its own strategy in the global automobile market. In other words, every other major car company is working on this as well.
46 "Facial Recognition Technology: Current and Planned Uses by Federal Agencies," Government Accountability Office, August 24, 2021, https://www.gao.gov/products/gao-21-526.
47 Adam Satariano, "Real Time Surveillance Will Test the British Tolerance for Cameras," *New York Times*, September 15, 2019, https://www.nytimes.com/2019/09/15/technology/britain-surveillance-privacy.html; Shannon Flynn, "13 Cities Where Police Are Banned from Using Facial Recognition Tech," *Innovation & Tech Today*, November 18, 2020, https://innotechtoday.com/13-cities-where-police-are-banned-from-using-facial-recognition-tech/.
48 Francis Bacon, *The Advancement of Learning*, I. v, 11. Bacon also posits that science should be "for the glory of the Creator," but this aim is not as relevant for many AI researchers.
49 Demis Hasabis, "AlphaFold Reveals the Structure of the Protein Universe," *DeepMind*, July 28, 2022, https://www.deepmind.com/blog/alphafold-reveals-the-structure-of-the-protein-universe.
50 Hong Kong Smart City Blueprint, accessed December 14, 2022, https://www.smartcity.gov.hk/.
51 "Artificial Intelligence in High Performance Computing," Cybele, accessed November 11, 2022, https://web.archive.org/web/20221208024119/https://www.cybele-project.eu/post/artificial-intelligence-in-high-performance-computing.
52 Lee Vinsel, "You're Doing It Wrong: Notes on Criticism and Technology Hype," *STS News*, February 2, 2021, https://sts-news.medium.com/youre-doing-it-wrong-notes-on-criticism-and-technology-hype-18b08b4307e5.

53 The piper came to collect a year later. After Musk's baffling ascent, he fumbled his way into owning the social media platform Twitter, National Highway Traffic Safety Administration recalled 362,000 cars, Tesla stock plummeted, and Musk lost around two hundred billion dollars of value.
54 Minsky, in fact, declared the field of AGI "'brain-dead' since the 1970s," a reference to what most call the "AI Winter." Josh McHugh, "Why A.I. Is Brain-Dead," *Wired*, August 1, 2003, https://www.wired.com/2003/08/why-a-i-is-brain-dead/. See also: Julia Bobak, "Why Did AI Research Drift from Strong AI to Weak AI?" *TechnoPreneurPH*, September 20, 2017, https://technopreneurph.wordpress.com/2017/09/20/why-did-ai-research-drift-from-strong-to-weak-ai-by-julia-bobak/.
55 "About," DeepMind.
56 See, e.g., Ben Goertzel, "From Narrow AI to AGI via Narrow AI?" *Medium*, August 1, 2019, https://medium.com/@bengoertzel/from-narrow-ai-to-agi-via-narrow-agi-8d828d8c2aa2.

CHAPTER 1

1 See: Jacques Ellul, *The Technological Society*, trans. John Wilkinson (Toronto: Alfred A. Knopf, 1964), 6; Arendt, *The Human Condition*, 145; Gunkel, *The Machine Question*, 31.
2 Robert Owen, *A New View of Society and Other Writings* (London: Everyman's Library, 1966), 143.
3 Paul Mozur, "Life inside Foxconn's Facility in Shenzhen," *The Wall Street Journal*, December 19, 2012, https://www.wsj.com/articles/BL-CJB-17008.
4 Christian de Looper, "Thousands of Jobs Lost as Apple Supplier Foxconn Fully Automates Its Factories," *Digital Trends*, December 30, 2016, https://www.digitaltrends.com/mobile/foxconn-three-phases-factory-automation/.
5 Gabriel Hallevy, "The Criminal Liability of Artificial Intelligence Entities—from Science Fiction to Legal Social Control," *Akron Intellectual Property Journal* 4, no. 2 (2010): 171–72. Interestingly, Hallevy's account differs from the source material he draws from: "In 1981, a 37-year-old factory worker named Kenji Urada entered a restricted safety zone at a Kawasaki manufacturing plant to perform some maintenance on a robot. In his haste, he failed to completely turn it off. The robot's powerful hydraulic arm pushed the engineer into some adjacent machinery, thus making Urada the first recorded victim to die at the hands of a robot." Yueh-Hsuan Weng, Chien-Hsun Chen, and Chuen-Tsai Sun, "Toward the Human–Robot Co-Existence Society: On Safety Intelligence for Next Generation Robots," *International Journal of Social Robotics* (April 2009): 273. Whether Hallevy intentionally embellished the story to give the machine more agency than the original authors is unclear, but it does demonstrate the sense of autonomy that pervades AI discourse.
6 Hubert Dreyfus, *What Computers* Still *Can't Do* (Cambridge, MA: MIT Press, 1992), 311 n.102.

7 Oscar Schwartz, "In the 17th Century, Leibniz Dreamed of a Machine That Could Calculate Ideas," *IEEE Spectrum*, November 4, 2019, spectrum.ieee.org/tech-talk/artificial-intelligence/machine-learning/in-the-17th-century-leibniz-dreamed-of-a-machine-that-could-calculate-ideas. Cf: Gottfried Wilhelm Leibniz, *Dissertation on Combinatorial Art*, trans. Massimo Mugnai, Han van Ruler, and Martin Wilson (Oxford: Oxford University Press, 2020).
8 Ada Augusta Lovelace, "Notes by Translator," in *Scientific Memoirs, Selected from the Transactions of Foreign Academies of Science and Learned Societies, and from Foreign Journals* vol. 3, ed. Richard Taylor (Richard & John E. Taylor: London, 1843), 722.
9 Claude Shannon, "A Mathematical Theory of Communication," *The Bell System Technical Journal* 27, no. 3 (July 1948): 394
10 Shannon, "A Mathematical Theory," 379.
11 Turing, "Computing Machinery," 440.
12 Turing, 433.
13 Norbert Wiener, *The Human Use of Human Beings: Cybernetics and Society* (London: Free Association Books, 1950), 130.
14 Wiener, *The Human Use*, 48.
15 John McCarthy and Patrick J. Hayes, "Some Philosophical Problems from the Standpoint of Artificial Intelligence," *Machine Intelligence* 4 (1969): 463–502.
16 John McCarthy, "Ascribing Mental Qualities to Machines," in *Philosophical Perspectives in Artificial Intelligence*, ed. Martin Ringle (Atlantic Highlands, NJ: Humanities Press, 1979), 161–95.
17 McCarthy, "Ascribing Mental Qualities."
18 Dreyfus, *What Computers* Still *Can't Do*, 129.
19 It is interesting to note that, while cybernetics *seems* to have gone out of favor, the ideas of cyberneticists have saturated popular culture in ways we often take for granted. Cybernetics' focus on feedback systems like an engine governor (from Latin: *gubernator*, originating from the Greek *xybernetes*) was adapted by Clynes and Kline in 1960 to propose that feedback machines could be integrated into organic systems, creating "cybernetic organisms" or "cyborgs." Manfred Clynes and Nathan Kline, "Cyborgs and Space," *Astronautics* (September 1960): 26–27, 74–76. "Cyborg," in turn, was adapted by William Gibson to describe a network of linked minds called "cyberspace." William Gibson, *Neuromancer* (New York: Penguin, 1984), 51. Today, "cyberspace" may be an outdated moniker for the internet, but the hearkening to Wiener and Shannon appears in such portmanteaus as "cybersecurity," "cybercrime," or "cyberwar." Indeed, there is something poetic about the concept of cyberwar: warfare fought through information attacks on enemy machinery rather than persons, vindicating Wiener's thesis that material is insignificant to information.
20 Hans Moravec, *Mind Children: The Future of Robot and Human Intelligence* (Cambridge, MA: Harvard University Press, 1988), 68.

21 Ben Goertzel, *The Hidden Pattern: A Patternist Philosophy of Mind* (Boca Raton: Brown Walker, 2006), 156; Kurzweil, *The Singularity Is Near.*

22 Goertzel, *The Hidden Pattern*, 156.

23 Kurzweil, *The Singularity Is Near*, 258.

24 Dreyfus, "Why Heideggerian AI Failed and How Fixing It Would Require Making It More Heideggerian," *Artificial Intelligence* 171, no. 18 (December 2007): 1138.

25 Dreyfus, "Why Heideggerian AI Failed." Dreyfus repeats this claim in his work, and it is repeated by other scholars, including M. Keith Wright, who says, "Marvin Minsky, once estimated that commonsense knowledge is composed of about forty million facts about the world we live in." M. Keith Wright, "Using Open Source Tools in Text Mining Research," paper presented at Southwest Design Sciences Institute Conference in Dallas, TX, March 3, 2005, 312. The closest corroboration for this I've found in Minsky's own work is "We all remember millions of frames, each representing some stereotyped situation like meeting a certain kind of person, being in a certain kind of room, or attending a certain kind of party." Marvin Minsky, *The Society of Mind* (New York: Simon & Schuster, 1985), 244. Later, Minsky made the claim that the brain is "400-odd different pieces of computer architecture with their own busses and somewhat different architecture." Marvin Minsky, "Why Freud Was the First Good AI Theorist," in *The Transhumanist Reader: Classical and Contemporary Essays on the Science, Technology and Philosophy of the Human Future*, ed. Max More and Natasha Vita-More (Malden, MA: Wiley-Blackwell, 2013), 172.

26 Janelle Shane, "AI Recipes Are Bad (and a Proposal for Making Them Worse)," *AI Weirdness*, January 31, 2020, https://www.aiweirdness.com/ai-recipes-are-bad-and-a-proposal-20-01-31/.

27 Arthur Samuel, "Some Studies in Machine Learning Using the Game of Checkers," *IBM Journal of Research and Development* 44 (1959): 206–29.

28 Dreyfus, *What Computers* Still *Can't Do*, xxxvi.

29 Metz, "In Two Moves."

30 김현길, "매너 좋고 인간적인 '알파고'도 가능할까," *국민일보*, March 18, 2021 http://news.kmib.co.kr/article/view.asp?arcid=0924183344&code=13150000&cp=du. The fact that this moment is only reported by Korean media and not by Western media is telling of the way technical precision, and not the protocol of Go, was the major focus among Western reporters.

31 Warren McCulloch and Walter Pitts, "A Logical Calculus of the Ideas Immanent in Nervous Activities," *Bulletin of Mathematical Biophysics* 5 (1943): 115–33.

32 Marvin Minsky and Seymour Papert, *Perceptrons: An Introduction to Computational Geometry*, expanded ed. (Cambridge, MA: MIT Press, 1988), 251.

33 James McClelland and David Rumelhart, "Distributed Memory and the Representation of General and Specific Information," *Journal of Experimental Psychology* 114, no. 2 (1985): 159–88.

34 Karen Hao, "AI Consumes a Lot of Energy. Hackers Could Make It Consume More," *MIT Technology Review*, May 6, 2021, https://www.technologyreview.com/2021/05/06/1024654/ai-energy-hack-adversarial-attack/; Roel Dobbe and Meredith Whitaker, "AI and Climate Change: How They're Connected and What We Can Do about It," *AI Now Institute*, October 18, 2019, https://medium.com/@AINowInstitute/ai-and-climate-change-how-theyre-connected-and-what-we-can-do-about-it-6aa8d0f5b32c.
35 Minsky, "Why Freud Was the First Good AI Theorist."
36 As we will see in the next chapter, it is here where the question of "consciousness" most clearly comes into play. John Searle's "Chinese Room" thought experiment draws out precisely the sort of problems tied to thinking and language that NLP tries to address.
37 Aaron Saenz, "Cleverbot Chat Engine Is Learning from the Internet to Talk Like a Human," *Singularity Hub*, January 13, 2010, https://singularityhub.com/2010/01/13/cleverbot-chat-engine-is-learning-from-the-internet-to-talk-like-a-human/.
38 James Vincent, "Twitter Taught Microsoft's AI Chatbot to Be a Racist Asshole in Less Than a Day," *The Verge*, March 24, 2016, https://www.theverge.com/2016/3/24/11297050/tay-microsoft-chatbot-racist.
39 "Facebook Researchers Shut Down AI Bots That Started Speaking in a Language Unintelligible to Humans," *Firstpost*, August 1, 2017, https://www.firstpost.com/tech/news-analysis/facebook-researchers-shut-down-ai-bots-that-started-speaking-in-a-language-unintelligible-to-humans-3876197.html. This is not really developing a language. At best, it can be described as adaptation, the way Modern English is different from Old English. Nobody really believes the machines have understanding, but that did not stop sensationalist media from using apocalyptic language to report it.
40 Toney Bradley, "Facebook AI Creates Its Own Language in Creepy Preview of Our Own Future," *Forbes*, July 31, 2017, https://www.forbes.com/sites/tonybradley/2017/07/31/facebook-ai-creates-its-own-language-in-creepy-preview-of-our-potential-future/?sh=7d9f9d5a292c.
41 Alec Radford, Jeffrey Wu, Dario Amodei, Daniela Amodei, Jack Clark, Miles Brundage, and Ilya Sutskever, "Better Language Models and Their Implications," *OpenAI*, February 14, 2019, https://openai.com/blog/better-language-models/.
42 Sofia Barnett, "ChatGPT Is Making Universities Rethink Plagiarism," *Wired*, January 30, 2023, https://www.wired.com/story/chatgpt-college-university-plagiarism/.
43 Janus Rose, "School Apologises after Using ChatGPT to Write Email about Mass-Shooting," *Vice*, February 22, 2023, https://www.vice.com/en/article/88qwqg/school-apologizes-after-using-chatgpt-to-write-email-about-mass-shooting.

44 Michael Grothaus, "A Science Fiction Magazine Closed Submissions after Being Bombarded with Stories Written by ChatGPT," *Fast Company*, February 23, 2023, https://www.fastcompany.com/90853591/chatgpt-science-fiction-short-stories-clarkesworld-magazine-submissions.
45 Nick Cave, "ChatGPT, What Do You Think?" *The Red Hand Files* no. 218, January 2023, https://www.theredhandfiles.com/chat-gpt-what-do-you-think/.
46 Randall Reed, "The Theology of GPT-2: Religion and Artificial Intelligence," *Religion Compass* 15, no. 11 (November 2021): e12422.
47 The humor site Engrish.com, a subsidiary of Cheezburger.com (an early meme site), has long documented examples of poor translations into "English" ("Engrish" being a racist caricature of the lack of distinction between R and L sounds in some East Asian countries, which occasionally leads to spelling mistakes), many of which were rendered by some translation software.
48 See: Dreyfus, *What Computers* Still *Can't Do*, 197–201.
49 Hubert Dreyfus outlined a similar set of underlying beliefs in *What Computers* Still *Can't Do*, 159–224. Like Dreyfus, I highlight the epistemological and ontological assumptions of AI, and references to him below demonstrate this. Dreyfus adds to this a "biological assumption," namely, that the brain operates "as a large telephone switchboard or . . . as an electronic computer" (159), and a "psychological assumption," that there is an "information-processing level" in the brain and "that on this level the mind uses computer processes such as comparing, classifying, searching lists, and so forth, to produce intelligent behavior" (163). I subsume part of the psychological assumption into the methodological assertion of AI below, while the biological assumption is part of the broader ontological assumption.
50 It is important to note that this philosophy may not be at play in all computer science work. A computer scientist can appreciate a computer's sophisticated computational power without assuming that the computer is doing anything like what human beings do. AI, however, assumes that the computer's activity is at least analogous to human cognition, so these philosophical assumptions remain.
51 Immanuel Kant, *Critique of Pure Reason*, ed. Paul Guyer and Allen W. Wood (Cambridge: Cambridge University Press, 1999), 27.
52 Brad Templeton, "Teslas Are Crashing into Emergency Vehicles too Much, So NHTSA Asks Other Car Companies about It," *Forbes*, September 20, 2021, https://www.forbes.com/sites/bradtempleton/2021/09/20/teslas-are-crashing-into-emergency-vehicles-too-much-so-nhtsa-asks-other-car-companies-about-it/?sh=7c5bd77160a7.
53 Rich McCormick, "Odds Are We're Living in a Simulation, Says Elon Musk," *The Verge*, June 2, 2016, http://www.theverge.com/2016/6/2/11837874/elon-musk-says-odds-living-in-simulation; Kurzweil, *The Singularity Is Near*, 271.
54 This is at the root of what Dreyfus refers to in his "biological assumption" and "psychological assumption." The biological assumption posits that the brain's

neurological firing is like a computer, and the psychological assumption posits that the brain's neurological functioning is essentially the same sort of activity as a computer executing a program. This view is held by many uploaders like Ray Kurzweil and Hans Moravec, but others, like Randal Koene, are not as optimistic. Koene believes "decoding" the mind is too great a task, so "whole brain emulation" will be necessary, where every neuron of a person's brain is recreated exactly in a computer emulation. See: Randal A. Koene, "Uploading to Substrate-Independent Minds," in *The Transhumanist Reader*, 149.

55 John Jumper et al., "Applying and Improving AlphaFold at CASP14," *Proteins* 89, no. 12 (October 2, 2021): 1711–21.

56 Hubert Dreyfus, "A History of First Step Fallacies," *Minds and Machines* 22 (2012): 91.

57 Minsky, "Why Freud Was the First Good AI Theorist."

58 See: "How to Reduce Bias in AI," *Appen*, June 7, 2021 https://appen.com/blog/how-to-reduce-bias-in-ai/; Emily Sokol, "Overcoming Bias in Artificial Intelligence, Machine Learning," *Health IT Analytics*, January 9, 2020, https://healthitanalytics.com/news/overcoming-bias-in-artificial-intelligence-machine-learning; Lance Eliot, "Overcoming Racial Bias in AI Systems and Startlingly Even in Self-Driving Cars," *Forbes*, January 4, 2020, https://www.forbes.com/sites/lanceeliot/2020/01/04/overcoming-racial-bias-in-ai-systems-and-startlingly-even-in-ai-self-driving-cars/?sh=455cc5b723b7. In the next chapter, we will see arguments from scholars like Ruha Benjamin and Safiya Nobel, who contend it isn't data alone but also the aims, goals, and frameworks of AI programmers.

59 "Purity," *xkcd*, accessed March 9, 2022, https://xkcd.com/435/.

60 AI theorist researchers like Ben Goertzel and Louie Helm have pointed out that Asimov's laws are poor models because they may be impossible to program and, as demonstrated in Asimov's own writings, might easily lead to contradictions. George Dvorsky, "Why Asimov's Three Laws of Robotics Can't Protect Us," *Gizmodo*, March 28, 2014, https://gizmodo.com/why-asimovs-three-laws-of-robotics-cant-protect-us-1553665410.

61 Dylan Matthews, "How Effective Altruism Went from a Niche Movement to a Billion-Dollar Force," *Vox*, August 8, 2022, https://www.vox.com/future-perfect/2022/8/8/23150496/effective-altruism-sam-bankman-fried-dustin-moskovitz-billionaire-philanthropy-crytocurrency.

62 Max Weber, *Economy and Society: An Outline of Interpretive Sociology*, ed. Guenther Roth and Claus Wittich (Berkeley: University of California Press, 1978), 24. The notion of "rationalism" as the social tendency that justifies capitalism is persistent through Weber's work, but he rarely appends the term "instrumental." Further readers of Weber, such as Max Horkheimer, Robert Nozick, and John Rawls, have emphasized this notion as distinct from other forms of rationalism. As we shall see later (conclusion), it really does not make much difference as all forms of rationalism seek to justify their position.

63 The general problem of "misaligned goals" is a problem we will look at in the next chapter. Existential Risk theorists consider this to be a greater general threat than the so-called "malevolent AI" threat *a lá* the *Terminator* movies.

CHAPTER 2

1 Mar Hicks, *Programmed Inequality: How Britain Discarded Women Technologists and Lost Its Edge in Computing* (Cambridge, MA: MIT Press, 2017).
2 Nathan Ensmenger, *Computer Boys Take Over: Computers, Programmers, and the Politics of Technical Expertise* (Cambridge, MA: MIT Press, 2017).
3 Brenda D. Frink, "Researcher Reveals How 'Computer Geeks' Replaced 'Computer Girls,'" *Gender News*, The Clayman Institute for Gender Research, June 1, 2011, https://web.archive.org/web/20150312130252/http://gender.stanford.edu/news/2011/researcher-reveals-how-%E2%80%9Ccomputer-geeks%E2%80%9D-replaced-%E2%80%9Ccomputergirls%E2%80%9D.
4 Catherine Ashcraft, Brad McLain, and Elizabeth Eger, *Women in Tech: The Facts* (National Center for Women in Information Technology, 2016), 6.
5 Sara Tangdall, "Google's Handling of the Echo Chamber Manifesto," Markkula Center for Applied Ethics, September 11, 2017, https://www.scu.edu/ethics/focus-areas/business-ethics/resources/googles-handling-of-the-echo-chamber-manifesto/.
6 Robert Williams, "I Was Wrongfully Arrested Because of Facial Recognition. Why Are Police Allowed to Use It?" *Washington Post*, June 24, 2020, https://www.washingtonpost.com/opinions/2020/06/24/i-was-wrongfully-arrested-because-facial-recognition-why-are-police-allowed-use-this-technology/.
7 Williams, "I Was Wrongfully Arrested."
8 Nick Bostrom, *Superintelligence: Paths, Dangers, Strategies* (Oxford: Oxford University Press, 2014), 211, 214; Nick Bostrom and Eliezer Yudkowsky, "The Ethics of Artificial Intelligence," in *Cambridge Handbook of Artificial Intelligence*, ed. Keith Frankish and William Ramsey (Cambridge: Cambridge University Press, 2014) 332; Coeckelbergh, *AI Ethics*, 51; Andreia Martinho, Adam Poulsen, Maarten Kroesen, and Caspar Chorus, "Perspectives about Artificial Moral Agents," *AI and Ethics* 1 (2021): 486.
9 Immanuel Kant, *Groundwork for the Metaphysics of Morals*, ed. and trans. Allen W. Wood (New Haven: Yale University Press, 2002), 49.
10 Kant, *Groundwork for the Metaphysics*, 58.
11 See: David Collings, "The Monster and the Imaginary Mother: A Lacanian Reading of Frankenstein," in *Frankenstein: Complete, Authoritative Text with Biographical, Historical, and Cultural Contexts; Critical History; and Essays from Contemporary Critical Perspectives*, 3rd ed., ed. Johanna M. Smith (Boston: Bedford/St. Martin's, 2016), 323–39.; Will W. Adams, "Making Daemons of Death and Love: Frankenstein, Existentialism, Psychoanalysis," *Journal of Humanistic Psychology* 41, no. 4

(2001): 57–89; Selen Baranoğlu, *An Analysis of Mary Shelley's Frankenstein and Robert Louis Stevenson's Dr. Jekyll and Mr. Hyde in Relation to Lacanian Criticism* (master's thesis, Middle East Technical University, 2008); Haidee Kotze, "Desire, Gender, Power, Language: A Psychoanalytic Reading of Mary Shelley's *Frankenstein*," *Literator* 21, no. 1 (2000): 53–67.

12 *Hackers* (1995); Andrew Leonard, "The Tech Industry's God Complex Is Getting Out of Control," *Salon*, June 13, 2014, https://www.salon.com/2014/06/13/the_tech_industrys_god_complex_is_getting_out_of_control/; Stephen Grocer, Maureen Farrell, and Telis Demos, "The 'God Complex' in Silicon Valley," *The Wall Street Journal*, April 8, 2017, https://www.wsj.com/podcasts/the-god-complex-in-silicon-valley/a17337f1-ad37-4720-9922-771b6dd7680e.

13 Dan Robitzski, "Former Google Exec Warns That AI Researchers Are 'Creating God,'" *The Byte*, September 30, 2021, https://futurism.com/the-byte/google-exec-ai-god; Mark Harris, "Inside the First Church of Artificial Intelligence," *Wired*, November 15, 2017, https://www.wired.com/story/anthony-levandowski-artificial-intelligence-religion/.

14 Tony Ho Tran, "The Radical Movement to Worship AI as a New God," *Daily Beast*, February 26, 2023, https://www.thedailybeast.com/the-radical-movement-to-worship-ai-chatbots-like-chatgpt-as-gods.

15 Karel Čapek, *R.U.R.*, trans. Paul Selver and Nigel Playfair, I–7.

16 Philip Hefner, "Technology and Human Becoming," *Zygon* 37, no. 3 (September 2002): 655.

17 Gunkel, *The Machine Question*, 215.

18 Bostrom and Yudkowsky, "The Ethics of Artificial Intelligence," 322.

19 "Frequently Asked Questions," Sentientism, accessed November 11, 2022, https://sentientism.info/faq; Francesca Ferrando, *Philosophical Posthumanism* (London: Bloombsury Academic, 2019), 187.

20 Bostrom and Yudkowsky, "The Ethics of Artificial Intelligence," 331; Daniel Wikler, "Paternalism in the Age of Cognitive Enhancement: Do Civil Liberties Presuppose Roughly Equal Mental Ability?" in *Human Enhancement*, ed. Julian Savulescu and Nick Bostrom (Oxford: Oxford University Press, 2009), 354.

21 Peter Singer, "Isaac Asimov's Laws of Robotics Are Wrong," Brookings Institute, May 18, 2009, https://www.brookings.edu/opinions/isaac-asimovs-laws-of-robotics-are-wrong/.

22 Koene, "Uploading to Substrate-Independent Minds," 155.

23 See: Bostrom and Yudkowsky, "The Ethics of Artificial Intelligence." Cf: Julian Savulescu and Ingmar Persson, "Moral Enhancement," *Philosophy Now* 91 (2012): https://philosophynow.org/issues/91/Moral_Enhancement.

24 See: L. Righetti, Q. Pham, R. Madhavan, and R. Chatila, "Lethal Autonomous Weapon Systems [Ethical, Legal, and Societal Issues]," *IEEE Robotics & Automation Magazine* 25, no. 1 (March 2018): 123–26.

25 Thomas Brewster, "DARPA Pays $1 Million for an AI App That Can Predict an Enemy's Emotions," *Forbes*, July 15, 2020, https://www.forbes.com/sites/thomasbrewster/2020/07/15/the-pentagons-1-million-question-can-ai-predict-an-enemys-emotions/?sh=3e64dad632b4.

26 Rory Cellan-Jones, "Stephen Hawking Warns Artificial Intelligence Could End Mankind," *BBC*, December 2, 2014, https://www.bbc.com/news/technology-30290540.

27 Although the internet might be said to only go back as far as 1989, and though the concept of "cyberspace" that stirred popular interest in internet technology goes back to William Gibson's 1984 novel *Neuromancer*, the 1977 film *Demon Seed* features a super-powerful AI capable of utilizing a network of computers to carry out its interests, and even the 1970 *Colossus: The Forbin Project* involves two AIs in the US and USSR linking through transatlantic cables to become a single super-AI. Indeed, AM from Harlan Ellison's "I Have No Mouth, and I Must Scream" is an AI that emerges from the synthesis of three different global defensive computer programs, so the idea dates back at least to the 1960s.

28 Hans Moravec, "Pigs in Cyberspace," in *The Transhumanist Reader*, 180.

29 Nick Bostrom, *Superintelligence*, 123–24.

30 Hans Jonas, "Cybernetics and Purpose: A Critique," in *The Phenomenon of Life: Toward a Philosophical Biology* (New York: Dell Publishing, 1966), 126. Jonas insightfully notes that telos is tied to metabolic functioning, i.e., we have organic needs that lead us to seek goods and avoid evils. Lawrence Vogel thus interprets Jonas's "biological philosophy" as a type of "natural law" thinking that mirrors the views scholastic natural law thinkers. See: Lawrence Vogel, "Natural Law Judaism? The Genesis of Bioethics in Hans Jonas, Leo Strauss, and Leon Kass," in *The Legacy of Hans Jonas: Judaism and the Phenomenon of Life*, ed. Hava Tirosh-Samuelson and Christian Wiese (Leiden: Brill, 2008), 287–314.

I disagree with the articulation of Jonas's position as natural law but find his argument, specifically the development of value from metabolism, to be quite convincing. Such a view accommodates itself well to various environmental philosophies, such as deep ecology or sentientism, while still maintaining an anthropic preference that many have found lacking in these views. In Jonas's view, ethics, and specifically concepts of right and wrong, are uniquely human, but are really the evolutionary outcome of emotion that we find in animals, which itself is an evolutionary outcome of the basic values of metabolism. See: Hans Jonas, *Philosophical Essays* (New York: Atropos Press, 2010), 187–225; and Hans Jonas, *Mortality and Morality: A Search for the Good after Auschwitz*, ed. Lawrence Vogel (Evanston, IL: Northwestern University Press, 1996), 59–74, 87–98.

From Jonas's view, then, an AI, which is itself an outgrowth of the cybernetic philosophy, would only be capable of moral action (properly speaking) if it had organic metabolic functioning, that is, if it had an innate drive to consume and avoid being killed.

31 Consider, e.g., Kant's view. For Kant, the morally right thing is what corresponds to autonomous reason, but more importantly, for Kant, "the only thing good is a good will." Autonomous reason *may* be achievable by a machine, but without apprehending that autonomous reason as the morally correct action, that is, one that must be chosen freely in opposition to any heteronomous act, the act will not be good. Unless the machine can choose the correct act, which entails also that it can choose the wrong act, it cannot be said to be good.

On a consequentialist scale, we may say that yielding maximal preferential outcomes is good, and this can be programmed into the machine. This may be true, but then the act of the machine would be good only from an external, not internal, perspective. The machine would not be considered "good" from this perspective any more than another machine would be said to be good or bad; that is, the AI would have to be treated with the same normative consideration that we consider "dumb" machines like automobiles, hair dryers, and coin mints. Thus, from any normative view that prioritizes intention (deontology, virtue, natural law, etc), the AI cannot be said to be good or bad, but from any view prioritizing outcome (consequentialism, social ethics models, etc.), the question of AI ethics is no more challenging than any technology ethics problem.

32 It is not by accident that words like animal and animate are related, or emotion and motivation. In antiquity, the idea of self-contained movement was linked to life—an animal possessed a soul (*anima*), which animated it, just as emotions and motivations were part of motility. Modern technology, however, mimics this idea, with new words like animatronic or motor indicating movement of mechanical things. This analogous use of these roots is not the same as attributing "motivation" or "animation" to lifeless machines; although a car has a "motor," we would never say car is "motivated" to seek out gasoline. Indeed, the discrepancy we can recognize—that a "motor" does not have "emotion" or that an "animatronic" is not an "animal" suggests more than anything else that Hefner's thesis is correct—technology functions as a mirror for how we envision ourselves. In this line, it is not at all surprising that Hawking, Elon Musk, Hans Moravec, and others, brilliant as they are (or claim to be), make such a fundamental error, namely, in attributing to computers' organic motivations to grow, reproduce, and perpetuate their existence. Why an adding machine would be driven to this is never fully explained, except that we humans are driven to this.

33 Michael Matteson and Chris Metivier, "Case: The Ford Pinto," *Business Ethics*, University of North Carolina Greensboro, accessed March 30, 2022, https://philosophia.uncg.edu/phi361-matteson/module-1-why-does-business-need-ethics/case-the-ford-pinto/.

34 John Searle, "Minds, Brains, and Programs," in *Philosophy of Mind: A Guide and an Anthology*, ed. John Heil (Oxford: Oxford University Press, 2004), 236–37. One thing that Searle seems to neglect is that there is no "one" answer to a given question. If I ask, "What sort of animal is a human being?" the answers "mammal,

primate, ape, hominin, rational, political, divine" are all appropriate and correct. Likewise, Searle does not take into consideration either that sometimes understanding is expressed through false answers, such as when a child is asked their name but provides a fake name, or when making a joke. In fact, this is part of the reason why, in 2014, it was reported that a computer had passed the Turing test: a chatbot created to imitate broken English and mannerisms of a Ukrainian teen was able to convince human judges that its peculiar responses were due either to poor English or to teenage colloquialisms. Vladimir Veselov, "Computer AI Passes Turing Test in 'World First,'" *BBC*, June 9, 2014, https://www.bbc.com/news/technology-27762088.

35 Searle, "Minds, Brains, and Programs," 249.

36 Searle, 251.

37 Jaron Lanier, *You Are Not a Gadget: A Manifesto* (Toronto: First Vintage Books, 2011), 10. Lanier's argument about "lock-in" is highly reminiscent of Heidegger's notion of "enframing." Martin Heidegger argued that technology closes off other possibilities. See: Martin Heidegger, "The Question Concerning Technology," in *The Question Concerning Technology and Other Essays*, trans. William Lovitt (New York: Harper Perennial, 1977), 27.

38 Lanier, *You Are Not a Gadget*, 21.

39 Lanier, 23.

40 Donna Haraway, "Cyborg Manifesto," in *Simians, Cyborgs, and Women: The Reinvention of Nature* (New York: Routledge, 1991), 150.

41 Haraway, "Cyborg Manifesto," 164.

42 Donna Haraway, "Situated Knowledges," in *Simians, Cyborgs, and Women*, 188.

43 Haraway, "Situated Knowledges," 189.

44 Haraway, David Bloor, Bruno Latour, and many others argue forcefully that science is a social construct. But they do not believe "social construct" means "arbitrary." Rather, as Latour writes, construction describes "a more realistic version of what it is for anything to *stand* . . . to say that something is constructed has always been associated with an appreciation of its robustness, quality, style, durability, worth, etc." Bruno Latour, *Reassembling the Social: An Introduction to Actor-Network-Theory* (Oxford: Oxford University Press, 2005), 89.

45 Haraway, "Situated Knowledges," 195.

46 Sherry Turkle and Seymour Papert, "Epistemological Pluralism: Styles and Voices within the Computer Culture," *Signs: Journal of Women in Culture and Society* 16, no. 1 (Autumn 1990): 128–57.

47 Turkle and Papert, "Epistemological Pluralism," 151.

48 Turkle and Papert, 156.

49 Sherry Turkle, *Alone Together: Why We Expect More from Technology and Less From Each Other* (New York: Basic Books, 2011), 224.

50 Turkle, *Alone Together*, 66.

51 See the concluding section of chapter 1 of this work.

52 Dreyfus, *What Computers* Still *Can't Do*, 232.
53 Dreyfus, *What Computers* Still *Can't Do*, 241.
54 Dreyfus, *What Computers* Still *Can't Do*, 257, 261
55 Dreyfus, *What Computers* Still *Can't Do*, 277.
56 Dreyfus, *What Computers* Still *Can't Do*, 303–4.
57 Noreen Herzfeld, *In Our Image: Artificial Intelligence and the Human Spirit* (Minneapolis: Fortress Press, 2002), 74. Note: Martine Rothblatt has also been advocating for consciousness uploading since 2004 through her Terasem Movement, a mere two years after Herzfeld's book was published. Rothblatt supports consciousness uploading through an argument tied to transgenderism and what she calls "morphological freedom." Rothblatt contends humans should have the freedom to reconfigure their bodies and minds in any way they please, free from legal constraint or social approbation. The feminists cited below tend to disagree with this point, noting that the idea of a "neutral" body position is inherently hegemonic and leads to further denigration of women's experience. See: Martine Rothblatt, "Mind Is Deeper Than Matter: Transgenderism, Transhumanism, and Freedom of Form," in *The Transhumanist Reader*, 317–26.
58 Cade Metz and Daisuke Wakabayashi, "Google Researcher Says She Was Fired Over Paper Highlighting Bias in A.I.," *The New York Times*, December 3, 2020, https://www.nytimes.com/2020/12/03/technology/google-researcher-timnit-gebru.html.
59 Paresh Dave and Jeffrey Dastin, "Google Fires Second AI Ethics Leader as Dispute over Research, Diversity Grows," *Reuters*, February 20, 2021, https://www.reuters.com/article/us-alphabet-google-research-idUSKBN2AJ2JA.
60 Bender, Gebru, McMillan-Major, and Shmitchell. While the *New York Times* article above claims Gebru was fired over highlighting bias, the "Stochastic Parrots" article only addresses bias in a small way. The focus of the article is NLP models, noting the models require massive amounts of energy to train, the way that language samples perpetuate bias, and the problem of overreliance on programs that do not "understand" what they "say."
61 Cathy O'Neil, *Weapons of Math Destruction: How Big Data Increases Inequality and Threatens Democracy* (New York: Crown, 2016), 31.
62 O'Neil, *Weapons of Math Destruction*, 25–26.
63 The US has both the highest rate and largest total number of people in its penal system. In 2013, nearly seven million adult Americans were either incarcerated or under parole or probation. Lauren E. Glaze and Danielle Kaeble, "Correctional Populations in the Untied States, 2013," US Bureau of Justice Statistics, December 2014, https://bjs.ojp.gov/library/publications/correctional-populations-united-states-2013. Within five years of release, around three-fourths of inmates are rearrested. Liz Benecchi, "Recidivism Imprisons American Progress," *Harvard Political Review*, August 8, 2021, https://harvardpolitics.com/recidivism-american-progress/. Racial disparities in the prison population have been detailed in many places, including the Michelle Alexander's *The New Jim Crow*. It is also

important to note that the majority of those in prison come from under the poverty line, an issue that is noted in the following chapter. We should note, then, that the inhumane machinery already in place in the US justice system is given legitimation by hardcoding its cruelties into algorithmic processes.

64 O'Neil, *Weapons of Math Destruction*, 20.

65 O'Neil, 21.

66 Safiya Noble, *Algorithms of Oppression: How Search Engines Reinforce Racism* (New York: New York University Press, 2018), 17.

67 Noble, *Algorithms of Oppression*, 22.

68 Noble, 31.

69 Ruha Benjamin, *Race after Technology: Abolitionist Tools for the New Jim Code* (Cambridge: Polity Press, 2019), 5–6.

70 Benjamin, *Race after Technology*, 12.

71 Benjamin, 47.

72 O'Neil notes, "Racism, at the individual level, can be seen as a predictive model whirring away in billions of human minds around the world." It should be no surprise, then, that some predictive models take racist assumptions as normative. O'Neil, *Weapons of Math Destruction*, 25.

73 Benjamin, *Race after Technology*, 80–84.

74 Benjamin, 155. *Pharmakon* means both "medicine" and "poison" in its original Greek usage. Jacques Derrida, "Plato's Pharmacy," in *Dissemination*, trans. Barbara Johnson (Chicago: University of Chicago Press, 1981), 63–171. Korean has a common phrase "병주고 약준다" ["Who brings the disease brings the cure"], referring to a person who promises to sell a miracle cure to something they created in the first place.

75 Jason Edward Lewis, ed. *Indigenous Protocol and Artificial Intelligence Position Paper* (Honolulu: The Initiative for Indigenous Futures and the Canadian Institute for Advanced Research, 2020), 20.

76 Lewis, *Indigenous Protocol*, 21–22.

77 Timnit Gebru, "Race and Gender," in *The Oxford Handbook of Ethics of AI*, ed. Markus Dubber, Frank Pasquale, and Sunit Das (Oxford: Oxford University Press, 2020), 264.

78 Gebru, "Race and Gender," 259–60.

79 Gebru, 261–64.

80 Ferrando, 69. Similar views are expressed by Haraway and Benjamin.

81 Joy Buolamwini and Timnit Gebru, "Gender Shades: Intersectional Accuracy Disparities inCommercial Gender Classification," *Proceedings of Machine Learning Research* 81 (2018): 1–15.

82 Gebru, Benjamin, and Noble do discuss class, but they tend to discuss it within the context of race. This is an important reality of the social matrix, but their main focus is on the way AI reinscribes *racism* within social orders, not the way it supports

classism. Virginia Eubanks and Daniel Greene, as we will see in chapter 5, do focus on this specific aspect of AI, and do so from the perspective from policy.

83 Matthew Johnston, "Biggest Companies in the World by Market Cap," *Investopedia*, December 21, 2021, https://www.investopedia.com/biggest-companies-in-the-world-by-market-cap-5212784. Note: Nvidia has yielded the most massive return on investments over 2021, with a 136 percent increase of its share values. Such seems strange given that the company's main product is graphics processing units (GPUs) for computers, i.e., the technology that allows brand new video games to look as nice as they do. But because GPUs are hardware that processes massive amounts of data relatively quickly, they are *very* useful for machine learning. As a result, Nvidia has produced and sold many more GPUs in recent years with the explosion of machine learning and AI.

84 Dan Moskowitz, "The 10 Richest People in the World," *Investopedia*, October 27, 2021, https://www.investopedia.com/articles/investing/012715/5-richest-people-world.asp.

85 Pfeiffer, *Digital Capitalism*, 114.

86 "EU-Funded Projects on Artificial Intelligence Technology: A Selection of Projects Funded by the Horizon 2020 Programme," European Commission, April 21, 2021, https://digital-strategy.ec.europa.eu/en/news/eu-funded-projects-use-artificial-intelligence-technology.

87 Yu Hong, "Reading the 13th Five Year Plan."

88 "Distribution of Household Wealth in the U.S. since 1989," Board of Governors of the Federal Reserve, September 23, 2022, https://www.federalreserve.gov/releases/z1/dataviz/dfa/distribute/table/.

CHAPTER 3

1 "Elon Musk Warns of Existential Risk from AI," Cambridge University Centre for Existential Risk, October 28, 2014, https://www.cser.ac.uk/news/elon-musk-warns-of-existential-risk-from-ai/.

2 Matt McFarland, "Elon Musk Just Added a Robot to His List of Things Always Coming 'Next Year.' For Now He's Got a Guy in a Suit," *CNN Business*, August 20, 2021, https://www.cnn.com/2021/08/20/tech/tesla-ai-day-robot/index.html.

3 Rebecca Elliott, "Tesla Posts First Full Year of Profitability," *Wall Street Journal* January 27, 2021, https://www.wsj.com/articles/tesla-tsla-4q-earnings-report-2020-11611708257.

4 Hank Tucker, "Elon Musk Gets Almost $13 Billion Richer in One Week as Tesla Stock Hits 8-Month High," *Forbes,* October 16, 2021, https://www.forbes.com/sites/hanktucker/2021/10/16/elon-musk-gets-almost-13-billion-richer-in-one-week-as-tesla-stock-hits-8-month-high/?sh=74dd195830b3.

5 Robert Woods, "Thomas Newcomen and the Steam Engine," *Mechanical Engineering Magazine*, December 2003, republished in *Engineering and Technology History*

Wiki, October 1, 2019, https://ethw.org/Thomas_Newcomen_and_the_Steam_Engine.

6 Linton Weeks, "Lazy in America: An Incomplete Social History," *National Public Radio*, July 1, 2011, https://www.npr.org/2011/07/01/137531711/lazy-in-america-a-brief-social-history.

7 "Humphrey Potter," Grace's Guide to British Industrial History, https://www.gracesguide.co.uk/Humphrey_Potter.

8 "Choose a Lazy Person to Do a Hard Job Because That Person Will Find an Easy Way to Do It," Quote Investigator, July 6, 2015, https://quoteinvestigator.com/2014/02/26/lazy-job/.

9 Max Weber, *The Protestant Ethic and the "Spirit" of Capitalism and Other Writings*, ed. and trans. Peter Baehr and Gordon C. Wells (London: Penguin Books, 2002), 16–17.

10 Pfeiffer, *Digital Capitalism*, 34.

11 Eugene Kim, "Amazon CEO Jeff Bezos Joins a Group Led by Ex-Google CEO Eric Schmidt to Advise the Pentagon," *Business Insider*, Aug 2, 2016, https://www.businessinsider.com/amazon-ceo-jeff-bezos-joins-pentagon-defense-advisory-board-2016-8.

12 Mohit Mookim, "The World Loses under Bill Gates' Vaccine Colonialism," *Wired*, May 19, 2021, https://www.wired.com/story/opinion-the-world-loses-under-bill-gates-vaccine-colonialism/.

13 See: Marcuse, *One-Dimensional Man*, 145–69; Jacques Ellul, *The Technological System*, trans. Joachim Neugroschel (New York: Continuum Publishing, 1980), 6; Langdon Winner, "Do Artifacts Have Politics?" *Daedalus* 109, no. 1 (Winter 1980): 121–36; Andrew Feenberg, *Transforming Technology: A Critical Theory Revisited* (Oxford: Oxford University Press, 2002), 16–19.

14 Pfeiffer, "Distributive Forces and (Digital) Capitalism: What Is New?" in *Digital Capitalism* .

15 O'Neil, *Weapons of Math Destruction*, 21.

16 Sheila Jasanoff, "Future Imperfect: Science, Technology, and the Imaginations of Modernity," in *Dreamscapes of Modernity: Sociotechnical Imaginaries and the Fabrication of Power*, ed. Sheila Jasanoff and Sang-Hyun Kim (Chicago: University of Chicago Press, 2015), 19.

17 Sang-Hyun Kim, "Social Movements and Contested Sociotechnical Imaginaries in South Korea," in *Dreamscapes of Modernity*, 159

18 J. Benjamin Hurlbut, "Remembering the Future: Science, Law, and the Legacy of Asilomar," in *Dreamscapes of Modernity*, 128.

19 Nancy N. Chen, "Consuming Biotechnology: Genetically Modified Rice in China," in *Dreamscapes of Modernity*, 229.

20 Michael S. Burdett, "The Religion of Technology: Transhumanism and the Myth of Progress," in *Religion and Transhumanism*, ed. Calvin Mercer and Tracy Trothen (Santa Barbara: Praeger, 2015), 136–38.

21 Broussard, *Artificial Unintelligence*, 8.
22 Kate Crawford, *Atlas of AI* (New Haven: Yale University Press, 2021), 7.
23 See conclusion, "Artificial Dignity."
24 Theodor Mommsen, "Petrarch's Conception of the Dark Ages," *Speculum* 17, no. 2 (April 1942): 226–42.
25 If one takes a look at centers of learning across the Old World ca. 1200, they will notice something quite interesting. Simultaneously, there were several European universities, Confucian schools, and Islamic universities. Each of these saw the goal of education and the outcomes quite differently. Europe emphasized theology as the "Queen of the Sciences," and priests were often the faculty members of these institutions. Islamic universities had a similar emphasis on understanding God, but jurisprudence was the typical outcome, as theology was a more Christian discipline. The Confucian schools, in contrast, emphasized studying the classics and rote memorization of long texts for the purpose of governing.
26 Trevor J. Pinch and Wiebe E. Bijker, "The Social Construction of Facts and Artifacts: Or How the Sociology of Science and the Sociology of Technology Might Benefit Each Other," in *The Social Construction of Technological Systems: New Directions in the Sociology and History of Technology*, ed. Wiebe E. Bijker, Thomas P. Hughes, and Trevor Pinch (Cambridge, MA: MIT Press, 1987), 18; Bruno Latour and Steve Woolgar, *Laboratory Life: The Construction of Scientific Facts* (Princeton: Princeton University Press, 1986), 176.
27 William Isaac Thomas and Dorothy Swaine Thomas, *The Child in America* (Oxford: Alfred A. Knopf, 1928), 572.
28 Dominic Rushe, "Wage Gap between CEOs and US Workers Jumped to 670-to-1 Last Year, Study Finds," *The Guardian*, June 7, 2022, https://www.theguardian.com/us-news/2022/jun/07/us-wage-gap-ceos-workers-institute-for-policy-studies-report.

The obscenely high CEO compensation rate stands as the exception that proves the rule for the bourgeoisie. It is the contradiction that maintains the internal logic. I have long been flabbergasted to note my business ethics students justify CEO pay rates saying that somehow the top executive is *worth* that much for what he (almost all are male still) contributes to the company. At no point, however, has any student of mine been able to give a reasonable explanation of how a single person can contribute over 600 times harder than their average employee. This amounts to saying the executive generates more revenue up to his morning coffee break than their average employee does in a full year.
29 Peter L. Berger and Thomas Luckmann, *The Social Construction of Reality: A Treatise in the Sociology of Knowledge*, (New York: Open Road Integrated Media, 2011), 178.
30 Latour, *Science in Action*, 78.
31 Thomas S. Kuhn, *The Structure of Scientific Revolutions*, 50th anniversary ed. (Chicago: University of Chicago Press, 2012), 72; Steven Shapin and Simon Schaffer, *Leviathan and the Air-Pump: Hobbes, Boyle, and the Experimental Life*

(Princeton: Princeton University Press, 1985), 141, 207; David Bloor, "Wittgenstein and Mannheim on the Sociology of Mathematics," *Studies in the History and Philosophy of Science* 4, no. 2 (1973): 173–91

32 Latour, *Science in Action*, 57.

33 Latour, *Science in Action*, 61. Latour differentiates between "facts" and "artifacts," with the latter meaning something like "relic." A scientist does not want their work to become an "artifact," an outdated concept disproven by newer work. But the main difference between an idea as "fact" and "artifact" is merely the strength of the network supporting it, per Latour. One must be careful in STS, however, lest one start to believe that the social context of science means science itself is arbitrary. As David Bloor argues, even mathematics is a socially constructed science; this does not mean it is mere opinion. Science fact being constructed merely means its social impact and its recognition as true depends on networks of connection and consensus. Debates in the early days of quantum mechanics demonstrate some of the difficulties of sorting this out, as demonstrated by Erwin Schrödinger's infamous "cat" thought experiment intended to demonstrate what he saw as the absurdity of superposition (although it has typically been misread to say the opposite).

The problem with AI is that "intelligence" is even less of a "neutral" scientific notion than terms like "lepton," "phlogiston," or "Growth Hormone Releasing Factor." These do exist within normative frameworks, but intelligence is a way we evaluate human worth and potential, so any claim suggestion that AI is a neutral project is either mistaken or bad faith.

34 Latour and Woolgar, *Laboratory Life*, 139.

35 Daniel Greene, *The Promise of Access: Technology, Inequality, and the Political Economy of Hope* (Cambridge, MA: MIT Press, 2021), 34.

36 Cf. Bruno Latour, "Where Are the Missing Masses? The Sociology of a Few Mundane Artifacts," in *Shaping Technology/Building Society: Studies in Sociotechnical Change*, ed. Wiebe E. Bijker and John Law (Cambridge, MA: MIT Press, 1992), 227.

37 mindgam3 [pseud.], "We Can't Trust AI Systems Built on Deep Learning Alone," *Hacker News*, September 29, 2019, https://news.ycombinator.com/item?id=21109017.

38 Latour, *Science in Action*, 202.

39 Adam Smith, *An Inquiry into the Nature and Cause of the Wealth of Nations*, (London: W. Strahan, 1776), 8; Pfeiffer, *Digital Capitalism*, 32.

40 Kurzweil, *The Singularity Is Near*, 73.

41 Zahidi et al., *The Future of Jobs*, 5.

42 Jacques Bughin, Jeongmin Seong, James Manyika, Michael Chui, and Raoul Joshi, *Notes from the AI Frontier: Modeling the Impact of AI on the World Economy*, McKinsey & Company, September 2018; Tara Balakrishnan, Michael Chui, Bryce Hall, and Nicolaus Henke, *Global Survey: The State of AI in 2020*, McKinsey & Company,

November 17, 2020, https://www.mckinsey.com/capabilities/quantumblack/our-insights/global-survey-the-state-of-ai-in-2020.

43 Raghunandhan Kuppuswamy and Ritu Jyoti, *Artificial Intelligence Software and Strategies*, IDC, accessed November 9, 2022, https://www.idc.com/getdoc.jsp?containerId=IDC_P38649.

44 Deloitte Technology, Media and Telecommunications Industry, "Global Artificial Intelligence Industry Whitepaper," Deloitte, accessed November 9, 2022, https://www2.deloitte.com/cn/en/pages/technology-media-and-telecommunications/articles/global-ai-development-white-paper.html.

45 Bughin et al., *Notes from the AI Frontier*, 3.

46 Arnand Rao and Gerard Verweij, "Sizing the Prize: What's the Real Value of AI for Your Business and How Can You Capitalise?" PwC, 2017, https://www.pwc.com/gx/en/issues/data-and-analytics/publications/artificial-intelligence-study.html.

47 Paul R. Daugherty and H. James Wilson, *Human + Machine: Reimagining Work in the Age of AI* (Boston: Harvard Business Review Press, 2018), 4, emphasis original.

48 Ajay Agrawal, Joshua S. Gans, and Avi Goldfarb, "What to Expect from Artificial Intelligence," *MIT Sloan Management Review*, February 7, 2017, https://sloanreview.mit.edu/article/what-to-expect-from-artificial-intelligence/.

49 Pfeiffer, *Digital Capitalism*, 182.

50 Free market advocates have claimed since at least Adam Smith that capitalism is more "efficient" as a model of distribution than other economic models, including mercantilism or socialism. Given the exacerbated wealth inequality and persistence of poverty across industrialized nations, this seems questionable. If AI can truly be "efficient" in the market, it may be able to solve the problem of resource distribution in a way that benefits all. However, the developers, promoters, and users of AI are committed to the capitalistic growth model.

51 Pfeiffer, *Digital Capitalism*, 182ff.

52 Hong, "Reading the 13th Five-Year Plan," 1758.

53 Pfeiffer, *Digital Capitalism*, 109.

54 Nick Lynn, "The AI CEO," *Medium*, September 7, 2019, https://nickl4.medium.com/the-ai-ceo-734f9970db3c.

In August 2022, a Chinese web-game developer company "appointed" an AI to be its new CEO. The description of the tasks of the new "boss" show, however, that the robot will really be functioning more as an important tool for other executives in the company, such as its chairman Liu Dejian. Shareholders, to say nothing of other C-suite executives, are hardly likely to allow an AI to make decisions such as acquisitions, mergers, restructures, corporate direction, and so forth, though logistical functions are just fine. Thus, this news should be read cynically as a publicity stunt. Nonetheless, it does herald a change in understanding of which jobs are "essential." Anugraha Sundaravelu, "Chinese Company Appoints Female Robot as Its CEO," *Metro*, August 30, 2022, https://metro.co.uk/2022/08/30/chinese-company-appoints-female-robot-as-its-ceo-17266313/.

55 Douwe Miedema and Sarah N. Lynch, "UK Speed Trader Arrested over Role in 2010 'Flash Crash,'" *Reuters*, April 22, 2015, https://www.reuters.com/article/us-usa-security-fraud-idUSKBN0NC21220150421.
56 Broussard, *Artificial Unintelligence*, 72.
57 Daugherty and Wilson, *Human + Machine*, 7; Jerry Kaplan, *Humans Need Not Apply: A Guide to Wealth & Work in the Age of Artificial Intelligence* (New Haven: Yale University Press, 2015), 11.
58 Kaplan, *Humans Need Not Apply*, 14.
59 Daugherty and Wilson, *Human + Machine*, 13.
60 Zahidi, et al., *The Future of Jobs*, 6.
61 Milton Friedman, "The Social Responsibility of Business Is to Increase Its Profits," *New York Times*, September 13, 1970.
62 This is the basic argument laid out by Adam Smith in *Wealth of Nations*, that the free market will be to the greatest advantage of all at stake because the "invisible hand" will self-regulate (i.e., will best distribute goods and services).
63 Kurzweil, *The Singularity Is Near*, 74.
64 Pfeiffer, *Digital Capitalism*, 65.
65 Pfeiffer, 244.
66 Ernst Friedrich Schumacher, "Buddhist Economics," Schumacher Center for a New Economics, accessed November 9, 2022, https://centerforneweconomics.org/publications/buddhist-economics/.
67 Consider the deeply bourgeois ethos of Michael Schur's *The Good Place*. While the TV series focuses on moral theory, often providing useful (if reductive) summaries of ethical theory, the show reduces morality in the end to a numerical function. Despite legitimate discussions about whether the proper moral framework should be consequentialist, deontological, or virtue-based, the condition for entry into "The Good Place" (i.e., heaven) is earning a sufficiently high score through moral actions assigned specific numerical weight.
68 Guanlin Wang et al., "Different Impacts of Resources on Opposite Sex Ratings of Physical Attractiveness by Males and Females," *Evolution and Human Behavior* 39, no. 2 (March 2018): 220–25.
69 Michael Walzer, *Spheres of Justice: A Defense of Pluralism and Equality* (New York: Basic Books, 1983), 100–103.
70 Karl Marx, "Capital, Volume I," in *The Marx-Engels Reader*, 2nd ed., ed. R. C. Tucker (New York: W. W. Norton, 1978), 321.
71 Slavoj Žižek, *The Sublime Object of Ideology* (London: Verso, 1989), 31.
72 Latour, "Where Are the Missing Masses?" 232.
73 Of course, this is, at present, not remotely true. The example above of the "Flash Crash" of 2010 demonstrates astutely the ill use of stock-trading AI programs. But AGI is meant to be its own agent, meaning it is not subject to the specific instructions of a given user.
74 David Levy, *Love and Sex with Robots: The Evolution of Human-Robot Relations* (New York: Harper Perennial, 2007), 22.

75 Bostrom, *Superintelligence*, 123–24.
76 Jak Connor, "Ex-Google Executive Warns of Apocalypse, 'We're Creating God,'" *TweakTown*, October 1, 2021, https://www.tweaktown.com/news/81931/ex-google-executive-warns-of-apocalypse-were-creating-god/index.html.
77 E.g., Benjamin Todd, "Misconceptions about Effective Altruism," 80000 Hours, August 7, 2020, https://80000hours.org/2020/08/misconceptions-effective-altruism/.
78 Kate Taylor and Avery Hartmans, "Amazon Drivers Say Peeing in Bottles Is an 'Inhumane' Yet Common Part of the Job, Despite the Company Denying It Happens," *Business Insider*, March 26, 2021, https://www.businessinsider.com/amazon-drivers-say-peeing-in-bottles-common-despite-company-denials-2021-3.
79 Michael Sainato, "'Go Back to Work': Outcry over Deaths on Amazon's Warehouse Floor," *The Guardian*, October 18, 2019, https://www.theguardian.com/technology/2019/oct/17/amazon-warehouse-worker-deaths.
80 David Streitfeld, "How Amazon Crushes Unions," *The New York Times*, March 16, 2021, https://www.nytimes.com/2021/03/16/technology/amazon-unions-virginia.html.
81 Dominick Reuter and Andy Kiersz, "Elon Musk Has a $2.5 Billion Reason to Move to Texas: Avoiding California Capital Gains Tax," *Business Insider*, December 1, 2021, https://www.businessinsider.com/why-did-elon-musk-move-texas-wealth-tax-capital-gains-2021-11.
82 Nellie Bowles, "They Can't Leave the Bay Area Fast Enough," *The New York Times*, January 14, 2021, https://www.nytimes.com/2021/01/14/technology/san-francisco-covid-work-moving.html.
83 Virginia Eubanks, *Automating Inequality: How High-Tech Tools Profile, Police, and Punish the Poor* (New York: Picador, 2018), 73.
84 O'Neil, *Weapons of Math Destruction*, 132–34.
85 Benjamin, *Race after Technology*, 113.
86 Eubanks, *Automating Inequality*, 16.
87 Lindsey Earner-Byrne, *Letters of the Catholic Poor: Poverty in Independent Ireland, 1920–1940* (Cambridge, UK: Cambridge University Press, 2017), 86.
88 Earner-Byrne, *Letters of the Catholic Poor*, 12, 68, 79 et passim.
89 Eubanks, *Automating Inequality*, 78–79.
90 Brady Meixell and Ross Eisenbrey, "Wage Theft is a Much Bigger Problem than Other Forms of Theft—But Workers Remain Mostly Unprotected," Economic Policy Institute, September 18, 2014, https://www.epi.org/publication/wage-theft-bigger-problem-forms-theft-workers/.
91 Amanda Michelle Gomez, "States Waste Hundreds of Thousands on Drug Testing for Welfare, but Have Little to Show for It," The Center for Law and Social Policy, May 7, 2018, https://www.clasp.org/press-room/news-clips/states-waste-hundreds-thousands-drug-testing-welfare-have-little-show-it/.
92 Eubanks, *Automating Inequality*, 29.
93 Eubanks, 7.

94 Eubanks, 179–80.
95 Eubanks, 62–63.
96 Eubanks, 82.
97 Arendt, *The Human Condition*, 45.
98 Friedrich Engels, "The Origin of the Family, Private Property, and the State," in *The Marx-Engels Reader*, 742.
99 Ruby K. Payne, *A Framework for Understanding Poverty*, 4th rev. ed. (Highlands, TX: aha! Process, 2005), 45; Pierre Bourdieu, *Distinction: A Social Critique of the Judgment of Taste*, trans. Richard Nice (Cambridge, MA: Harvard University Press, 1984), 85.
100 Payne, *A Framework for Understanding*, 69–70.
101 Erving Goffman, *The Presentation of the Self in Everyday Life* (New York: Anchor Books, 1959), 36.
102 Michel Foucault, *Discipline and Punish: The Birth of the Prison*, trans. Alan Sheridan (New York: Vintage Press), 145.

CHAPTER 4

1 Kate Tinney, "New Food Delivery Service Kiwi Brings Robots to Campus," *Daily Californian*, May 15, 2017, https://www.dailycal.org/2017/05/15/new-food-delivery-service-kiwi-brings-robots-campus/.
2 Supriya Yelimeli "Berkeley's Biggest Homeless Camps Were Closed. Where Are the Residents Now?" *Berkeleyside*, September 2, 2021, https://www.berkeleyside.org/2021/09/02/berkeleys-biggest-homeless-camps-were-closed-where-are-the-residents-now.
3 Emilie Raguso, "Police: Berkeley Man, Fed Up With Kiwibot Delivery Robots, Steals One," *Berkeleyside*, April 26, 2019, https://www.berkeleyside.org/2019/04/26/police-berkeley-man-fed-up-with-kiwibot-delivery-robots-steals-one.
4 Talia Desch, "Kiwibot Delivery Robot Catches Fire after 'Human Error,'" *BBC*, December 17, 2018, https://www.bbc.com/news/technology-46593190.
5 Jessice Lynn, "Why Do I Want to Kick Those Cute Little Food-Delivery Robots?" *The Bold Italic*, January 7, 2020, https://thebolditalic.com/why-do-i-want-to-kick-those-cute-little-food-delivery-robots-ba0555a144d9.
6 "Senate Resolution No. 2019/2020-028: Condemning Kiwi Campus for Its Low Compensation of Columbian Workers," The Associated Students University of California, https://docs.google.com/document/d/1UWPbKTWLPJJgdlaZdI8m_24YNJkDFQG7ukUSqdDrZIo/edit?fbclid=IwAR1X4az6fFXszbem9NMu2c2oXBb-7IyWcttNzriPVa9GX1kg_dap60prCBE.
7 Rebecca Bellan, "Kiwibot Partners with Hospitality Giant Sodexo to Bring Food Delivery Robots to More College Campuses," *Tech Crunch*, August 11, 2021, https://techcrunch.com/2021/08/10/kiwibot-partners-with-hospitality-giant-sodexo-to-bring-food-delivery-robots-to-college-campuses/.

8 "Start-Up Uses Robots to Deliver Food to Hungry UC Berkeley," *CBS San Francisco*, May 16, 2017, https://www.cbsnews.com/sanfrancisco/news/start-up-uses-robots-to-deliver-food-to-hungry-uc-berkeley-students/.
9 Julia Carrie Wong, "San Francisco Tech Worker: 'I Don't Want to See Homeless Riff-Raff,'" *The Guardian*, February 17, 2016, https://www.theguardian.com/technology/2016/feb/17/san-francisco-tech-open-letter-i-dont-want-to-see-homeless-riff-raff.
10 Michael E. Miller, "S.F. 'Tech Bro' Writes Open Letter to Mayor: 'I Shouldn't Have to See the Pain, Struggle, And Despair of Homeless People', 'Riff Raff,'" *The Washington Post*, February 18, 2016, https://www.washingtonpost.com/news/morning-mix/wp/2016/02/18/s-f-tech-bro-writes-open-letter-to-mayor-i-shouldnt-have-to-see-the-pain-struggle-and-despair-of-homeless-people/.
11 "Poverty in San Francisco," City and County of San Francisco, accessed December 14, 2022, https://sfgov.org/scorecards/safety-net/poverty-san-francisco.
12 Karen Chapple, et al., "Mapping Displacement, Gentrification, and Exclusion in the San Francisco Bay Area," Urban Displacement Project, accessed December 14, 2022, https://www.urbandisplacement.org/maps/sf-bay-area-gentrification-and-displacement/.
13 Rebecca Solnit, "Get Off the Bus," *London Review of Books* 36, no. 4, February 20, 2014, https://www.lrb.co.uk/the-paper/v36/n04/rebecca-solnit/diary.
14 Bowles, "They Can't Leave the Bay Area Fast Enough."
15 Jürgen Habermas, *Moral Consciousness and Communicative Action*, trans. Christian Lenhardt and Shierry Weber Nicholsen (Cambridge, MA: MIT Press, 1990), 65.
16 Friedrich Nietzsche, *Beyond Good and Evil*, trans. Helen Zimmerman (Stilwell, KS: Digireads.com, 2005), 145.
17 See, e.g., Levi Checketts, "Recognizing the Face and Facial Recognition," in *Social Epistemology and Technology*, ed. Frank Scalambrino (London: Rowman & Littlefield, 2016), 177–86.
18 Jon Sobrino, *No Salvation outside the Poor: Prophetic-Utopian Essays* (Maryknoll: Orbis, 2008), 23.
19 See, e.g., Marcella Althaus-Reid, *Indecent Theology: Theological Perversions in Sex, Gender and Politics* (New York: Routledge, 2000), 5; Sobrino, *No Salvation outside the Poor*, 22; Elsa Tamez, "Poverty, the Poor, and the Option for the Poor: A Biblical Perspective," in *The Option for the Poor in Christian Theology*, ed. Daniel Groody (Notre Dame, IN: University of Notre Dame Press, 2007), 50; Virgilio Elizondo, "Culture, the Option for the Poor, and Liberation," in *The Option for the Poor in Christian Theology*, 156; Gustavo Gutiérrez, "Memory and Prophecy," in *The Option for the Poor in Christian Theology*, 26.
20 Kimberle Crenshaw, "Mapping the Margins: Intersectionality, Identity Politics, and Violence against Women of Color," *Stanford Law Review* 43, no. 6 (July 1993): 1241–99.

21 See, e.g., Hartnett, Daniel, "Remembering the Poor: An Interview with Gustavo Gutierrez," *America Magazine*, February 3, 2003, https://www.americamagazine.org/faith/2003/02/03/remembering-poor-interview-gustavo-gutierrez.
22 Gayatri Spivak, *Can the Subaltern Speak? Reflections on an Idea*, ed. Rosalind C. Morris (New York: Columbia University Press, 2010), 37.
23 See, e.g., Spivak, *Can the Subaltern Speak?*, 63–66; the other essays in her volume.
24 Emmanuel Levinas, *Otherwise than Being: Or Beyond Essence*, trans. Alphonso Lingis (Pittsburgh: Duquesne University Press, 1998), 7.
25 Cf., Martin Heidegger, "The Turning," in *The Question Concerning Technology*, 45.
26 Jacques Lacan, *Écrits*, trans. Bruce Fink (New York : W. W. Norton, 2006), 371.
27 Jiyoung Ko, *Destruction and Creation ex Nihilo: Mary of Bethany's and Margery Kempe's Spiritualities of Nonconformity from the Perspective of Lacanian Ethics of Desire* (PhD Doctoral Dissertation, The Graduate Theological Union, Berkeley, CA, 2022), 12.
28 Berger and Luckmann, *The Social Construction of Reality*, 130.
29 While *Nicomachean Ethics* is about the cultivation of virtue (Book II) and is often cited for the specific virtues it lists (Books III–VI), Aristotle also emphasizes the need for proper education (Book II.1), the role of friendship (Books VIII–IX), the need for external goods (Book I.8), and even the proper place of pleasure (Book X) for cultivation of virtue and, consequently, happiness.
30 In Lacanian psychoanalysis, perversion is the typical way in which individuals transgress the law, but this transgression is itself a recognition of the authority of the law. See Jacques Lacan, *The Seminars of Jacques Lacan IV: The Object Relation*, ed. Jacques-Alain Miller, trans. A. R. Price (Medford: Polity Press, 2020), 76–77; and Jacques Lacan, *The Seminar of Jacques Lacan Book VII: The Ethics of Psychoanalysis 1959–1960*, ed. Jacques-Alain Miller, trans. Dennis Porter (New York: W.W. Norton & Company, 1992), 109. Judith Butler also notes this phenomenon in gender critiques that reinforce gender binaries by reifying them as objects to reject. See: Judith Butler, *Gender Trouble: Feminism and the Subversion of Identity* 2nd ed. (New York: Routledge, 2007), 30.
31 Karl Marx, "The German Ideology: Part I," in *The Marx-Engels Reader*, 150.
32 Latour, *Reassembling the Social*, 147.
33 See Andrew Feenberg, *Technosystem: The Social Life of Reason* (Cambridge, MA: Harvard University Press, 2017), 51.
34 Žižek, *The Sublime Object of Ideology*, 31.
35 Bourdieu, *Distinction*, 56, 16.
36 Bourdieu, 5.
37 Payne, *A Framework for Understanding*, 7.
38 Bourdieu, *Distinction*, 100.
39 Payne, *A Framework for Understanding*, 3.
40 Payne, 77. Payne's view here is more revealing of her own middle-class biases than it is of the poor; she writes, "The notion that discipline should be instructive and

change behavior is not part of the culture in generational poverty." Rather than questioning the value of the bourgeois sense of discipline, Payne takes it as normative and assumes that poor children's at-times maladaptive behaviors to the bourgeois situation are deficiencies. In other words, her own expectations demonstrate the point below that taste is primarily "distaste."

41 Payne, 33–34. She raises this issue specifically to suggest to other educators reasons why poor children may not be as easily conformed to bourgeois styles of language comprehension, an important task of formal education.

42 Payne, 42–43.

43 Bourdieu, *Distinction*, 188–89.

44 Bourdieu, 32–33.

45 Bourdieu, 53, 132. Note that Payne's work is, not accidentally, also focused on education, a tool for lifting the poor out of their poverty. Bourdieu further notes that "legitimate" culture of the educated upper classes differs from the culture of the wealthy business class, which tends to lack the same "cultural capital" despite possessing greater economic capital.

46 Bourdieu, 106.

47 Bourdieu, 92. The sociologist Ervin Goffman said that all social relations could be viewed through a dramaturgical lens. For Goffman, successfully "playing a role" was the primary prerequisite for occupying a given location in society. Goffman, *The Presentation of the Self*, 75. Taken together, Goffman's and Bourdieu's insights assure us that what lets the upper classes occupy the place they do is the ability to successfully play their role, not the possession of any physical object.

48 Bourdieu, *Distinction*, 47.

49 Angela McRobbie, *Postmodernism and Popular Culture* (London: Routledge, 1994), 13; Malcolm Waters, *Globalization*, 2nd ed. (London: Routledge, 2001), 198.

50 Martin Scorsese, "I Said Marvel Movies Aren't Cinema. Let Me Explain," *The New York Times*, November 11, 2019, https://www.nytimes.com/2019/11/04/opinion/martin-scorsese-marvel.html.

51 See, e.g., Mark D. White, ed. *The Avengers and Philosophy: Earth's Mightiest Thinkers* (Hoboken: John Wiley & Sons, 2012).

52 Payne, *A Framework for Understanding*, 44. I had never left the United States until after getting married, when I went with my wife to stay with her family for a few months in Korea. There isn't enough space here to articulate the sense of disorientation and anxiety that this first venture outside of the US provoked in me, but one experience the following year (my second trip outside the US) stands out significantly. A college friend was getting married in Seoul while I was there, so I attended the wedding. His only other non-Korean guests were a friend he went to boarding school with in the UK and two classmates from the London School of Economics. All of them were quite well-off and referenced traveling to Beijing, Bangkok, Tokyo, Taipei, and other major Asian cities (all of them were European) very casually. Listening to their experiences was entirely alienating—I had no

experience to compare the sort of luxury they took for granted. Fortunately, because my undergraduate alma mater skews massively toward the upper classes, this secondary socialization helped provide me with enough frames of reference to "bluff" my way through the conversation. It was clear to me, however, that I would never be (nor want to be) good friends with these men; their entire experiential world was utterly foreign to mine and the values they embraced too distant from the realities of the poor.

53 Bourdieu, *Distinction*, 56.
54 Bourdieu, 57.
55 Žižek, *The Sublime Object of Ideology*, 80.
56 Lacan says "woman is a symptom" of man. Jacques Lacan, *The Seminar of Jacques Lacan XXII: R.S.I.*, trans. Cormac Gallagher, (Lacan in Ireland, 2010), 65, http://www.lacaninireland.com/web/wp-content/uploads/2010/06/RSI-Complete-With-Diagrams.pdf. By this, Lacan means that the sexual definition of man is intrinsic upon a sexual essentialism of "woman." For man to articulate himself as "masculine," he first must delineate the "feminine," despite the fact that no *actual* woman corresponds to the symptom of "woman." In this way, fantasy and symptom are intrinsically bound up.
57 See: Žižek, *The Sublime Object of Ideology*, 81. Žižek also gives a good example of this on page 118 with the case of Dickensian articulations of the poor as virtuous.
58 Bourdieu, *Distinction*, 68.
59 Payne, *A Framework for Understanding*, 42–43.
60 Norbert Elias, *The Civilizing Process: Sociogenetic and Psychogenetic Investigations*, rev. ed., trans. Edmund Jephcott, ed. Johan Goudsblom and Stephen Mennell (Malden: Blackwell), 200, part 2, chapter 4.
61 Bourdieu, *Distinction*, 41.
62 Marx, "The German Ideology, Part I," 174.
63 Frantz Fanon, *The Wretched of the Earth*, 60th anniversary ed., trans. Richard Philcox (New York: Grove Press, 2021), 18; Karl Marx, *Contribution to the Critique of Hegel's Philosophy of Right*, trans. Joseph O'Malley (Oxford: Oxford University Press, 1970), Introduction.
64 Henry Shue's argument in *Basic Rights: Subsistence, Affluence and U.S. Foreign Policy* (Princeton: Princeton University Press, 1996) is particularly interesting on this point. Shue notes that the right to subsistence is one of three "basic rights" along with the liberty and security. The right to security is most obviously threatened by violence, but the right to liberty (especially freedom of movement) is also threatened by violence or the threat of violence by the state. However, he notes that, while most people conflate the "right to subsistence" with a *positive* duty (e.g., food must be provided), it also entails a *negative* duty (e.g., my food must not be taken from me). Thus, subsistence is also threatened by violence, such as the Irish Potato Famine where one eighth of the Irish population died and another eighth emigrated due to British colonial demands for potato crops amid scarcity.

65 See: Fanon, *The Wretched of the Earth*, chapter 1.

66 Herbert Marcuse, *Eros and Civilization: A Philosophical Inquiry into Freud* (New York: Vintage Press, 1962), chapter 4.

67 Paulo Freire, *Pedagogy of the Oppressed*, trans. Myra Bergman (New York: Penguin, 2017); Gustavo Gutiérrez, *A Theology of Liberation: History, Politics and Salvation*, trans. Caridad Inda and John Eagleson (Maryknoll: Orbis Books, 1973), 65.

68 See, e.g., Foucault, *Discipline and Punish*; Jacques Ellul, *Propaganda: The Formation of Men's Attitudes*, trans. Konrad Kellen (New York: Vintage, 1973); Arendt, *The Human Condition*, 42–43.

69 Jon Delano, "Donald Trump Jr. Refers to Dad as 'The Blue-Collar Billionaire' During Pittsburgh Campaign Stop," *KDKA2 CBS Pittsburgh*, September 14, 2016, pittsburgh.cbslocal.com/2016/09/14/donald-trump-jr-refers-to-dad-as-the-blue-collar-billionaire-during-pittsburgh-campaign-stop/.

70 Bourdieu frequently juxtaposes teachers with similarly paid workers, like clerks or skilled laborers, but notes that their tastes tend to be more "legitimate" than is typical of the lower classes. As such, he tends to connect them more with the upper classes despite their obviously lower economic status.

71 Bourdieu, *Distinction*, 16

72 Spivak, *Can the Subaltern Speak?*, 27.

73 Fanon, *The Wretched of the Earth*, 13.

74 Or, as Martin Luther King Jr. more eloquently stated, "Hate cannot drive out hate; only love can do that."

75 Georg W. F. Hegel, *Phenomenology of Spirit*, trans. A. V. Miller (Oxford: Oxford University Press, 1977), section 431.

76 Daniel Groody and Gustavo Gutierréz, "Introduction," in *The Preferential Option for the Poor Beyond Theology*, ed. Daniel Groody and Gustavo Gutiérrez (Notre Dame, IN: University of Notre Dame Press, 2014), 4.

77 See, e.g., Goffman, *The Presentation of the Self*, 172. Goffman did not dive into this question, but the issue of "front region profanation" is one that resonates strongly with the poor. To be able to mock the sensibilities and values of the upper classes privately, all while behaving publicly as though they were completely docile, is the purview of the poor. However, Goffman also notes the problem of backstage infiltrators, the spy for example. Wealthy "poor-coded" culture-makers thus often engage in the same sort of ritual profanation, generating sympathy among the actual poor, but in fact promoting the values and interests of the upper classes against the poor. This is, after all, the function of right-wing news media like Fox News, which cultivates a "salt of the earth" image among its viewers as a way of attacking the "liberal elite" image of other media, despite the fact that Rupert Murdoch is a multibillionaire who has no interest in helping the common American.

78 Maurice Merleau-Ponty, *Phenomenology of Perception*, trans. D. Landes (London: Routledge, 2012), 177.

79 Marx, "The German Ideology, Part I," 175.

80 Georg Lukács, *History and Class Consciousness* (New York: Bibliotech Press, 2017), 50.
81 See Freire, *Pedagogy of the Oppressed*, 41.
82 Freire, 19. Lukács popularizes the concept of "false consciousness" into Marxist dialogue, but he means by this a class consciousness that lacks key understanding of either the reality of social relations, the world-historic process of economic development, or the genuine interests of the class. See Lukács, *History and Class Consciousness*, 39–41.
83 Fanon, *The Wretched of the Earth*, 23.
84 Lukács, *History and Class Consciousness*, 47.
85 Fanon, *The Wretched of the Earth*, 23.
86 Michel Foucault, *Power/Knowledge: Selected Interviews and Other Writings 1972–1977*, trans. Colin Gordon, Leo Marshall, John Mepham, and Kate Sopher, ed. Colin Gordon (New York: Vintage Press, 1980), 138.
87 Althaus-Reid, *Indecent Theology*, 5.
88 Spivak, *Can the Subaltern Speak?*, 38.
89 Žižek, *The Sublime Object of Ideology*, 81.
90 Jean-Paul Sartre, *Being and Nothingness*, trans. Hazel E. Barnes (New York: Washington Square, 1984), 400.
91 Frantz Fanon, *Black Skin, White Masks*, trans. C. Markmann (London: Pluto, 1986), 115.
92 Cf. Bourdieu, *Distinction*, 376.
93 See, e.g., Joan C. Williams, "What So Many People Don't Get about the U.S. Working Class," *Harvard Business Review*, November 10, 2016, https://hbr.org/2016/11/what-so-many-people-dont-get-about-the-u-s-working-class.
94 John D. Huber and Piero Stanig, "Why Do the Poor Support Right-Wing Parties? A Cross-National Analysis," Presented at RSF Inequality Conference, University of California Los Angeles, January 2007.
95 Forrest Wickman, "Working Man's Blues," *Slate*, May 1, 2012, https://slate.com/business/2012/05/blue-collar-white-collar-why-do-we-use-these-terms.html.
96 A startling example of this can be seen in music. The socialist, anti-fascist, self-described redneck Woody Guthrie stands sharply against the GOP-aligned entirety of country-western "redneck" music of today. One only need recall how the Dixie Chicks (now "the Chicks") became pariahs among country-western fans when they criticized George W. Bush for the invasion of Iraq in 2003.
97 Ruth Igielnik, Scott Keeter, and Hannah Hartig, "Behind Biden's 2020 Victory," Pew Research Center, June 30, 2021, https://www.pewresearch.org/politics/2021/06/30/behind-bidens-2020-victory/.
98 Joan C. Williams, "How Biden Won Back (Enough of) the Working Class," *Harvard Business Review*, November 10, 2020, https://hbr.org/2020/11/how-biden-won-back-enough-of-the-white-working-class.

99 "Exit Polls of the 2020 Presidential Election in the United States on November 3, 2020, Share of Votes By Income," *Statista*, November 2020, https://www.statista.com/statistics/1184428/presidential-election-exit-polls-share-votes-income-us/; "Exit Polls," *CNN*, accessed December 14, 2022, https://edition.cnn.com/election/2020/exit-polls/president/national-results.

100 "2018: ACS 1-Year Estimates Selected Population Profiles," US Census Bureau, accessed November 11, 2022, https://data.census.gov/cedsci/table?t=-A0&d=ACS%201-Year%20Estimates%20Selected%20Population%20Profiles&tid=ACSSPP1Y2018.S0201.

101 Ben Leonard, "QAnon Shaman' Granted Organic Food in Jail after Report of Deteriorating Health," *Politico*, February 3, 2021, https://www.politico.com/news/2021/02/03/qanon-shaman-organic-food-465563.

102 See: Emilie Townes, *Womanist Ethics and the Cultural Production of Evil* (New York: Palgrave MacMillan, 2006), 71; Arthur K. Spears, "Race and Ideology: An Introduction," in *Race and Ideology: Language, Symbolism and Popular Culture* (Detroit: Wayne State University Press, 1999), 11–58.

103 See: Allyson Drinkard, "White Trash," in *The Social History of the American Family: An Encyclopedia*, Vol. 3, ed. Marilyn J. Coleman and Lawrence H. Ganong (Los Angeles: Sage, 2014), 1452–53; Annalee Newitz and Matthew Wray, "What Is 'White Trash?' Stereotypes and Economic Conditions of Poor Whites in the U.S." *Minnesota Review* 47 (Fall 1996): 57–72.

104 Cf. Fanon, *Black Skins, White Masks*, 17.

105 Jennifer Lee and Tiffany Huang, "Why the Trope of Black-Asian Conflict in the Face of Anti-Asian Violence Dismisses Solidarity," Brookings Institute, *How We Rise*, March 11, 2021, https://www.brookings.edu/blog/how-we-rise/2021/03/11/why-the-trope-of-black-asian-conflict-in-the-face-of-anti-asian-violence-dismisses-solidarity/.

106 Kyeyoung Park, "Use and Abuse of Race and Culture: Black-Korean Tension in America," *American Anthropologist* 98, no. 3 (September 1996): 492–99. Spike Lee's 1989 drama *Do the Right Thing* plays on this very trope, with the predominantly Black residents of the Bed-Stuy projects frequently disparaging the Korean immigrant family who successfully run the nearby corner shop. At the film's climax, a riot breaks out after police kill Radio Raheem. After trashing the Italian American family's pizza shop, the residents move in on the corner store, but back down when defensive store owner Sonny shouts, "I'm Black! I'm Black!" disarming the hostility of the crowd.

107 See: Max Weber, *The Protestant Ethic*, 77.

108 Thomas Malthus, *An Essay on the Principle of Population* (London: J. Johnson, 1798), 123.

109 Gutiérrez, *A Theology of Liberation*, 296–97.

110 Sobrino, *No Salvation outside the Poor*, 72.

111 Elizondo, 157. Emphasis mine.

112 An ironic example of this can be seen in Gutiérrez, "Memory and Prophecy." In an essay in which he speaks authoritatively on behalf of the poor, he then notes the poor "are not simply objects to pity or help but, above all, persons destined to be the subjects of their own destiny and history. The theological reflection that begins from these people takes into account all these elements and does not pretend to be . . . 'the voice of the voiceless'" (31). Then he concludes his essay with an exegesis on the anointing of Jesus at Bethany, in which he describes Jesus and the "anonymous" woman as follows: "He is a victim who cannot delay the threat that hangs over him. . . . Neither can the woman do anything; she is insignificant, being a woman and being anonymous" (34). In stark contrast to this reading is that of Jiyoung Ko, who reads Mary (John's Gospel *names* her) as acting in a deeply authentic and autonomous way. Ko reads Mary as actually being a subject, but Gutiérrez, who just pages before had declared the poor to be "the subjects of their own destiny and history," is quick to reduce the anonymous woman in the Gospel to a victim with no autonomy. See: Jiyoung Ko, 139–42.

113 Dorothy Day, "Poverty and Precarity," in *Selected Writings: By Little and By Little*, ed. Robert Ellsberg (Maryknoll: Orbis Books, 2011), 108.

114 Arthur C. Brooks, *Who Really Cares: The Surprising Truth about Compassionate Conservatism* (Philadelphia: Basic Books, 2006), 80.

115 Pravin J. Patel, "Trade Union Participation and Development of Class-Consciousness," *Economic and Political Weekly* 29, no. 36 (September 3, 1994): 2376.

116 "Union Members Summary," US Bureau of Labor Statistics (January 22, 2020). In recent years, some sectors have seen new unions arise, such as adjunct professors, coffee shop baristas, and tech workers. None of these are considered traditional "blue collar" occupations, though economically some of them are paid poverty wages. It may be the case that an adjunct professor of English literature may feel class consciousness, but most likely they will not have the same cultivated tastes of the poor (see above section), nor that the other poor will have solidarity with them as an over-educated professional.

117 Williams, "What So Many People Don't Get about the U.S. Working Class."

118 The idea that the poor are "voiceless" as liberation theologians are wont to claim is a great disfavor to most of the poor. It is true their choices are less free, and it is further true that they have less opportunity to make public pronouncements. But in calling the poor "voiceless," liberation theologians reduce the agency of the poor, making them, once again, objects against the subjectivity of the bourgeoisie. It is better to recognize that (most of) the poor make choices in a different constellation of values and opportunities from the upper classes.

119 Žižek, *The Sublime Object of Ideology*, 84.

120 Aristotle, *Nicomachean Ethics*, Book I.8.

121 On this note, we may highlight Ellacuría and Sobrino's definition of the poor as "those who cannot take their life for granted" as particularly fitting. Cf. Sobrino, *No Salvation outside the Poor*, 16.

122 The sense of crime may not correlate to an actual danger. The "broken-windows" model of crime prevention is a well-known anti-poor (and largely racist) tactic that does not actually correspond to true dangers. However, the belief that poorer neighborhoods are more dangerous persists, even among the poor. See: Stephen Lurie, "There's No Such Thing as a Dangerous Neighborhood," *Bloomberg City Lab*, February 25, 2019, www.bloomberg.com/new/articles/2019-02-25/beyond-broken-windows-what-really-drives-urban-crime.

123 E.g., M. Shawn Copeland, "Poor Is the Color of God," in *The Option for the Poor in Christian Theology*, 219. Copeland says, most likely as hyperbole rather than as fact, "The poor are brought to resignation; they have no options." The first part of this sentence is true, but the latter part treats the poor as non-subjects.

124 Friedrich Engels, *The Conditions of the Working-Class in England* (London: George Allen & Unwin, 1892), 115.

125 The literature on economic desperation and sex work is quite vast. See, for example, Whitney Moret, *Economic Strengthening for Female Sex Workers: A Review of the Literature* (United States Agency for International Development, 2014), 8–9.

To take an example, the production of pornography in the United States is subject to a lot of regulation—if it is done properly. However, the internet offers many ways to produce and disseminate pornography in ways that circumvent legal strictures. As a result, it is unclear how many women who perform in pornography (to say nothing of minors coerced into it) do so out of anything resembling free choice. More to the point, even many of the women who do so "freely," typically do so out of desperation—the San Fernando Valley (dubbed "San Pornando" because of its high concentration of pornography production) is full of women who moved to the Los Angeles area on the hope of becoming actresses. See, e.g., Laura Donavan, "The Disturbing Reason Many Girls Enter Amateur Porn," *Attn:*, June 15, 2015, https://archive.attn.com/stories/2058/rashida-jones-documentary-amateur-porn.

126 E.g., Payne, *A Framework for Understanding*, 52; Copeland, 219.

127 Susan Moller Okin, *Justice, Gender and the Family* (New York: Basic Books, 1989), 167.

128 Karl Marx, "Capital, Volume I," in *The Marx-Engels Reader*, 336.

129 Arendt, "The Labor of Our Bodies and the Work of Our Hands," in *The Human Condition*

130 Weber, *The Protestant Ethic*, 17.

131 Bruce Bartlett, "The Whiners Who Earn $200,000 and Complain They're Broke," *The New Republic*, July 20, 2020, https://newrepublic.com/article/158555/whiners-earn-200000-complain-theyre-broke.

132 Erika Giovanetti, "Places with the Most Payday Lenders Tend to Be Low-Income Communities," Lending Tree, July 28, 2020, https://www.lendingtree.com/debt-consolidation/places-with-most-payday-lenders-study/.

133 Payne, *A Framework for Understanding*, 41.

134 Arendt, *The Human Condition*, 99.

135 Paul Mosley and Arjan Verschoor refer to this as a "survival algorithm." "A state of mind brought about by chronic poverty, which we measure with an index of perceived vulnerability, reduces one's willingness to undertake the risky investment that may offer an escape from poverty, which completes the circle." Paul Mosley and Arjan Verschoor, "Risk Attitudes in the 'Vicious Circle of Poverty,'" *European Journal of Developmental Research* 17, no. 1 (March 2005): 59.

136 Bourdieu, *Distinction*, 92.

137 "10 Conditions Linked to Stress," *Health Plus*, May 4, 2018, https://www.mountelizabeth.com.sg/healthplus/article/health-conditions-linked-to-stress.

138 Ajai R. Singh and Shakuntala A. Singh, "Diseases of Poverty and Lifestyle, Well-Being and Human Development," *Mens Sana Monogr* 6, no. 1 (January 2008): 187–225, https://www.ncbi.nlm.nih.gov/pmc/articles/PMC3190550/.

139 "Understanding the Relationship between Poverty and Addiction," St Joseph Institute for Addiction, July 18, 2018, https://stjosephinstitute.com/understanding-the-relationship-between-poverty-and-addiction/. Of course, the wealthy also abuse substances but benefit from economic opportunities to seek help. As Ruby Payne notes, part of what separates economic classes is the support systems available. Payne, *A Framework for Understanding*, 69.

140 Matt Bloom, "Are the Poor Happier? Perspectives from Business Management," in *The Preferential Option for the Poor beyond Theology*, 70.

141 Bloom, "Are the Poor Happier?" 77. Cf. Aristotle, *Nicomachean Ethics*, I.8.

142 Ben Fells and Miles Hewstone, "Psychological Perspectives on Poverty," Joseph Rowntree Foundation, June 4, 2015, https://www.jrf.org.uk/report/psychological-perspectives-poverty; Paul D. Hastings, Lisa A. Serbin, William Bukowski, Jonathan L. Helm, Dale M. Stack, Daniel J. Dickson, Jane E. Ledingham, Alex E. Schwartzman, "Predicting Psychosis-Spectrum Diagnosis in Adulthood from Social Behaviors and Neighborhood Contexts in Childhood," *Development and Psychopathology* 32, no. 2 (2019): 465–79.

143 Morgan Kelly, "Poor Concentration: Poverty Reduces Brainpower Needed for Navigating Other Areas of Life," Princeton University, August 29, 2013, https://www.princeton.edu/news/2013/08/29/poor-concentration-poverty-reduces-brainpower-needed-navigating-other-areas-life. See also: Eldar Shafir and Sendhil Mullainathan, "Scarcity: Why Having Too Little Means So Much," *Behavioral Scientist*, September 12, 2013, https://behavioralscientist.org/scarcity-excerpt-mullainathan-shafir/.

Of course, IQ itself is a metric that reinforces racist (middle-class) ideologies, but it is sufficient to note that stress and scarcity effect biological triggers that affect our ability to think and adapt.

144 Angela Jones, *Camming: Money, Power, and Pleasure in the Sex Work Industry* (New York: New York University Press, 2020), 91.

145 Paul Houston Blankenship, *Soul Woundedness* (PhD diss., The Graduate Theological Union, Berkeley, CA, 2020), 145.

146 Ironically, as demonstrated by any number of crises created by the upper classes, like the housing market collapse of 2009 or the continual degradation of the environment, the bourgeoisie themselves seem to lack the ability to make reasonable long-term choices. The great difference between the poor and the middle class is that, while the poor often make poor short-term choices for themselves, they are better at looking after long-term survival for the community and the reverse is the case for the middle class. Of the two, it goes without saying that the bourgeois tendency to externalize consequences on others for their own benefit is the much more pernicious.

147 Emile P. Torres, "Selling 'Longtermism': How PR and Marketing Drive a Controversial New Movement," *Salon*, September 10, 2022, https://www.salon.com/2022/09/10/selling-longtermism-how-pr-and-marketing-drive-a-controversial-new-movement/; Emile P. Torres, "Against Longtermism," *Aeon*, October 19, 2021, https://aeon.co/essays/why-longtermism-is-the-worlds-most-dangerous-secular-credo.

148 Shafir and Mullainathan, "Scarcity."

149 Neil Metz and Mariya Burdina, "Neighbourhood Income Inequality and Property Crime," *Urban Studies* 55, no. 1 (April 2016): 133–50.

150 Metz and Burdina, "Neighbourhood Income Inequality."

151 Foucault, *Discipline and Punish*, 85.

152 Earner-Byrne, *Letters of the Catholic Poor*, 88.

153 Earner-Byrne, 68.

154 See, e.g., the cases Virginia Eubanks raises regarding poor Hoosiers rallying, persevering, and resisting the automated welfare assistance program the State of Indiana adopted ostensibly to combat welfare fraud in chapter 2 of her book. Eubanks quotes one mother who fought desperately to regain the necessary medical coverage for her disabled daughter saying, "During [the time we lost coverage], my mind was muddled because it was so stressful. All my focus was getting [my daughter] back on that Medicaid. Then crying afterwards because everybody was calling us white trash, moochers. It was like being sucked into this vacuum of nothingness." 82.

155 Paul K. Piff, Michael W. Kraus, Stéphane Côté, Bonnie Hayden Cheng, and Dacher Keltner, "Having Less, Giving More: The Influence of Social Class on Prosocial Behavior," *Journal of Personality and Social Psychology* 99, no. 5 (2010): 771–84.

156 Brooks, *Who Really Cares*, 80.

157 Cf. Fanon, *Wretched of the Earth*, 11; Sobrino, *No Salvation outside the Poor*, 10.

158 Piff, et al., "Having Less, Giving More," 780.

159 See, e.g., Sergi Castellano et al., "Patterns of Coding Variation in the Complete Exomes of Three Neanderthals," *Proceedings of the National Academy of the Sciences of the United States of America* 111, no. 18 (March 2014): 6666–71.

160 Cf. Sobrino, *No Salvation outside the Poor*, 39.

161 Marx, "Capital Volume I," 336.
162 See: Fanon, *Wretched of the Earth*, 57.
163 AI has long been applied to Game Theory to simulate decision-making outcomes. One of the earliest cases found that, in a "prisoner's dilemma" scenario, an AI designed to cooperate consistently fared better than a selfish AI. See: Moravec, *Mind Children*, 141–46.
164 Raj Patel and Jason W. Moore, *A History of the World in Seven Cheap Things: A Guide to Capitalism, Nature, and the Future of the Planet* (Berkeley: University of California Press, 2017), 2.
165 Bourdieu, *Distinction*, 47.

CHAPTER 5

1 Kevin Binfield, ed., *Writings of the Luddites* (Baltimore: Johns Hopkins University Press, 2015), 74.
2 Lord Byron, "Maiden Speech to the House of Lords," in *Recollections of the Life of Lord Byron*, by Robert Charles Dallas (London: Charles Knight, 1824), 205–18.
3 Eric Hobsbawn, "The Machine Breakers," *Past & Present* 1, no. 1 (February 1952): 57–70.
4 Ned Ludd [pseud.], "8th January 1813: The Execution of George Mellor, William Thorpe & Thomas Smith," *Luddite Bicentenary—1811–1817*, January 8, 2013, https://ludditebicentenary.blogspot.com/2013/01/8th-january-1812-execution-of-george.html; "Luddites in Marsden," Luddite History Group, accessed March 26, 2012, https://web.archive.org/web/20120326170835/http://www.marsdenhistory.co.uk/people/luddites.html.
5 Michael Andrew Žmolek, *Rethinking the Industrial Revolution: Five Centuries of Transition from Agrarian to Industrial Capitalism in England* (Leiden: Brill, 2013), 645.
6 Anonymous_EA [pseud.], "What We Owe the Future Is an NYT Best Seller," Effective Altruism Forum, August 25, 2022, https://forum.effectivealtruism.org/posts/Xhm3vshLdufaDfC5Y/what-we-owe-the-future-is-an-nyt-bestseller.
7 Gideon Lewis-Kraus, "The Reluctant Prophet of Effective Altruism," *The New Yorker*, August 8, 2022, https://www.newyorker.com/magazine/2022/08/15/the-reluctant-prophet-of-effective-altruism.
8 Malaka Gharib, "How Can We Help Humans Thrive Trillions of Years from Now? This Philosopher Has a Plan," *National Public Radio*, August 16, 2022, https://www.npr.org/sections/goatsandsoda/2022/08/16/1114353811/how-can-we-help-humans-thrive-trillions-of-years-from-now-this-philosopher-has-a.
9 Eric Levitz, "Why Effective Altruists Fear the AI Apocalypse: A Conversation with the Philosopher William MacAskill," *New York Magazine*, August 30, 2022, https://nymag.com/intelligencer/2022/08/why-effective-altruists-fear-the-ai-apocalypse.html.

10 William MacAskill, "What Is Longtermism?" *BBC*, August 8, 2022, https://www.bbc.com/future/article/20220805-what-is-longtermism-and-why-does-it-matter.
11 William MacAskill, "The Beginning of History: Surviving Catastrophic Risk," *Foreign Affairs*, August/September 2022, https://www.foreignaffairs.com/world/william-macaskill-beginning-history.
12 "Home," What We Owe the Future, accessed November 11, 2022, https://whatweowethefuture.com/.
13 Lewis-Kraus.
14 See: Peter Singer, "The Singer Solution to World Poverty," *The New York Times*, September 5, 1999, Section 6, 60.
15 "About," 80000 Hours, accessed November 11, 2022, https://80000hours.org/about/.
16 "Our Donors," 80000 Hours, https://80000hours.org/about/donors/; "About Us," Open Philanthropy, accessed November 11, 2022, https://www.openphilanthropy.org/about-us/.
17 William MacAskill, "Longtermism," *Effective Altrusim Blog*, accessed November 11, 2022, https://forum.effectivealtruism.org/posts/qZyshHCNkjs3TvSem/longtermism.
18 Nick Bostrom, "Existential Risks," *Journal of Evolution and Technology* 9, no. 1 (2002).
19 "Research Areas," The Future of Humanity Institute, accessed November 11, 2022, https://www.fhi.ox.ac.uk/research/research-areas/#macro_tab.
20 Leon Kass, *Life, Liberty and the Defense of Dignity: The Challenge for Bioethics* (San Francisco: Encounter Books, 2002).
21 Michael Sandel, *The Case Against Perfection* (Cambridge, MA: Belknap Press, 2007).
22 Francis Fukuyama, *Our Posthuman Future: Consequences of the Biotechnology Revolution* (New York: Farrar, Straus & Giroux, 2002).
23 Extropy Institute, accessed November 11, 2022, https://www.extropy.org/.
24 Humanity+, accessed November 11, 2022, http://www.humanityplus.org.
25 James Hughes, "The Politics of Transhumanism," *Zygon: Religion of Journal and Science* 47, no. 4 (December 2012): 758
26 Benjamin Todd, "Misconceptions about Effective Altruism," 80000 Hours, August 7, 2020, https://80000hours.org/2020/08/misconceptions-effective-altruism/.
27 Aristotle, *Nicomachean Ethics*, Book I.
28 *Universal Declaration of Human Rights*, articles 23 and 25, https://www.un.org/en/about-us/universal-declaration-of-human-rights.
29 John Rawls, *A Theory of Justice* (Cambridge, MA: Belknap Press, 1971). 75.
30 Robert Nozick, *Anarchy, the State and Utopia* (New York: Basic Books, 1974), 213.
31 Rawls, *A Theory of Justice*, 11.
32 Cf. Gutiérrez, "Memory and Prophecy," 22–23.
33 Cf. Gutiérrez, *A Theology of Liberation*, 293.

34 Marvin L. Chaney, "Accusing Whom of What? Hosea's Rhetoric of Promiscuity," in *Distant Voices Drawing Near: Essays in Honor of Antoinette Clark Wire*, ed. Holly E. Hearon (Collegeville, MN: Liturgical Press, 2004), 101.
35 Friedrich Nietzsche, *On the Genealogy of Morals*, trans. Carol Diethe (Cambridge, UK: Cambridge University Press, 2006), 17.
36 Nietzsche, *On the Genealogy of Morals*.
37 Yara Nadi and Philip Pullella, "World Has Become Deaf to Plight of the Poor, Pope Says in Assisi," *Reuters*, November 12, 2021, https://www.reuters.com/world/world-has-become-deaf-plight-poor-pope-says-assisi-2021-11-12/.
38 Gutiérrez, *A Theology of Liberation*, 137.
39 William Doino Jr., "The Errors of Liberation Theology," *First Things*, July 27, 2015, https://www.firstthings.com/web-exclusives/2015/07/the-errors-of-liberation-theology.
40 Leo XIII, *Rerum Novarum: On Capital and Labor* (Vatican City: Libreria Editrice Vaticana, 1891), 19.
41 Gutiérrez, *A Theology of Liberation*, 87, 174. Cf. Sobrino, *No Salvation outside the Poor*, 9–10.
42 See: Pius XI, *Quadragesimo Anno: On Reconstruction of the Social Order* (Vatican City: Libreria Editrice Vaticana, 1931), 112.
43 Gutiérrez, *A Theology of Liberation*, 32.
44 Gutiérrez, 11.
45 Marx, "The German Ideology," 175.
46 Gutiérrez, *A Theology of Liberation*, 91.
47 Gutiérrez, 24; Sobrino, *No Salvation outside the Poor*, 14.
48 Gutiérrez, "Theology: A Critical Reflection," in *A Theology of Liberation*.
49 See: Bernard Lonergan, *Method in Theology* (Toronto: University of Toronto Press, 1990), 303.
50 Leo XIII, *Rerum Novarum*.
51 Leo XIII, Aeterni Patris: On the Restoration of Christian Philosophy (Vatican City: Libreria Editrice Vaticana, 1879).
52 Pius X, *Pascendi Dominis Gregis: On the Doctrines of the Modernists* (Vatican City: Libreria Editrice Vaticana, 1907).
53 Second Vatican Council, *Pastoral Constitution on the Church in the Modern World: Gaudium et Spes* (Vatican City: Libreria Editrice Vaticana, 1963), 1.
54 Second Vatican Council, *Gaudium et Spes*, 44.
55 Accounting for the last thirty-plus years would be difficult to do here. The concluding decade or so of John Paul II's papacy saw a shift from a rather congenial pontiff oriented toward the broad church to a power-consolidating autodidact. His "reconsecration" of the priesthood in 2000, his single-minded emphasis on abortion, and his clear undermining of lay theologians in *Veritatis Splendor* have all undercut any efforts to develop theology since the 1990s. His successor, Pope Benedict XVI, maintained John Paul's single-minded focus on abortion until his abdication in

2013. Pope Francis, the first pope ever elected from outside of Europe, has taken on a much more pastoral, contextual focus than his two predecessors, but the cultural conservatism propped up by John Paul and Benedict, embraced by numerous bishops installed by these pontiffs and financially underwritten by groups like the Napa and Acton institutes, remains a powerful influence on catechesis, liturgy, and social orientation.

56 John Paul II, *Sollicitudo Rei Socialis* (Vatican City: Libreria Editrice Vaticana, 1987), 42.

57 E. J. Dionne Jr., "Catholics Debate Morality of Capitalism, U.S. Style," *The New York Times,* November 29, 1986, https://www.nytimes.com/1986/11/29/us/catholics-debate-morality-of-capitalism-us-style.html.

58 Althaus-Reid, *Indecent Theology*, 23.

59 Althaus-Reid, 4–5.

60 Josef Ratzinger [prefect], *Instruction on Certain Aspects of the "Theology of Liberation"* (Vatican City: Libreria Editrice Vaticana, 1984).

Note: Ratzinger's analysis is more nuanced than this, but it mostly boils down to a denial of the contextual nature of theology, the way he takes his own sociocultural position as normative, a justified concern about violence, and a trite repetition of the old idea that Christians should avoid Marxism for fear of becoming atheists.

61 Anselm Min, *The Solidarity of Others in a Divided World: A Postmodern Theology after Postmodernism* (New York: T & T Clark, 2004), 134.

62 Sobrino, *No Salvation outside the Poor*, 9.

63 Sobrino, 14.

64 Sobrino, 17.

65 Sobrino, 15.

66 Sobrino, 17.

67 See: Brian Patrick Green, "A Roman Catholic View: Technological Progress? Yes. Transhumanism? No." In *Religious Transhumanism and Its Critics*, ed. Arvin Gouw, Brian Patrick Green, and Ted Peters (Lanham: Lexington Books, 2022), 151.

68 Sobrino, *No Salvation outside the Poor*, 80; Gutiérrez, *A Theology of Liberation*, 22.

69 Hans Jonas, *The Imperative of Responsibility: In Search of an Ethics for the Technological Age* (Chicago: University of Chicago Press, 1984), 188.

70 Broussard, *Artificial Unintelligence*, 72.

71 Broussard, 79. Note: Minsky was also named as one of Jeffrey Epstein's clients. Minsky's widow has denied this, but the "boys club" atmosphere Broussard reports certainly lends credence to this claim.

72 Broussard, 70.

73 Max More, "The Proactionary Principle: Optimizing Technological Outcomes," in *The Transhumanist Reader*, 258–67.

74 Nick Bostrom, "Is the Default Outcome Doom?" in *Superintelligence: Paths, Dangers, Strategies* (Oxford: Oxford University Press, 2014).

75 Gutiérrez, *A Theology of Liberation*, 25; Sobrino, *No Salvation outside the Poor*, 14.
76 Sobrino, *No Salvation outside the Poor*, 1.
77 "Augmented Intelligence in Medicine," American Medical Association, accessed November 11, 2022, https://www.ama-assn.org/practice-management/digital/augmented-intelligence-medicine.
78 Eubanks, *Automating Inequality*, 37.
79 Earner-Byrne, *Letters of the Catholic Poor*, 8.
80 Earner-Byrne, 68.
81 Eubanks, 28.
82 Javier Maria Iguiñiz Echeverria, "The Multidimensionality of Poverty," in *The Preferential Option for the Poor Beyond Theology*, 50.
83 Arendt, "The Rise of the Social," in *The Human Condition*.
84 O'Neil, *Weapons of Math Destruction*, 86.
85 Benjamin, *Race after Technology*, 83.
86 Eubanks, *Automating Inequality*, 48.
87 Eubanks, 74.
88 Eubanks, 53.
89 Eubanks, 51.
90 Eubanks, 74.
91 Eubanks, 64.
92 Eubanks, 67.
93 Eubanks, 75.
94 Greene, *The Promise of Access*, 21.
95 Greene, 15–16.
96 Greene, 26.
97 Feenberg, *Transforming Technology*, 18.
98 Feenberg, *Transforming Technology*, 9.
99 Feenberg, *Technosystem*, 23.
100 Marcuse, *One-Dimensional Man*, 73.
101 Marcuse, *Eros and Civilization*, 101.
102 Feenberg, *Transforming Technology*, 149.
103 Feenberg, *Transforming Technology*, 165.
104 Feenberg, *Technosystem*, 67.
105 Marcella Althaus-Reid, "Becoming Queens: Bending Gender and Poverty on the Websites of the Excluded," in "Cyberethics—Cyberspace—Cybertheology," ed. Erik Borgman, Stephen van Erp and Hille Haker, *Concilium*, no. 1 (2005): 99. Althaus-Reid uses the term "transvestite" to refer to these sex workers. While some may find such a term offensive, it is important to note that some of these sex workers are cisgender men who crossdress as part of their work, and do not actually identify as another gender.
106 Althaus-Reid, "Becoming Queens," 100.

107 Bourdieu, *Distinction*, 47.
108 Althaus-Reid, "Becoming Queens," 104.
109 Benjamin, *Race after Technology*, 104.
110 Papert and Turkle, 135.
111 See: O'Neil, *Weapons of Math Destruction*, 25–30, 85–86.
112 Audre Lorde, "The Master's Tools Will Never Dismantle the Master's House," in *Sister Outsider: Essays and Speeches* (Berkeley: Crossing Press, 1984): 110–14.
113 Scharper, 99.
114 Gutiérrez, "Memory and Prophecy," 31.
115 Sobrino, *No Salvation outside the Poor*, 58.
116 Sobrino, *No Salvation outside the Poor*, 71.
117 Sobrino, *No Salvation outside the Poor*, 72.
118 Cf. Leonardo Boff, *When Theology Listens to the Poor*, trans. Robert R. Barr (San Francisco: Harper & Row, 1988), 25.
119 Sobrino, "The Latin American Martyrs," 99–101.
120 Gutiérrez, "Memory and Prophecy," 31.
121 See: Gutiérrez,"Memory and Prophecy," 34.
122 Lukács, *History and Class Consciousness*, 55.
123 Freire, *Pedagogy of the Oppressed*, 42.
124 Spivak, *Can the Subaltern Speak?*, 27.
125 Spivak, 26.
126 Spivak, 61.
127 Spivak, 63.
128 Hans Jonas, *Philosophical Essays*, 252; Jacques Derrida, "Des tours de Babel," in *Psyche I* (Stanford: Stanford University Press, 2007), 222.
129 Habermas, *Moral Consciousness*, 93.
130 Goffman, *The Presentation of the Self*, 36.
131 Younghak Hyun, "A Theological Look at the Mask Dance in Korea," in *Minjung Theology: People as the Subjects of History*, ed. Yongbock Kim (Singapore: Christian Conference of Asia, 1981), 48.
132 Jae-sik Ko, "Minjung Theology and Liberation Theology," *Theological Studies* (Chinese) 28 (July 1987): 213.

CONCLUSION

1 *Buck v Bell*, 274 US 200 (1927).
2 Alison White and Ina Hofland, "Origins of Eugenics: From Sir Francis Galton to Virginia's Racial Integrity Act of 1924," University of Virginia, 2007, http://exhibits.hsl.virginia.edu/eugenics/2-origins/.
3 Edwin Black, "Eugenics and the Nazis—The California Connection," *SF Gate*, November 9, 2003, https://www.sfgate.com/opinion/article/Eugenics-and-the-Nazis-the-California-2549771.php.

4 Collette Leung, "Kellogg, John Harvey," *Eugenics Archive*, http://eugenicsarchive.ca/discover/connections/512fa0d334c5399e2c000005.
5 Harry Laughlin, "Eugenical Sterilization in the United States," Psychopathic Laboratory of the Municipal Court of Chicago, December 1922, https://web.archive.org/web/20110709175251/http://www.people.fas.harvard.edu/~wellerst/laughlin/.
6 Virginia Sterilization Act of 1924.
7 Paul A. Lombardo, "Three Generations, No Imbeciles: New Light on *Buck v Bell*," *New York University Law Review* 60, no. 1 (1985): 30–62
8 *Buck v Bell*, 207.
9 Lutz Kaelber, "Eugenics: Compulsory Sterilization in 50 American States," University of Vermont, 2009, https://www.uvm.edu/%7Elkaelber/eugenics/VA/VA.html.
10 Karl Stampfl, "He Came Ted Kaczynski, He Left the Unabomber," *Michigan Daily*, March 16, 2006, https://web.archive.org/web/20170114062259/https://www.michigandaily.com/content/he-came-ted-kaczynski-he-left-unabomber.
11 "The Unabomber's Targets: An Interactive Map," *Cable News Network*, 1997, https://web.archive.org/web/20080613131220/http://www.cnn.com/SPECIALS/1997/unabomb/victims/.
12 Unabomber [pseudonym], "Industrial Society and Its Future," *Washington Post*, September 22, 1995, paragraph 183.
13 James Brooke, "New Portrait of Unabomber: Environmental Saboteur Around Montana Village for 20 Years," *The New York Times*, March 14, 1999, https://www.nytimes.com/1999/03/14/us/new-portrait-unabomber-environmental-saboteur-around-montana-village-for-20.html.
14 Alston Chase, "Harvard and the Making of the Unabomber," *The Atlantic*, June 2006, https://www.theatlantic.com/magazine/archive/2000/06/harvard-and-the-making-of-the-unabomber/378239/.
15 Alston Chase, *A Mind for Murder: The Education of The Unabomber and the Origins of Modern Terrorism* (New York: W. W. Norton, 2003), 107–8.
16 Chase, "Harvard and the Making of the Unabomber,"
17 James D. Moreno, "Harvard's Experiment on the Unabomber, Class Of '62: An Odd Footnote to Kaczynski's Class Reunion," *Psychology Today*, May 25, 2012, https://www.psychologytoday.com/intl/blog/impromptu-man/201205/harvards-experiment-the-unabomber-class-62.
18 Stampfl, "He Came Ted Kaczynski."
19 Stampfl.
20 Cal Thomas, "Did Liberalism Spur Unabomber?" *Lawrence Journal-World*, April 11, 1996.
21 Chase, "Harvard and the Making of the Unabomber."
22 The examples I provide and the conversation are largely oriented toward contemporary US culture. The US's predilection for "intelligence" is a vestige of the broader western philosophical trend. Arguably, one could contend that this does not translate to Eastern cultures, but one should be careful not to exoticize "the

East" for the sake of critique. Confucianism, for example, prizes academic study as the most worthy pursuit of life, and as illustrated above, China is jockeying for world leadership in AI research. Though there are certainly contradicting views within individual societies and even perhaps among whole cultures, the reality is the US set the standard for economic, scientific, and technological progress in the twentieth century (in competition with the Soviet Union, seeking the same "smart" ends), and China and other new players on the world stage are following the trend.

23 Emmanuel Levinas, *Totality and Infinity: An Essay on Exteriority*, trans. Alphonsus Lingis (Pittsburgh: Duquesne University Press, 1969), 39.

24 Aquinas, *Summa Theologiae*, I–II Q94 A4.

25 Indeed, the Book of Ruth, replete with questions of inheritance, widow status, and obligations to the poor, demonstrates in a clear way how Israelite society conceived of ownership in vastly different terms from late-capitalist cultures.

26 Nozick, 167.

27 Walzer, chapter 9, esp. 228.

28 Marx, "German Ideology," 154.

29 Weber, *The Protestant Ethic*, 5.

30 Elias, 457. Freud, of course, applies this repression to all of society. However, the key difference between Elias and Freud is exhibited more in, for example, Erving Goffman. Goffman notes that all social roles have expectations and can fall subject to *faux pas*. The poor are marked by an affect economy and social expectations as much as the rich. The cost for the poor is different of course—they will not lose economic standing, but they may lose the community they are a part of if they act "too big for their breeches." See: Goffman, *The Presentation of the Self*, 210.

31 Foucault, *Discipline and Punish*, 85.

32 Gunkel, *The Machine Question*, 46.

33 Gunkel, 47.

34 Hans Jonas, "To Move and To Feel: On the Animal Soul," in *The Phenomenon of Life: Toward a Philosophical Biology* (New York: Dell Publishing, 1966), 99–107; Pierre Teilhard de Chardin, *The Phenomenon of Man*, trans. Bernard Wall (New York: Harper Colophon, 1975), 148.

35 Ben Goertzel, *Ten Years to Singularity If We Really, Really Try* (NP: Humanity+ Press, 2014), 231.

36 Hector J. Levesque, "On Our Best Behavior," *Artificial Intelligence* 212 (July 2014): 27–35.

37 Mark O. Reidl, "The Lovelace 2.0 Test of Artificial Creativity and Intelligence," arXiv:1410.6142v3, December 22, 2014.

38 Davide Michielin, "Bot or Scientist? The Controversial Use of ChatGPT in Science," *Foresight*, The CMCC Observatory on Climate Policies and Futures, February 6, 2023, https://www.climateforesight.eu/articles/chatgpt-science/.

39 Sakaguchi, Le Bras, Bhagavatula and Choi, "WinoGrande: An Adversarial Winograd Schema Challenge at Scale," arXiv:1907.10641v2, November 21, 2019.

40 Ahmed Elgammal, "How Artificial Intelligence Completed Beethoven's Unfinished Tenth Symphony," *Smithsonian Magazine*, September 24, 2021, https://www.smithsonianmag.com/innovation/how-artificial-intelligence-completed-beethovens-unfinished-10th-symphony-180978753/.
41 Elizabeth Penava, "AI Art Is in Legal Greyscale," *The Regulatory Review*, January 24, 2023, https://www.theregreview.org/2023/01/24/penava-ai-art-is-in-legal-greyscale/.
42 David Gunkel, *Person, Thing, Robot: A Moral and Legal Ontology for the 21st Century and Beyond* (Cambridge, MA: MIT Press, 2023).
43 Leon Kass, "Defending Human Dignity," in *Human Dignity and Bioethics*, ed. Adam Schulman and Thomas W. Merrill, (Washington, DC: President's Council on Bioethics, 2008), 308–9.
44 Thomas Aquinas, *Summa Theologiae*, II–II 63 A1 Reply 1.
45 E.g., *Universal Declaration of Human Rights*, article 1, 1948, https://www.un.org/en/about-us/universal-declaration-of-human-rights.
46 Cf. Ferrando, 81.
47 Fanon, *Wretched of the Earth*, 16.
48 See: William Max Nelson, "Making Men: Enlightenment Ideas of Racial Engineering," *American Historical Review* 115, no. 5 (December 2010): 1364–94. South Africa famously carried this out during Apartheid, with a caste system of whites, Blacks, coloreds (mixed race), and Indian (South Asian). The US had a similar system in place, where the census from 1850 to 1920 had categories like "mulatto" (half-Black and half-white), "quadroon" (one quarter Black), and even "octoroon" (one-eighth Black).
49 Ferrando, 81.
50 Plato, *The Republic*, Book VI.
51 Aristotle, *Nicomachean Ethics*, Book VI.7
52 Aquinas, *Summa Theologiae*, prelude to Secunda Pars.
53 Kant, *Groundwork for the Metaphysics of Morals*, 58, 46.
54 John Stuart Mill, *Utilitarianism*, Kindle ed. (London: Longmans, Green, 1879), 147.
55 One can find notably divergent positions here, such as Levinas's position that it is the encounter with an Other face-to-face that provides moral knowledge (first philosophy) and that the position of starting from metaphysics to go to philosophy leads to moral failure. The tradition of feminist care ethics likewise emphasizes the centrality of relationship over the purity of abstracted "justice" and the importance of embodiment over detached rationality.
56 Wikler, "Paternalism in the Age of Cognitive Enhancement," 354.
57 Mill, *Utilitarianism*, loc. 1082.
58 Cf. Michel Foucault, *A History of Madness*, trans. Jonathan Murphy and Jean Khalfa (London: Routledge, 2006), 463–511; Martha C. Nussbaum, *Frontiers of Justice: Disability, Nationality, Species Membership* (Cambridge, MA: Belknap Press, 2006), 98.

59 It is significant to note, on this point, that many people who advocate for consideration of AI rights are bourgeois, white men. Among the most prominent in these discussions include Nick Bostrom, Ben Goertzel, and Peter Singer. On the other hand, many opponents of this view challenge the dehumanizing tendency of AI rights toward marginalized people. See: Abeba Birhane and Jelle van Dijk, "Robot Rights? Let's Talk about Human Welfare Instead," *arXiv:* 2001.05046v1, January 14, 2020; Shannon Vallor (@ShannonVallor), "The constant excitement at giving machines rights while we gleefully strip them from women, trans people, workers . . . telling. Twitter, March 6, 2023, 7:08 p.m., https://twitter.com/ShannonVallor/status/1632699738213560321.

60 Bruce Bartlett, "He Is Even Dumber Than We Thought," *The New Republic*, June 8, 2020, https://newrepublic.com/article/158069/donald-trump-not-smart-polls.

61 Tanya Lewis, "The 'Shared Psychosis' of Donald Trump and His Loyalists," *Scientific American*, January 11, 2021 https://www.scientificamerican.com/article/the-shared-psychosis-of-donald-trump-and-his-loyalists/.

62 James Hamblin, "Is Something Neurologically Wrong with Donald Trump?" *The Atlantic*, January 3, 2018, https://www.theatlantic.com/health/archive/2018/01/trump-cog-decline/548759/.

63 Katherine Cross, "Donald Trump Is a Rich Man's Idea of a Rich Man," *Medium*, March 13, 2017, https://medium.com/the-establishment/donald-trump-is-a-rich-mans-idea-of-a-rich-man-bc5cea992c81.

64 Tina Nguyen, "Is Donald Trump Not Really a Billionaire?" *Vanity Fair*, May 31, 2016, https://www.vanityfair.com/news/2016/05/donald-trump-net-worth.

65 A similar, parallel connotation can be found in sexual health in, e.g., the "social hygiene" movement, wherein in sexually transmitted infections are cast as natural punishment for moral failings, and thus moral disapproval follows those who have STIs. In purely "logical" terms, health and morality are not inherently connected, but, as should be clear by now, the socio-logics of a given society (e.g., Protestant Anglophone nations) entail a corollary association between health and goodness, one where those who are good are healthy and those who are bad are unhealthy (e.g., lung cancer, STIs, cirrhosis).

66 Jonathan M. Metzl, Jennifer Piemonte, and Tara McKay, "Mental Illness, Mass Shootings, and the Future of Psychiatric Research into American Gun Violence," *Harvard Review of Psychiatry* 29, no. 1 (January 2021): 81–89.

One should note that, among the key talking points about mass shootings are the following: the influence of video games (or popular culture generally), mental illness, and gun legislation. Firearm advocacy groups, like the National Rifle Association, quickly dismiss conversations about gun legislation as irrelevant. The claim they maintain is that guns themselves do not increase violence. In fact, one of their slogans is "Only a good guy with a gun can stop a bad guy with a gun," maintaining the paradox that somehow an increase in weapons will decrease weapon violence. Associating violence with neurodivergence benefits the gun culture by giving them a convenient scapegoat (one they can avoid taking responsibility for) while maintaining the illusion that treating the Second Amendment as sacrosanct has no bearing on the culture of violence in the US.

67 The term "bedlam" meaning a state of chaos is a shortened version of "Bethlehem" from the hospital of St Mary of Bethlehem, a psychiatric institution in London particularly notable for its inhumane treatment of patients.

68 "Why the R-Word Is the R-Slur," *Special Olympics*, accessed November 9, 2022, https://www.specialolympics.org/stories/impact/why-the-r-word-is-the-r-slur.

69 Julian Quinones and Arijeta Lajka, "'What Kind of Society Do You Want to Live in?': Inside the Country Where Down Syndrome Is Disappearing," *CBS News*, August 15, 2017, https://www.cbsnews.com/news/down-syndrome-iceland/.

70 Anne Thériault, "What Vaxxers and Anti-Vaxxers Are Missing: Autism Isn't the Worst Thing to Happen to a Child," *Quartz*, February 11, 2015, https://qz.com/340623/what-vaxxers-and-anti-vaxxers-are-missing-autism-isnt-the-worst-thing-to-happen-to-a-child/.

71 Jack McCullough, "The Psychopathic CEO," *Forbes*, December 9, 2019, https://www.forbes.com/sites/jackmccullough/2019/12/09/the-psychopathic-ceo/?sh=e484423791e3.

72 Consider the Oscar-winning 1997 film *Good Will Hunting*, where the main character, Will Hunting, is significant because, despite being a certifiable genius (according to various bourgeois metrics), he is stuck in poverty. The discordance of this reality is made clear by his mental superiority to, but inability to study among, students of Boston-area premier educational institutions. The film portrays Hunting as a victim of circumstance, though he clearly acknowledges the deeply unjust system of self-justifying reward and punishment inherent in capitalism. Nonetheless, the film concludes with him deciding to pursue a bourgeois life.

73 Sam Altman (@sama), Twitter, February 19, 2023, 9:00 a.m., https://twitter.com/sama/status/1627110889508978688?s=46&t=3zImHRVTW7lV-ALMATAJ5Q.

74 Emily Reynolds, "The Agony of Sophia, the World's First Robot Citizen Condemned to a Lifeless Career in Marketing," *Wired*, January 6, 2018, https://www.wired.co.uk/article/sophia-robot-citizen-womens-rights-detriot-become-human-hanson-robotics.

75 Peter Arcidiacono, Josh Kinsler, and Tyler Ransom, "Legacy and Athlete Preferences at Harvard," *Journal of Labor Economics* 40, no. 1 (January 2022): 133–56.

76 Goffman, *The Presentation of the Self*, 52. The 2002 film *Catch Me If You Can*, a biopic about real-life fraudster Frank Abagnale Jr. depicts this well. Abagnale successfully occupies several high-profile careers successively, from medical doctor to lawyer to airline pilot by making forgeries of degrees and licenses. Combined with an impressive amount of bluffing (see: Bourdieu, *Distinction*, 92) and actual dedicated study of these careers, he successfully "passed" in these positions until the FBI caught him.

77 Efforts to circumvent the "tyranny of authority" in the US tend to be bad faith power plays by the elite to replace one established group with another. Those who hawk homeopathic medicines as alternatives to FDA-approved drugs do so more for their own enrichment than for legitimate scientific inquiry. On the other hand, US culture tends to regard Chinese medicine with suspicion because the medical science does not fit into the authoritative paradigm of western medical knowledge, despite many Chinese universities developing rigorous Chinese medical programs.
78 "2022–2023 Best Global University Rankings," *US News*, accessed March 23, 2023, https://www.usnews.com/education/best-global-universities/rankings; "World University Rankings 2022," *Times Higher Education*, accessed March 23, 2023, https://www.timeshighereducation.com/world-university-rankings/2022.Even the QS list places five in the top ten (MIT, Stanford, Harvard, CalTech and U of Chicago), with four of the others being British, and the last (number 9) ETH Zurich. "QS World University Rankings 2023," QS Top Universities, accessed March 23, 2023, https://www.topuniversities.com/university-rankings/world-university-rankings/2023.
79 Organization for Economic Cooperation and Development, *Education at a Glance 2016* (Paris: OECD Publishing, 2016), 44, https://read.oecd-ilibrary.org/education/education-at-a-glance-2016_eag-2016-en#page44.
80 Bourdieu, *Distinction*, 88.
81 Payne, *A Framework for Understanding*, 3
82 See: Payne, 8–9.
83 Cf. Goffman, *The Presentation of the Self*, 78.
84 Payne, *A Framework for Understanding*, 28.
85 Broussard, *Artificial Unintelligence*, 54.
86 Amber Dance, "Many Colleges Dropped Their SAT and ACT Requirements during the Pandemic—Here's How It Affected Admissions," *Knowable Magazine*, July 15, 2021, https://www.businessinsider.com/dropping-sat-act-requirement-affected-college-admissions-2021-7?op=1.
87 Not surprisingly, there exists a sexual fetish called "pygmalionism," where a person is sexually attracted to inanimate humanoid objects, like a statue or mannequin, which is conceptually linked to robot fetishism. See: WinterRose [pseud.], "Technosexuality," *The Pygmalion Syndrome*, accessed March 23, 2023, http://www.p-synd.com/winterrose/technosexuality.html.

Consequently, one can see that even in sexual fetishism, there remains a tension between the humanization of inanimate machines and the dehumanization of the human poor.
88 Cf. Kuhn, 165.
89 Foucault, *Power/Knowledge*, 88.
90 Søren Kierkegaard, *Either/Or: A Fragment of Life*, trans. Alastair Hannay (New York: Penguin Books, 1992), 49.

91 Friedrich Nietzsche, *Thus Spake Zarathustra: A Book for All and None*, trans. Adrian del Caro (Cambridge, UK: Cambridge University Press, 2006), "Zarathustra's Prologue."
92 Cf: Derrida, "Des Tours de Babel," 197.
93 Fanon, *Wretched of the Earth*, 23.
94 Jennifer Schuessler, "Hoaxers Slip Breastaurants and Dog-Park Sex into Journals," *The New York Times*, October 4, 2018, https://www.nytimes.com/2018/10/04/arts/academic-journals-hoax.html; Alan D. Sokal, "A Physicist Experiments with Cultural Studies," New York University, June 5, 1996, https://physics.nyu.edu/faculty/sokal/lingua_franca_v4/lingua_franca_v4.html.
95 See: Ian Hacking, *The Social Construction of What?* (Cambridge, MA: Harvard Press, 1999), 6.
96 See: Fanon, *Wretched of the Earth*, 23, 44.
97 Nietzsche, *Genealogy of Morals*, 21.
98 A phrase I owe to *Wall Street Journal* reporter Rebecca Feng in personal conversation.
99 Ted Peters, *God—The World's Future: Systematic Theology for a New Era*, 3rd ed. (Minneapolis: Fortress Press, 2015), 274.
100 Søren Kierkegaard, *Fear and Trembling*, trans. Alastair Hannay (London: Penguin Books, 1985), 75–76.
101 Dietrich Bonhoeffer, *The Cost of Discipleship*, trans. R. H. Fuller (New York: Touchstone, 1995), 44.
102 Nietzsche, *Thus Spoke Zarathustra*, 10.
103 The Mentor [pseud.] "The Conscience of a Hacker," *Phrack* 1, no. 7 (1986): Phile 3 of 10, http://www.phrack.org/issues/7/3.html.

When I was in my late teens and early twenties, as someone good (but not a prodigy by any means) at math, parts of the manifesto resonated with me. In reading it today, though, I see the obvious ageism, misanthropy, and hubris. The hacker (as professed in the manifesto) is the logical counterpart to Kaczynski. If the internet had existed in the 1960s, perhaps Kaczynski would have become a Silicon Valley mogul by finding the affirmation he craved as a young man.

104 The Mentor.
105 Technology ethicist Shannon Vallor recently captured this idea as technology no longer "increasingly less a center of joy and excitement in our lives" and "technology is [not] for us. It's for a company trying to extract some value from us." Philip Drost, "Tech Made Our Lives Easier. Now It's Taking More than It Gives, Says Researcher," *CBC News*, January 23, 2023, https://www.cbc.ca/radio/thecurrent/technology-change-philosopher-1.6703933.
106 Jiyoung Ko, 31; Cf.: Lacan, *The Ethics of Psychoanalysis*, 314.
107 William Shakespeare, *MacBeth*, 1623. Act 5, Scene 5, line 30.
108 Reinhold Niebuhr, "The Serenity Prayer," from *Alcoholics Anonymous Resource Center.*

109 Bonhoeffer, 59.
110 Levinas, *Otherwise than Being*, 7.
111 Cf. Aquinas, *Summa Theologiae*, I Q14 A1.
112 Hefner, "Technology and Human Becoming," 656.
113 Ludwig Feuerbach, *The Essence of Christianity*, trans. Marian Evans (London: Chapman's Quarterly, 1854), chapter 1, section 2
114 Hefner, 657–60.
115 Feuerbach, chapter 2.
116 Hefner, 662.
117 Jean-Luc Marion, *God without Being*, 2nd ed., trans. Thomas A. Carlson (Chicago: University of Chicago Press, 2012), 12.
118 Hefner, 655.
119 Lydia H. Liu, *The Freudian Robot: Digital Media and the Future of the Unconscious* (Chicago: University of Chicago Press, 2010), 225.
120 Liu, *The Freudian Robot*, 206.
121 See: Liu; Isabell Millar, *The Psychoanalysis of Artificial Intelligence* (Cham, Switzerland: Palgrave MacMillan, 2021).
122 See: Liu, 214, 255; Millar, *The Psychoanalysis of Artificial Intelligence*, 136–37.
123 Jacques Lacan, *The Seminar of Jacques Lacan Book X: Anxiety*, trans. A. R. Price, ed. Jacques-Alain Miller (Cambridge, UK: Polity Press, 2014), 315.
124 Lacan, *Anxiety* 332.
125 Liu, *The Freudian Robot*, 213.
126 Millar, *The Psychoanalysis of Artificial Intelligence*, 137.
127 Lacan, *Anxiety*, 332.
128 *The Stepford Wives* brilliantly illustrates Lacan's concept of anxiety. The entire story revolves around men in the fictional town of Stepford, Connecticut, who engineer "perfect" wives out of robots. Within castration anxiety lies male desire as desire of the Other, of the hope of satisfying the Other. But because the Other is always barred from us, there remains a gap that can never be filled, even in the physical uniting of sexual intercourse. This structure of lack constitutes a site of uncertainty for the man; he can never be sure of his position in relation to the woman. On the other hand, the woman also cannot know what the man's intention is, but regards him with suspicion (Lacan, *Anxiety*, 262–64). The story moves from unsettling to horrific, as good horrors do, when Eberhart begins to realize her husband aims to replace her as well.
129 Wong, "San Francisco Tech Worker."
130 Lacan, *Anxiety*, 315. Lacanian scholar and psychoanalyst Dr. Ali Chavoshian noted in one of his seminars that he had a patient who was so disturbed by his own memory of infant sexuality that, as an adult, he tore out his own eye.
131 Ursula Le Guin, "The Ones Who Walk Away from Omelas," in *New Dimensions 3*, ed. Robert Silverberg (Garden City, NY: Doubleday, 1973), 5.

109. Ibid.
110. Lacan, [illegible] 9.
111. Cf. Augustine, Sermon [illegible] 1.
112. [illegible] Theology [illegible] Repentance [illegible].
113. Ludwig Feuerbach, *The Essence of Christianity*, trans. George Eliot (Amherst, [illegible] Prometheus, 1989), [illegible].
114. Hegel, [illegible]/[illegible].
115. [illegible] chapter 2.
116. Hegel, 662.
117. Jean-Luc Marion, *God without Being*, 2nd ed., trans. Thomas A. Carlson (Chicago: University of Chicago Press, 2012), [illegible].
118. Hegel, 655.
119. Cyril O'Regan, [illegible] (Albany: State University of New York Press, [illegible]).
120. [illegible] 30.
121. See [illegible] Isabel Kinlilla, [illegible] (Cham, Switzerland: Palgrave Macmillan, [illegible]).
122. See [illegible].
123. Jacques Lacan, [illegible], ed. Jacques-Alain Miller (Cambridge, UK: [illegible]).
124. Lacan, [illegible].
125. [illegible], 213.
126. Miller, [illegible] 147.
127. [illegible].
128. [illegible] illustrates Lacan's conception [illegible] early [illegible] around men at the fictional town of [illegible] who [illegible] perfect [illegible] of [illegible] Oedipal [illegible] is always [illegible] that can never be filled, even in the physical [illegible] of sexual intercourse. This structure [illegible] uncertainty [illegible] the man can never be sure of his position [illegible]. On the other hand, the woman also cannot know what the man [illegible] (Lacan, [illegible], 262–[illegible]). The [illegible] from [illegible] when [illegible] begins to realize her husband [illegible].
129. [illegible] (San Francisco: [illegible] Worker).
130. Lacan, [illegible], 385. Lacanian scholar and psychoanalyst Dr. [illegible] noted [illegible] that he had a patient [illegible] was so disturbed by his own [illegible] of [illegible].
131. [illegible] Walk [illegible] of Robert [illegible] (Oxford [illegible] 1978).

BIBLIOGRAPHY

Adams, Will W. "Making Daemons of Death and Love: Frankenstein, Existentialism, Psychoanalysis." *Journal of Humanistic Psychology* 41, no. 4 (2001): 57–89.

Agrawal, Ajay, Joshua S. Gans, and Avi Goldfarb. "What to Expect from Artificial Intelligence." *MIT Sloan Management Review*, February 7, 2017. https://sloanreview.mit.edu/article/what-to-expect-from-artificial-intelligence/.

Alexander, Michelle. *The New Jim Crow: Mass Incarceration in the Age of Colorblindness*. New York: The New Press, 2012.

Althaus-Reid, Marcella. "Becoming Queens: Bending Gender and Poverty on the Websites of the Excluded." *Concilium*, no. 1 (2005): 99–108.

———. *Indecent Theology: Theological Perversions in Sex, Gender and Politics*. New York: Routledge, 2000.

Aquinas, Thomas. *Summa Theologiae*. Amazon Kindle E-book edition. Translated by the Blackfriars. Claremont, CA: Coyote Canyon Press, 2010.

Arcidiacono, Peter, Josh Kinsler, and Tyler Ransom. "Legacy and Athlete Preferences at Harvard." *Journal of Labor Economics* 40, no. 1 (January 2022): 133–56.

Arendt, Hannah. *The Human Condition*. 2nd ed. Chicago: University of Chicago Press, 1958.

Ashcraft, Catherine, Brad McLain, and Elizabeth Eger. *Women in Tech: The Facts*. National Center for Women in Information Technology, 2016. https://ncwit.org/resource/thefacts/.

Bacon, Francis. *The Advancement of Learning*. London: Cassell & Company, 1893.

Balakrishnan, Tara, Michael Chui, Bryce Hall, and Nicolaus Henke. *Global Survey: The State of AI in 2020*. McKinsey & Company. November 17, 2020. https://www.mckinsey.com/capabilities/quantumblack/our-insights/global-survey-the-state-of-ai-in-2020.

Baranoğlu, Selen. "An Analysis of Mary Shelley's Frankenstein and Robert Louis Stevenson's Dr. Jekyll and Mr. Hyde in Relation to Lacanian Criticism." Master's thesis, Middle East Technical University, 2008, https://etd.lib.metu.edu.tr/upload/12610151/index.pdf.

Barnett, Sofia. "ChatGPT Is Making Universities Rethink Plagiarism." *Wired*, January 30, 2023. https://www.wired.com/story/chatgpt-college-university-plagiarism/.

Bartlett, Bruce. "He Is Even Dumber Than We Thought." *The New Republic*, June 8, 2020. https://newrepublic.com/article/158069/donald-trump-not-smart-polls.

———. "The Whiners Who Earn $200,000 and Complain They're Broke." *The New Republic*, July 20, 2020. https://newrepublic.com/article/158555/whiners-earn-200000-complain-theyre-broke.

Bellan, Rebecca. "Kiwibot Partners with Hospitality Giant Sodexo to Bring Food Delivery Robots to More College Campuses." *Tech Crunch*, August 11, 2021. https://techcrunch.com/2021/08/10/kiwibot-partners-with-hospitality-giant-sodexo-to-bring-food-delivery-robots-to-college-campuses/.

Bender, Emily M., Timnit Gebru, Angelina McMillan-Major, and Shmargaret Shmitchell. "On the Dangers of Stochastic Parrots: Can Language Models Be Too Big?" Paper presented at the Conference on Fairness, Accountability, and Transparency (FAccT '21), virtual event, March 3–10, 2021.

Benecchi, Liz. "Recidivism Imprisons American Progress." *Harvard Political Review*, August 8, 2021. https://harvardpolitics.com/recidivism-american-progress/.

Benjamin, Ruha. *Race after Technology: Abolitionist Tools for the New Jim Code*. Cambridge: Polity Press, 2019.

Berger, Peter L., and Thomas Luckmann. *The Social Construction of Reality: A Treatise in the Sociology of Knowledge*. New York: Open Road Integrated Media, 2011.

Binfield, Kevin, ed. *Writings of the Luddites*. Baltimore: Johns Hopkins University Press, 2015.

Black, Edwin. "Eugenics and the Nazis—The California Connection." *SF Gate*, November 9, 2003. https://www.sfgate.com/opinion/article/Eugenics-and-the-Nazis-the-California-2549771.php.

Blankenship, Paul Houston. "Soul Woundedness." PhD diss., The Graduate Theological Union, Berkeley, CA, 2020.

Bloor, David. "Wittgenstein and Mannheim on the Sociology of Mathematics." *Studies in the History and Philosophy of Science* 4, no. 2 (1973): 173–91.

Bobak, Julia. "Why Did AI Research Drift from Strong AI to Weak AI?" *TechnoPreneurPH* (blog), September 20, 2017. https://technopreneurph.wordpress.com/2017/09/20/why-did-ai-research-drift-from-strong-to-weak-ai-by-julia-bobak/.

Boff, Leonardo. *When Theology Listens to the Poor*. Translated by Robert R. Barr. San Francisco: Harper & Row, 1988.

Bonhoeffer, Dietrich. *The Cost of Discipleship*. Translated by R. H. Fuller. New York: Touchstone, 1995.

Bostrom, Nick. "Existential Risks." *Journal of Evolution and Technology* 9, no. 1 (2002).

———. *Superintelligence: Paths, Dangers, Strategies*. Oxford: Oxford University Press, 2014.

Bostrom, Nick, and Eliezer Yudkowsky. "The Ethics of Artificial Intelligence." In *Cambridge Handbook of Artificial Intelligence*, edited by Keith Frankish and William Ramsey, 316–34. Cambridge: Cambridge University Press, 2014.

Bourdieu, Pierre. *Distinction: A Social Critique of the Judgment of Taste*. Translated by Richard Nice. Cambridge, MA: Harvard University Press, 1984.

Bowles, Nellie. "They Can't Leave the Bay Area Fast Enough." *The New York Times*, January 14, 2021. https://www.nytimes.com/2021/01/14/technology/san-francisco-covid-work-moving.html.

Bradley, Toney. "Facebook AI Creates Its Own Language in Creepy Preview of Our Own Future." *Forbes*, July 31, 2017. https://www.forbes.com/sites/tonybradley/2017/07/31/facebook-ai-creates-its-own-language-in-creepy-preview-of-our-potential-future/?sh=7d9f9d5a292c.

Brewster, Thomas. "DARPA Pays $1 Million for an AI App That Can Predict an Enemy's Emotions." *Forbes*, July 15, 2020. https://www.forbes.com/sites/thomasbrewster/2020/07/15/the-pentagons-1-million-question-can-ai-predict-an-enemys-emotions/?sh=3e64dad632b4.

Brooke, James. "New Portrait of Unabomber: Environmental Saboteur around Montana Village for 20 Years." *The New York Times*, March 14, 1999. https://www.nytimes.com/1999/03/14/us/new-portrait-unabomber-environmental-saboteur-around-montana-village-for-20.html.

Brooks, Arthur C. *Who Really Cares: The Surprising Truth about Compassionate Conservatism*. Philadelphia: Basic Books, 2006.

Broussard, Meredith. *Artificial Unintelligence: How Computers Misunderstand the World*. Cambridge, MA: MIT Press, 2019.

Bughin, Jacques, Jeongmin Seong, James Manyika, Michael Chui, and Raoul Joshi. *Notes from the AI Frontier: Modeling the Impact of AI on the World Economy*. McKinsey & Company. September 2018.

Buck v Bell, 274 US 200 (1927).

Buolamwini, Joy, and Timnit Gebru. "Gender Shades: Intersectional Accuracy Disparities in Commercial Gender Classification." *Proceedings of Machine Learning Research* 81 (2018): 1–15.

Burdett, Michael S. "The Religion of Technology: Transhumanism and the Myth of Progress." In *Religion and Transhumanism*, edited by Calvin Mercer and Tracy Trothen, 131–48. Santa Barbara: Praeger, 2015.

Butler, Judith. *Gender Trouble: Feminism and the Subversion of Identity*, 2nd ed. New York: Routledge, 2007.

Byron, George Gordon (Lord). "Maiden Speech to the House of Lords." In *Recollections of the Life of Lord Byron*, by Robert Charles Dallas, 205–18. London: Charles Knight, 1824.

Čapek, Karel. *R.U.R.* Translated by Paul Selver and Nigel Playfair.

Castellano, Sergi, Genís Parra, Federico A. Sánchez-Quinto, Fernando Racimo, Martin Kuhlwilm, Martin Kircher, Susanna Sawyer, Qiaomei Fu, Anja Heinze, Birgit Nickel, Jesse Dabney, Michael Siebauer, Louise White, Hernán A. Burbano, Gabriel Renaud, Udo Stenzel, Carles Lalueza-Fox, Marco de la Rasilla, Antonio Rosas, Pavao Rudan, Dejana Brajković, Željko Kucan, Ivan Gušic, Michael V. Shunkov, Anatoli P. Derevianko, Bence Viola, Matthias Meyer, Janet Kelso, Aida

M. Andrés, and Svante Pääbo. "Patterns of Coding Variation in the Complete Exomes of Three Neandertals," *Proceedings of the National Academy of the Sciences of the United States of America* 111, no. 18 (March 2014): 6666–71.

Cave, Nick. "ChatGPT, What Do You Think?" *The Red Hand Files*, January 2023, https://www.theredhandfiles.com/chat-gpt-what-do-you-think/.

Cellan-Jones, Rory. "Stephen Hawking Warns Artificial Intelligence Could End Mankind." *BBC*, December 2, 2014. https://www.bbc.com/news/technology-30290540.

Chaney, Marvin L. "Accusing Whom of What? Hosea's Rhetoric of Promiscuity." In *Distant Voices Drawing Near: Essays in Honor of Antoinette Clark Wire*, edited by Holly E. Hearon, 97–116. Collegeville, MN: Liturgical Press, 2004.

Chapple, Karen, Renee Roy Elias, Tim Thomas, Miriam Zuk, Alex Ramiller, Dori Ganetsos, Carson Hartmann, Ayesha Yusuf, Rachel Schten, Shayan Ghosh, and Jen Hu. "Mapping Displacement, Gentrification, and Exclusion in the San Francisco Bay Area." Urban Displacement Project, https://www.urbandisplacement.org/maps/sf-bay-area-gentrification-and-displacement/.

Chase, Alston. "Harvard and the Making of the Unabomber," *The Atlantic*, June 2006. https://www.theatlantic.com/magazine/archive/2000/06/harvard-and-the-making-of-the-unabomber/378239/.

———. *A Mind for Murder: The Education of The Unabomber and the Origins of Modern Terrorism*. New York: W. W. Norton, 2003.

Checketts, Levi. "Idle Hands and the Omega Point: Labor Automation and Catholic Social Teaching." *Agathon: A Journal of Ethics and Value in the Modern World* 5 (2018): 153–71.

———. "Recognizing the Face and Facial Recognition." In *Social Epistemology and Technology*, edited by Frank Scalambrino, 177–86. London: Rowman & Littlefield, 2016.

Chee, Wilvin, and Michael Shirer, "IDC Forecasts Strong 12.3% Growth for AI Market in 2020 Amidst Challenging Circumstances," International Data Corporation, August 4, 2020. http://web.archive.org/web/20220203155144/https://www.idc.com/getdoc.jsp?containerId=prUS46757920. Accessed on March 9, 2022.

Chen, Li. "Engaging Digital News Audiences with an AI-Powered News Chatbot." Hong Kong Baptist University. https://interdisciplinary-research.hkbu.edu.hk/research/research-projects/engaging-digital-news-audiences-with-an-ai-powered-news-chatbot.

Clynes, Manfred, and Nathan Kline. "Cyborgs and Space." *Astronautics* (September 1960): 26–27, 74–76.

Coeckelbergh, Mark. *AI Ethics*. Cambridge, MA: MIT Press, 2020.

Cole, Alistair. "Trust in the Smart City." Hong Kong Baptist University. https://research.hkbu.edu.hk/page/detail/472. Accessed March 23, 2023.

Collings, David. "The Monster and the Imaginary Mother: A Lacanian Reading of Frankenstein." In *Frankenstein: Complete, Authoritative Text with Biographical,*

Historical, and Cultural Contexts; Critical History; and Essays from Contemporary Critical Perspectives, 3rd ed., edited by Johanna M. Smith, 323–39. Boston: Bedford/St. Martin's, 2016.

Connor, Jack. "Ex-Google Executive Warns of Apocalypse, 'We're Creating God.'" *TweakTown*, October 1, 2021. https://www.tweaktown.com/news/81931/ex-google-executive-warns-of-apocalypse-were-creating-god/index.html.

Crawford, Kate. *Atlas of AI*. New Haven: Yale University Press, 2021.

Crenshaw, Kimberle. "Mapping the Margins: Intersectionality, Identity Politics, and Violence against Women of Color." *Stanford Law Review* 43, no. 6 (July 1993): 1241–99.

Cross, Katherine. "Donald Trump Is a Rich Man's Idea of a Rich Man." *Medium*, March 13, 2017. https://medium.com/the-establishment/donald-trump-is-a-rich-mans-idea-of-a-rich-man-bc5cea992c81.

Dance, Amber. "Many Colleges Dropped Their SAT and ACT Requirements during the Pandemic—Here's How It Affected Admissions." *Knowable Magazine*, July 15, 2021. https://www.businessinsider.com/dropping-sat-act-requirement-affected-college-admissions-2021-7?op=1.

Daugherty, Paul R., and H. James Wilson. *Human + Machine: Reimagining Work in the Age of AI*. Boston: Harvard Business Review Press, 2018.

Dave, Paresh, and Jeffrey Dastin. "Google Fires Second AI Ethics Leader as Dispute over Research, Diversity Grows." *Reuters*, February 20, 2021. https://www.reuters.com/article/us-alphabet-google-research-idUSKBN2AJ2JA.

Day, Dorothy. "Poverty and Precarity." In *Selected Writings: By Little and By Little*, edited by Robert Ellsberg, 106–9. Maryknoll: Orbis Books, 2011.

Delano, Jon. "Donald Trump Jr. Refers to Dad as 'The Blue-Collar Billionaire' during Pittsburgh Campaign Stop." *KDKA2 CBS Pittsburgh*, September 14, 2016. pittsburgh.cbslocal.com/2016/09/14/donald-trump-jr-refers-to-dad-as-the-blue-collar-billionaire-during-pittsburgh-campaign-stop/.

Deloitte Technology, Media and Telecommunications Industry. "Global Artificial Intelligence Industry Whitepaper." Accessed March 23, 2023. https://www2.deloitte.com/cn/en/pages/technology-media-and-telecommunications/articles/global-ai-development-white-paper.html.

Derrida, Jacques. "Des tours de Babel." In *Psyche: Inventions of the Other*, Vol. 1, edited by Peggy Kamuf and Elizabeth G. Rottenberg, 191–225. Stanford: Stanford University Press, 2007.

———. "Plato's Pharmacy." In *Dissemination*, trans. Barbara Johnson, 63–171. Chicago: University of Chicago Press, 1981.

Desch, Talia. "Kiwibot Delivery Robot Catches Fire after 'Human Error.'" *BBC*, December 17, 2018. https://www.bbc.com/news/technology-46593190

Dionne, E. J., Jr. "Catholics Debate Morality of Capitalism, U.S. Style." *The New York Times*, November 29, 1986. https://www.nytimes.com/1986/11/29/us/catholics-debate-morality-of-capitalism-us-style.html

Dobbe, Roel, and Meredith Whitaker. "AI and Climate Change: How They're Connected and What We Can Do about It." *AI Now Institute*, October 17, 2019. https://ainowinstitute.org/publication/ai-and-climate-change-how-theyre-connected-and-what-we-can-do-about-it.

Doino, William, Jr. "The Errors of Liberation Theology." *First Things*, July 27, 2015. https://www.firstthings.com/web-exclusives/2015/07/the-errors-of-liberation-theology.

Donavan, Laura. "The Disturbing Reason Many Girls Enter Amateur Porn." *Attn:*, June 15, 2015. https://archive.attn.com/stories/2058/rashida-jones-documentary-amateur-porn.

Dreyfus, Hubert. "A History of First Step Fallacies." *Minds and Machines* 22 (2012): 87–99.

———. *What Computers* Still *Can't Do*. Cambridge, MA: MIT Press, 1992.

———. "Why Heideggerian AI Failed and How Fixing It Would Require Making It More Heideggerian." *Artificial Intelligence* 171, no. 18 (December 2007): 1137–60.

Drinkard, Allyson. "White Trash." In *The Social History of the American Family: An Encyclopedia*, Vol. 3, edited by Marilyn J. Coleman and Lawrence H. Ganong, 1452–53. Los Angeles: Sage, 2014.

Drost, Philip. "Tech Made Our Lives Easier. Now It's Taking More Than It Gives, Says Researcher." *CBC News*, January 23, 2023. https://www.cbc.ca/radio/thecurrent/technology-change-philosopher-1.6703933

Dvorsky, George. "Why Asimov's Three Laws of Robotics Can't Protect Us." *Gizmodo*, March 28, 2014. https://gizmodo.com/why-asimovs-three-laws-of-robotics-cant-protect-us-1553665410.

Earner-Byrne, Lindsey. *Letters of the Catholic Poor: Poverty in Independent Ireland, 1920–1940*. Cambridge, UK: Cambridge University Press, 2017.

Elgammal, Ahmed. "How Artificial Intelligence Completed Beethoven's Unfinished Tenth Symphony." *Smithsonian Magazine*, September 24, 2021. https://www.smithsonianmag.com/innovation/how-artificial-intelligence-completed-beethovens-unfinished-10th-symphony-180978753\/.

Elias, Norbert. *The Civilizing Process: Sociogenetic and Psychogenetic Investigations*. Rev. ed. Translated by Edmund Jephcott. Edited by Johan Goudsblom and Stephen Mennell. Malden: Blackwell, 2000.

Eliot, Lance. "Overcoming Racial Bias in AI Systems and Startlingly Even in Self-Driving Cars." *Forbes*, January 4, 2020. https://www.forbes.com/sites/lanceeliot/2020/01/04/overcoming-racial-bias-in-ai-systems-and-startlingly-even-in-ai-self-driving-cars/?sh=455cc5b723b7.

Elliott, Rebecca. "Tesla Posts First Full Year of Profitability." *The Wall Street Journal*, January 27, 2021. https://www.wsj.com/articles/tesla-tsla-4q-earnings-report-2020-11611708257.

Ellul, Jacques. *Propaganda: The Formation of Men's Attitudes*. Translated by Konrad Kellen. New York: Vintage, 1973.

———. *The Technological Society*. Translated by John Wilkinson. Toronto: Alfred A. Knopf, 1964.

———. *The Technological System*. Translated by Joachim Neugroschel. New York: Continuum Publishing, 1980.

Engels, Friedrich. *The Conditions of the Working-Class in England*. London: George Allen & Unwin, 1892.

Ensmenger, Nathan. *Computer Boys Take Over: Computers, Programmers, and the Politics of Technical Expertise*. Cambridge, MA: MIT Press, 2017.

Eubanks, Virginia. *Automating Inequality: How High-Tech Tools Profile, Police, and Punish the Poor*. New York: Picador, 2018.

Fanon, Frantz. *Black Skin, White Masks*. Translated by C. Markmann. London: Pluto, 1986.

———. *The Wretched of the Earth*, 60th anniversary ed. Translated by Richard Philcox. New York: Grove Press, 2021.

Feenberg, Andrew. *Technosystem: The Social Life of Reason*. Cambridge, MA: Harvard University Press, 2017.

———. *Transforming Technology: A Critical Theory Revisited*. Oxford: Oxford University Press, 2002.

Fells, Ben, and Miles Hewstone. "Psychological Perspectives on Poverty." Joseph Rowntree Foundation, June 4, 2015. https://www.jrf.org.uk/report/psychological-perspectives-poverty.

Ferrando, Francesca. *Philosophical Posthumanism*. London: Bloomsbury Academic, 2019.

Feuerbach, Ludwig. *The Essence of Christianity*. Translated by Marian Evans. London: Chapman's Quarterly, 1854.

Flynn, Shannon. "13 Cities Where Police Are Banned from Using Facial Recognition Tech." *Innovation & Tech Today*, November 18, 2020. https://innotechtoday.com/13-cities-where-police-are-banned-from-using-facial-recognition-tech/.

Foucault, Michel. *Discipline and Punish: The Birth of the Prison*. Translated by Alan Sheridan. New York: Vintage Press, 1977.

———. *A History of Madness*. Translated by Jonathan Murphy and Jean Khalfa. London: Routledge, 2006.

———. *Power/Knowledge: Selected Interviews and Other Writings 1972–1977*. Edited by Colin Gordon. Translated by Colin Gordon, Leo Marshall, John Mepham, and Kate Sopher. New York: Vintage Press, 1980.

Freire, Paulo. *Pedagogy of the Oppressed*. Translated by Myra Bergman. New York: Penguin, 2017.

Friedman, Milton. "The Social Responsibility of Business Is to Increase Its Profits." *New York Times*, September 13, 1970.

Frink, Brenda D. "Researcher Reveals How 'Computer Geeks' Replaced 'Computer Girls.'" *Gender News*. The Clayman Institute for Gender Research, June 1, 2011. https://tinyurl.com/mryz683r.

Fukuyama, Francis. *Our Posthuman Future: Consequences of the Biotechnology Revolution*. New York: Farrar, Straus & Giroux, 2002.

Ge, Xiaohu, John Thompson, Yonghui Li, Xue Liu, Weiyi Zhang, and Tao Chen. "Applications of Artificial Intelligence in Wireless Communications," *IEEE Communications Magazine* 57, no. 3 (March 2019): 12–13.

Gebru, Timnit. "Race and Gender." In *The Oxford Handbook of Ethics of AI*, edited by Markus Dubber, Frank Pasquale, and Sunit Das, 253–70. Oxford: Oxford University Press, 2020.

Gharib, Malaka. "How Can We Help Humans Thrive Trillions of Years from Now? This Philosopher Has a Plan." *National Public Radio*, August 16, 2022. https://www.npr.org/sections/goatsandsoda/2022/08/16/1114353811/how-can-we-help-humans-thrive-trillions-of-years-from-now-this-philosopher-has-a.

Gibson, William. *Neuromancer*. New York: Penguin, 1984.

Giovanetti, Erika. "Places with the Most Payday Lenders Tend to Be Low-Income Communities." Lending Tree, July 28, 2020. https://www.lendingtree.com/debt-consolidation/places-with-most-payday-lenders-study/.

Glaze, Lauren E., and Danielle Kaeble. "Correctional Populations in the United States, 2013." US Bureau of Justice Statistics, December 2014, https://bjs.ojp.gov/library/publications/correctional-populations-united-states-2013.

Goertzel, Ben. "From Narrow AI to AGI via Narrow AI?" *Medium*, August 1, 2019. https://medium.com/@bengoertzel/from-narrow-ai-to-agi-via-narrow-agi-8d828d8c2aa2.

———. *The Hidden Pattern: A Patternist Philosophy of Mind*. Boca Raton: Brown Walker, 2006.

———. *Ten Years to Singularity If We Really, Really Try*. NP: Humanity+ Press, 2014.

Gomez, Amanda Michelle. "States Waste Hundreds of Thousands on Drug Testing for Welfare, but Have Little to Show for It." *The Center for Law and Social Policy*, May 7, 2018. https://www.clasp.org/press-room/news-clips/states-waste-hundreds-thousands-drug-testing-welfare-have-little-show-it/.

Green, Brian Patrick. "A Roman Catholic View: Technological Progress? Yes. Transhumanism? No." In *Religious Transhumanism and Its Critics*, edited by Arvin Gouw, Brian Patrick Green, and Ted Peters, 143–60. Lanham: Lexington Books, 2022.

Greene, Daniel. *The Promise of Access: Technology, Inequality, and the Political Economy of Hope*. Cambridge, MA: MIT Press, 2021.

Grocer, Stephen, Maureen Farrell, and Telis Demos. "The 'God Complex' in Silicon Valley." *The Wall Street Journal*. April 8, 2017. https://www.wsj.com/podcasts/the-god-complex-in-silicon-valley/a17337f1-ad37-4720-9922-771b6dd7680e.

Groody, Daniel, ed. *The Option for the Poor in Christian Theology*. Notre Dame, IN: University of Notre Dame Press, 2007.

Groody, Daniel, and Gustavo Gutiérrez, eds. *The Preferential Option for the Poor Beyond Theology*. Notre Dame, IN: University of Notre Dame Press, 2014.

Grothaus, Michael. "A Science Fiction Magazine Closed Submissions after Being Bombarded with Stories Written by ChatGPT." *Fast Company*, February 23, 2023. https://www.fastcompany.com/90853591/chatgpt-science-fiction-short-stories-clarkesworld-magazine-submissions.

Guariglia, Matthew. "Police Use of Artificial Intelligence: 2021 in Review." *Electronic Frontier Foundation*, January 1, 2022. https://www.eff.org/deeplinks/2021/12/police-use-artificial-intelligence-2021-review.

Gunkel, David. *The Machine Question: Critical Perspectives on AI, Robots, and Ethics*. Cambridge, MA: MIT Press, 2012.

———. *Person, Thing, Robot: A Moral and Legal Ontology for the 21st Century and Beyond*. Cambridge, MA: MIT Press, 2023.

Gutiérrez, Gustavo. *A Theology of Liberation: History, Politics and Salvation*. Translated by Caidad Inda and John Eagleson. Maryknoll: Orbis Books, 1973.

Habermas, Jürgen. *Moral Consciousness and Communicative Action*. Translated by Christian Lenhardt and Shierry Weber Nicholsen. Cambridge, MA: MIT Press, 1990.

Hacking, Ian. *The Social Construction of What?* Cambridge, MA: Harvard Press, 1999.

Hallevy, Gabriel. "The Criminal Liability of Artificial Intelligence Entities—from Science Fiction to Legal Social Control." *Akron Intellectual Property Journal* 4, no. 2 (2010): 171–201.

Hamblin, James. "Is Something Neurologically Wrong with Donald Trump?" *The Atlantic*, January 3, 2018. https://www.theatlantic.com/health/archive/2018/01/trump-cog-decline/548759/.

Hao, Karen. "AI Consumes a Lot of Energy. Hackers Could Make It Consume More." *MIT Technology Review*, May 6, 2021. https://www.technologyreview.com/2021/05/06/1024654/ai-energy-hack-adversarial-attack/.

Haraway, Donna. *Simians, Cyborgs, and Women: The Reinvention of Nature*. New York: Routledge, 1991.

Hardy, Maryann, and Hugh Harvey. "Artificial Intelligence in Diagnostic Imaging: Impact on the Radiography Profession." *The British Journal of Radiology* 93, no. 1108 (2020). doi: 10.1259/bjr.20190840.

Harris, Mark. "Inside the First Church of Artificial Intelligence." *Wired*, November 15, 2017. https://www.wired.com/story/anthony-levandowski-artificial-intelligence-religion/.

Hartnett, Daniel. "Remembering the Poor: An Interview with Gustavo Gutierrez." *America Magazine*, February 3, 2003. https://www.americamagazine.org/faith/2003/02/03/remembering-poor-interview-gustavo-gutierrez.

Hasabis, Demis. "AlphaFold Reveals the Structure of the Protein Universe." *DeepMind* (blog), July 28, 2022. https://www.deepmind.com/blog/alphafold-reveals-the-structure-of-the-protein-universe.

Hastings, Paul D., Lisa A. Serbin, William Bukowski, Jonathan L. Helm, Dale M. Stack, Daniel J. Dickson, Jane E. Ledingham, and Alex E. Schwartzman.

"Predicting Psychosis-Spectrum Diagnosis in Adulthood from Social Behaviors and Neighborhood Contexts in Childhood." *Development and Psychopathology* 32, no. 2 (2019): 465–79.

Heidegger, Martin. *The Question Concerning Technology and Other Essays*. Translated by William Lovitt. New York: Harper Perennial, 1977.

Herzfeld, Noreen. *In Our Image: Artificial Intelligence and the Human Spirit*. Minneapolis: Fortress Press, 2002.

Hefner, Philip. "Technology and Human Becoming." *Zygon* 37, no. 3 (September 2002): 655–66.

Hegel, Georg W. F. *Phenomenology of Spirit*. Translated by A. V. Miller. Oxford: Oxford University Press, 1977.

Hicks, Mar. *Programmed Inequality: How Britain Discarded Women Technologists and Lost Its Edge in Computing*. Cambridge, MA: MIT Press, 2017.

Hobsbawn, Eric. "The Machine Breakers." *Past & Present* 1, no. 1 (February 1952): 57–70.

Hong, Yu. "Reading the 13th Five Year Plan: Reflections on China's ICT Policy." *International Journal of Communication* 11 (2017): 1755–74.

Hosny, Ahmed, Chintan Parmar, John Quackenbush, Lawrence H. Schwartz, and Hugo J. W. L. Aerts. "Artificial Intelligence in Radiology." *Nature Reviews Cancer* 18 (2018): 500–510.

Huber, John D., and Piero Stanig. "Why Do the Poor Support Right-Wing Parties? A Cross-National Analysis." Presented at RSF Inequality Conference, University of California Los Angeles, January 2007.

Hughes, James. "The Politics of Transhumanism." *Zygon: Religion of Journal and Science* 47, no. 4 (December 2012): 757–76.

Hume, David. *A Treatise on Human Nature*. London: John Noon, 1739.

"Humphrey Potter." *Grace's Guide to British Industrial History*. Accessed March 23, 2023. https://www.gracesguide.co.uk/Humphrey_Potter.

Hyun, Younghak. "A Theological Look at the Mask Dance in Korea." In *Minjung Theology: People as the Subjects of History*, edited by Yongbock Kim, 47–54. Singapore: Christian Conference of Asia, 1981.

Igielnik, Ruth, Scott Keeter, and Hannah Hartig. "Behind Biden's 2020 Victory." *Pew Research Center*, June 30, 2021. https://www.pewresearch.org/politics/2021/06/30/behind-bidens-2020-victory/.

Jackson, Maggie. "Would You Let a Robot Take Care of Your Mother?" *The New York Times*, December 13, 2019. https://www.nytimes.com/2019/12/13/opinion/robot-caregiver-aging.html.

Jaffe, Eric. "Americans Think Upward Mobility Is Far More Common Than It Really Is." *CityLab*. February 3, 2015. https://www.bloomberg.com/news/articles/2015-02-02/americans-think-upward-mobility-is-far-more-common-than-it-really-is.

Jasanoff, Sheila, and Sang-Hyun Kim, eds. *Dreamscapes of Modernity: Sociotechnical Imaginaries and the Fabrication of Power*. Chicago: University of Chicago Press, 2015.

John Paul II. *Sollicitudo Rei Socialis*. Vatican City: Libreria Editrice Vaticana, 1987.

Johnson, Leif, and Michelle Fitzsimmons. "Uber Self-Driving Cars: Everything You Need to Know." *Tech Radar*, May 26, 2018. https://www.techradar.com/news/uber-self-driving-cars.

Johnston, Matthew. "Biggest Companies in the World by Market Cap." *Investopedia*, December 21, 2021. https://www.investopedia.com/biggest-companies-in-the-world-by-market-cap-5212784.

Jonas, Hans. *The Imperative of Responsibility: In Search of an Ethics for the Technological Age*. Chicago: University of Chicago Press, 1984.

———. *Mortality and Morality: A Search for the Good after Auschwitz*. Edited by Lawrence Vogel. Evanston, IL: Northwestern University Press, 1996.

———. *The Phenomenon of Life: Toward a Philosophical Biology*. New York: Dell Publishing, 1966.

———. *Philosophical Essays*. New York: Atropos Press, 2010.

Jones, Angela. *Camming: Money, Power, and Pleasure in the Sex Work Industry*. New York: New York University Press, 2020.

Jumper, John, Richard Evans, Alexander Pritzel, Tim Green, Michael Figurnov, Olaf Ronneberger, Kathryn Tunyasuvunakool, Russ Bates, Augustin Žídek, Anna Potapenko, Alex Bridgland, Clemens Meyer, Simon A. A. Kohl, Andrew J. Ballard, Andrew Cowie, Bernardino Romera-Paredes, Stanislav Nikolov, Rishub Jain, Jonas Adler, Trevor Back, Stig Petersen, David Reiman, Ellen Clancy, Michal Zielinski, Martin Steinegger, Michalina Pacholska, Tamas Berghammer, David Silver, Oriol Vinyals, Andrew W. Senior, Koray Kavukcuoglu, Pushmeet Kohli, and Demis Hassabis. "Applying and Improving AlphaFold at CASP14." *Proteins* 89, no. 12 (October 2, 2021): 1711–21.

Kaelber, Lutz. "Eugenics: Compulsory Sterilization in 50 American States." University of Vermont, 2009. https://www.uvm.edu/%7Elkaelber/eugenics/VA/VA.html.

Kant, Immanuel. *Critique of Pure Reason*. Edited by Paul Guyer and Allen W. Wood. Cambridge: Cambridge University Press, 1999.

———. *Groundwork for the Metaphysics of Morals*. Edited and translated by Allen W. Wood. New Haven: Yale University Press, 2002.

Kaplan, Jerry. *Humans Need Not Apply: A Guide to Wealth & Work in the Age of Artificial Intelligence*. New Haven: Yale University Press, 2015.

Kass, Leon. "Defending Human Dignity." In *Human Dignity and Bioethics*, edited by Adam Schulman and Thomas W. Merrill, 297–332. Washington, DC: President's Council on Bioethics, 2008.

———. *Life, Liberty and the Defense of Dignity: The Challenge for Bioethics*. San Francisco: Encounter Books, 2002.

Kelly, Morgan. "Poor Concentration: Poverty Reduces Brainpower Needed for Navigating Other Areas of Life." Princeton University, August 29, 2013. https://www.princeton.edu/news/2013/08/29/poor-concentration-poverty-reduces-brainpower-needed-navigating-other-areas-life.

Kewalramani, Manoj. *China's Quest for AI Leadership Prospects*. Takshashila Working Paper, October 1, 2018. http://dx.doi.org/10.2139/ssrn.3414883.

Kierkegaard, Søren. *Either/Or: A Fragment of Life*. Translated by Alastair Hannay. New York: Penguin Books, 1992.

———. *Fear and Trembling*. Translated by Alastair Hannay. London: Penguin Books, 1985.

Kim, Eugene. "Amazon CEO Jeff Bezos Joins a Group Led by Ex-Google CEO Eric Schmidt to Advise the Pentagon." *Business Insider*, August 2, 2016. https://www.businessinsider.com/amazon-ceo-jeff-bezos-joins-pentagon-defense-advisory-board-2016-8.

Kim, Hyeun-gil, 김현길, "매너 좋고 인간적인 '알파고'도 가능할까" *국민일보*, March 18, 2021. http://news.kmib.co.kr/article/view.asp?arcid=0924183344&code=13150000&cp=du.

Kim, Hyo-Eun, Hak Hee Kim, Boo-Kyung Han, Ki Hwan Kim, Kyunghwa Han, Hyeonseob Nam, Eun Hye Lee, and Eun-Kyung Kim. "Changes in Cancer Detection and False-Positive Recall in Mammography Using Artificial Intelligence: A Retrospective, Multireader Study." *The Lancet* 2, no. 3 (March 2020): e138–e148.

Ko, Jae-sik. "Minjung Theology and Liberation Theology." *Theological Studies* (Chinese) 28 (July 1987): 199–227.

Ko, Jiyoung. "Destruction and Creation Ex Nihilo: Mary of Bethany's and Margery Kempe's Spiritualities of Nonconformity from the Perspective of Lacanian Ethics of Desire." PhD diss., The Graduate Theological Union, Berkeley, CA, 2022.

Kotze, Haidee. "Desire, Gender, Power, Language: A Psychoanalytic Reading of Mary Shelley's Frankenstein." *Literator* 21, no. 1 (2000): 53–67.

Kuhn, Thomas S. *The Structure of Scientific Revolutions*, 50th anniversary ed. Chicago: University of Chicago Press, 2012.

Kuppuswamy, Raghunandhan, and Ritu Jyoti. *Artificial Intelligence Software and Strategies*. International Data Corporation. https://www.idc.com/getdoc.jsp?containerId=IDC_P38649.

Kurzweil, Ray. *The Singularity Is Near: When Humans Transcend Biology*. New York: Viking, 2005.

Lacan, Jacques. *Écrits*. Translated by Bruce Fink. New York: W. W. Norton, 2006.

———. *The Seminars of Jacques Lacan IV: The Object Relation*. Edited by Jacques-Alain Miller. Translated by A. R. Price. Medford: Polity Press, 2020.

———. *The Seminar of Jacques Lacan VII: The Ethics of Psychoanalysis 1959–1960*. Edited by Jacques-Alain Miller. Translated by Dennis Porter. New York: W.W. Norton, 1992.

———. *The Seminar of Jacques Lacan X: Anxiety*. Edited by Jacques-Alain Miller. Translated by A. R. Price. Cambridge, UK: Polity Press, 2014.

———. *The Seminar of Jacques Lacan XXII: R.S.I.* Translated by Cormac Gallagher. Jacques Lacan in Ireland, 2010. http://www.lacaninireland.com/web/wp-content/uploads/2010/06/RSI-Complete-With-Diagrams.pdf.

Lanier, Jaron. *You Are Not a Gadget: A Manifesto.* Toronto: First Vintage Books, 2011.

Lat, David. "How Artificial Intelligence Is Transforming Legal Research." *ThomsonReuters*, 2020. https://abovethelaw.com/law2020/how-artificial-intelligence-is-transforming-legal-research/.

Latour, Bruno. *Reassembling the Social: An Introduction to Actor-Network-Theory.* Oxford: Oxford University Press, 2005.

———. *Science in Action: How to Follow Scientists and Engineers through Society.* Cambridge, MA: Harvard University Press, 1987.

———. "Where Are the Missing Masses? The Sociology of a Few Mundane Artifacts." In *Shaping Technology/Building Society: Studies in Sociotechnical Change*, edited by Wiebe E. Bijker and John Law, 225–58. Cambridge, MA: MIT Press, 1992.

Latour, Bruno, and Steve Woolgar. *Laboratory Life: The Construction of Scientific Facts.* Princeton: Princeton University Press, 1986.

Laughlin, Harry. "Eugenical Sterilization in the United States." Psychopathic Laboratory of the Municipal Court of Chicago, December 1922. https://web.archive.org/web/20110709175251/http://www.people.fas.harvard.edu/~wellerst/laughlin/.

Le Guin, Ursula. "The Ones Who Walk Away from Omelas." In *New Dimensions 3*, edited by Robert Silverberg, 1–9. Garden City, NY: Doubleday, 1973.

Lee, Jennifer, and Tiffany Huang. "Why the Trope of Black-Asian Conflict in the Face of Anti-Asian Violence Dismisses Solidarity." Brookings Institute, *How We Rise*, March 11, 2021. https://www.brookings.edu/blog/how-we-rise/2021/03/11/why-the-trope-of-black-asian-conflict-in-the-face-of-anti-asian-violence-dismisses-solidarity/.

Lemoine, Blake. "Is LaMDA Sentient? An Interview." *Medium*, June 11, 2022. https://cajundiscordian.medium.com/is-lamda-sentient-an-interview-ea64d916d917.

———. "May Be Fired Soon for Doing AI Ethics Work." *Medium*, June 7, 2022. https://cajundiscordian.medium.com/may-be-fired-soon-for-doing-ai-ethics-work-802d8c474e66.

Leibniz, Gottfried Wilhelm. *Dissertation on Combinatorial Art.* Translated by Massimo Mugnai, Han van Ruler, and Martin Wilson. Oxford: Oxford University Press, 2020.

Leo XIII. *Aeterni Patris: On the Restoration of Christian Philosophy.* Vatican City: Libreria Editrice Vaticana, 1879.

———. *Rerum Novarum: On Capital and Labor.* Vatican City: Libreria Editrice Vaticana, 1891.

Leonard, Andrew. "The Tech Industry's God Complex Is Getting Out of Control." *Salon*, June 13, 2014. https://www.salon.com/2014/06/13/the_tech_industrys_god_complex_is_getting_out_of_control/.

Leonard, Ben. "'QAnon Shaman' Granted Organic Food in Jail after Report of Deteriorating Health." *Politico*, February 3, 2021. https://www.politico.com/news/2021/02/03/qanon-shaman-organic-food-465563.

Leung, Collette. "Kellogg, John Harvey." *Eugenics Archive*, https://web.archive.org/web/20230310110854/http://eugenicsarchive.ca/discover/connections/512fa0d334c5399e2c000005.

Levesque, Hector J. "On Our Best Behavior." *Artificial Intelligence* 212 (July 2014): 27–35.

Levinas, Emmanuel. *Otherwise than Being, or beyond Essence*. Translated by Alphonso Lingis. Pittsburgh: Duquesne University Press, 1998.

———. *Totality and Infinity: An Essay on Exteriority*. Translated by Alphonso Lingis. Pittsburgh: Duquesne University Press, 1969.

Levinovitz, Alan. "The Mystery of Go, the Ancient Game that Computers Still Can't Win." *Wired*, May 12, 2014. https://www.wired.com/2014/05/the-world-of-computer-go/.

Levitz, Eric. "Why Effective Altruists Fear the AI Apocalypse: A Conversation with the Philosopher William MacAskill." *New York Magazine*, August 30, 2022. https://nymag.com/intelligencer/2022/08/why-effective-altruists-fear-the-ai-apocalypse.html.

Levy, David. *Love and Sex with Robots: The Evolution of Human-Robot Relations*. New York: Harper Perennial, 2007.

Lewis, Jason Edward, ed. *Indigenous Protocol and Artificial Intelligence Position Paper*. Honolulu: The Initiative for Indigenous Futures and the Canadian Institute for Advanced Research, 2020. 10.11573/spectrum.library.concordia.ca.00986506.

Lewis-Kraus, Gideon. "The Reluctant Prophet of Effective Altruism." *The New Yorker*, August 8, 2022. https://www.newyorker.com/magazine/2022/08/15/the-reluctant-prophet-of-effective-altruism.

Lewis, Tanya. "The 'Shared Psychosis' of Donald Trump and His Loyalists." *Scientific American*, January 11, 2021. https://www.scientificamerican.com/article/the-shared-psychosis-of-donald-trump-and-his-loyalists/.

Liu, Lydia H. *The Freudian Robot: Digital Media and the Future of the Unconscious*. Chicago: University of Chicago Press, 2010.

Lombardo, Paul A. "Three Generations, No Imbeciles: New Light on Buck v. Bell." *New York University Law Review* 60, no. 1 (1985): 30–62.

Lonergan, Bernard. *Method in Theology*. Toronto: University of Toronto Press, 1990.

de Looper, Christian. "Thousands of Jobs Lost as Apple Supplier Foxconn Fully Automates Its Factories." *Digital Trends*, December 30, 2016. https://www.digitaltrends.com/mobile/foxconn-three-phases-factory-automation/.

Lorde, Audre. "The Master's Tools Will Never Dismantle the Master's House." In *Sister Outsider: Essays and Speeches*, 110–14. Berkeley: Crossing Press, 1984.

Lovelace, Ada Augusta. "Notes by Translator." In *Scientific Memoirs, Selected from the Transactions of Foreign Academies of Science and Learned Societies, and from Foreign Journals*, Volume 3. Edited by Richard Taylor and John E. Taylor, 691–731. London: 1843.

Ludd, Ned [pseud.]. "8th January 1813: The Execution of George Mellor, William Thorpe & Thomas Smith," *Luddite Bicentenary–1811–1817* (blog), January 8,

2013. https://ludditebicentenary.blogspot.com/2013/01/8th-january-1812-execution-of-george.html.

Lukács, Georg. *History and Class Consciousness*. New York: Bibliotech Press, 2017.

Lurie, Stephen. "There's No Such Thing as a Dangerous Neighborhood." *Bloomberg City Lab*, February 25, 2019. https://www.bloomberg.com/news/articles/2019-02-25/beyond-broken-windows-what-really-drives-urban-crime.

Lynn, Jessica. "Why Do I Want to Kick Those Cute Little Food-Delivery Robots?" *The Bold Italic*, January 7, 2020. https://thebolditalic.com/why-do-i-want-to-kick-those-cute-little-food-delivery-robots-ba0555a144d9.

Lynn, Nick. "The AI CEO." *Medium*, September 7, 2019. https://nickl4.medium.com/the-ai-ceo-734f9970db3c.

MacAskill, William. "The Beginning of History: Surviving Catastrophic Risk." *Foreign Affairs*, August/September 2022. https://www.foreignaffairs.com/world/william-macaskill-beginning-history.

———. "Longtermism." *Effective Altrusim Blog*, July 25, 2019. https://forum.effectivealtruism.org/posts/qZyshHCNkjs3TvSem/longtermism.

———. "What Is Longtermism?" *BBC*, August 8, 2022. https://www.bbc.com/future/article/20220805-what-is-longtermism-and-why-does-it-matter.

Malthus, Thomas. *An Essay on the Principle of Population*. London: J. Johnson, 1798.

Marcuse, Herbert. *Eros and Civilization: A Philosophical Inquiry into Freud*. New York: Vintage Press, 1962.

———. *One-Dimensional Man: Studies in the Ideology of Advanced Industrial Society*. Boston: Beacon Press, 1991.

Marion, Jean-Luc. *God without Being*, 2nd ed. Translated by Thomas A. Carlson. Chicago: University of Chicago Press, 2012.

Marsden History Group. "Luddites in Marsden." Accessed March 26, 2012. https://web.archive.org/web/20120326170835/http://www.marsdenhistory.co.uk/people/luddites.html.

Martinho, Andreia, Adam Poulsen, Maarten Kroesen, and Caspar Chorus. "Perspectives about Artificial Moral Agents." *AI and Ethics* 1 (2021): 477–90.

Marx, Karl. *Contribution to the Critique of Hegel's Philosophy of Right*. Translated by Joseph O'Malley. Oxford: Oxford University Press, 1970.

Matteson, Michael, and Chris Metivier. "Case: The Ford Pinto." *Business Ethics*. University of North Carolina Greensboro. https://philosophia.uncg.edu/phi361-matteson/module-1-why-does-business-need-ethics/case-the-ford-pinto/.

Matthews, Dylan. "How Effective Altruism Went from a Nice Movement to a Billion-Dollar Force." *Vox*, August 8, 2022. https://tinyurl.com/2s35wc9n.

McCarthy, John. "Ascribing Mental Qualities to Machines." In *Philosophical Perspectives in Artificial Intelligence*. Edited by Martin Ringle, 161–95. Atlantic Highlands, NJ: Humanities Press, 1979.

McCarthy, John, and Patrick J. Hayes. "Some Philosophical Problems from the Standpoint of Artificial Intelligence." *Machine Intelligence* 4 (1969): 463–502.

McClelland, James, and David Rumelhart. "Distributed Memory and the Representation of General and Specific Information." *Journal of Experimental Psychology* 114, no. 2 (1985): 159–88.

McCormick, Rich. "Odds Are We're Living in a Simulation, Says Elon Musk." *The Verge*, June 2, 2016. http://www.theverge.com/2016/6/2/11837874/elon-musk-says-odds-living-in-simulation.

McCulloch, Warren, and Walter Pitts. "A Logical Calculus of the Ideas Immanent in Nervous Activities." *Bulletin of Mathematical Biophysics* 5 (1943): 115–33.

McCullough, Jack. "The Psychopathic CEO." *Forbes*, December 9, 2019. https://www.forbes.com/sites/jackmccullough/2019/12/09/the-psychopathic-ceo/?sh=e484423791e3.

McFarland, Matt. "Elon Musk Just Added a Robot to His List of Things Always Coming 'Next Year.' For Now He's Got a Guy in a Suit." *CNN Business*, August 20, 2021 https://www.cnn.com/2021/08/20/tech/tesla-ai-day-robot/index.html

McHugh, Josh. "Why A.I. is Brain-Dead." *Wired*, August 1, 2003. https://www.wired.com/2003/08/why-a-i-is-brain-dead/.

McRobbie, Angela. *Postmodernism and Popular Culture*. London: Routledge, 1994.

Meixell, Brady, and Ross Eisenbrey, "Wage Theft Is a Much Bigger Problem than Other Forms of Theft—But Workers Remain Mostly Unprotected." *Economic Policy Institute*, September 18, 2014. https://www.epi.org/publication/wage-theft-bigger-problem-forms-theft-workers/.

The Mentor [pseud.]. "The Conscience of a Hacker." *Phrack* 1, no. 7 (1986): Phile 3 of 10. http://www.phrack.org/issues/7/3.html.

Merleau-Ponty, Maurice. *Phenomenology of Perception*. Translated by D. Landes. London: Routledge, 2012.

Metz, Cade. "In Two Moves, AlphaGo and Lee Sedol Redefined the Future." *Wired*, March 16, 2016. https://www.wired.com/2016/03/two-moves-alphago-lee-sedol-redefined-future/.

Metz, Cade, and Daisuke Wakabayashi. "Google Researcher Says She Was Fired Over Paper Highlighting Bias in A.I." *The New York Times*, December 3, 2020. https://www.nytimes.com/2020/12/03/technology/google-researcher-timnit-gebru.html.

Metz, Neil, and Mariya Burdina. "Neighbourhood Income Inequality and Property Crime." *Urban Studies* 55, no. 1 (April 2016): 133–50.

Metzl, Jonathan M., Jennifer Piemonte, and Tara McKay. "Mental Illness, Mass Shootings, and the Future of Psychiatric Research into American Gun Violence." *Harvard Review of Psychiatry* 29, no. 1 (January 2021): 81–89.

Michielin, Davide. "Bot or Scientist? The Controversial Use of ChatGPT in Science." *Foresight*, February 6, 2023. https://www.climateforesight.eu/articles/chatgpt-science/.

Miedema, Douwe, and Sarah N. Lynch. "UK Speed Trader Arrested over Role in 2010 'Flash Crash.'" *Reuters*, April 22, 2015. https://www.reuters.com/article/us-usa-security-fraud-idUSKBN0NC21220150421.

Mill, John Stuart. *Utilitarianism*. London: Longmans, Green, 1879.

Miller, Michael E. "S.F. 'Tech Bro' Writes Open Letter to Mayor: 'I Shouldn't Have to See the Pain, Struggle, and Despair of Homeless People', 'Riff Raff.'" *The Washington Post*, February 18, 2016.

Millar, Isabell. *The Psychoanalysis of Artificial Intelligence*. Cham, Switzerland: Palgrave MacMillan, 2021.

Min, Anselm. *The Solidarity of Others in a Divided World: A Postmodern Theology after Postmodernism*. New York: T & T Clark, 2004.

Minsky, Marvin. *The Society of Mind*. New York: Simon & Schuster, 1985.

Minsky, Marvin, and Seymour Papert. *Perceptrons: An Introduction to Computational Geometry*. Expanded ed. Cambridge, MA: MIT Press, 1988.

Mommsen, Theodor. "Petrarch's Conception of the Dark Ages." *Speculum* 17, no. 2 (April 1942): 226–42.

Mookim, Mohit. "The World Loses under Bill Gates' Vaccine Colonialism." *Wired*, May 19, 2021, https://www.wired.com/story/opinion-the-world-loses-under-bill-gates-vaccine-colonialism/

Moravec, Hans. *Mind Children: The Future of Robot and Human Intelligence*. Cambridge, MA: Harvard University Press, 1988.

More, Max, and Natasha Vita-More, eds. *The Transhumanist Reader: Classical and Contemporary Essays on the Science, Technology and Philosophy of the Human Future*. Malden, MA: Wiley-Blackwell, 2013.

Moreno, James D. "Harvard's Experiment on the Unabomber, Class Of '62: An Odd Footnote to Kaczynski's Class Reunion." *Psychology Today*, May 25, 2012. https://www.psychologytoday.com/intl/blog/impromptu-man/201205/harvards-experiment-the-unabomber-class-62.

Moret, Whitney. *Economic Strengthening for Female Sex Workers: A Review of the Literature*. United States Agency for International Development, May 2014.

Moskowitz, Dan. "The 10 Richest People in the World." *Investopedia*, October 27, 2021. https://www.investopedia.com/articles/investing/012715/5-richest-people-world.asp.

Mosley, Paul, and Arjan Verschoor. "Risk Attitudes in the 'Vicious Circle of Poverty.'" *European Journal of Developmental Research* 17, no. 1 (March 2005): 59–88.

Mozur, Paul. "Life inside Foxconn's Facility in Shenzhen." *The Wall Street Journal*, December 19, 2012. https://www.wsj.com/articles/BL-CJB-17008.

Nadi, Yara, and Philip Pullella. "World Has Become Deaf to Plight of the Poor, Pope Says in Assisi." *Reuters*, November 12, 2021. https://www.reuters.com/world/world-has-become-deaf-plight-poor-pope-says-assisi-2021-11-12/.

Nelson, William Max. "Making Men: Enlightenment Ideas of Racial Engineering." *American Historical Review* 115, no. 5 (December 2010): 1364–94.

Newitz, Annalee and Matthew Wray. "What Is 'White Trash?' Stereotypes and Economic Conditions of Poor Whites in the U.S." *Minnesota Review* 47 (Fall 1996): 57–72.

Nguyen, Tina. "Is Donald Trump Not Really a Billionaire?" *Vanity Fair*, May 31, 2016 https://www.vanityfair.com/news/2016/05/donald-trump-net-worth

Nietzsche, Friedrich. *Beyond Good and Evil*. Translated by Helen Zimmerman. Stilwell, KS: Digireads.com, 2005.

———. *On the Genealogy of Morals*. Translated by Carol Diethe. Cambridge, UK: Cambridge University Press, 2006.

———. *Thus Spake Zarathustra: A Book for All and None*. Translated by Adrian del Caro. Cambridge, UK: Cambridge University Press, 2006.

Noble, Safiya. *Algorithms of Oppression: How Search Engines Reinforce Racism*. New York: New York University Press, 2018.

Nozick, Robert. *Anarchy, the State and Utopia*. New York: Basic Books, 1974.

Nussbaum, Martha C. *Frontiers of Justice: Disability, Nationality, Species Membership*. Cambridge, MA: Belknap Press, 2006.

Okin, Susan Moller. *Justice, Gender and the Family*. New York: Basic Books, 1989.

O'Neil, Cathy. *Weapons of Math Destruction: How Big Data Increases Inequality and Threatens Democracy*. New York: Crown, 2016.

Organization for Economic Cooperation and Development. *Education at a Glance 2016*. Paris: OECD Publishing, 2016. https://read.oecd-ilibrary.org/education/education-at-a-glance-2016_eag-2016-en#page44.

Owen, Robert. *A New View of Society and Other Writings*. London: Everyman's Library, 1966.

Park, Kyeyoung. "Use and Abuse of Race and Culture: Black-Korean Tension in America." *American Anthropologist* 98, no. 3 (September 1996): 492–99.

Patel, Pravin J. "Trade Union Participation and Development of Class-Consciousness." *Economic and Political Weekly* 29, no. 36 (September 3, 1994): 2376.

Patel, Raj, and Jason W. Moore. *A History of the World in Seven Cheap Things: A Guide to Capitalism, Nature, and the Future of the Planet*. Berkeley: University of California Press, 2017.

Payne, Ruby K. *A Framework for Understanding Poverty*, 4th rev. ed. Highlands, TX: aha! Process, 2005.

Penava, Elizabeth. "AI Art Is in Legal Greyscale." *The Regulatory Review*, January 24, 2023. https://www.theregreview.org/2023/01/24/penava-ai-art-is-in-legal-greyscale/.

Peters, Ted. *God—The World's Future: Systematic Theology for a New Era*, 3rd ed. Minneapolis: Fortress Press, 2015.

Pinch, Trevor J., and Wiebe E. Bijker. "The Social Construction of Facts and Artifacts: Or How the Sociology of Science and the Sociology of Technology Might Benefit Each Other." In *The Social Construction of Technological Systems: New Directions in the Sociology and History of Technology*, edited by Wiebe E. Bijker, Thomas P. Hughes, and Trevor Pinch, 17–50. Cambridge, MA: MIT Press, 1987.

Piff, Paul K., Michael W. Kraus, Stéphane Côté, Bonnie Hayden Cheng, and Dacher Keltner. "Having Less, Giving More: The Influence of Social Class on

Prosocial Behavior." *Journal of Personality and Social Psychology* 99, no. 5 (2010): 771–84.

Pius X. *Pascendi Dominis Gregis: On the Doctrines of the Modernists.* Vatican City: Libreria Editrice Vaticana, 1907.

Pius XI. *Quadragesimo Anno: On Reconstruction of the Social Order.* Vatican City: Libreria Editrice Vaticana, 1931.

Pfeiffer, Sabine. *Digital Capitalism and Distributive Forces.* Bielefeld, Germany: Transcript Verlag, 2022.

Plato. *The Republic.* Translated by Benjamin Jowett. 3rd ed. Oxford: Clarendon Press, 1888.

"Poverty in San Francisco," City and County of San Francisco. Accessed November 11, 2022. https://sfgov.org/scorecards/safety-net/poverty-san-francisco.

Quinones, Julian, and Arijeta Lajka. "'What Kind of Society Do You Want to Live in?': Inside the Country Where Down Syndrome Is Disappearing." *CBS News*, August 15, 2017. https://www.cbsnews.com/news/down-syndrome-iceland/.

Radford, Alec, Jeffrey Wu, Dario Amodei, Daniela Amodei, Jack Clark, Miles Brundage, and Ilya Sutskever. "Better Language Models and Their Implications." *OpenAI*, February 14, 2019. https://openai.com/blog/better-language-models/.

Raguso, Emilie. "Police: Berkeley Man, Fed Up with Kiwibot Delivery Robots, Steals One." *Berkeleyside*, April 26, 2019. https://www.berkeleyside.org/2019/04/26/police-berkeley-man-fed-up-with-kiwibot-delivery-robots-steals-one.

Rao, Arnand, and Gerard Verweij. "Sizing the Prize: What's the Real Value of AI for Your Business and How Can You Capitalise?" PwC. 2017. https://www.pwc.com/gx/en/issues/data-and-analytics/publications/artificial-intelligence-study.html.

Ratzinger, Josef [prefect]. *Instruction on Certain Aspects of the "Theology of Liberation."* Vatican City: Libreria Editrice Vaticana, 1984.

Rawls, John. *A Theory of Justice.* Cambridge, MA: Belknap Press, 1971.

Reed, Randall. "The Theology of GPT-2: Religion and Artificial Intelligence." *Religion Compass* 15, no. 11 (November 2021): e12422.

Reidl, Mark O. "The Lovelace 2.0 Test of Artificial Creativity and Intelligence." *arXiv* 1410.6142v3 (2014): December 22, 2014. https://doi.org/10.48550/arXiv.1410.6142.

Reuter, Dominick, and Andy Kiersz. "Elon Musk Has a $2.5 Billion Reason to Move to Texas: Avoiding California Capital Gains Tax." *Business Insider*, December 1, 2021. https://www.businessinsider.com/why-did-elon-musk-move-texas-wealth-tax-capital-gains-2021-11.

Reuters Staff. "USA: Uber Critiqué pour un Accident Fatal en 2018." *Reuters*, November 20, 2019. https://www.reuters.com/article/usa-uber-idFRKBN1XU0IC.

Reynolds, Emily. "The Agony of Sophia, the World's First Robot Citizen Condemned to a Lifeless Career in Marketing." *Wired*, January 6, 2018. https://www.wired.co.uk/article/sophia-robot-citizen-womens-rights-detriot-become-human-hanson-robotics.

Righetti, L., Q. Pham, R. Madhavan, and R. Chatila, "Lethal Autonomous Weapon Systems [Ethical, Legal, and Societal Issues]." *IEEE Robotics & Automation Magazine* 25, no. 1 (March 2018): 123–26.

Robitzski, Dan. "Former Google Exec Warns That AI Researchers Are 'Creating God.'" *The Byte*, September 30, 2021. https://futurism.com/the-byte/google-exec-ai-god.

Rose, Janus. "School Apologises after Using ChatGPT to Write Email about Mass-Shooting." *Vice*, February 22, 2023. https://www.vice.com/en/article/88qwqg/school-apologizes-after-using-chatgpt-to-write-email-about-mass-shooting.

Rushe, Dominic. "Wage Gap between CEOs and US Workers Jumped to 670-to-1 Last Year, Study Finds." *The Guardian*, June 7, 2022. https://www.theguardian.com/us-news/2022/jun/07/us-wage-gap-ceos-workers-institute-for-policy-studies-report.

Saenz, Aaron. "Cleverbot Chat Engine Is Learning from the Internet to Talk like a Human." *Singularity Hub*, January 13, 2010. https://singularityhub.com/2010/01/13/cleverbot-chat-engine-is-learning-from-the-internet-to-talk-like-a-human/.

Sainato, Michael. "'Go Back to Work': Outcry over Deaths on Amazon's Warehouse Floor." *The Guardian*, October 18, 2019. https://www.theguardian.com/technology/2019/oct/17/amazon-warehouse-worker-deaths.

Sakaguchi, Keisuke, Ronan Le Bras, Chandra Bhagavatula, and Yejin Choiy. "WinoGrande: An Adversarial Winograd Schema Challenge at Scale," *arXiv* (2019): 1907.10641v2.

Samuel, Arthur. "Some Studies in Machine Learning Using the Game of Checkers." *IBM Journal of Research and Development* 44 (1959): 206–29.

Sandel, Michael. *The Case Against Perfection*. Cambridge, MA: Belknap Press, 2007.

Sartre, Jean-Paul. *Being and Nothingness*. Translated by Hazel E. Barnes. New York: Washington Square, 1984.

Satariano, Adam. "Real Time Surveillance Will Test the British Tolerance for Cameras." *The New York Times*, September 15, 2019. https://www.nytimes.com/2019/09/15/technology/britain-surveillance-privacy.html.

Savulescu, Julian, and Ingmar Persson. "Moral Enhancement." *Philosophy Now* 91 (2012). https://philosophynow.org/issues/91/Moral_Enhancement.

Schuessler, Jennifer. "Hoaxers Slip Breastaurants and Dog-Park Sex into Journals." *The New York Times*, October 4, 2018. https://www.nytimes.com/2018/10/04/arts/academic-journals-hoax.html.

Searle, John. "Minds, Brains, and Programs." In *Philosophy of Mind: A Guide and an Anthology*, edited by John Heil, 235–52. Oxford: Oxford University Press, 2004.

Schumacher, Ernst Friedrich. "Buddhist Economics." Schumacher Center for a New Economics. https://centerforneweconomics.org/publications/buddhist-economics/.

Schwartz, Oscar. "In the 17th Century, Leibniz Dreamed of a Machine That Could Calculate Ideas." *IEEE Spectrum*, November 4, 2019.

spectrum.ieee.org/tech-talk/artificial-intelligence/machine-learning/in-the-17th-century-leibniz-dreamed-of-a-machine-that-could-calculate-ideas.

Second Vatican Council. *Pastoral Constitution on the Church in the Modern World: Gaudium et Spes*. Vatican City: Libreria Editrice Vaticana, 1963.

"Senate Resolution No. 2019/2020-028: Condemning Kiwi Campus for Its Low Compensation of Columbian Workers." The Associated Students University of California. https://tinyurl.com/yc7v5v7c.

Shafir, Eldar, and Sendhil Mullainathan. "Scarcity: Why Having Too Little Means So Much." *Behavioral Scientist*, September 12, 2013. https://behavioralscientist.org/scarcity-excerpt-mullainathan-shafir/.

Shane, Janelle. "AI Recipes Are Bad (and a Proposal for Making Them Worse)." *AI Weirdness*, January 31, 2020. https://www.aiweirdness.com/ai-recipes-are-bad-and-a-proposal-20-01-31/.

Shannon, Claude. "A Mathematical Theory of Communication." *The Bell System Technical Journal* 27, no. 3 (July 1948): 379–423, 623–56.

Shapin, Steven, and Simon Schaffer. *Leviathan and the Air-Pump: Hobbes, Boyle, and the Experimental Life*. Princeton: Princeton University Press, 1985.

Shue, Henry. *Basic Rights: Subsistence, Affluence and U.S. Foreign Policy*. Princeton: Princeton University Press, 1996.

Silver, David, Thomas Hubert, Julian Schrittwieser, Ioannis Antonoglou, Matthew Lai, Arthur Guez, Marc Lanctot, Laurent Sifre, Dharshan Kumaran, Thore Graepel, Timothy Lillicrap, Karen Simonyan, and Demis Hassabis. "A General Reinforcement Learning Algorithm That Masters Chess, Shogi, and Go through Self-Play." *Science* 362, no. 6419 (December 7, 2018): 1140–44.

Singer, Peter. "Isaac Asimov's Laws of Robotics Are Wrong." Brookings Institute, May 18, 2009. https://www.brookings.edu/opinions/isaac-asimovs-laws-of-robotics-are-wrong/.

———. "The Singer Solution to World Poverty." *The New York Times*, September 5, 1999, sec. 6.

Singh, Ajai R., and Shakuntala A. Singh. "Diseases of Poverty and Lifestyle, Well-Being and Human Development." *Mens Sana Monogr* 6, no. 1 (January–December 2008): 187–225. https://www.ncbi.nlm.nih.gov/pmc/articles/PMC3190550/.

Smith, Adam. *An Inquiry into the Nature and Cause of the Wealth of Nations*. London: W. Strahan, 1776.

Sobrino, Jon. *No Salvation outside the Poor: Prophetic-Utopian Essays*. Maryknoll: Orbis, 2008.

Sokal, Alan D. "A Physicist Experiments with Cultural Studies." New York University, https://physics.nyu.edu/faculty/sokal/lingua_franca_v4/lingua_franca_v4.html.

Sokol, Emily. "Overcoming Bias in Artificial Intelligence, Machine Learning." *Health IT Analytics*, January 9, 2020. https://healthitanalytics.com/news/overcoming-bias-in-artificial-intelligence-machine-learning.

Solnit, Rebecca. "Get Off the Bus." *London Review of Books* 36, no. 4, February 20, 2014. https://www.lrb.co.uk/the-paper/v36/n04/rebecca-solnit/diary.

Spears, Arthur K. "Race and Ideology: An Introduction." In *Race and Ideology: Language, Symbolism and Popular Culture*, 11–58. Detroit: Wayne State University Press, 1999.

Spivak, Gayatri. *Can the Subaltern Speak? Reflections on an Idea*. Edited by Rosalind C. Morris. New York: Columbia University Press, 2010.

Stampfl, Karl. "He Came Ted Kaczynski, He Left the Unabomber." *Michigan Daily*, March 16, 2006. https://web.archive.org/web/20170114062259/https://www.michigandaily.com/content/he-came-ted-kaczynski-he-left-unabomber.

Streitfeld, David. "How Amazon Crushes Unions." *The New York Times*, March 16, 2021. https://www.nytimes.com/2021/03/16/technology/amazon-unions-virginia.html.

Stromberg, Joseph. "The Forgotten History of How Automakers Invented the Crime of 'Jaywalking.'" *Vox*, November 4, 2015. https://www.vox.com/2015/1/15/7551873/jaywalking-history.

Sundaravelu, Anugraha. "Chinese Company Appoints Female Robot as Its CEO." *Metro*, August 30, 2022. https://metro.co.uk/2022/08/30/chinese-company-appoints-female-robot-as-its-ceo-17266313/.

Tangdall, Sara. "Google's Handling of the Echo Chamber Manifesto." Markkula Center for Applied Ethics, September 11, 2017. https://www.scu.edu/ethics/focus-areas/business-ethics/resources/googles-handling-of-the-echo-chamber-manifesto/.

Teilhard de Chardin, Pierre. *The Phenomenon of Man*. Translated by Bernard Wall. New York: Harper Colophon, 1975.

Templeton, Brad. "Teslas Are Crashing into Emergency Vehicles Too Much, So NHTSA Asks Other Car Companies about It." *Forbes*, September 20, 2021. https://tinyurl.com/348v337f.

Thalassery. "LaMDA: The AI That Google Engineer Blake Lemoine Thinks Has Become Sentient." *The Indian Express*, June 19, 2022. https://indianexpress.com/article/technology/tech-news-technology/lamda-the-program-that-a-google-engineer-thinks-has-become-sentient-7967050/.

Thériault, Anne. "What Vaxxers and Anti-Vaxxers Are Missing: Autism Isn't the Worst Thing to Happen to a Child." *Quartz*, February 11, 2015. https://qz.com/340623/what-vaxxers-and-anti-vaxxers-are-missing-autism-isnt-the-worst-thing-to-happen-to-a-child/.

Thomas, Cal. "Did Liberalism Spur Unabomber?" *Lawrence Journal-World*, April 11, 1996.

Thomas, William Isaac, and Dorothy Swaine Thomas. *The Child in America*. Oxford: Alfred A. Knopf, 1928.

Tinney, Kate. "New Food Delivery Service Kiwi Brings Robots to Campus." *Daily Californian*, May 15, 2017. https://www.dailycal.org/2017/05/15/new-food-delivery-service-kiwi-brings-robots-campus/.

Todd, Benjamin. "Misconceptions about Effective Altruism." *80000 Hours*, August 7, 2020. https://80000hours.org/2020/08/misconceptions-effective-altruism/.

Torres, Emile P. "Against Longtermism." *Aeon*, October 19, 2021. https://aeon.co/essays/why-longtermism-is-the-worlds-most-dangerous-secular-credo.

———. "Selling 'Longtermism': How PR and Marketing Drive a Controversial New Movement." *Salon*, September 10, 2022. https://www.salon.com/2022/09/10/selling-longtermism-how-pr-and-marketing-drive-a-controversial-new-movement/.

Townes, Emilie. *Womanist Ethics and the Cultural Production of Evil*. New York: Palgrave MacMillan, 2006.

Tran, Tony Ho. "The Radical Movement to Worship AI as a New God." *Daily Beast*, February 26, 2023. https://www.thedailybeast.com/the-radical-movement-to-worship-ai-chatbots-like-chatgpt-as-gods.

Trout, C. "There's a New Sex Robot in Town: Say Hello to Solana." *Engadget*, January 10, 2018. https://www.engadget.com/2018-01-10-there-s-a-new-sex-robot-in-town-say-hello-to-solana.html.

Tucker, Hank. "Elon Musk Gets Almost $13 Billion Richer in One Week as Tesla Stock Hits 8-Month High." *Forbes*, October 16, 2021. https://www.forbes.com/sites/hanktucker/2021/10/16/elon-musk-gets-almost-13-billion-richer-in-one-week-as-tesla-stock-hits-8-month-high/?sh=74dd195830b3.

Tucker, R. C., ed. *The Marx-Engels Reader*, 2nd ed. New York: W. W. Norton, 1978.

Turing, Alan. "Computing Machinery and Intelligence." *Mind* 49 (1950): 433–60.

Turkle, Sherry. *Alone Together: Why We Expect More from Technology and Less from Each Other*. New York: Basic Books, 2011.

Turkle, Sherry, and Seymour Papert. "Epistemological Pluralism: Styles and Voices within the Computer Culture." *Signs: Journal of Women in Culture and Society* 16, no. 1 (Autumn 1990): 128–57.

US Census Bureau, "2018: ACS 1-Year Estimates Selected Population Profiles," 2018, https://data.census.gov/cedsci/table?t=-A0&d=ACS%201-Year%20Estimates%20Selected%20Population%20Profiles&tid=ACSSPP1Y2018.S0201.

Unabomber [pseudonym]. "Industrial Society and Its Future." *Washington Post*, September 22, 1995.

"Union Members Summary." US Bureau of Labor Statistics (January 22, 2020).

The Universal Declaration of Human Rights. United Nations, December 1948. https://www.un.org/en/about-us/universal-declaration-of-human-rights.

Vinsel, Lee. "You're Doing It Wrong: Notes on Criticism and Technology Hype." *STS News*, February 2, 2021. https://sts-news.medium.com/youre-doing-it-wrong-notes-on-criticism-and-technology-hype-18b08b4307e5.

Vincent, James. "Google Is Poisoning Its Reputation with AI Researchers." *The Verge*, April 13, 2021. https://www.theverge.com/2021/4/13/22370158/google-ai-ethics-timnit-gebru-margaret-mitchell-firing-reputation.

———. "Twitter Taught Microsoft's AI Chatbot to Be a Racist Asshole in Less Than a Day." *The Verge*, March 24, 2016. https://www.theverge.com/2016/3/24/11297050/tay-microsoft-chatbot-racist.

Virginia Sterilization Act of 1924.

Vogel, Lawrence. "Natural Law Judaism? The Genesis of Bioethics in Hans Jonas, Leo Strauss and Leon Kass." In *The Legacy of Hans Jonas: Judaism and the Phenomenon of Life*, edited by Hava Tirosh-Samuelson and Christian Wiese, 287–314. Leiden: Brill, 2008.

Walzer, Michael. *Spheres of Justice: A Defense of Pluralism and Equality*. New York: Basic Books, 1983.

Wang, Guanlin, Minxuan Cao, Justina Sauciuvenaite, Ruth Bissland, Megan Hacker, Catherine Hambly, Lobke M. Vaanholt, Chaoqun Niu, Mark D. Faries, and John R. Speakman. "Different Impacts of Resources on Opposite Sex Ratings of Physical Attractiveness by Males and Females." *Evolution and Human Behavior* 39, no. 2 (March 2018): 220–25.

Wang, Kelly. "'iPal' Robot Companion for China's Lonely Children." *Phys.Org*, June 14, 2018. https://phys.org/news/2018-06-ipal-robot-companion-china-lonely.html.

Waters, Malcolm. *Globalization*, 2nd ed. London: Routledge, 2001.

Wayland, Michael. "General Motors Unveils New High-End GMC Sierra Denali and AT4X Pickup Trucks." *CNBC*, October 21, 2021. https://www.cnbc.com/2021/10/21/general-motors-unveils-new-high-end-gmc-sierra-denali-and-at4x-pickups.html.

Weber, Max. *Economy and Society: An Outline of Interpretive Sociology*. Edited by Guenther Roth and Claus Wittich. Berkeley: University of California Press, 1978.

———. *The Protestant Ethic and the "Spirit" of Capitalism and Other Writings*. Edited and translated by Peter Baehr and Gordon C. Wells. London: Penguin Books, 2002.

Weeks, Linton. "Lazy in America: An Incomplete Social History." *National Public Radio*, July 1, 2011. https://www.npr.org/2011/07/01/137531711/lazy-in-america-a-brief-social-history.

Weng, Yueh-Hsuan, Chien-Hsun Chen, and Chuen-Tsai Sun. "Toward the Human–Robot Co-Existence Society: On Safety Intelligence for Next Generation Robots." *International Journal of Social Robotics* (April 2009): 267–82.

White, Alison, and Ina Hofland. "Origins of Eugenics: From Sir Francis Galton to Virginia's Racial Integrity Act of 1924." University of Virginia, 2007. http://exhibits.hsl.virginia.edu/eugenics/2-origins/.

White, Mark D., ed. *The Avengers and Philosophy: Earth's Mightiest Thinkers*. Hoboken: John Wiley & Sons, 2012.

"Why the R-Word Is the R-Slur." Special Olympics. https://www.specialolympics.org/stories/impact/why-the-r-word-is-the-r-slur.

Wickman, Forrest. "Working Man's Blues." *Slate*, May 1, 2012. https://slate.com/business/2012/05/blue-collar-white-collar-why-do-we-use-these-terms.html.

Wiener, Norbert. *The Human Use of Human Beings: Cybernetics and Society*. London: Free Association Books, 1950.

Wikler, Daniel. "Paternalism in the Age of Cognitive Enhancement: Do Civil Liberties Presuppose Roughly Equal Mental Ability?" In *Human Enhancement*, edited by Julian Savulescu and Nick Bostrom, 341–56. Oxford: Oxford University Press, 2009.

Williams, Joan C. "How Biden Won Back (Enough of) the Working Class." *Harvard Business Review*, November 10, 2020. https://hbr.org/2020/11/how-biden-won-back-enough-of-the-white-working-class.

———. "What So Many People Don't Get about the U.S. Working Class." *Harvard Business Review*, November 10, 2016. https://hbr.org/2016/11/what-so-many-people-dont-get-about-the-u-s-working-class.

Williams, Robert. "I Was Wrongfully Arrested Because of Facial Recognition. Why Are Police Allowed to Use It?" *Washington Post*, June 24, 2020. https://www.washingtonpost.com/opinions/2020/06/24/i-was-wrongfully-arrested-because-facial-recognition-why-are-police-allowed-use-this-technology/.

Winner, Langdon. "Do Artifacts Have Politics?" *Daedalus* 109, no. 1 (Winter 1980): 121–36.

Wong, Julia Carrie. "San Francisco Tech Worker: 'I Don't Want to See Homeless Riff-Raff.'" *The Guardian*, February 17, 2016. https://www.theguardian.com/technology/2016/feb/17/san-francisco-tech-open-letter-i-dont-want-to-see-homeless-riff-raff.

Woods, Robert. "Thomas Newcomen and the Steam Engine." *Mechanical Engineering Magazine*, December 2003, republished in *Engineering and Technology History Wiki*, October 1, 2019. https://ethw.org/Thomas_Newcomen_and_the_Steam_Engine.

Wright, M. Keith. "Using Open Source Tools in Text Mining Research." Paper presented at Southwest Design Sciences Institute conference, Dallas, TX, March 3, 2005, 312.

Yelimeli, Supriya. "Berkeley's Biggest Homeless Camps Were Closed. Where Are the Residents Now?" *Berkeleyside*, September 2, 2021. https://www.berkeleyside.org/2021/09/02/berkeleys-biggest-homeless-camps-were-closed-where-are-the-residents-now.

Zahidi, Saadia, Vesselina Ratcheva, Guillaume Hingel, and Sophie Brown. *The Future of Jobs Report 2020*. World Economic Forum. October 2018.

Zastrow, Mark. "South Korea Trumpets $863-Million AI Fund after AlphaGo 'Shock.'" *Nature*, March 16, 2016. https://www.nature.com/articles/nature.2016.19595.

Zhao, Zhongying. "HKBU Team Developing Portable Rapid Detection Platform for Cancer and GMOs." Hong Kong Baptist University. https://interdisciplinary-research.hkbu.edu.hk/research/featured-articles/hkbu-team-developing-portable-rapid-detection-platform-for-cancer-and-gmos.

Zhou, Changsong. "Machine Learning Utilised for Understanding Cognitive Behavior." Hong Kong Baptist University. https://interdisciplinary-research.hkbu.edu.hk/research/featured-articles/machine-learning-utilised-for-understanding-cognitive-behaviour.

Žižek, Slavoj. *The Sublime Object of Ideology*. London: Verso, 1989.

Žmolek, Michael Andrew. *Rethinking the Industrial Revolution: Five Centuries of Transition from Agrarian to Industrial Capitalism in England*. Leiden: Brill, 2013.

INDEX